Dear Max,
Thanks for helping
Paul start the AFB!
We both loved you and
Barbara —
Miss you

Love
Diane

Dec. 6, 2013

DADDY'S LEDGER

SONNENCRAFT RESIDENCE OF C. E. HUTCHINSON, FAIRMONT, W. VA.

By
Diane Hutchinson Parker

First Printing, September 2013
ISBN 978-0-615-88982-5

First Edition

For more information, to contact the author, or to order additional copies of this book, please contact:

Diane Hutchinson Parker
714 Venture Drive, #106
Morgantown, WV 26508

Table of Contents

FOREWORD

Carol J. Ballah Amos

A.B. in Education, Fairmont State College, 1968
Master of Arts, West Virginia University, 1980
Marion County Educator, 1969-2006 and Teacher of the Year, 2002

Diane Hutchinson Parker, a novice published writer, has maintained her father's mine ledger filled with newspaper articles, (many from The Fairmont Times and The West Virginian as well as state and national publications), family photos, and journals. The 20" x 15" ledger provides a history of a family's entrepreneurship and the impact on an industry as revealed through meticulous documentation and a daughter's devotion to preserve the family history. The explosive growth of the coal boom is lead by "Coal Baron" extraordinaire and family patriarch Clyde E. Hutchinson.

Mesmerized by the massive book when she first revealed the contents of the ledger, I remain fascinated by the intertwining of the family and the city of Fairmont -- inextricably bonded through the economy and community philanthropy. She writes her recollections as a collection of stories that are sometimes heartwarming, sometimes shocking, but always providing insight to one of the premier families of Fairmont.

With the birth of Diane and her early years at the castle, the readers experience a glimpse of the golden era at Sonnencroft, an icon of the city on Morgantown Avenue in the Palatine district of the Friendly City. Designed and built to replicate Inverness Castle in Scotland, the beautiful structure and gorgeous gardens, lost during the Great Depression, was razed in the 1961 with property bought by the Marion County Board of Education.

Through legend and lore, Mrs. Parker recounts the family traditions and experiences of Clyde E. and Mary Lyda Hutchinson, Papa and Mammam to the family.

Diane's engrossing stories captivate me; I am convinced they will do the same for her readers.

****

FOREWORD

Roger D. Curry, JD
Fairmont West Virginia

I considered it a rare privilege to read the proofs of "Daddy's Ledger" by my dear friend Diane Hutchinson Parker. And now being asked to pen a foreword is both an honor and quite a treat. The reader's hands are filled with nothing less than a living history.

Diane Parker is the scion of the Hutchinson family, genuine pioneers of the coal industry in West Virginia. Their reach was much more than a local phenomenon. Really, the coal of northern Appalachia including all of West Virginia powered most of the 20th Century America. Coal was the energy source, which won two World Wars and built a modern society. Without the coal developed by people of vision and dug by hardy workers from beneath these mountains, there would have been no electricity, no steel, no automobiles, no skyscrapers and no large factories.

I met Diane Parker 35 years ago through her husband, the late Paul E. Parker, Jr. Mr. Parker was a senior attorney in Fairmont, Marion County, West Virginia. When I came to the Bar, Paul became a mentor and my great friend. And yet, through these pages that the reader holds, I have gotten to know Paul so much better than I ever did. Diane reveals what a vibrant Renaissance man Paul really was.

Diane also leads us through a fascinating first person account of American life in small towns from the 30s through the 70s. Lately I have been walking up and down the same streets the history of which is recounted by Diane Parker. Her vivid descriptions take me body and soul to the world as it was all of those many years ago.

A work such as this has considerably greater value than simply amusing the odd jackleg historian such as this Poor Scribe. These are the windows into the story of our culture. These are the accounts by and about the people who lived the history of our culture and formed the society in which we live today. Diane has given us a worthy addition to the story of life in America - and life in West Virginia - and I, for one, am profoundly grateful.

FOREWORD

Robert H. Quenon
Retired President and CEO
Peabody Holding Company Inc., now Peabody Energy Corporation

As a native of West Virginia and a long time participant in the coal industry, I maintain a great interest in the contemporary and historical aspects of my chosen field. Diane Hutchinson Parker has made a great contribution to the historical records of the early years through her research and writing that has gone into Daddy's Ledger. Using family records and other sources, she has reconstructed a period of development of the northern West Virginia coal field which has been the source of a major contribution to national energy supply for over 150 years.

Other writers, including Harry M. Caudill and John Knowles, have contributed through factual and fictional publications to memorialize the drama of the families and the financial and social struggles that went into this significant historical development. Diane Hutchinson Parker's effort will add to and supplement all earlier documentation of these years.

****

FOREWORD

Eddie Barrett

Fairmont native, now of Huntington, WV and Naples, FL
Former Sports Information Director, West Virginia University
Former Athletic Director, Marshall University
Member of WVU Sports Hall of Fame

Fairmont is lucky that so many sons and daughters, with talent, have left a legacy about those who went before. From E. E. Meredith's "Do You Remember?" to C. E. (Ned) Smith and Bill Evans with their "Good Morning!" and Sport Talk columns, through to John Knowles the novelist and Cleveland Amory in the Saturday Evening Post, Glenn Hamilton's "I Love the Name of Fairmont" and Fuzzy Knight's one hundred and eighty six B-grade movies, not much about Fairmont has gone unnoted. Until now, when there is still time, thank God.

Diane Parker, with help from her father's (Brooks Hutchinson) journal or ledger, has put together as close to a "You Are There" book as the real thing, and everyone who loves Fairmont is the richer for it as will generations to come. Her husband Paul Parker, a Morgantowner who passed away in 2000, deeply approves, and Paul E. III, "Eddie", daughter Sylvia and grandsons Brooks and Brett will carry on the Hutchinson legacy.

A word about Diane, or de-AWN' as the French pronounce it. She writes about the past, but she very much lives in the present. She takes on a project for the benefit of her hometown and runs with it or beats the drum for it. There is no middle ground for Diane Parker.

****

DEDICATION

"As long as rivers run down to the sea, or shadows touch the mountain slopes, or stars gaze in the vault of heaven, so long shall your honour, your name, your praises endure."

~ Virgil

With love and devotion, I dedicate this book to:

my parents, Ray and Brooks Hutchinson, who documented and validated my memories through Mother's jottings and over 200 love letters she saved; and Daddy's preservation of every newspaper article that was interesting to him, carefully pasted in a large coal ledger he made into a scrapbook;

my beloved, Paul, "Meminerunt omnia amantes." Ovid;

my son and advocate, Eddie, "A man for all seasons", who has always encouraged and advised many of the endeavors I have undertaken; sanctioning them while cheering me onward;

my daughter, my precious angel, Sylvia, "Holy, fair and wise is she, the heaven such grace did lend her", all my love and thanks for her constant encouragement praise and love that she provides, not only for me, but also for so many others;

and to those imaginative romantics, the East Fairmont High School students, lovers of the "Castle", who took my place growing up in the ruins of Sonnencroft, keeping alive the beautiful dreams and memories of past splendor. It has been your questions and interest that encouraged me to write this book.

EPIGRAPH

"To be ignorant of what happened before you were born is ever to be a child".

~ Cicero

Diane Hutchinson Parker, age two and a half

INTRODUCTION

Holden Caulfield said in J.D. Salinger's "Catcher in the Rye",

"What really knocks me out is a book that, when you're all done reading it, you wish the author that wrote it was a terrific friend of yours and you could call him up on the phone whenever you felt like it."

This novice author was born on December 30, 1932. I arrived with the new president, Franklin Delano Roosevelt and the worst depression ever remembered. My birth was announced shortly before midnight at the Junior League's Charity Ball at the Fairmont Hotel. The bandleader was about to announce the Grand March, instead he announced, "Brooks and Ray Hutchinson have another girl!" The crowd responded, "Oh, no, not another girl!" Daddy, the second of eight sons, always said he was delighted to have three daughters as he had helped raise seven brothers.

My grandparents, parents and sisters had been millionaires. I arrived after the 1929 Wall Street crash. Banks closed, fortunes lost, suicides were common, in not only our town, but across the United States. But I remember the castle my grandfather built for his wife and eight sons named Sonnencroft (Home of Sons); and the elegant, opulent times in Fairmont, West Virginia, often called "The Coal Capital of the world".

My father kept a huge cloth covered coal ledger filled with local newspapers' articles of interest to him- obituaries, murders and gossip - starting in 1864, when his grandfather was murdered. I have grown up with the ledger and write about our family, friends and enemies, elaborating the untold, true stories behind the headlines.

An old friend and author, John Knowles (A Separate Peace) wrote about Fairmont, West Virginia and the coal industry in his novel "A Vein of Riches". Jack said at a book signing, "You write about the real people, Diane, you knew them all. You are a part of that history".

Checking Daddy's ledger for facts, I recalled the old man who was cleaning an attic and found a box full of short pieces of string. On the lid of the box was written in an old, shaky script, "String too short to be saved". I have been reading these too short excerpts of lives and personal tragedies for many years, remembering the rest of each story, but never realizing how to tie them all together. I have told the true tales to my friends who have always asked for more.

I thank those who loved me, who listened and enjoyed my stories. This includes my dear husband, Paul, whom I married at the age of nineteen; no sad stories here! It has been a wonderful life. We walked together in the shadow of a rainbow for 48 years.

When we tell our stories to others we not only entertain and enlighten them, we create a bond with those who listen. Please, savor these unique moments as I have while tying them together into a journey; a book about many things you have never heard or read before.

"Daddy's Ledger" is a memory book of five generations by one who listened, learned, laughed, loved and remembers. I hope you will, like Holden, want to read it more than once. If we have never met, please, realize you are not alone, that you will consider me a terrific friend. Call me on the phone whenever you feel like it. Enjoy!

~ DIANE

CHAPTER ONE

SONNENCROFT: HOME OF SONS

Architect's Rendering of Sonnencroft

"East Side Castle"
"Sonnencroft remembered as 'opulent, gorgeous, and lavish'."
By Jonathan Williams
The Times West Virginian, March 6, 2012

"In its day, Sonnencroft stood on 11 acres of land on Morgantown Avenue, near what is now East Fairmont Junior High School. Diane Hutchinson Parker, granddaughter of the original builder, says the castle, modeled after Inverness castle in Scotland, fueled the dreams and imagination of East Side students. Fairmont was once a wealthy, happening place. Money from local coal companies enriched the town and spawned a class of millionaires, with ties to the coal companies, who poured their money and efforts into building a place for themselves in history."

The coal magnate, Clyde E. Hutchinson, built many structures in Fairmont, which was then known as the "Coal Capital of the world". The other Coal Kings built their buildings, each trying to exceed the other's height and grandeur, which made Fairmont an architectural delight.

It was the era to name your home and my grandmother's friend Susan Maxwell Moore, Dean of Women at WVU and Elizabeth Moore's daughter, from Morgantown, suggested Sonnencroft, German for home of sons.

Sonnencroft was built during 1912 - 1913, and opened for friends with a grand ball on New Year's Eve, welcoming 1914 and becoming a social magnet for Fairmont for 20 years. Why was it allowed to deteriorate for 25 years, finally demolished by fire and a wrecking ball in April of 1961? Why has the image prevailed on the empty acreage for all these many years?

One hundred years later, there is a strange but understandable fascination and intrigue about the Hutchinson mansion. To understand the allure, one must step back in time and get to know the owners: the family and the sons. The scandals and loves of eight handsome, debonair, charming young men with more charisma than was good for them.

Last night I dreamed I was at Sonnencroft again…

THE GILDED AGE

It is New Year's Eve of 1913. Exquisite in a creation of frosty white billows accented by diamonds that gleam in the moonlight, Sonnencroft stands gowned in heavy snow on that memorable night of her debut.

At midnight, thousands of candles that encircle her burst into red flame. From the music room, just off the conservatory where sits the magnificent Steinway grand, an orchestra becomes sentimental with strains of Old Lang Syne. The red glow of the candles cast a strange illumination upon the coral draperies of silver velour; it deepens the hue of the rose and blue in the Persian rugs and accents the shadows on the rich portieres.

Four hundred people have danced and celebrated here tonight. Thus Sonnencroft launched upon her sea of fate, destined to live high while she lived and to die-hard when her brief day expired, leaving behind her but a shell of framework, grim skeleton of once she was, soon to be destroyed with only a legend remaining.

I dreamed of the fantastic house parties with crowds of young beautiful people in gorgeous gowns and plumed combs in their glamorous coiffed hair; gentlemen, not to be outdone, in their spotless white tie and tails. My grandmother and grandfather are overseeing each guest's need - matchmaking with delight and introducing out of town guests - the perfect hosts.

4

Mammam and Papa found their chief happiness in sharing their pleasures with others and, in addition to their private entertaining, they delighted in having the various local and state organizations hold their meetings at Sonnencroft. Although Papa is president of West Virginia Coal and Coke Company and the Hutchinson Coal Company, there is little evidence of the tired businessman about him looking scarcely older than his sons.

On the greyest winter day one turns from the fireplace to catch glimpses of the spring gardens brought into the conservatory. There is the large dining room with walls hung with tapestry above the paneled wainscot and a large table that seats thirty persons and is never made smaller. Mammam added personal touches from many countries and there is evidence of her artistic ability in many of the candles and lampshades that would do credit to the smartest of the shops where she makes her purchases.

In my dream Sonnencroft is a fairyland covered in beautiful snow; all of the growing things are sleeping to awake to a greater beauty when the sky and earth are warmer. Very soon the first bulbs will shoot up, the magnolias will bloom; the yellow blossoms of the golden bells will distract the eye from the ivy covered castle to be followed by almost every plant and shrub of the flower kingdom. I pray another dream will allow me to stroll through the formal gardens onto the cascade ending at the lily pond where lovely drooping weeping willows, ferns and iris have voluntarily appeared. I will take the long way around through the vegetable and fruit gardens to the pergola leading the entrance and have tea or lemonade at one of the charming spots arranged for that purpose.

I hate to awaken but as I do I take one last glance of the inscription on the half stained glass window which has been engraved on my mind over the years- "East, West, Home's Best" and I will add reflectively, a home where hate is locked out and love is locked in.

ULTIMATE BETRAYAL - An Untold Tale

My father, Brooks, wrote February 20, 1956, many years later to Aunt Jet Joliffe Post, who was lamenting how she could not stand Mel Hutchinson, his father's brother and her Grandmother's (Catherine Ann Joliffe) oldest son.

Brooks writes, "I, too, had had a terrible experience with the man, He was, without the least semblance of a doubt, the most selfish, jealous, and self centered individual within my memory or misfortune to know". [This was so unlike my father to feel this way about anyone. I never heard him say an unkind word about a soul, although my mother had alluded to this hatred felt by many in the family and the town.]

Daddy went onto explain, "Uncle Mel had to be dragged out of the store in Smithtown to keep the books so that Father could do the work of running the mines and the brokering necessary that made them so successful. After Father's death, Uncle Mel and I were appointed as Administrators of the estate. Everything had to be sold eventually, to provide funds for the settlement of debts, the majority of which were obligations of others and he was security. All of our property was accordingly sold before the Court House and bid in mainly by Uncle Mel. The other bidders thought he was bidding for our family and consequently did not bid up the price in any instance. I felt that he was protecting us to the limit and so depended on him implicitly. When all was concluded, he totally ignored us all, including Mother. He would have none of the boys in the Hutchinson Coal business that Father had founded and originated in Beachwood. Uncle Mel would have been in Smithtown if it had not been for Father's surprising success and Uncle Mel's envious and eager craving to share the same. "

"Uncle Mel bought up all of Father's coal stock at $1.00 per share, the stock being worth $150 per share at the time. Father had 6000 shares the same that Mel had. Mel purchased the Hutchinson Building, belonging to father for $5000, which was conservatively worth $175,000. He purchased several other properties of the estate, on the same relative nominal bids. Father's estate was appraised at $1,250,000.00. When Uncle Mel finished with it and the Administrators paid a relative amount of the debt, the family was left penniless and without a home. My mother was left dependent on her sons and principally me, as the only one in town and the oldest living child. It was my greatest pleasure to do all within my power to make life as easy as possible for her. I literally worshiped her, as did others in Fairmont;

but unfortunately, I could not do as much as I would have liked for her comfort and peace of mind.

"Uncle Mel literally stole or appropriated all of Father's life accumulation under false pretenses, supposedly bidding in our behalf. I might have arranged for sufficient finances to bid them in myself, had I thought that we were to be so betrayed by our own flesh and blood- a so-called brother and uncle. You may perhaps think we are somewhat bitter and you are absolutely correct, for we are. While we do not broadcast our troubles, most people here understand and know most of the story. What amazes me more is that Uncle Mel did not take it with him when he passed on- I know that it was his intention to do so."

Devotedly, Your cousin,
~ Brooks

The Fairmont Times
April 26, 1960

"The Marion County Board of Education has, at long last, acquired the "old Hutchinson property", on Morgantown Avenue. This purchase includes somewhat less than the original 11 acres of thicket and undergrowth that at one time was a fabulous estate and the remains of a decomposing castle, stripped by vandals of even its woodwork and its plumbing; home of Clyde, Lyda and their eight sons.

"The Hutchinson fortune was made in coal- made and lost in one short generation as were so many in those hectic years of prosperity and depression.

"Lyda and Clyde had first seen their castle in Scotland. Upon their return, they had hired architects Holmboe and Lafferty of Clarksburg to begin the gigantic task of duplicating the famous "Inverness" castle on Morgantown Avenue. Lyda's friend, Susan Maxwell Moore, dean of women at WVU at the time, proposed the name of Sonnencroft, German for house of Sons. After sitting derelict for 30 years and after the deaths of Harry and Victor Shaw, Thelma Skaggs Shaw (the daughter-in-law and only remaining family) had inherited, what she called, "the monstrosity"; and threatened by the city, sold the property to the Board of Education."

LOSS of SONNENCROFT

Sonnencroft was built in 1913 on 11 acres of ground. Six hundred and fifty feet fronted Morgantown Avenue and seven hundred feet fronted Mason Street. The architects, Holmboe and Lafferty, of Clarksburg worked very closely with the family, who designed their castle from Inverness castle in Scotland. The house, 100-feet long, was built of terra cotta tile faced with cement stucco. It had one square tower on the right facing Mason Street, and two round towers, one faced Morgantown Avenue and the other was on the middle back wall. The structure consisted of 32 rooms including nine bedrooms plus a sleeping porch which accommodated 10 to 12 in dormitory style, which pleased the eight Hutchinson sons and their many friends. The basement housed a 15'x 40' pool used by every youngster in the neighborhood followed usually by cookies and lemonade on the terrace.

In reading through Daddy's ledger there is a notice that Sonnencroft, Morgantown Avenue, was up for taxes, which is usually posted on the Court House doors. Brooks and the boys were unable to pay the back taxes on Sonnencroft and when asked, Uncle Mel refused. Harry Shaw, Judge of the Circuit Court at the time, who, in his avarice, resembled Uncle Mel, paid the back taxes for Sonnencroft and allowed Mammam to live there for a monthly rent. To pay the rent each month, the sons had to sell off the furniture. Uncle Frank, Aunt Bonnie, Jack and Frank, Jr. sold their home in Logan and came back to take care of the old homestead and Mammam.

Eventually there was an eviction notice. Daddy found a house across the street from their dear old friend Mattie Watson (Mrs. James Edwin Watson) who, after selling their estate, Highgate, to the Sisters of St. Joseph, had moved to First Street and Gaston Avenue.

The townspeople have blamed the City of Fairmont all these years for not buying the Castle to use as a school, museum or a bed and breakfast. It is important not to blame the City; they tried! The Shaws, who over the years hated the happiness and success of their old neighbors, allowed the beautiful ivy covered home of sons to befall a decline that no one but they could prevent. Even after Judge Harry and his son Victor died, Thelma did nothing. I understand many guests of Sonnencroft's parties and balls would drive up the Judge's driveway thinking his house was our gatekeeper's cottage. This, I know, infuriated the three who lived there even though the Judge, and his children, "Vick" and Thelma, had always been invited to the parties.

The following article by the late Jim Comstock who did everything to save the Castle since the 1940's really tells the truth, but the Judge refused to give or sell the deteriorating structure to anyone. This is an explanation by the late Mr. Comstock, when asked to help save the Watson's Highgate from its sale to Hardees, and why he felt he was a failure in "saving old structures":

"The Comstock Lode", Editorial
From "Sonnencroft to Highgate"
The West Virginia Hillbilly
September 22, 1988

"I first visited the mansion of C.E. Hutchinson in the late 1940s. This was the famous Castle.

"I had started my newspapering, working night and day, and there coming a mid-summer lull, I fulfilled a promise to take my family on a vacation to New England in our first car. I had heard about Sonnencroft, Hutchinson's castle and I wanted to see it. It was in the early stages of ruin. The plumbing had been plundered. Winos used the place as a refuge. Boys hid out here to learn to smoke. I came here with an inkling of the castle's story. Hutchinson was foreign to most individuals, a lover of Shakespeare, especially the Bard's Macbeth. When he reached the stage of great wealth, Hutchinson gave life to a childhood promise that someday he would live in a replica of Macbeth's castle. He dispatched 2 Clarksburg architects, Messrs. Holmboe and Laffery to Scotland for a model and they returned with one (Inverness Castle) and built it. There is doubt among scholars about the authenticity of it all, they holding that Macbeth couldn't have lived in a castle as we visualize a castle. Nevertheless, Hutchinson got his castle. In time, sadly, the owners fell on hard times and lost everything, including the castle, which he had named Sonnencroft, German for "Home of Sons".

"The idea that the castle should be saved, restored, and made into a museum occurred to me a few days later, when I was face to face with another castle in Connecticut on the first leg of a vacation trip. I followed a sign, which directed me to "Gillett's Castle". I wanted to compare the two, and upon arrival found it to be a museum of kind and run by the State. The castle had been owned by the famous actor, William Gillett, known for his portrayal of Sherlock Holmes on the stage. He had built it on a whim and had willed it to the state when he died in 1937 at the age of 82.

"If Connecticut could save its castle then West Virginia could do no less with Sonnencroft. That was the first article in my NEWS LEADER-HILLBILLY had not been born yet. I mailed the editorial to other papers, and made considerable noise, all to no avail. After a few weeks of urging, I received a phone call from a Fairmonter telling me I might be interested to know that bulldozers were at that minute clearing Sonnencroft off of the land. I had lost my first battle in the war of preservation. So maybe, I'd better remain silent about Highgate."

Harry Shaw died on October 28, 1952 at 8:20 am in his house at 425 Morgantown Avenue, a few months after his son, Victor, had expired. He lay bedfast in his home from January until his death. The West Virginian reported, "Judge Shaw, the son of Joshua and Emily West Shaw from Prickett's Creek in Union District, was born on February 15, 1872. Shaw had married Willa Berry and they had three children, Olive and Robert Shaw who both died in infancy and Victor Hugo Shaw who died on August 30 of this year (1952)."

Judge Shaw's estate, a matter of public record, was published in the West Virginian June 3, 1954 and listed his property, as appraised by John W. Meredith, S.A. Shuttlesworth, and Fred W. Wilson, at $577,432.31. Other property in Wetzel County was listed at $76, 503.55.

Marion County's Commissioner of Accounts, James F. Burns, listed his real estate in Marion County at $350,432.31, which includes his residence on Morgantown Avenue, at $35,000. He owned the Home Savings bank building, more than a score of residential properties in Fairmont and Mannington, including the old Hutchinson estate, $18,000, and the former John A. Clark residence in South Fairmont. His daughter-in-law was left the whole estate.

Thelma Shaw struggled to keep her home intact; but instead of leaving it to the city, where we could have made it into a museum; she willed it to the college who really did not know what to do with it. It was supposed to be the President's home and called the Shaw House, but they already had a President's home. It was a real albatross for them.

While writing this segment, I cannot help but think of Mr. Potter in "It's a Wonderful Life" or Scrooge. Uncle Mel and the Judge were such good examples of "a little power is a dangerous thing". I do not ask for forgiveness for the schadenfreude I feel when I write of these two.

But as Daddy ends his letter to Aunt Jet, "Such is life, Aunt Jet, and we have to live and make the most of it. I try not to think of this phase of the past history and existence for we gain nothing by such reminiscence of bitterness, we only make ourselves miserable without profit to anyone."

"The evil that men do live after them; the good is oft interred with their bones."

~ Julius Caesar

(Photo credit: John C. Veasey)

THE LEGEND: FORTY-SEVEN YEARS LATER

From Mason Street, two broad driveways intercept the stone wall my great grandfather, Jacob Watkins, built, and this approach was most used. I told my little son, Eddie, "Here stood the carriage house, later converted to a garage, and beyond it, the stable. Once, seven horses were lodged here as well as the pet pony. Five were carriage horses and two were for riding." My five-year-old son, Eddie, always fascinated by cars, was interested in hearing about the ones that were at Sonnencroft. When the "horseless carriage" came into vogue, processions of vehicles rolled down the concrete driveway and through the archway under the house. Mammam called them the "boys' toys". There was a Maxwell, a Buick Roadster, a Cadillac, a Packard, a 1912 Rochet Schneider that Daddy had brought home from Yale, and Mammam had an electric car with a constant demand for batteries. I told him about Uncle Jimmy, the youngest of the uncles, who would sleep all night in one of the cars so he could claim it first the next morning.

Standing here in the shadow of the vanished pergola, it is hard to recall the August seasons of rich purple, savory grapes clustered on the cypress wood arbor, or the scent of roses, which framed the passageway with fragrance so rare. Here is where the garden furniture was placed and where we gathered for afternoon tea. As a little girl, I learned from Daddy that you could eat the grapes two ways, by squeezing the skin off and throwing it away, or simply putting the whole grape into the mouth, which I preferred.

Sometimes on hot afternoons you could hear the laughter and splashing of the grandchildren and neighborhood boys coming from the pool. My first cousins, Jack and "Justie" (Frank, Jr.) were living there with their parents, Aunt Bonnie and Uncle Frank. The family had returned from Logan where Frank had run the southern mines. I have been told the friends from Pittsburgh Avenue were Jack Carpenter, Bob Williams, George May, Ralph Weekly, and Paul Hutchinson, son of A.D. Hutchinson from Columbia Street. There was not so much as an echo now. Silence has settled like an appalling fog over the ghosts of the garden.

Eddie and I fought our way around to the front of the building, climbing over the bramble-cane and briar, the clinging vines, the stubble and the weeds; dead limbs piled around us obstruct our way, but I must show my five year old what seems like a forgotten grave. Buried beneath our feet are the spacious lawns, the terraced gardens and the crystal pool my mother and so many others wrote about many years ago. Where was the sundial that marked the shining hours? And where were the rock gardens and the lily pads, like mermaids from the blue? Where are the Great Danes that strutted the promenade? I remember Polly, a beautiful, silky, red setter that was bigger than I, always within my sight, taking care of me.

The grounds have been cleared a bit, sunlight filters through the branches of the giant oaks, and you can hear a rabbit or squirrels scamper amidst the ruins, but from inside the castle walls, no sign of light, movement or sound. Once all friendliness and warmth and cheer, she stands cold, silent and forbidding. We climb what is left of the crumbled steps leading to the once white double doors. The stucco has fallen off the outside displaying the broken red tile underneath. Like countless sunken eyes are the innumerable glassless windows revealing everything and nothing, stripped of the rare dignity that was ever a part of her. Sonnencroft stands shamefully naked.

The entrance hall projects out from the house and its roof forms a parapet accessible from the second floor. Huge granite benches had flanked the doors and massive jardinières once sat on the pillars of the steps. Mammam had the benches taken to our lots at Woodlawn Cemetery where one still exists today.

Inside, the gigantic hall creates an impressive entry. Only indications are left of what were closets for wraps on either side of the vestibule. Evidence remains of doors on the left, which led to the living room, the conservatory, music room, dining room, breakfast room, and servants' quarters in the rear. On the right, the library, the billiard room, where a bas-relief of Washington crossing the Delaware is still discernable on a dark red brick fireplace, the sun porch and side entrance. This was known as the east wing. Above it were the bedrooms for the boys and a long dormitory or sleeping porch enclosed in glass, containing rows of beds to accommodate twenty boys.

It is impossible to climb what is left of the massive steps in their state of devastation, retaining not even a baluster to accompany them upstairs. On the landing of the once magnificent staircase is the most beloved of all the memories; it is of the 22-foot stained glass window imported from Scotland and bearing the inscription within a shield "East- West, Home's best." Only a large gaping hole is left.

It was said that Mammam never set a table for less than 16, never knowing how many swimmers or friends would be invited from school. The Hutchinsons were never known to turn down a request to share their home and grounds with any responsible organization or individual. Church, civic, and social clubs held many meeting here. Many of the groups Mammam founded and served as first president, such as The Woman's Association of Cook Hospital (1916), now called The Volunteer Association of Fairmont General Hospital. I am proud to say I served as president of this group fifty years later, 1969 to 1973. Mammam was also the founder and first president of the YWCA Board of Directors.

Numberless guests were entertained and overnight visitors had a wing of the house to themselves. They could choose the guest room with its orchid walls, ivory furniture and purple rug, or the yellow room, with its lovely four-poster mahogany bed. There were many private baths. The master bedroom where memories of Mammam predominate; her hand-blocked linen draperies of eggshell blue blossoming with faded roses, the soft carpet bringing out the subdued tones of the blue. Here, my mother's memories of Mammam unpacking the many trunks of gifts brought home from foreign lands. I can imagine all the daughters-in-law crowded around her, faces flushed with excitement and warmth from the fire reflected in the mirror above the white mantle and in the wardrobe's mirrored doors. This room is located over the living room, there is space unlimited and in the one end, again the curvature of the tower.

Above is the third floor, where the housekeeper and maids' rooms and baths had been. A narrow, enclosed stairway led upwards to the roof where one could walk as a sentry on lookout behind the crenellated battlements, down onto the sprawling city of Fairmont. Comfort throughout the maze of rooms was assured in winter by steam heated radiators open grates and gas. A monstrous furnace in the basement devoured coal by the ton. Water from a deep well outside could be pumped inside to the house electrically should there be an inadequate city supply. Its quality was preferred for drinking by the family and many of the neighbors. There was also a reserve or auxiliary General Electric Delco power plant in the garage to provide electricity in an emergency. The rooms and the beautiful oriental rugs were cleaned through an elaborate hotel type Lux System in the walls, sucking up the dirt and depositing it with ashes from the furnace. The Lux system was brought to Old Greenwich, Connecticut in 1919 from Sweden and was later called Electrolux. Mammam insisted on using nothing but suction on the hand loomed wool Persian rugs.

Eddie and I wander through the archway, out of the conservatory to another porch. Here are the steps where pictures of the family were often taken. Each boy, from oldest to youngest sat on each of the steps downwards. Uncle Jimmy, the "baby", whom Mammam dressed in dresses and kept in long blond, curls for so long, always wishing for a daughter, was always in the middle of the last step. These steps lead down to the formal gardens and more granite benches. Eddie and I turn and go back inside rather than to risk the poison ivy and growth of brambles. We stand where the graceful, six-foot, alabaster fountain stood in the center of the tiled dance floor. Mother and Daddy had the fountain stored in our basement on Fairmont Avenue for years, too heavy to use or get rid of.

Eddie is tiring now, and I am getting homesick for my real home, my real life. We meander back on the path to the east wing, not quite ready to leave or break the spell. I take one last look at the library and recall the countless books, shelved in cases of transparent leaded glass, holding, not only leather bound classics and encyclopedias, but lower rows of many beautiful children's books that I once sat on the floor and read. Beyond the library, I could still smell the smoked-filled billiard room, with its dark red fireplace, where such laughter, jests and wagers billowed forth. Today I still love the hint of stale tobacco smoke reminiscent of these two rooms. I was fascinated by the smoke rings each of the uncles would blow to amuse me. More French doors leading to the sun porch looking out on the grape arbor and pergola and our 1957 blue Chevy station wagon. Eddie runs to it eager to go home. I stand there and think of Papa. I feel his presence, like a time traveler - he is always here but he isn't.

Clyde Hutchinson invested his money in living and letting live. He never lost sight of the fact this is just a world we are only passing through. He loved the story of Macbeth, and built a castle similar to his. Macbeth's philosophy is certainly reflected in these empty, lifeless halls. "A home where hate was shut out and love was locked in."

"Out out brief candle. Life is but a walking shadow, a poor player that struts and frets his hour upon the stage, and then, is heard no more."

~ Shakespeare, Macbeth

I HAVE ALWAYS LIVED IN A CASTLE

Eddie and I arrive home to our real life, to our own little castle that my husband Paul had built for us in 1958 at 931 Coleman Avenue, a three-bedroom ranch house, using one as a sitting room-den. When Sylvia was born they brought this real life doll-baby to me in her pink blanket. I thought how wonderful! Now I have three beautiful people to love - one in each bedroom. "God's in his heaven, all's right with the world."

This is my castle - smaller, perhaps, but filled with the same amount of love as Sonnencroft and nestled among some of the furnishings from Mammam's castle. The Steinway grand, dated 1898; the Canterbury Tales, an ink sketch with an over-brush of watercolor in a three paneled mural of Chaucer's Pilgrims arriving at Canterbury; the Rose medallion punch bowl and the Imari and Canton ware; Mammam's rosewood desk from Grover Cleveland's honeymoon cottage that Mammam bought from the Deer Park Hotel. She used it at our beautiful summer home in Deer Park, MD. Our living room's rose and blue Oriental rug with eleven borders that Eddie used for highways when he played with his Matchbox cars. Mother taught me good Persian rugs are two colors, depending on the nap. If you lay it one way, this rug is predominantly rose and turned around, it is predominantly a dark blue.

The large commercial mangle came to our house at 741 and I remember Iona, our laundry woman using that mangle to iron a double bed sheet in a minute or two after the laundry had been done in a large copper washing machine that rocked the clothes back and forth until you turned it off.

My mother had saved all the children's books for her grandchildren, who much preferred the Little Golden Books, so brightly illustrated. But I have saved some of my favorites, those that have been long out of print.

We moved from Coleman Avenue to West End Drive in 1967 when we outgrew our first little house. I have the same furniture we used on Coleman with some of Paul's home intertwined with Sonnencroft and 741 Fairmont Avenue. This house and grounds truly has been my castle - with deep roots and, I pray, from where I will never leave until death. All my family and friends have visited us here. I can still hear the laughter and hear our neighbors, Bernie Sampson, Chuck Critchfield and Dick Albright telling their jokes on the front porch. And who can forget Joe Woodward's British accent: "No, just now when I roared".

This home has witnessed births, deaths and memories never to be forgotten - so many more than the short-lived Sonnencroft. I have pampered peonies, hostas and mystery lilies that grew in my grandmother's gardens, transplanted to my mother's on Fairmont Avenue, to Coleman and to West End. I have planted and outlived dogwoods and apple trees; and I still try some new tree or shrub each year, keeping the gardens new with heirloom plants.

I put out the porch furniture every year - one old wicker rocker from my nursery. Daddy would rock me to sleep every night singing, "Baby's Boat's a Silver Moon". I did the same with my two babies singing the same songs in the same chair. Many years later Eddie called me to make sure of the words, so he could sing "Baby's Boat" to his first son.

This has been my castle and with the wild life I feed every day - white tailed deer, raccoons, feral cats, wild turkeys; I might even call it my "Dear Park".

With all these poignant memories and stories to tell Paul and the children, I have always felt that every home we bought or built was our castle, both physically and spiritually. "Where hate has been shut out, and love locked in."

I refuse to let all those glorious "yesteryears" be lost to "dusty death!"

FIVE WESTEND DRIVE

"Castle Razed"
The Fairmont Times
April 30, 1961

"What remained of the interior of "Sonnencroft," the old Hutchinson mansion on Morgantown Avenue, was gutted by flames kindled yesterday by the Fairmont fire department, but the walls are still standing and will have to be pulled down. The 30-room residence, long abandoned and now owned by the Marion County Board of Education, is being razed to make way for a new school building.

"Just the gray, smoking stuccoed walls of Sonnencroft, Fairmont's only "castle" remained standing last night following an attempt by city firemen to destroy the structure by fire yesterday.

"The 46-year-old mansion, built by Fairmont coal magnate Clyde Effington Hutchinson on a hill overlooking Morgantown Avenue, was apparently "built to last" according to Fire Chief Ralph L. Gump who directed the destruction and will have to be further demolished by mechanical means.

"Although all frame sections in the mansion were smoldering ashes lying at the base of the foundation by yesterday afternoon, the walls did not seem prone to fall. Gump explained that a great deal of structural steel honeycombs the walls, making impossible his plan of allowing them to get hot as a result of the flames and then cooling them with fire hoses, causing them to crack and give way.

"The property is now owned by the Marion County Board of Education and the eleven acres upon which it stands will later be used as the site of a new school.

"The mansion presented a hazard as it was before yesterday's operation. As a result of standing unused as it had for so many years, supporting beams and flooring were rotten and most of the plaster was gone. Over the years, much of the imported marble, leaded windows, wiring and mahogany woodwork had been stripped from the interior."

The new East Side High School was built in Pleasant Valley and the old school is being used as Fairmont Junior High School. In June of 2012, excavation was begun on the Sonnencroft site for the new East Fairmont Middle School. The officers of the Most Worshipful Grand Lodge of Ancient Free and Accepted Masons officially performed the ceremony of the laying of the cornerstone on Saturday, June 9th. A time capsule, known as a casket, was filled with various artifacts, including "a tile from Sonnencroft Castle". I am sure that Papa and Daddy, both 32nd degree Masons, would heartily approve.

The front steps leading to the castle have been cemented across as they had become dangerous and unusable.

The stately sycamore trees my grandmother had planted, lining Morgantown Avenue, were cut down in the late nineties by Allegheny Power Company, even though their power lines were across the avenue not near the trees.

Many from East Side wrote letters to the editor of the Times-West Virginian complaining about the waste of healthy, beautiful trees that lined the avenue, as did I, but to no avail.

****

In March of 2012, my friend JoAnne Lough offered the following poem, which was written by her father, the late Glenn D. Lough, in 1951. A local writer and historian, he was living near Enterprise, WV at the time. He wrote it in response to Fairmont's painfully extended neglect, vandalism and ultimate loss of Sonnencroft (c. 1914) the Clyde E. Hutchinson family home on Morgantown Avenue, which was indeed a castle. Saved it could have served the people of Fairmont and the upper Monongahela Valley in so many ways-situated on 11 lush acres with its marble swimming pool, ballroom, grand dining hall, conservatory, gardens, and more.

HUTCHINSON HOUSE

Thor drums his sky- troops to the field knob
Palatine draws on a mall of dism
And here amidst the weeds and bramble-cane
An aura, humid, pulses of decay.

Pale lichen'd walls a shatter of neglect;
All of gloom, and drear, the escarpment break;
A hush'd cadence the living leaves do
As Thor, with hammer, clangs the welkin- plate

Once here rare beauty throve most lush
Huge, gentle canines strode the promenade
And boyish laughter laced the galleries
As song-birds trilled a wondrous serenade.

Then came, a chore of Circumstance, this Doom
Transposing of events that named an end
To the promise of a money'd dynasty
Re: crumbled castle, dank, and direful fen

'Tis close and scarcely breathful in the dark
No stir down on the Avenue
The heavy waiting quite becomes a sound
Murmurs the hopeful founders' waning rue

'Tis an atmosphere here inciting to reflect
As 'twere this were an old'n year, medieval
And there a-crouch behind that highway wall
Lurk heathen brigades, evil

Now, should I, anon, shout out the guard
And join the defenders at yon barbican
Or should I hold my silence while the enemy
Swarm the wall and breast the moat'd tarn

If gentle Madame were but there
Up yon beside the turret'd don-jon keep
To signal, then I'd know what I should do
Cry out the guard, or flee the craggy steep

But no figure moves along the cranny-watch
The stillness gasps as lancing lightening breaks
Along Valhalla's vast and darking pall
A tremor strikes as Thor his harness shakes

And all about me, limn'd in heaven's glow
Is ruin rampant, long-moldering neglect
And I wonder what strange humor makes it so
And why civic minds lack so in circumspect

Here, once again, the flowers could bloom
And children skip the shining promenade
A haven or healing place could it be
And gladness sing to make a serenade.

Glenn D. Lough
Enterprise, WV
Published by The Fairmont Times
April 5, 1951
Sonnencroft

CHAPTER TWO

MURDER MOST FOUL

Tintypes of Catherine Ann Joliffe, James Jeremiah Hutchison and photo of Hutchison General Store in Smithtown, WV taken in 1956 before it was torn down for the new Route 73.

Where did this happy breed of men come from? My father, Brooks, never spoke of his paternal grandparents - James Jeremiah Hutchinson and his wife Catherine Ann (Joliffe). Nor do I recall what pet name he used for either of them. Mother had told us pieces of the scandal but she knew little more than Daddy did. I found the following article in Daddy's Ledger:

"Horrible Affair at Smithtown"
"Jerry Hutchison's Throat Slit From Ear to Ear"
Morgantown Weekly Post
November 12, 1864

"On Friday night last, Mr. James Jeremiah Hutchison, a merchant doing business at Smithtown was most horribly murdered at his store at an early hour in the evening. Although nothing has yet been heard of the murderer, but from all the circumstantial evidence that can be elicited from persons residing in the town, we are enabled to give the full particulars in regard to the murder.

"Jerry Hutchison was a man about 35 years of age when he was murdered, in his store, in the early part of the evening, about 7 or 8 o'clock. The General store, as is the case, in a small country town, was deserted and no one about apparently, except Mr. H. It is said that Hutchison was in the habit, occasionally, of taking a little too much liquor, but on the evening in question he was duly sober.

"At about 9 o'clock in the dark, dreary, rainy evening, something was heard fall in Hutchison's store. Mr. Powell, a neighbor who lives next to the store, supposing that Jerry was probably under the influence of liquor, had fallen over a box or something of the kind, thought nothing more about the matter and did not go to see the cause of the noise. Nothing more was heard that night.

"The next morning Mr. H's wife, Catherine Anne Joliffe Hutchison, feeling uneasy about his whereabouts, came down very early to the store to see if he was there. It was unusual for him to be absent from home at night and of course she felt very apprehensive.

"When she arrived at the store, the front door was ajar, and all was dark within. She called to him, but received no answer and being rather timid, she did not go in the store, but went to Mr. Powell's to inquire if they knew anything of her husband.

"After informing him that the door to the store was partly open, Mr. Powell's fears were naturally aroused and he communicated this intelligence to a number of his neighbors, who agreed to go with him and Mrs. H. to the store.

"Upon entering the store, a horrible sight was presented to their view. Stretched upon the floor in the cold embrace of death lay the unfortunate man, weltering in his blood—his skull terribly bruised and throat cut, the head being nearly severed from the body!

"A search was instantly begun to ascertain if any weapons could be discovered and a large hickory club was found near the door. Upon a doorknob were the marks of the blood of the murdered man imprinted there by the hands of the murderer that had killed his fellow man.

"The sight was a terrible one to the on-lookers, especially to his wife.

"Her agony can better be imagined than described.

"They had to ascertain if any money had been taken from the murdered man, and upon a search of the store and his purse, it was found that only about $200 had been abstracted from his side pocket and that $1500 yet remained in the pocket of his pantaloons.

"It is generally supposed that the murder was committed about 9 o'clock at night, the time the noise was heard by Mr. Powell and that the murderer, meeting with more opposition than was anticipated, a scuffle ensued and the noise was the falling of the murdered man after being struck on the head with the club.

"Lest the sounds might arouse the neighbors, the murderer took his flight with only $200 as he was evidently scared and overlooked the $1500 in his pants pocket.

"This information we have derived from various sources and whether strictly correct or not, we are unprepared to say.

"The murderer has not yet been found out."

****

Several days after the murder a peddler in the area called "Mad" (Madden) Carter was tried for the murder, but was acquitted.

****

The facts we have gathered over the years... my great grandfather, James Jeremiah Hutchison was born in 1824 and married Catherine Ann Joliffe on October 10, 1856. Catherine was born on Christmas day, 1830, and was six years younger than her husband.

James Jeremiah Hutchison and Catherine Anne (Joliffe) had three children:

The oldest child was Melville Lee (Uncle Mel) (1853-1943) He married Alice Maud Post and they had five children:

The first-Martha Hutchinson married Andrew Jackson Colborn; Irene married George Phillips; Laura Lee married Dr. Carl Carter; Florence married Robert Ritchie; and, a son, Melville Lee, Jr. who died in his twenties.

Clyde Effington (Papa) (1861-1926) married Mary Lyda Watkins and they had eight sons:

Claude, Brooks, Lee, Frank, Harold, Paul, Robert, and Jimmy. (Brooks was my father)

Their third child was born several months after her father was murdered:

Lily Jay (Aunt Jay) (1865-1891) married Thomas Watson Arnett.

Three children were born to them: Bernard Lee Arnett married Frances Haymond; Susan married Fannie Haymond's brother, Frank Haymond; and Katherine married Andrew Henry.

****

At the time of the murder, Catherine was a young woman of 34, evidently healthy and strong after bearing two sons and pregnant with a third child, Lily Jay, who was born in the next year. Her two boys, Melville and Clyde, were just seven and three years of age and probably did not know or realize what was going on.

The oldest son, Melville might have been suspicious, which perhaps in later years created one of the meanest Mr. Potters our town of Fairmont ever knew. As an adult, Melville served as president of the National Bank for many years, dispensing his greed to many with a certain relish and satisfaction that was most unbecoming. How could two brothers be so different? Lastly, we knew that Jerry Hutchison had returned the day before from a buying trip to New York, accompanied by a young woman.

One day when I was in high school, I was first told about the murder by old Dr. Sturm, a retired, gossipy dentist that lived near Sixth Street Pharmacy. The retired dentist was outside the pharmacy in his straw bowler licking an ice cream cone, just waiting for an eager ear to listen to some of his old stories. He was the bearer of past scandals and must have felt I was grown up enough to hear the gory details of my own family.

Dr. Sturm had related the tale of my first cousin, twice removed, Uncle Mel Hutchinson's only son - Melville, Junior, who, as a child had shot and killed the little Faulkner girl in her house near Sixth Street. Mother had confirmed that story, but it had happened in 1912 before she married Daddy and came to Fairmont.

Now the Doctor was dying to tell me about my great grandfather and his throat slit ear to ear! He knew all the rumors and delighted to pass them on to a naive little girl who had never heard such stories about her family. That is when I found out what we knew was true. But Mother warned me not to speak of it to Daddy, who evidently knew nothing more than she did and was extremely sensitive about the history.

According to Dr. Sturm, "Many swore your great grandmother murdered her husband in cold blood."

POST MORTEM

Jerry Hutchison owned the General Store and Post Office in Smithtown, Monongalia County, West Virginia, a new state, and the only one born out of the Civil War. Smithtown had been a plantation and had always been the hub of the locale until the city of Fairmont was established in January of 1820 and in 1842 became the seat of Marion County, alienating Smithtown left in the outskirts of Monongalia County. The intervening space was built up to the edge of the new Marion County line.

A stagecoach inn had been built across the road from Jerry's General Store on the route between Uniontown, Pennsylvania and Clarksburg, Virginia. The stage line had been put into operation in the late 1830s and it is believed the hotel was built at that time. The stagecoach had been held up over at the inn three days before Jerry's murder, but that robber had escaped and was never found.

It was known that Jerry had just returned the day before his murder from a buying trip to New York and it was rumored he had taken his sales clerk, a pretty little thing, with him. Catherine might have caught wind of this. Being several months pregnant for the third time carrying his daughter, Lilly Jay, I think the women of the community would have sided with Catherine, telling her of the tryst and keeping quiet if she confided her plans to them.

Another family legend is that Jerry was reputed to have been in love with his wife's younger sister, Mary, who could not marry until her older sister did, as was the custom at that time, and that he might have taken her to New York, unbeknownst to Catherine, until their return. To most, the former story seems more plausible.

Others suspected that there was general unrest at the time in the Smithtown neighborhood and some blamed itinerant "Rebs" on their way home from the Civil War. What we know as fact is what we have discovered by Catherine's actions after her husband's murder.

In 2001, 137 years after the murder, my daughter Sylvia and I took a trip to Pisgah Cemetery where Daddy took me often as a child. He would do rubbings of the extremely old stones searching for ancestors. Sylvia and I found the grave of James Jeremiah. His stone is far away from the other stones, and lies at the end of the grounds; but the unusual thing is that his headstone is facing west. It should have been facing east as all the other stones in Pisgah Cemetery. The Christian belief is that when Christ returns, he will arise from the east. Christian altars are usually placed so the parishioners will be facing east during services.

After his death, Catherine added an N to the family name making it HutchiNson, denying her husband's existence and refusing his name. When Catherine Ann died on April 15, 1908 at the age of seventy-eight, Uncle Melville and Clyde bought one lone lot in the relatively new Woodlawn Cemetery for her; and on her gravestone is Catherine Ann Joliffe Hutchinson, with the N that she had added. The sons did not place her next to her husband and his family in Pisgah Cemetery, nor within either of their large Hutchinson parcels at Woodlawn Cemetery. She lies near the entrance of Woodlawn, all alone.

The old general store in Smithtown was eventually torn down in 1956, still bearing the blood soaked floorboards of Jerry Hutchison.

"Who would have thought the old man had so much blood in him!"

~ Macbeth

CHAPTER THREE

HARD TIMES: MOM'S STORY

Clockwise: Mary Catherine – "Mom"; Lucinda & Johnnie; George Gumbert – "Daddy" and First House in Boise

At the same time my father's grandfather was murdered in November of 1864, my mother's grandmother was crossing the plains on the Oregon Trail with her family to escape the terrible Civil War in the east. Mom, my maternal great-grandmother, was born in 1851 on a plantation in Kentucky. The Turner family had money to emigrate to the west and decided to join the wagon train to Oregon that left from Independence, Missouri and took six months to complete.

I remember the article in The West Virginian- February 1, 1943, "Mary Chatter", written by our family friend, the late Medora Mason (Wolfe),

"On Thursday after noon the frail and spent body of a little old lady, whose first memories went back in time more than 90 years ago when she crossed the plains in a covered wagon, was laid to rest under a blanket of snow in Woodlawn Cemetery. Fairmont had been her home for more than 20 years far removed from the western prairies that had been her home for 60 odd years. She was Mrs. George Gumbert, grandmother of Mrs. Brooks S. Hutchinson and a grand old lady, indeed, who, had she lived until April, would have been 92 years old."

****

That frail little old lady was my great grandmother, Mary Catherine Turner Gumbert, "Mom" to all who knew and loved her. The mailman, Mr. Byrd, delivered the morning mail and The Idaho Statesman, the oldest newspaper in Idaho (est. 1864) to her every day and always came in to talk with Mom. She always sat in the same beautiful, old brocaded wing back chair next to the window and radiator in the front hall, the same chair I am sitting in right now as I write this book. Here she could keep an eye on the streetcars and Fairmont Avenue and Eighth Street traffic. A new mailman came in the afternoon. Ah --- the days of two mail deliveries and two-cent stamps! They would sit on the bench over the radiator and discuss politics and the world news with their 82-year-old friend. They all warmed up sitting on that radiator, but had to share it with a multitude of books and magazines: Time, Look, Life, McCall's, Good Housekeeping, Saturday Evening Post, Reader's Digest. Mom was an avid reader.

I sat on her lap. No place in the world was safer or softer than Mom's lap! She had read Uncle Wiggily (Howard R. Garris), The Curley Top, The Bobbsey Twins (Laura Lee Hope), The Hole Book (Peter Newell), the Wizard of Oz (L. Frank Balm), Queen Zixie of Ix (my favorite Balm book)

Marjorie Marigold, and hundreds of others to her three little 'darlings' since 1922 when Elaine was born.

I saved several of these books for my children, but they preferred the new, beautifully illustrated, colorful Little Golden Books. Isn't it wonderful that all these books can be found today just by going on the Internet?

By the time I was born, Mom was pretty tired of all of them, but she patiently read each of them over and over again, to satisfy me. She often confided to Mother that she was concerned about the relationship between Uncle Wiggily and Nurse Jane Fuzzywuzzy, the muskrat lady housekeeper!

Often she would scrape an apple and feed it to me and never forget a line. She wore a long, usually blue, dress with a long white apron over it every day. The apron pocket held a large ring of keys to all the cupboards in the butler's pantry. Not used to strangers in the house, she didn't trust " the help" who might walk away with food or the good china.

Her eyes were a bright blue, slightly faded with time and her silvery white hair was always severely pulled back into a bun. A barber in Boise pierced her ears so she could wear her only jewelry, a wedding present from Daddy Gumbert, a pair of tiny lavender blue enameled pansies, he had said, "to match your eyes". Both of the small pansies had diamonds in the center.

We buried her wearing those earrings. But, let her tell you her story.

MOM'S STORY

"In my day," said Mom, "we didn't call it depression or any other high-sounding words. It was just hard times!"

There she sat by the fire, white haired, apple cheeked, darning the socks of her great-grandchildren and listening to her favorite radio show, Amos and Andy. Always busy, full of energy, hardly seeming the ninety years she was. Not a bit concerned with the terrible depression we were suffering in the thirties:

"You children don't know what hard times are. Here you are with telephones, radios, fires at the stroke of a match, lights at the turn of a switch, food and clothes ever so cheap; why, when we first went to Idaho, Mother had to spin all the cloth for our clothes then make them—no sewing machines in those days either. Father had to pay a dollar a pound for flour and the same for potatoes and then carry them on his back about five miles to the ranch. We had a barrel of beans and one of sorghum and that is about all the variety we had. I've hated beans and sorghum ever since.

"That summer we crossed the Great Plains," and she began the ever-interesting story we had heard many times.

"You know I was born on April 30, 1851 in Lincoln County, Kentucky, near Crab Orchard, on a plantation. I was too small to remember my life there for when we children were very little Father and Mother decided to emigrate west, so we went to Kansas. From old Fort Leavenworth, we went in a covered wagon, with about fifty other wagons in the same train, across the plains headed for Oregon."

[Author's Note: The Oregon Trail was 2000 miles long from Independence Missouri to Vancouver, WA and took about six months to complete. "Oregon Fever" started in 1843 and men, women, and children had started to use the dangerous trail in 1848. The Gold Rush in California reduced the number heading for the Comstock Lode. These pioneers suffered and died by Indian attacks, cholera, epidemics, grass fires, storms, and even quicksand in Nebraska around the river crossings. Floods also killed many of these frontiersmen.]

"It was summer and boiling hot most of the time. I was only about eight years old, but I can remember mother made me wear mitts of red flannel and cut a hole in the top of my hat and tied my hair through it so I would keep my good complexion. We never knew from one hour to the next whether the Indians would kill us or not, but mother being from Kentucky where a woman just had to be beautiful, thought of us girls' complexion and smiles just the same. They had all our teeth pulled and fitted with dentures so we wouldn't suffer the toothaches along the trail and our smiles would stay pretty.

"Then I remember walking back of the wagons in the dust with the other children and playing games as we skipped along. I had a little Pinto pony I rode sometimes."

"What's a Pinto pony?" we asked, "I wish I had a pony. What fun you must have had, Mom!"

"It was a spotted brown and white Indian pony. Father bought it from some friendly Indians for us children. Another thing I remember was the cows being milked every morning. Then the cans of milk were tied on the backs of the wagons, where it would jog the most, and at night when we camped we would have butter.

"The nights around the campfire were the most fun. We always sang hymns and told stories. Of course, nighttime was more dangerous for the Indians might see the fires and attack, but we children never realized that. The wagon train ahead of us and the one behind us were both massacred by the Indians, but we were never bothered. Three months we were on those hot dry prairies with never a tree in sight, just sagebrush for miles and miles of flat, level country. During that crossing one poor baby died and had to be buried out there on the prairie. The poor young mother lost her mind and kept trying to run back to find her baby's grave.

"The wagon train traveled along the Platte River to Fort Laramie, Wyoming and went through the Rockies by the South Pass and on north to Fort Hill, Idaho. The next trek was to follow the Snake River all the way to Fort Boise, where their food and water were getting low. "There wasn't much there in that little frontier town, but saloons, gambling houses, dance halls and a fort, but it seemed like Heaven to us. Great excitement that day for our prairie schooners [Conestoga wagons that looked like ships from afar] added quite a bit to the population. Everyone was glad to see us and hear news from the east.

"We lived in our wagons awhile longer until we couldn't decide whether to stay or push on to Oregon. If we left Fort Boise it was by water to Fort Vancouver, Washington. We were so tired, though, and we liked it so well we just decided to stay in Boise, which meant 'beautiful mountains' in Blackfoot. The Fort was built in 1834 by the Hudson Bay Company for fur trading and everyone lived in adobe huts. They were so nice and so glad to have us settle there. Father was offered what's now the best corner on Main Street for his span of mules, but he wouldn't trade, as the mules were the most valuable then. He would say, 'Don't worry if the mule goes blind, just keep the wagon loaded'.

"He finally got some land quite a distance from town and we lived in a log cabin all that winter. I can remember all of us sitting around the big stone fireplace at night, tired but cozy and happy because we were together. Mother and Father, both smoking their pipes. They got real comfort out of it. These cigarette-smoking girls these days don't really enjoy it, they just do it to look smart.

"It was a hard winter, though. We all had to work to keep alive. Father finally had to sell the mules so we could get enough to eat.

"Every once in awhile the Indians would go on a rampage over on Snake River. The big bell would ring in town and we'd drop everything and run for the Fort. Everybody would be scared to death, but they'd finally go back to their ranches." [These were Blackfoot and Shoshone Indians, who lived in skin tepees and were renowned for horse stealing. The Comanche tribe used conical, brush, communal tepees.]

"One time, Mother looked up from her work to find three big Indians standing in the doorway. She almost died of fright, especially when they demanded to see my father. He was out in the field and she didn't know what to do. She was afraid they wanted to kill him. She gave them some food and when they kept insisting on seeing him, she sent one of the boys for him. We smaller children clung to her skirts but were too scared to cry.

"Father came immediately. They stood up and saluted him and said they were going to make war on the whites soon, but as he had befriended one of their tribe he and his family would be safe. After that they left. We were all so relieved we almost gave a war-hoop ourselves. In a few days we heard the same Shoshone Tribe (Snake Indians) killed a little white girl and started their war over on Snake River, but we were never bothered in any way.

"The years passed and I was growing up. I wasn't much more than a little girl though, when I met George [Gumbert]. He was just back from fighting Indians and hunting gold in California. He was about forty-three, [30 years older than Mom who was only 13] the sort of dashing kind, and looking for a wife. I was just at the smart age, and knew it all, so I ran off with him. We were married on New Year's Day. [1865]

"I often wonder how he had so much patience with me. I was such a child. I couldn't keep house or cook a thing. I'd go on a picnic or swimming with the other girls, and then rush home at six o'clock to cook a roast for dinner. Once he brought home sauerkraut, first I'd ever seen and I cooked it without any water.

"I guess I worried him a little bit, too, for I flirted now and then. I wasn't good looking, but I was witty and full of fun, and women were scarce out there then. I never had any girlhood really, for my two children, Lucinda (Oct. 22, 1866) and Johnny (1867), were born before I was seventeen. But George was good in lots of ways and we managed to go through life together. Most of my friends were divorced three and four times. Men were easy to get those days. Women were hard to find.

"We moved to Nevada and it was my first time away from Mother. I thought I'd die of homesickness. I made thirteen trips home on the stagecoach with my babies. There was always danger of Indians, but it was kind of exciting. Once when I was going home to my brother's funeral, my cheeks were frozen it was so cold.

"We lived in Virginia City during the exciting gold rush, at the time when the famous (Henry TP) Comstock Lode was at its height. It was a wonderful mine. All its machinery was tipped with gold. I went down in it once, thirty-five hundred feet below the ground. The miners were stripped to the waist, too hot for shirts. They worked in four-hour shifts, couldn't stand it any longer and then wore ice on their heads all that time. I swore if I ever got out alive, I'd never go underground again until I was put under.

"We had a nice home there in Nevada, a big house well furnished. But the Indians used to get up on a hill back of us and yell and dance all night around their fires. We never knew whether they were serious or not; when the Indians weren't yelling the coyotes were.

"Then George got restless and went to California. When he sent for us, I had to sell everything in a hurry so I sold the house, lot and furniture for fifty dollars and went to him. Money didn't mean much in those days. Once I made eighty thousand dollars on the stock market and kept it hidden under a board in the kitchen floor. Then I got smart, played some more and doubled it. I kept on playing 'till I lost it all. It didn't worry me though. Now, you all take losing money too seriously. Money is the least of life.

"After several years, we went back to Boise to live. Father and my three brothers had died, so only Mother (Lucinda Turner "Baba") and my sister (Ellen Defonda Turner) were left. They were so lonesome we just lived with them. That's where my children grew up. My Johnny was such a dear, affectionate boy, but he wasn't very strong and died when he was just seventeen, just when I could hardly live without him.

"My daughter, "Ludee" (Lucinda), was a beauty. She had lots of beaux, but Ray Pefley, dark haired with a crisp mustache, was the one she wanted, so she ran away and married him just as I had done before her. It struck me funny when Ray, your mother, had such a big church wedding. Half expected her to run away, too.

"I reckon I was the strongest of all the family, for I've buried them all. I'm the last one and you'll have to look after me. Ray, when your father, Ray, died of the measles 5 weeks after you were born, Lucinda brought you home to live with us. Wonder that you weren't spoiled to death, being brought up with your great-grandmother and grandfather and grandmother. It helped a lot to have a baby with us through all the sickness and trouble we had. Ray, you've always been a comfort to me. You're all I have left to link me with the past - you and the movies.

"You make fun of me for liking Western movies but you know, they aren't so far-fetched, as you say. Those old days were pretty exciting. It's grand to live here in the East with you but it's a long way from home.

"Funny how my life's been. I've known six generations, starting with my grandfather on down to your children, my great-grandchildren. Seems like I love them best of all. Like all the loves of my life are centered in them. Here I am over ninety years old and my life's run in a circle. Clear from Kentucky way out west in a covered wagon, with the horses crawling along in the hot sun for months and months. Then after sixty years, east again in a drawing room of a Pullman car, with electric fans and iced drinks, in only five days. And you talk of depression!"

****

After Mom's death in January of 1943, Miss Mason wrote once more in her "Mary Chatter" column,

"Her family and community are grieving, but although her body is no more, she lives today and her spirit will go on in her great granddaughters, who it seemed, "I loved the best of all". Her story will be heard by their little children and so on and on through the years and it will always be an exciting adventure...part and parcel of this great land which is America."

****

Mother, Diane, Elaine, Mom, Sylvia in 1933

FIRST GRIEF

It was a cold, dreary Thursday on January 28, 1943. I had walked home from Butcher School where I was in Miss Ruth Poling's fifth grade. My sister Sylvia was a sophomore at Fairmont Senior High School and we both came home every day for lunch. When upstairs, freshening up to go back to school, we could hear Mom's rattle in her bedroom. She had not responded much to anything for about a week and Dr. John Paul Trach had been called in several days before. I had heard Mother and the doctor discussing she had pneumonia, the "old man's friend" and that her breathing was the "rattle of death."

I was tiptoeing past her room and there was a dead silence. Frightened, I yelled to Sylvia who was up in her room. She came tearing down the stairs and listened with me. We both ran down the back stairs to Mother who hurried us off to afternoon classes. She must have taken care of the rest. When we came home from school- my Mom was gone.

That night I wrote Mom a letter and hid it under the mattress of my bed. I prayed that she would forgive me for all the times she cried and pleaded for me to just sit down and listen to her old stories. I knew she was lonesome, but I seldom had time. She sat day after day in her bedroom window in an old Windsor rocker looking out at the high school children going and coming from school. Why, oh why didn't I go in and sit once more at her knees? I loved her so.

It was my first trip to a funeral home. The first thing that hit me was the heavy aroma of roses, a scent I would never forget - always reminding me of Mom. The dimness from lights in heavy globes directed to the ceiling was frustrating - surely that pale, waxen, peaceful little old woman lying in all the tufted white satin was not my great-grandmother. When no one was looking, I tucked two of her favorite pink roses in her transparent hand; the icy cold penetrated my whole being.

That night I read my letter to her and told her how beautiful she looked, and then tucked it back under the mattress, for her eyes only. It was snowing that cold January night in 1943. When I climbed into that warm bed, the lights were out and I could think of nothing but Mom, all alone at Woodlawn, deep in that cold, cold ground. My grief overwhelms me again. I refused to be comforted and sobbed myself to sleep.

SYLVIA REMEMBERS

My sister Sylvia has lived in Hawaii for the last fifty years. Due to a six-hour time difference, she writes me on the Internet. When she goes to bed I am just getting up and checking my mail. We can instant message frequently. She writes,

"Mom was so much a part of my life and I loved her more than anybody. "I thought I was adopted, but knew I belonged to Mom and could not figure out how we were mixed up in this family. Of course, I never asked anyone-how Daddy would have laughed! I finally decided we must have been walking by 741 Fairmont Avenue one day and they had invited us to come in and stay.

"Mom and I had breakfast together every morning as I was the only one up and Elaine was in school. About nine, Daddy would come down and I remember hugging him and he smelled so good…powder and Colgate. After Daddy left, Mom would read The Curly Tops, The Bobbsey Twins, Honey Bunch and the Oz books, which I didn't like as well as Elaine did. We waited for the Wednesday Idaho Statesman newspaper as it had comics, which we both loved.

"She went to the movies about twice a week and I'd go with Daddy to pick her up. She would be sitting with Mrs. Boyer at the ticket window of the old Nelson Theatre that showed nothing but old Western movies, which she loved. I'd run in to get her, as Daddy could never park out front.

"We always had dinner at 6:30 and I sat next to Mom, who sat on Daddy's right. After eating she always went to the Butler's pantry to chat with Nanny who did the dishes in the huge copper sink. Nanny's children were always sitting on the steps of the back porch. I supposed they got dinner that way. It never occurred to me that they might be hungry, but Mom would make sure they were fed.

"Mom and I were always concerned about money and the depression. I would find ads in the magazines- don't remember what they promised- but we were sure we could win a thousand dollars. She would give me the money to enter the contests, usually a fifty-cent piece. I remember how she cried when Daddy told her she had to hand in her $100 gold piece when we went off the gold standard.

"I worried so about Mom. I know she did not feel good some days and would stay in her room. I remember going alone to see Shirley Temple in "Captain January" and worrying through the whole movie about Mom dying alone in her room without me."

ELAINE'S STORY

Left to right: Mom; Mother and Elaine in 1923

My sister Elaine, Mom's first great-grandchild, wrote a beautiful description of her great grandmother for a high school English class,

"To look at her spotted old hands and faded blue eyes, one would never guess that this ancient being had a history as colorful as the era that fostered her. Born in 1851, those uproarious years preceding the Civil War, she had crossed the plains in a covered wagon, lived in Virginia City at the time of the famous Comstock Lode, gambled away thousands on the game tables of San Francisco, and is never tired of repeating these stories to anyone who will listen.

"Garrulous and grey, she sits in her chair by the window, for the time has passed when she could board the streetcars and go to the movies. Westerns were her favorites as they reminded her of her youth, when she had been on familiar terms with both cowboys and Indians.

"Now she is bent and shapeless, but from the tales of her youth, one can see her promenading the boardwalks of the crude western town, Fort Boise, Idaho. A splendid figure in her heavy black alpaca, correctly bustled with parasol in hand; never possessed with true beauty, yet blessed with a sparkling, infectious love of life; and made friends with the owners of the Comstock Lode to the Chinese who sold her vegetables each morning.

"Though withered and aged she has never lost that love of life and of people. Streetcar conductors and waitresses, banker and senators, never have forgotten her. Her pile of Christmas cards is enormous and each year on Mother's Day her room is crowded with flowers.

"Never pretentiously religious, her life has been an example of God's teachings. She is sincerely interested in everything and everybody and no bit of human misery is too small for her to comfort. Here and there on her worn face is a line etched by sorrow, but there are lines of laughter too. She has looked into the depths of life as well as touched the heights, and now she is tired and feeble. She sits and nods by the fire dreaming of days long forgotten. Here is a soul at peace."

CHAPTER FOUR

HOW GREEN WAS OUR VALLEY

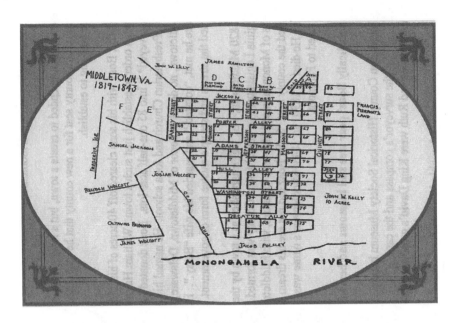

Middletown, Virginia 1819 – 1843

Fairmont, West Virginia

INRODUCTION to Chapter 4

"A VEIN of RICHES"

John Knowles, well known as the author of "A Separate Peace", (1959), his first, world-renowned novel, mentioned much of this valley's history-though fictional -in his novel "A Vein of Riches", (1978).

Jack grew up at 706 Coleman Avenue right behind 700 Benoni Avenue where Papa built his first large home in 1904. Jack was born to Beatrice and Jim Knowles on September 16, 1926 in Fairmont soon after his father was transferred here by CONSOL. Jack had two older siblings. Marjorie (Johnson) and a brother James ("Brud") and a little sister, Dorothy ("Doss") who married Bob Maxwell of Pittsburgh in December of 1952, a month after Paul and I were married. "Doss" and I were good friends and shared several wedding showers together.

Jack attended Saint Peter's elementary school here in Fairmont and then entered Phillips Exeter Academy, graduating from there in 1945. He attended Yale, where he majored in English. He was a typical preppie wearing messy linen jackets, button down shirts - with the first button opened, chino pants - a little too short, and always sockless.

Jack was a good friend of my sister, Sylvia, and spent many hours at our home, 741 Fairmont Avenue. He often talked to Mother and Daddy about "old" Fairmont and was enchanted with Sonnencroft, putting a facsimile of it on his book cover. I am glad he wrote a fictional novel about fictitious people, leaving me the opportunity to tell the true stories of the real people.

In his book, "A Vein of Riches", he writes about the coal barons of Fairmont, with fictional characters in real settings. He explained to Paul and me, "All of my stories are based on places I know and remember very well and places I feel very deeply about. When I wrote "A Separate Peace", I wrote about Exeter Academy and call it Devon. I wanted to write about Fairmont, where I was born and grew up, as a town of the rich and powerful, describing the majestic homes and lavish lifestyles, so I used the coal industry as a framework." Jack's father was an executive with CONSOL, so Jack was very knowledgeable about the coal industry.

"I never knew your grandparents, Diane, but I knew their grandchildren very well; and heard about the money, the terrific industrial strife and the fun of the roaring twenties from our parents - hence "A Vein of Riches".

He even describes in detail Mother's seven-foot tall portrait painted by Vincent Nesbitt of Pittsburgh, when, in this novel, he used our living room at 741 for his description of the fictitious "Catherwood" home. He had never been in Sonnencroft, nor did he know Mammam or Papa. I loved reading how Jack remembered our home after 30 years,

"Big walnut furniture with elaborately carved doors and drawers filled the Catherwood home, which they had tried to name the Towers, but everyone called it Catherwood Castle. The high-ceilinged rooms contained natural and hothouse flowers in cut glass vases; there were colored glass lampshades with cut glass pendants over circular marble-topped tables holding knick-knacks and mementos and framed silhouettes in black against white of children in profile. There were sliding doors, burgundy colored Oriental rugs, tall thrusting potted plants and trees, big enveloping leather and plush armchairs and couches filled rooms shadowed by heavy velvet and brocade draperies, with a very grand portrait of "Minnie" (my mother - Ray) in full evening regalia, egret feathers starting up out of her hair, a pearl dog collar at her throat, in a heavy gilt frame dominating the front living room." He concluded that the Castle was "first and foremost, despite its self-conscious exterior, a comfortable home for a family."

Jack cleverly combined the edifices of Highgate and Sonnencroft to depict the exterior of two homes in the book and called the town Middleburg instead of the first name of Fairmont, Middletown. He even used the telephone number of Minnie's as 93. Our number was 92.

He depicted several people I knew such as Aunt Ophelia (McKay) and Clarence Stallings Robinson. Ophelia looked like the movie grand matron, Edna May Oliver, who played Aunt March in the first Little Women movie with Katherine Hepburn. The Robinsons lived in a great grey stucco house at the corner of Sixth Street and Fairmont Avenue and had no children. She would exclaim, "All the children of Fairmont are mine", and we believed it! She had a lovely shower for Doss Knowles and me; and she and Mrs. M.M. Neely (Alberta Ramage) poured at my wedding reception in 1952. She and Mr. Robinson died within a week of each other in March of 1957. They were both in their late eighties.

Jack writes, "Aunt Ophelia was no blood kin but an aunt by virtue of old family intimacy, as were so many old friends". These dear friends were too close to the family to be called Mrs. Robinson and we were too young to be so rude as to call them by their first names, so we were taught to use the familial term of Aunt and Uncle, but only when asked. Many of us carried this little courtesy through to our children. I always felt my closest friends were like family; and do so even more at my age today. Jack said he was, "trying to establish West Virginia as a southern state - at least - culturally speaking." We are two hours from Charleston, and only one hour from Pittsburgh; I think of us as the most northern of the southern states.

Jack would come back for weddings quite often and be eager to hear about Sylvia and our lives and many of his old friends. He would be thrilled to see others from his past and relied on us to keep him aware of who had died and who to ask about, since his last visit.

Paul and I went to the Morgantown Public Library to meet with Jack on March 14, 1978. He was on a book signing tour for "A Vein of Riches", and with his permission, I taped his speech. I had not seen Jack for several years and it was good to listen to his explanation of his fictional characters while looking right at me. I could see a lot of my mother in "Minnie", but most of the novel was stories she or Daddy, and probably many other parents of friends, had told him combined with his rich imagination. My friend, Eddie Barrett of Huntington, WV always thought "Doris Lee Pence" in the novel was his mother, Jesse Church Barrett, another beautiful woman, but Eddie assures us, she was no one's "paramour".

Jack said, "When my publishers told me in 1960 that they were going to bring out my first novel, "A Separate Peace" on February 29, I should have expected that something unusual was going to happen; a day that happens only once every 4 years. I remember looking back and thinking, maybe three thousand copies will be sold- if I am lucky. Who will want to read about a bunch of high school boys and what happened to them long ago in the past. That was something like nine million copies ago. The one limiting result of this success, my later work was expected to resemble "A Separate Peace"; they wanted all my books to be set in schools." (Esquire, March 1985)

Jack died on November 29, 2001 at the age of seventy-five in Fort Lauderdale Florida.

What a witty, charming, fascinating friend we lost. I have missed him.

THE BLOODY YEAR OF THE THREE SEVENS

After the French and Indian War, in July of 1775 the State of Virginia formed the District of West Augusta on their western frontier. In 1776 West Augusta was sub-divided into three huge counties - Monongalia, Yohogania, and Ohio. [Author's Note: these were the old spellings of the two rivers – Monongahela – Youghiogheny – Ohio - all names of Indian Chiefs] Since that time, many counties in Pennsylvania and present West Virginia have been formed from the original Monongalia County. The county's present size is 368.8 square miles.

The 2006 edition of the West Virginia Encyclopedia reports, "In the 1720s, settlers started coming into the area of the Eastern Panhandle which was the first part of (West Augusta - Virginia) to be settled."

Morgan Morgan, traditionally recognized as the first white settler in West Virginia, was born in Wales on November1, 1688. Morgan, a Welshman immigrating to Delaware in 1712, brought his wife, Catherine Garretson, whom he had met and married in 1714, and five of their nine children into Orange County, Virginia, in 1729. He had been a successful merchant tailor and coroner in the Delaware colony and built a home for the family in what is now called Berkeley County, WV. By 1735, Morgan had acquired 1000 of acres land claimed by Lord Fairfax. Other emigrants followed Morgan, building many homesteads around his. Today it is known as Bunker Hill on Mill Creek, six miles from Martinsburg.

In 1777, the earliest settlers began to move into Monongalia after the French and Indian Wars (1689-1763). Prominent among these settlers were two of the Morgan Morgan's sons, Colonel Zackwell Morgan and David Morgan. Zackwell Morgan built a log house which became Fort Morgan, becoming Morgan's Town; and David Morgan, Captain James Booth, and Jacob Prickett trekked on down into what was to become Marion Co., but not until 1842. David Morgan's son, another Morgan Morgan, was born here in Fairmont and when Captain William Haymond organized his company of Monongalia County Militia in 1777, young Morgan Morgan, assuming his grandfather's role, became its first lieutenant. Thus the first Unit of the 201st Field Artillery Battalion came into being. This 201st Unit, the oldest in the United States, has served in every war for 300 years, from the Revolutionary up to and including today's Iraq and Afghanistan wars.

Even in these unsettled conditions, the general assembly created Monongalia County and they extended every effort to create an effective government.

In the year of the three sevens these pioneers, who were actually invading and pushing this Nation of Indians farther westward, were fighting and clearing the natives' territory claiming it theirs. The Six Nations, the Iroquois Confederacy, consisted of the original tribes of the Mohawks, the Onondagas, the Senecas, the Oneidas, the Cayugas, and the Tuscarawas, thought to be a subordinate group.

In their bark wigwams the braves danced their war dances and sang their war songs. When time to go on scalping expeditions they painted their bodies black and red and wore headdresses of panther skin, or the shaggy horned forehead of the buffalo.

Alexander Scott Withers wrote in his "Chronicles of Border Warfare" (1831),

"When we reflect on the dangers, the difficulties, the complicated distresses to which the inhabitants were exposed, it is really [a] matter of astonishment that they did not abandon the country. How women, with all their feminine weaknesses of the sex, could be prevailed upon to remain during the winter and encounter with the returning spring, the returning horrors of savage warfare is truly surprising. They flattered themselves with the hope that the ravages which had been checked by winter would not be repeated on the return of spring; they were sadly disappointed."

On December 13, 1776, Virginia's first Governor, Patrick Henry, sent messages to the frontier leaders warning them and advising using, "the utmost diligence in preparation for defense against probable Indian hostilities in the spring". How right he was. The Indians hiding in the heavily forested areas would attack a farmer working in his cornfields, or hunters looking for food, often becoming the prey. The savages would then kill the women and children left behind, torching their newly built cabins, then disappearing back to safety into the forests. So many were lost throughout the bloody year of 1777, but a young Monongahela Valley boy recalled: "We had the Reverend John Corbly among us and his prayers and his sermons tended to reanimate the feeble, many of them traveling ten miles to hear him. He represented our cause as the cause of heaven".

Many Indian threats and attacks created a need of forts and barricades to protect the settlers and several were built. The Jacob Prickett's Fort was an important stopping place for emigrants traveling through the area.

Glenn D. Lough tells about Keziah Batten Shearer in his book, "Now and Long Ago".

Mrs. Shearer, who was born in 1776 and lived to be 96, told the stories of the Fort to her younger relatives who recorded her memories. She recalled the settlers used to get an Indian alarm from a scout and men would ride from house to house to give the alarm. The scared families would scurry to the first Prickett's Fort.

Once in 1786 when she was ten years old, her family and many other families lived at the Fort for seven weeks. They stayed in little huts outside the Fort in the daytime and huddled together inside the Fort at night. "The Morgan men would come and go in the moonlight in their buckskin leggings and long shirts with rifles in their hands. Twice Daniel Boone was there with his wife and children and I played with the Boone children."

She said she had seen Gen. Clark (George Rogers Clark) several times; he and Zackwell Morgan would be signing up men for soldier duty. She told of Mr. Richard Taylor and his family coming from the south and riding their horses down the Tygart River with their black and white servants walking along beside them. They remained at the Fort for several days resting up, and Mrs. Shearer remembered the little Taylor boy, less than a year old, that she and all the children held in their arms. She remembered this so well, because that little baby, Zachary, grew up to be President of the United States.

THE SETTLERS

Ten years later the Indians had moved westward but there were still a few Shawnees, Delawares and Chippewas around from the Ohio Valley. In 1787 Boaz Fleming and his brothers, Nathan and Benoni Fleming, who came from the Fleming stock around the town of Milford, Delaware, led a party of relatives and friends into the area of the present Fairmont. Boaz was born in 1758 and fought in the Revolutionary War. After the war, he courted and married Miss Elizabeth Hutchinson from Middletown Delaware. He and his brothers and their wives emigrated to what were Harrison and Monongalia counties.

The Fleming party came with ox drawn wagons, many horses, sheep, turkeys, chickens, cows, and carefully wrapped in an often-wetted piece of flannel, a sprig of a pear tree. In the book, "Now and Long Ago", (1969) Glenn D. Lough tells about an article in the Fairmont Times, April 2, 1936. "M.D. Christie noted that, 'The old pear tree, with its body and limbs all black and dead, is still standing on the vacant lot opposite the hotel on the Hull alley side across from the (Fairmont) Hotel entrance. This lot adjoined the property where I was born and lived until manhood. I remember eating and filling my pockets with that luscious fruit." The old pear tree was removed in 1937 and at least one walking stick or cane was made from it as a memento.

Boaz Fleming had to ride a hundred miles to two different counties to pay his taxes. Today Fairmont and Clarksburg are only about 13 miles apart. One day, on his way home, Boaz stopped to see and complain about all this traveling to his cousins, Mrs. John G. Jackson, the former Mary Payne, who lived in Clarksburg, Harrison County, and Dolley Payne Madison, who was visiting her ill sister. Dolley said to Mr. Fleming, "Why don't you make a county of your own, Boaz, and stop all this traveling?" A seed of truth was planted!

[Author's Note- John G. Jackson and his second wife were grandparents of General Thomas Jonathan (Stonewall) Jackson, 1824-1863 who was born and reared in Clarksburg, Virginia. Dolley Payne Madison (1758-1849) became the fourth First Lady of the United States in 1809-1817.]

First Boaz had to develop a county seat, which he would call Middletown. It had to be bigger and better than all the other towns in the territory, worthy of being a "courthouse town". There is a map dated October of 1818, the oldest map of this new city, with 85 lots and the street names of past presidents. On the back of the map is the signature of surveyor. William Haymond Jr. Some say the Flemings named the new city Middletown because it was the overnight stop for travelers on a two-day stagecoach ride from Morgantown to Clarksburg. It is also said they named it for Elizabeth's birthplace –Middletown, Delaware. Middletown, Virginia was legally established in 1820.

Boaz Fleming named his son David after David Morgan who was the grandfather of the Hon. William S. Morgan, who was responsible for the county of Marion to be established in1842. Middletown was the county seat, but in 1843 the name was changed to Fairmont.

Allison Sweeny Fleming, in his book, "My Own Home Town" (1950), reported in this family history that his great-great grandfather was Nathan Fleming, the older brother of Boaz. His grave is in front of the Fleming Memorial Church. The entire Edgemont district was Nathan's farm and their homestead was a large grey stucco building next to the church, where Sweeny and his sister, Aunt Jean Fleming Wilshire, lived until their deaths.

Mr. Fleming said that many of the streets in Fairmont were named for several generations of Flemings: Benoni, Coleman, Joab (my street, but it was changed to West End Drive in the sixties) and Joseph and Harrison (Jo Harry) Street.

THE VALLEY MINES

More fortunes have been made and lost in Marion County than perhaps anywhere else in the country. There were 18 millionaires reported in Fairmont during 1900-1929 most of them living on Fairmont or Locust Avenues. This was a period when the Coal Barons' holdings soared to an astronomical figure.

In Daddy's Ledger there are many renditions about the first mine in Fairmont and where it was located. I am using quotes of James Otis Watson, II, son of Sylvanus Lamb Watson and grandson of James Otis Watson (1815-1902), "the Father of the Bituminous Coal Industry", and his family remembrances published in The Times-West Virginian newspaper articles in 1957.

J.O.II's daughter, Elinor Watson Carroll, also wrote a wonderful article, published in The West Virginian on Monday, September 20, 1954. Elaine Bennett Watson, widow of Bartlett Watson, son of J.O. II, contributed many interesting facts I have never heard or read about the Watson family. Elaine's sons, Jonathan Blair and Timothy Alan Watson are the last of the James Otis Watson family left around Fairmont.

The first bituminous coal mine in America was opened in 1842 at Eckhart between Cumberland, Maryland and Frostburg, Maryland and was known as the Eckhart Mine. Experienced miners from Wales were employed to teach their skills to local residents. Many of the Welsh built stone houses in Maryland similar to the ones they had to leave in Wales; and many of these houses are still standing and habitable today.

The movie "How Green Was My Valley" (October 31,1941), taken from the book by Richard Llewellyn, depicted the Welch leaving for America back in the late 1800s because their mine owners could not keep up with the experienced miners pay raises; so they lost many of them to America to teach us the rudiments of mining coal.

"Almost everyone in Fairmont had his own mine in his back yard." Glenn D. Lough wrote, "At first each farmer had a coal mine (coal bank) of his own. He dug a tunnel into the hillside with a pick and shovel then hauled the coal to his house on a sled." This coal was only for domestic purposes. If you did not have a vein on your land, your neighbor let you mine his at a rate of a penny a bushel. This method of mining was called "drift mining". The coal seam was usually visible at the side of a hill, known as outcrop coal. The coal was removed from the side of the hill and as the outcrop was reduced, the miner had to follow the seam further and further under the hill, until the working condition became unsafe. Then the mine was abandoned.

Lough wrote, "These coal banks in the area were opened long before 1800 and there is good history that three of these mines were opened before whites are known to have lived here. In Middletown history, coal banks were in operation and mentioned before the town was surveyed. In 1785 John Bunner, on good authority, burned coal at Rivesville to make lime (a limekiln). About 1850, Jimmy Burns opened a mine in Fairmont near the site of Cook Hospital, now the Board of Education on Gaston Avenue, from which he sold the coal".

The first rail shipping of bituminous coal west of the Allegheny Mountains was located within 100 yards of the now razed, B & O Railroad station at the foot of Madison Street in Fairmont WV. This mine was opened in 1852 by James Otis Watson and the astute politician Governor Francis H. Pierpont (1824-1899). Very few people today realize that this Fairmont mine and the Eckhart mine were the nucleus of what is today the best operated coal corporation in the world, the Consolidated Coal Company."

Francis H. (Frank) Pierpont, Governor of the "restored state of Virginia", lived in Fairmont, and helped develop a strategy to bring the railroad in to Marion County, thus giving the budding coal industry a real boost.

The first railroad in the United States was our own Baltimore and Ohio Railroad. The B&O was started in Baltimore in 1828. It was fashioned after the first steam railroad in the world built in England in1825 and called the Stockington and Darlington RR. Stephenson in England and Cooper in America designed the first steam locomotives and its first terminal was in Cumberland, Maryland. Frank Pierpont later served as an attorney for the B&O railroad.

Working closely with President Abraham Lincoln in creating the new state of West Virginia, Pierpont, from a historical standpoint, occupies a special niche in history. This led to Pierpont's statue being erected in Statuary Hall in the United State Capitol building, representing West Virginia. West Virginia is the only state created from the Civil War.

Julia Robertson Pierpont, the Governor's wife, her daughter Anna and friends decorated the graves of Union soldiers buried in Hollywood Cemetery in Richmond, and she was credited for initiating Decoration Day -

now called Memorial Day. She, her husband, daughter Anna (Siviter) and sons, William and Samuel are buried at our historic Woodlawn Cemetery and were significant for the cemetery being listed on the National Historic Register in April 2004.

Since the upper Monongahela Valley has been engaged in coal production for over 150 years, many people believe that the coal has been exhausted - not so! No matter that the southern coalfield owners are taking advantage of quick and easy mountain top removal, the entire northern corridor of Appalachia is in underground mining.

In 1942, George R. Higginbotham was transferred to Fairmont and became president of the Mountaineer Division of Consolidated Coal Company of WV (CONSOL). He bought a beautiful, first-of-its-kind, house from Eugene Holland in Fairmont Farms. This house was right across the street from LaGrange, J.O. Watson's homestead. Higginbotham's son, Attorney George R. Jr. and his wife, Janice, live there today. John, the youngest son of Josie and George, and his wife Jeanne Marie, also live in the Farms' log house built by David Morgan. [It is often called a cabin, but a cabin has only one floor and a loft; and a log house has two floors.]

According to Glenn Lough, David Morgan built this log house in 1779 and called it "Riversee". Riversee was 361 acreage of farmland and Morgan reserved 39 acres of the land for his home. The land was high enough to overlook the Tygart Valley River and the West Fork River where they meet at a little settlement called Pettyjohn. [These two rivers form the Monongahela River at the Watson Bridge, which flows 128 miles North to Pittsburgh, PA meeting with the Allegheny and creating the Ohio River].

The Pettyjohn brothers had opened a little store on their land that David Morgan had given them and soon it was authorized as a "mail-drop", (authorized Post Office). Today Pettyjohn is at 14th Street. The land where the East West stadium and the Municipal Pool both built by the Works Progress Administration (WPA) during Roosevelt's New Deal program in 1937 was David Morgan's cornfield. David Morgan heirs sold his log house in 1813 to Benoni Fleming's nephew, Alexander Fleming and several years later; Alexander sold it to J.O. Watson, who had ten children.

Mr. Higginbotham asked the CONSOL engineers to make an estimate of the remaining tonnage of coal available in the untapped seams of Appalachia. It should be of interest, and made known to the alarmists, that the study showed,

"Sixteen billion tons of recoverable coal is in seams of the small area between Clarksburg and the Pennsylvania boundary, and from the Ohio River to the coal out crop east of the Monongahela River. With the enormous amount of recoverable coal in the Appalachians - the largest coal field in the world - extending a distance of 908 miles, and including the large coal acreage in the northern and western states, our country has a coal supply for 2000 years."

My Grandfather, Clyde E. Hutchinson suspected this and took his wife, Mary Lyda, and four sons, Claude, Brooks Lee, and Frank to Chicago in 1895 for five years to learn the intricacies of becoming a coal broker in his Monongahela Valley, composed of the northern counties of Barbour, Harrison, Marion, Monongalia, and Preston. In 1900 they came back to make their fortune with a fifth son, Harold.

According to J.O.II, "The first explosion in this area was at the Gaston mine in 1880 when two men were killed." In 1883 the state legislature established the West Virginia Department of Mines with Oscar Veasey appointed as the first Mine Inspector. Three years later a second explosion was at Newburg, in Preston County, WV in 1886, when 39 men were killed. Many of these miners are buried at Woodlawn Cemetery in Fairmont.

"The greatest mine disaster in the world at that time was December 6, 1907, the Monongah, West Virginia mine explosion when 361 men lost their lives. The road to Monongah from Fairmont was not paved until 1914. So many hundreds of friends and relatives of the deceased rode the inter-urban streetcars to the site to help in any way they could.

"The French government sent four officials to study and investigate the Monongah catastrophe, but they were called back to France that same month because of another explosion that occurred in Charleroi, France in which more than 1000 miners were killed. There were many other explosions throughout the world, although no one could ever officially say the cause was gas, or dust, or a mixture of both."

Thank God the Hutchinson Coal Company suffered only one disaster in 1917 under Clyde Hutchinson's ownership. It was printed in the local newspaper in a Miner' Day supplement. Thanks to an old friend, Delegate Mike Caputo, majority whip of the West Virginia House of Delegates and Vice President of International District 31 of the United Mine Workers of America, who sent me the details from "Archives and History", State Capitol, Charleston West Virginia:

"Major Coal Mine Disasters in the United States not classified as Explosions: 1846-1962:

The Lynden Mine in Mason County West Virginia

"On Wednesday morning, April 18, 1917, about 7:00 a.m., an unusual happening occurred at Mason in Mason County, W.Va., when lightning struck a powder magazine at the Lynden mine, exploding thirty kegs of powder. There were five men working in the powder house and when the magazine was demolished all five men were killed."

****

Coal production in the state increased from more than two million tons in1883 to more than 11 million tons in 1894. By 1900 coal production had doubled to 22 million tons. The boom created more tragic explosions, because of employment of unskilled workers, including immigrants as well as white and black natives. Even sons of freed slaves were recruited from the South, all of them new to mining. In 1907 alone there were explosions at the Red Ash Mine, and the Stuart shaft mines in Fayette County, killing 46 and 81. "Thirty-seven of those 81 were listed as "Americans", meaning white natives." (West Virginia Encyclopedia)

From 1900 to 1910 there were 26 mine disasters in the United States. From 1910 to 1920 there were only 17. Each decade the explosions became fewer.

Clarence Edwin (Ned) Smith, who was born in Fairmont, July 11, 1885, was just three years older than my father, Brooks, and a good friend. Everyone in town read his front-page, above the fold column, "Good Morning!" to learn the truth behind the news, each day with their first cup of coffee, much as we do today with the Times West Virginian Editor, John C. Veasey.

"Ned" Smith attended the public schools here including Fairmont High School, then to finish his preparatory work at Virginia Military Institute in Lexington Virginia. He attended the University of Virginia in 1904 and 1905, returning home to be a cub reporter for the "Times", edited by his father, General Clarence Linden Smith. His mother was Margaret Virginia Fleming Smith whose ancestry ran back through the Barnes family to Captain Phillip Pindall, Captain of the Maryland militia in the Revolutionary War.

Soon after "Ned" became a reporter, one of his first major assignments was to cover the Monongah Mine disaster in 1907, at the age of 22. In August of 1926, as editor of the Times, he wrote about the Jamison Cole and Coke Co. No.8 mine in Farmington, where 19 were killed on January 14, 1926:

"About 9:o'clock last night we were sitting in Jock McNeil's (John H. McNeil Sr.) house talking about the No. 8 Mine. We had been upstairs talking to Jock as he lay in bed. He still had pain in his chest from the black damp and was nervous from his harassing experience. He had told Bob Lily, June Clark and our self the whole story from kiver to kiver. He told us about how the trapped men prayed for deliverance and how their prayers had been answered.

Jock spoke in deep reverence of how the little group of miners, foreign born, native born, and Negros - all Americans, had sat through the long hours in the icy darkness trembling on the brink of eternity. 'I am going to do a lot more reading of the bible than I used to,' he said simply.

"On Thursday night, shortly after 10 o'clock there was a local explosion in some of the new workings of the No. 8 mine know as the 7th Right Heading or Entry. The explosion killed every living thing within an area as big as the business section of Fairmont. In such mine explosions Death travels upon a path of dust. In No.8 there was no dust and only those whom death could reach with his fiery tongue were laid low. A mile away down near the face of the coal in the workings centering around the 20th right entry, 20 odd men were working. We, on the outside did not think these men had a gambler's chance to be alive.

"Just about dawn, Bill Riggleman, the veteran mine inspector told us he thought they might be alive and this cheered us, but they started to bring out the bodies of the dead. Each poor fellow was wrapped in canvas and lay upon a stretcher. One at a time they came up the coal shaft until we counted ten. Curiosity led us to follow the first one into the improvised morgue. He had been killed by concussion and flame but his watch was still ticking away as if to boast that neither fire nor flame nor blast nor death can halt Time in her flight. Then they brought in a young fellow, badly blasted but whose tiny electric safety light bulb still burned brightly on his cap.

"What a grim old monster is Death, we thought, to snap a man's life without breaking the filament of a tiny light bulb on his brow. Perhaps, we thought, the light is symbolic that it burns in death as a sign that God is not far away and is moving in mysterious ways His wonders to perform. "The third blackened form was laid beside the first and side by side lay the father and the son." We came home just before noon and slept."

Jock McNeil's little group of the 20th Right Entry were found alive. The next afternoon, Ned Smith received a call, "The voice at the other end of the line tried to be calm, 'Those men in the mine are alive. There are twenty men coming out of the mine now'. Only nineteen were lost.

Yesterday's Times with glaring headlines proclaiming all were dead lay on a chair, a sad commentary of man's knowledge of the unknown."

****

I remember well the huge Consolidated Coal Company's No.9 mine (the former Jamison No.9 mine) in the great Pittsburgh coal seam near Farmington, Marion County, a few miles from Fairmont, on November 20, 1968. I had friends who lost brothers, sons and fathers in this carnage. A huge burst of black smoke and flames burst from the pit opening and rocks and debris were shot everywhere. Seventy-eight men were lost, but 21 made it out safely. Because of this explosion, Congress passed the Federal Coal Mine Health and Safety Act of 1969 and President Richard Nixon signed it. This Farmington disaster also contributed to the eventual unseating of the UMW President Tony Boyle, who angered many by defending Consolidated Coal Company.

The West Virginia encyclopedia lists "as of January, 2006, 118 disasters have taken place in West Virginia at 104 different mines", but they did not start counting until 1883.

A local author and historian, George Ramsey, Jr., reported in the Times-West Virginian, September 3, 2010:

"The first Italian flag unfurled in the state was in Fairmont about 1903. This occurred when groups of Italian immigrants, along with others from the eastern and southern regions of Europe began to arrive on the scene to work in the mines and mills of West Virginia."

****

Evidently the Italian government, seeing an emerging immigrant problem, chose Fairmont, because of the location and the many mines in the area, to open a Consulate in the Skinner Tavern down near the B&O station on the

Monongahela River. Mr. John Marianni, a graduate of Yale University, served as consular agent.

Some six weeks later on July 24, 1903 the first Italian church in West Virginia was opened in Monongah, where, after the explosion in 1907, all the 361 dead covered the hillside around their new church.

In 1908, the Fairmont Times listed the number of foreign immigrants in Marion County as 2,964 Italians; 2,753 Hungarians; 1,540 Polish; 3,519 other nationalities, including the Irish who immigrated here as a result of the of the potato famine in Ireland. The list ended with 20,409 whites and 9,908 black Americans.

By 1910, Fairmont was called "Coal City", and the Fairmont Field was called the "Coal Capital of the Appalachian Valley", and became the greatest bituminous coal region in the world.

Where would the country be today without the coal mining workforce who strived daily to bring that energy to the surface of these West Virginia hills? The Welsh had taught us how to mine the coal from underground, but we did not have the workforce to execute the process. The Italians, and the Irish, were starving and eager to come from afar, often leaving their family behind, to send for later. They were promised homes and jobs, a prerequisite before boarding a ship. Many received passage money for their families to come to the "Land of Freedom and Wealth".

When they reached the new Ellis Island, opened in 1900, many kissed the ground. Some of their family names were changed, dropping the "I" or "O" at the ending, to facilitate the harried registrars. Many were called TONY, simplifying first names, because they wore badges explaining their destination: TO NY.

These are the people who mined the energy for the country and helped us create the greatest coal industry in the world.

The Hutchinson Coal Camp.

Hutchinson Coal Camp at Hutchinson, Inc.
Marion County, West Virginia

KINGS of COAL

Hutchinson Coal Company Ad; Clyde Effington Hutchinson; Brooks Hutchinson (left) and Frank Hutchinson (right) in Logan Country, WV

Robert Leroy Ripley's column, "Ripley's Believe It Or Not", always enjoyed in the Sunday's paper comic section, stated in the early 1920s,

> "There are more millionaires within one square mile in Fairmont, West Virginia than anywhere else in the world."

****

In 1890, the city of Fairmont census showed a population of 992. The beginning of the coal industry and the oil boom in Mannington, started by John Davison Rockefeller (1831-1937), founder of Standard Oil Company in 1870, and Michael L. Benedum of Harrison County brought many new comers into Marion County; many who would become million and billionaires. J.D. Rockefeller was purported to have 1.5 billion dollars at the time of his death on May 23, 1937; just four weeks before his great grandson, J.D. Rockefeller, IV was born on June 18, 1937. Many years later, "Jay" arrived in WV as a Peace Corp volunteer and, we were delighted he decided to stay. He first became our two term Governor and has been our U.S. Senator since 1984.

It all started here in Mannington, Marion County, West Virginia back in the late 1860s.

One hundred and forty years later, on 16 March 2010, The Fairmont Times West Virginian printed a front-page article by Michael Felberbaum, AP Business writer from Richmond, Virginia:

"CONSOL Energy Inc. has agreed to buy Dominion Resources, Inc.'s Appalachian exploration and production business for $3,475 billion substantially increasing its natural gas reserves and production capacity. The deal will give the coal and natural gas company a leading position in the strategic Marcellus Shale, a rock bed about 6,000 feet beneath New York, Pennsylvania, West Virginia, and Ohio that could be the country's most productive natural gas source." The part that really interested me, "CONSOL will acquire a total of 1.46 million oil and gas acres from Dominion along with over 9000 producing wells, the assets that were originally part of John D. Rockefeller's Standard Oil Empire."

****

Forbes magazine printed a Forbes 400-Photo Essay about Fairmont in the October 9, 2000 issue about Fairmont with a picture of Highgate, J.E. Watson's estate on Fairmont, Avenue:

"About 90 miles southwest of Pittsburgh, PA, Fairmont, W.Va. is identified as a hotbed of millionaires on several Web sites. Area authorities have heard the claims but cannot fully verify them. No Fairmont residents appear on the Tribune World Almanac lists. But the zenith was clearly around 1900, when the population was about 5,500 and coal was king, with numerous coal companies - and coal company presidents, in town. We figure the ratio of millionaires at one out of about 688. Many were partners or family members of James Otis Watson, coal tycoon. His son Clarence became a US Senator." [After the death of Republican-Stephen B. Elkins, Clarence-a Democrat was elected in a special election to serve out the remaining two-year term, 1911 to 1913. Clarence ran in the next regular election and lost to Republican Nathan B. Goff of Clarksburg, who was elected in 1913 and served out a full term.]

"Fairmont enjoyed excellent rail connections, but recessions, depressions, labor unrest, the ups and downs of the coal industry eventually dissipated most of the fortunes of Fairmont. Highgate, the Elizabethan style mansion of the J.E. Watson family, sat on a full city block. This mansion passed from family ownership in 1929 and for several decades has been an oversize funeral home". [Actually, J.E.'s widow, Matilda (Modderwell) Watson sold Highgate in 1929 to the Wheeling Diocese of the Catholic Church for the retired Sisters of Saint Joseph and was bought after WWII by the Ross family for their Funeral Home and they still own it.]

****

On September 26, 2009, The Times West Virginian headlined "STATE NO LONGER at BOTTOM of FORBES LIST". George Hohmann of the Charleston Daily Mail writes:

"Forbes Magazine has placed WV up from the bottom of the Annual List to 46." After a private interview with Governor Joe Manchin of Fairmont, who spoke with Editor Steve Forbes about how "WV is changing", Forbes, said, "You have a chance to surge ahead. You have a nice area, low electricity prices, low property taxes. Build on those. Build on reforms. Don't stop now."

****

In 1852 to 1885 the coal industry in Fairmont was in its infancy. Then, as an adolescent, it began to grow into maturity when J.E. Watson and Neil Gaskins constructed the Montana Mine on the Monongahela River and built the first successful beehive coke ovens, catching the attention of Standard Oil Co. multi millionaire, US Senator Johnston Newlon Camden, from Parkersburg, WV. Urged on by J.D. Rockefeller, the scoundrel, Camden, arrived in Fairmont as a guest of the Governor Fleming's oldest son George, carrying a shotgun, supposedly to shoot squirrels, but actually bent on acquiring a coal empire. He persuaded J. E. and Sylvanus Watson to sell him 70,000 acres or 700 million tons of recoverable coal along the West Fork River, a distance of 33 miles. Claiming the coal could not be recoverable "for ages," he kept the price down to five dollars per acre.

Senator Camden wanted to name the town of Monongah, Camden, but the Post Office refused as Monongah was already listed and, before 1890, the original name was Briartown. The new Fairmont suburb was named "Jayenne", for J.N. Camden, (now called Westchester). As initials were not allowed in a school's name, Jayenne School was built for the rural students of the area, as the city line lies a few feet west from Locust Avenue and still remains so.

The Rockefellers and the Camdens were the first of the "out of state barons" to come into our valley. Bobby Kennedy, Jr. asked, in 2010, in his debate with our latest scoundrel, Blankenship of Massey Coal, "Why is it that West Virginia has the richest resources and is still the poorest state? It is greed!"

J.N. opened mines with seams running into Harrison County and along Route 19 as far as Shinnston. Caroline Richards Carlot tells about her grandfather of Harrison County, Goff Joseph Richards, a member of the US Senator Nathan Goff family; and her father, Paul Joseph Richards who was one of ten sons. Ten years after the "crash" in 1939, father and son rescued abandoned Cameron mines around Shinnston, and called the corporation, Pitfair Coal Company. These Pittsburgh seams of bituminous coal were very productive into the 1970s, when the Richards brothers sold the Pitfair Company to the Galloway Land Company of New York City.

Caroline remembers her father telling of how demeaning the depression was and how, with nine brothers they had to share clothes with each other and how his mother had saved buttons for years as we all did, as buttons were an expensive commodity. She had no white buttons left so would add colored buttons to replace the lost ones. Paul Joseph remembered being chastised in front of his class by his seventh grade teacher for not having all white buttons on his shirt, and how humiliated he felt.

One of the Fairmont coal kings, Judge Aretas Brooks Fleming, was a capable and conservative lawyer and was the ultimate friend of his political opponent Nathan B. Goff of Clarksburg. In 1888, with the help and support of Camden, Fleming, after a bitter campaign, won the Democrat nomination for Governor of WV over Goff, the Republican candidate. In the initial count, Goff won by 106 votes. Fleming demanded a recount challenging the residency of many black voters in Mercer and McDowell counties. Both Fleming and Goff were sworn in on Inauguration Day, but Emanuel Willis Wilson, the incumbent Governor refused to give up the office. The state Supreme Court upheld Wilson. Finally, over a year later on January 1890, in a party line vote by the Legislature, Fleming was sworn in as West

Virginia's eighth Governor. Fleming served until 1893 and returned to his practice of Law in Fairmont, and his and J.O. Watson Fairmont Coal Co.

Fleming's and Watson's success in the coal business was marred by the terrible Monongah disaster that killed 361 men and boys in 1907. Fleming recognized that good mines must be safe mines, discouraging the use of children in any capacity in West Virginia; and in 1910 had considerable influence in establishing the U.S. Bureau of Mines. The Federal Government did not regulate the Child Labor Laws, minimum age and hours, until 1938.

J. O. Watson II reports:

"While Fleming knew nothing about coal operations and cared even less, he will go down in history as one of West Virginia's leading coal men."

"My grandfather, J. O, was a farmer, merchandise miner, and coal operator and he and Governor Francis Haymond Pierpont were partners and friends, but the two simply could not cooperate in coalmine operations. J. O. and Pierpont separated went into courts over some dispute and never spoke to each other again. Immediately after J. O. died in 1902 the representatives of both families held an amicable meeting and in a few moments, concluded the long drawn out dispute which was satisfactory to both parties."

****

James Roosevelt was the father of President Franklin Delano Roosevelt and Warren Delano was Franklin's grandfather. Warren Delano was a director of Consolidated Coal when it was formed in 1864 and continued in that position until 1875. The Delanos and John D. Rockefeller were prominent in the oil, gas and coal of the Fairmont area, and remembered the Watson name. In 1928, J. O. Watson II was proud that he was asked to wheel the future Governor of New York, Franklin Delano Roosevelt and aid him in walking to the podium to nominate Al Smith for President at the Houston, Texas Democratic Convention in 1928. Roosevelt had contracted poliomyelitis- which at that time was called Infantile Paralysis, at Campobello Island, their summer retreat in New Brunswick, Canada in August of 1921; and in his political career he was seen only twice in a wheel chair as it was politically fatal to show such weakness.

The fourth son of James Otis Watson, the "Father of the Bituminous coal industry", James Edwin (J.E.) Watson (1859-1926) assumed control of the Valley Coal operation in 1885 when his father turned seventy. J.E. organized the Bank of Fairmont, the Fairmont Development Company, later called the FDIC and was Director of the Fairmont-Clarksburg Transit Company. In 1890, J.E made many shrewd investments, which were instrumental in forming what was to become CONSOL in WV. By 1900 he had inherited and amassed a huge fortune. Associated with him were his brothers, Sylvanus and Clarence. Clarence was only 21 years old.

J.E. had always been frail and had been born with one leg much shorter than the other leg, preventing the luxury of any athletic endeavors and requiring a valet to dress and chauffeur him. I remember his tiny little wife, "Mattie" Modderwell Watson, a great friend of my grandmother's. She was only as tall as I was in Jr. High School, about 4ft. 8in. I recall she was easy to hug; but it would have been difficult for her to take care of any Watson, they were all very large, as were her children and grandchildren.

Carol Lee Bobet Gilmore, an old friend and schoolmate, told me about her father, who was J.E.'s valet as a very young man and became very attached to his charge. Carol Lee said, at the time of J.E.'s death in 1926, he had sponsored Chester Bobet in a franchised News Service, where all periodicals and newspapers arrived and were distributed to all the local outlets for sale. The building stood next to the Fairmont Theatre on Adams Street and was called Bobet News.

As J.E's. health was failing in 1910, he had resigned to a wheelchair, and had to turn the coal operation over to Clarence, the youngest brother, the scallywag. The patriarch, J.O. Watson, had not only disapproved of him, but had disowned his youngest son because of his total disregard for money and his irresponsible lifestyle.

****

"J.E. Watson is Dead"
"Business Leader is Taken After Bitter Battle with Death"
The Fairmont Times
Tuesday Morning, August 3, 1926

"After a valiant fight for his life, after years of untold and patient suffering, struggling against afflictions that came over him a quarter of a century ago, James Edwin Watson, aged 67 years, pioneer coal operator and banker, passed away to his eternal sleep at 10:25 o'clock at his home at Highgate on Fairmont Avenue.

"Coal was king to Mr. Watson and from his early manhood he had followed this industry beginning his career with his illustrious father, the late James Otis Watson, one of the very early coal operators of the Fairmont region. More than forty years ago he took charge of the J.O. Watson coal interests, which embraced practically all the operations in this area. And was head of the same for a long period."

****

According to J.O. II, "James Edwin was probably the best coal operator the Valley ever produced and could never be replaced." However, "Clarence had a number of able operation associates, his brother, Sylvanus Lamb, Clyde E. Hutchinson, John A. Clark, Rolf Hite, and several other men", that CE (Ned) Smith, editor of The Fairmont Times, aptly described as "Tall Timber". The younger generations included John A. Clark, Jr., Brooks S. Hutchinson, Frank Lyon, William Doolittle, the Showalters and Stoetzers, the Robinsons, the Dobbies, and "poor old Sam Brady".

I coin Daddy's expression of him because on Sunday afternoon drives we would go to the Fairmont Field Club. When we passed the yellow brick walled entrance leading up to the beautiful home called Pinelea, now the home of friends, Bob and Carol (Sorensen) LaFollette, my father would shake his head and say, "Poor old Sam Brady". Evidently Sam, a good friend, was a victim of the Crash and one of the barons who committed suicide by a fatal gunshot. Carol swears she has inherited his ghost.

These second-generation coal kings were good friends, having grown up together. A few were trapper boys and a few went to prep schools together. Their fathers were friends, compatible, but competitors who had learned the business of Coal, starting out with so little, and with primitive, crude techniques, yet gaining unheard of wealth through the sweat of their brow. They loved every minute of it and welcomed new competition, but not the out of state "scallywags", who had taken advantage of them. They made sure their sons, the younger generation, went to universities and became mining engineers or attorneys or business men, knowledgeable in this new industry so important to the world.

THE TRAPPER BOYS

Many of this younger generation of Coal Barons grew up in the mines working as "Trapper Boys", a term not heard of today. There were no West Virginia child labor laws until 1910 and the young boys, starting at the age of six, got paid 10 cents a day to be lifted down in to a narrow mine shaft, fill their bucket and drawn back up, time after time each day. The scenes of Roddy McDowell as a little trapper boy in HOW GREEN WAS MY VALLEY are difficult to forget.

J.O.II had many little friends, whose family owned mines, and served as trapper boys for their fathers or grandfathers. J.O. Watson II and John A. Clark, Jr. (June) were trapper boys along with Glenn D. Lough, Pete Sypult, James Gillis, Ted Jarrett and George Murray of Rachel. They brought in their friends to help and they each received 80 cents a day for a 10-hour day. Most of the children were under 10 years old, depending on their size.

Some of the small boys were stationed at traps (canvas flaps) or doors in various parts of the pit. The trapper opened the flaps so that the trams of coal could pass through, and then immediately closed it. Air ventilation was stringently controlled and if the trap was not closed correctly, parts of the mine would lack adequate ventilation and dangerous gases would build up.

The work was arduous and very scary to a little boy. It was pitch black, a candle or an oil lamp was all the light a child would have. Sir Humphrey Davy did not invent the safety lamp - a flame burning inside metallic gauze that cannot ignite the methane gas (fire damp), for several more years. The flame of the Davy lamp would change under various concentrations of gas.

If the young boy's candle or oil went out he would spend the rest of the day in complete darkness with the ominous sounds of strata moving, pieces of roof or sides falling and rats were common visitors. The walls of coal were draped with grey material to keep down the dust, and fluttered when the flap was raised and lowered, creating a ghost- like wavering. My friend, the late Rosemary Brunetti Tennant's father, Giuseppe (Joe) Brunetti, used to tell his children about how scary those depths of coal were. His mama worried so about him she gave him a prayer book in Italian to read by his candle lamp, but when he would get to the passage, "in the name of the Father, the Son and the Holy GHOST", he would be frightened all over again!

John A. Clark, Jr., a close friend of the family, hence Uncle June to me, grew up from a trapper boy in his daddy's mine to be one of the most influential coal operators in the nation. His father, John A. Clark, came to Monongah from Newburg, the site of the first recorded mine disaster in West Virginia history, in 1889, to help open up the Camden mines. Mr. Clark was the son of one of the first locomotive engineers of the Baltimore and Ohio RR who ran a powder train for General Beauregard's army during the War Between the States and died in 1870 at Elizabeth Town, Kentucky.

The senior Clark came to Newburg in 1877 from the George Creek section of Maryland. After 12 years with the Newburg Coal and Oil Co, he joined the J.N. Camden operations in Monongah. Clark opened his first mine called the Double X, in reference to the two $10 bills with which he was reputed to begin operations. As this mine prospered he started the Anderson Mine in the bend of the West Fork River in 1894 and then the Chiefton Mine in 1896. Working with him were his three sons, John A. Jr., Harry B. and Kenna Clark.

Uncle June would tell of seeing the first electric light in 1894 as coal officials gathered in the Watson Hotel Lobby on Adams and Madison Street. J.A. Sr. announced he would not be afraid to place that Edison light in a keg of powder, and the 6-year-old June was scared to death he might do it, fearing a terrible explosion.

Later, in 1907, Uncle June, a large, strong 18 year old, worked continuously at the Monongah mine explosion from December 6 until Christmas Eve. In the "West Virginian", Elinor Watson Carroll reported:

"June could always recall the names of the various men he discovered in the fated mine, as he knew 300 of the 361 victims personally; and could tell their families where each man was found after the blast."

Uncle June married Annette Murphy of Uniontown, Pennsylvania in 1911 and they had two sons, John A. III and Frank Jackson. Frank remained in Fairmont and ran the mines for many years with his father. J.O. Watson II reported in the mid 1950s that the Clark Coal mines had been in continuous operation since 1890. Today, Uncle June's grandson, Frank Jackson. Jr. and his wife Mary still live in the Monongah area.

When I was going to New York to visit my sisters in 1948, Aunt Annette Clark sent me the first one hundred dollar bill I had ever seen. I can still remember Mother crying over such an unexpected gift and I have always remembered her kindness to a little 16-year-old girl.

It was a terrible shock to us when Aunt Annette died on a City Lines Bus at the corner of Fairmont Avenue and Country Club Road on July 9, 1957 of a heart attack. She was on her way home from seeing her doctor, J.J. Jenkins, Jr., who had just given her "a clean bill of health".

Uncle June lived to be 69 and died at his home 67 West End Drive after three paralytic strokes in 1958. He knew everyone in Fairmont and had a nickname for each one of us. My moniker was "Curly Top".

The Fairmont Times reported on May 3, 1958:

> "June Clark took a paternal interest in his employees and often said, his men did not work for him - but with him. Clark numbered among his many friends, the heads of most of the Coal industry and virtually all of the United Mine Workers, from President John L. Lewis down."

****

Fifty years later, I was appointed Chairman of the Woodlawn Preservation Society. I was speaking to the Fairmont Rotary Club at the Fairmont Field Club trying to recruit trustees to be legally appointed to a new Board of Trustees for the Woodlawn National Historic Cemetery. I was pleading for those who might be interested to stand up and serve. Frank Jackson Clark, Jr. stood up and said, "All of my family is buried at Woodlawn, and, Diane, you made me feel guilty. I will serve as a trustee."

How proud Uncle June and Aunt Annette would be.

John A. Clark, Jr.

A FAMILY AFFAIR

Papa, Clyde Effington Hutchinson, was originally from Smithtown situated near White Day Creek, today - White Day Golf Course. Smithtown was six miles from Fairmont, but the intervening space has been so built up it has become the "outskirts" of the City. Clyde was one of the area's earliest pioneers in the coal industry. Starting what was to become a statewide coal empire at Beachwood near Catawba in the 1880s, Clyde had mines all over the state of West Virginia and in Cincinnati, Ohio.

He went to Chicago in 1895 to1900 to study how to broker coal. He left in 1895 when he was 35 and Lyda was 31, and with four sons, Claude 9, Brooks 8, Lee 6, and Frank 4, and returned in 1900 with a fifth son, Harold Herbert. While in Chicago they lived in a large house on Lexington Avenue, South Side first and then moved to 18 Wisconsin Street, North Side.

When the family returned to Fairmont, Clyde built a large stately house on the corner lot of Seventh Street and Benoni Avenue. This property has been restored by the Vandalia Heritage Foundation as a gesture of our Congressman Alan B. Mollohan to maintain the name of one of northern West Virginia's most prominent pioneers of the northern coal prosperity.

Clyde literally dragged his older brother, Melville Lee, from the general store that their father had managed before his premature death, into Fairmont to help keep the company's books. Uncle Mel preferred the quiet country life. The two brothers formed Hutchinson Coal Co. and soon opened a mine at Hutchinson in Grant District and several in Harrison County. These included one at Mt. Clare, Erie mine at Hephzibah, Robey and Laura Lee at Lumberport - the latter named for one of M. L's daughters- and the McCandlish Mine at Meadowbrook, the Gerard Mine at Dola and the York mine at Reynoldsville.

In the book, Great Coal Leaders of West Virginia (1988), Fred Toothman writes:

"Clyde and M.L. seemed to make a good business team. Clyde was the zealous, adventurous outside man, while M.L. was content to keeping a sharp eye on the cash flow and the bottom line.

"As the coal industry boomed, the brothers branched out to the southern part of the state and formed the Logan Mining Co. opening mines in Logan and Fayette counties.

74

"Their first venture was to buy the distressed mine at Omar where John Kelly and Jack Dalton were facing bankruptcy.

" This mine was later put into Clyde's West Virginia Coal and Coke Company in 1925, but the other two mines, Dabney and Macbeth were kept under the Hutchinson name.

"Several other mines were operated by the merged company in the Logan area mines including the Earling mine at Manbar, Mona mine at Monaville, Rossmore mine at Rossmore, and Manitoba and Wanda Mine at Ethel. These mines made up the Rich Creek Coal Co and were primarily operated by Brooks and Frank, sons of C. E. This company also operated two mines at Lybrun and one at Wilburn.

"Fifty-eight coal mines combined in southern West Virginia and merged with C.E. Hutchinson's group forming West Virginia Coal and Coke in February 1925. The deal combined a working capital of $25,000,000 and C.E. Hutchinson became president of the new corporation with offices in Cincinnati and Cleveland Ohio, and in Philadelphia, Pennsylvania."

****

Clyde built the Jacobs and Hutchinson building on the corner of Adams and Monroe Street in 1902. The Jacobs-Hutchinson block was designed by Andrew C. Lyons and built by S. Ray Holbert and W.H. Spedden. The other owners of the building were the Jacobs brothers, George M. and J. Melville. (Lyons had designed all these men's private residences).

Debra Ball McMillan in Ornament to the City (1996) writes:

'This neo-Classical structure is 92 feet x 82, five stories high and is built of Roman shaped pressed brick and trimmed with Euclid blue stone, with a terra cotta cornice."

****

When it was built it was to be used as four separate businesses. The fifth floor was the Hutchinson Coal Company and a passageway, only on the fifth floor, led into Mel Jacobs' office, as he was secretary of the coal company. His daughter, the late Nancy Lou Jacobs (Bosley) was a friend and member of my class (1950) at Fairmont Senior High School.

Cletus H. Jenkins (1871-1932) was the vice-president and had been associated with the Hutchinson Coal Company since 1898, starting as a clerk and advancing successfully to be secretary-treasurer and in 1917 vice-president. Mr. Jenkins was killed instantly in a car accident on the way home from Charleston where he and Charles Campbell Robb and Nelson Moran, fellow coal men, had attended hearings on the Davis- Kelly coal bill. The Jenkins family lived across the street from us on Fairmont Avenue in a large dark red brick house; and Cletus' son, Harold, my friend, Carole Jenkins Wilburn's father, worked in the offices of the Logan mines with Uncle Frank. It was a terrible loss for us all.

All of Clyde's sons worked for the company. Claude died at an early age, but had driven his father all over the state. Brooks got a law degree from Yale University and was corporate attorney, later becoming head of West Virginia Coal and Coke Company. Lee went to Cincinnati to run the sales offices and Frank was a part of management in the Logan field. Harold went to head up the Montgomery mines and Robert accompanied him. Paul received an engineering degree at Yale and superintended the Junior Mine near Elkins, and Jimmy stayed at the local office after college.

The coal industry had prospered in West Virginia as the source of power for the Industrial Revolution that began after the Civil War and extended up to World War I. Coal was king in supplying all the heat and power that is so needed in steel making. After this war was over, many mines were forced to close and war prosperity turned into peace poverty for a short time, until the rebuilding.

The Hutchinson's Lough's mines in Logan County where Uncles Harold and Uncle Frank lived and managed the mines; and in Cincinnati, Uncle Lee's Ohio mines, were all still thriving. Brooks bought The Annapolis Hotel in 1923, as they had bills before congress at that time; and many coal operators and owners from the northern fields spent many hours traveling back and forth to the Capitol on the B&O railroad to lobby for this area, which was suffering a slight depression after WW I. The coal kings were generally men of good will, deeply committed to family, church and country. Most of them shared their wealth by giving generously to the church, education, and charitable organizations. Papa provided a home for the Young Women's Christian Association, which Mammam (Mary Lyda) insisted on starting in Fairmont, and they were both staunch members of the First Baptist Church of Fairmont, which was on First Street and Walnut Avenue and a liberal contributor to the church's finances. Papa was a charter member of the Fairmont Elk's Lodge #294, The Masonic Lodge (32nd Degree) and the Sons of the American Revolution.

Unlike today, these barons of industry were always there for the community and helped provide for the city when asked. In the fall of 1919 Papa received this invitation from G.H. Colebank who was then Principal of Fairmont High School where Claude and Harold had attended. The letter read:

"For several years, it has been a custom of the second year class of the High School to elect a citizen of the community as their Class Sponsor. In making their selection, two or three requirements are considered by the students: character and reputation of the man as a citizen of the community and his attitude and interest in young people. You may feel assured that these young people hold you in high esteem and have entire confidence in your sterling worth as a citizen of Fairmont and in your ability to give them good wholesome counsel.

I wish to assure you, Mr. Hutchinson, that I have always appreciated your co-operation and also that of Mrs. Hutchinson's. Permit me to congratulate you upon being chosen by the Class of 1919 as their sponsor. We are highly pleased with your election and shall be glad to have the opportunity to become better acquainted with you.

I trust that you will be pleased with the students of this class and find inspiration in your relationship with them."

Very truly yours,

G.H. Colebank

****

Many of Uncle Harold's friends were still attending Fairmont High School and though Harold had left for Culver, Claude had graduated from there. Papa accepted the honor; making sure that each graduate received a class ring. Because of the War, it was decided there would be no class project that year.

George W. Ramsey uncovered an interesting item about the original High Level Bridge, or the Million Dollar Bridge, now restored by Congressman

Alan B. Mollohan and named in honor of his father, the late Congressman, Robert H. Mollohan.

Ramsey found that, "Back in 1920 the bridge was more than three-fourths completed; funds for the project had run out, partly because the funds available were also being used to build the new South Side Bridge. The city asked five local executives to sign notes for $35,000 so that work on the bridge could be completed. This group was called the "Fairmont Bridge Aid Syndicate" and the five local leaders were J.M. Hartley, C.E. Hutchinson, George T. Watson, W.S. Meredith, and R.T. Cunningham." When my husband read this excerpt 50 years later in John Veasey's column, he laughed and said, "I wonder if they were paid back with interest."

I remember hearing about the opening of the new Million Dollar Bridge on Decoration Day, May 30, 1921. All the city dignitaries met at Sonnencroft to welcome our hometown boy, Governor Ephraim Franklin Morgan, who had been invited to dedicate the Bridge. Mammam served a luncheon and reception for the Governor, and then all the guests walked, following Papa in the "open air" Packard which carried the honored speakers to the dedication ceremonies.

Governor Morgan was from Fairmont and was the great uncle of a schoolmate and friend, Donald Morgan West and his sisters Judy and Mrs. Charles Snider (Patty West).

On August 3, 1926 Clyde Hutchinson lost his good friend and mentor; his best ally. James Edwin Watson had died after years of illness and suffering at the age of 67, leaving the whole town saddened. Papa was only 58 and thought:

"But I have promises to keep,

And miles to go before I sleep,

And miles to go, before I sleep."

~ Robert Frost

78

MILES TO GO

His best friend had died eight weeks before, but Papa forged ahead to buy even more mines to leave to his sons. On Monday, September 27, 1926, Papa went to Logan and completed the transaction to acquire the Thurmond Coal Company for a consideration of $670,000. He drove on to Charleston Tuesday morning the 28th to complete the details. He was to meet with Attorney E. L. Michie for a conference at 4 o'clock at the Hotel Kanawha where he registered. When E.L. arrived and called Papa's room. Papa answered but complained about not feeling well, and had spent the last couple of hours lying down and would see him at dinner.

At 6 o'clock, Mr. Michie returned to the hotel to meet him for dinner and found him unconscious in his room. Physicians were summoned and pronounced him dead when they arrived at his bedside. Headlines from all over the state echoed the sad news. Papa's miles had turned into days.

"Heart Attack Proves Fatal to Fairmont Man in Hotel Here"
"Body is Sent Home for Burial"
The Charleston Daily Mail

"Clyde E. Hutchinson of Fairmont, prominent member of the Hutchinson family of coal operators died in his room at the Hotel Kanawha about 6 o'clock last evening after being ill during the day. The body was sent this morning over the Baltimore and Ohio railroad to his home in Fairmont. Mr. Hutchinson died of an apparent heart attack after negotiating to buy yet another mine in the territory. It was the mines that he opened and developed in Northern West Virginia that were first purchased by Consolidation Coal Company. Hutchinson Coal took an active interest in better housing conditions for miners throughout the state, and his mines were said to be the best equipped for the miners than any in the northern field."

"Clyde E. Hutchinson Dies in Charleston"
"Heart Attack Claims Local Business Man Before Aid Arrives"
"Fairmont in Mourning"
The Fairmont Times
September 28, 1926

"All of Fairmont is mourning the loss of its most prominent and substantial citizen in the sudden passing of Clyde E. Hutchinson. The body arrived here late yesterday afternoon from Charleston and was removed to

79

Sonnencroft, the beautiful family home on Morgantown Avenue, where streams of sympathizing friends have already called.

"Mr. Hutchinson's body was placed in the spacious living room overlooking the gardens in the array of fall greenery and flowers.

"The family of the deceased, which was scattered at the time of his death, arrived here at different times yesterday and all are now at Sonnencroft. Mrs. Hutchinson and her daughter-in-law, Mrs. Brooks S. Hutchinson and little daughter, Elaine, and Mrs. M. C. Gumbert (Mrs. Brooks Hutchinson's grandmother), who were together in Washington, D.C. came home yesterday accompanied by Mr. Robert H. Fatt, formerly of Fairmont, now the manager of the Annapolis Hotel of Washington."

****

A close friend of the family, Editor C.E. "Ned" Smith, wrote a poignant Good Morning Column:

The Fairmont Times
September 28, 1926

"Yesterday at Charleston Clyde E. Hutchinson, in the prime of life, was seized with indigestion and passed away as the drab twilight fell upon the land...

"Yesterday in the haze and the mist no shadow lay on Sonnencroft, the great home he had reared to house his boys and enjoy the fruits of his labors, but this morning Sonnencroft lies dark and still. Death had sent no messenger telling of his coming.

"Last night messages ticked over the wires to his boys in New York, in Cincinnati, in Kentucky, in the West Virginia mountain fastnesses of Lybrun and Manbar; and saddest of all to her in Washington.

"Messages also flashed into the ether destined to far off Costa Rica and the Sacra Familia Gold Mining Co., to men boring into the earth for gold. Also went forth tidings to the far west to seekers of Black Gold. Into the hills and narrow valleys of Logan and Fayette counties also went tidings.... For the Skipper of the Hutchinson Fleet had crossed the bar and dropped his anchor in the harbor of Eternity!"

The lead story on the front page of the evening edition of *The West Virginian:*

"Sonnencroft Receives Body of Late Master"
The West Virginian
Wednesday, September 29, 1926

"Clyde E. Hutchinson was one of the big men in the community and state, not only in mental caliber, but also in the coal business, his home, his church and his social life. His genial nature asserted itself and the visitor to his office was graciously welcomed.

Mr. Hutchinson meant much to Fairmont and to the state of West Virginia, and his keen business sagacity and vision has possibly done as much in the development of the state's natural resources as those of any other man."

"C.E. Hutchinson Laid to Rest Today"
"Rev. Wm. J. Eddy, Pastor and Friend of Deceased, Pays Eloquent Tribute"
"Sonnencroft Scene of Impressive Service"
"Seven Sons Bear Body to Grave"
The West Virginian
Friday Evening, October 1, 1926

"Mother Earth again claimed one of Fairmont's prominent and beloved citizens, when all that was mortal of Clyde E. Hutchinson, financier, businessman and Christian gentleman was consigned to the grave at Woodlawn Cemetery, while a large concourse of relatives, friends and business associates stood with bowed heads. The spirit which was claimed by its Giver last Tuesday evening, however, will continue to dominate the affairs of home and associates for many years.

"The body was borne from amid a profusion of flowers at Sonnencroft, his palatial residence on Morgantown Avenue which ever will stand as a monument to his sagacity, by his seven sons, whom he had cherished so fondly and served so loyally. It seemed fitting that these sons should perform the last sad service for their father and friend who they loved and revered.

"The services were conducted by the Rev. William J. Eddy, pastor of the First Baptist Church, of which the deceased was a member. The Rev. Mr. Eddy was assisted by the Rev. H. G. Stoetzer, pastor emeritus of the First Presbyterian Church. A quartet composed of Mr. and Mrs. Truman E. Johnson, Mrs. Forrest Fankhauser and Samuel H. Diemer, accompanied by Miss Katharine Moore, sang. Burial was made in the family plot in Woodlawn Cemetery by R. C. Jones.

"The reverend Mr. Eddy declared that, "Clyde was a student of the Bible and always carried a copy of the Bible in his pocket". He praised him for the "support and up-building of the church, and spoke of him as a philanthropist and a man most interested in his community and civic affairs. "The keynote of his life", the Reverend said, "was honesty in business and from this path he is believed never to have swerved".

A list of honorary pallbearer's, all-powerful executives of the period included:

"E. D. Kenna of N.Y.; J. D. Ayers and W. W. Keefer of Pittsburgh, PA; Frank Ehlen of Baltimore, MD; W.M. Wilshire of Cincinnati, OH; Robert H. Fatt of Washington, D. C.; Houston D. Young, Arthur S. Dayton, former Gov. E F. Morgan, E.L. Michie of Charleston; Virgil L. Highland and M.G. Sperry of Clarksburg; John E. Norval of Huntington; Gohen C. Arnold, of Buckhannon; R.J. Crogan and Frank Manown of Kingwood; D.H. Courtney and George C. Baker of Morgantown; H. A. McAllister, Fred Haislip and J. Carey Alderson of Logan; and C.J. Ryan of Hepzibah.

"Jim Jacobs, John S. Scott, Brooks Fleming Jr., J.A. Clark, Jr., J.M. Brownfield, George E. Amos, Major Duncan Sinclair, E.C. Jones, J. L. Hall, Frank C. Haymond, J.M.Hartley, Z.F. Davis, C.R. Hall, C.H. Jenkins, C.L. Shaver, Tusca Morris, J.O. Watson, II, T.I. Brett, E.C. Currey, Dr. L. D. Howard, Dr. C.W. Waddell, Judge W.S. Meredith, C.E. Smith, Judge Harry Shaw, W.J. Wiegel, Smith Hood, M.L. Brown, Clarence Hall, C.D. Robinson, Sam R. Nuzum, W.A. Wiedebusch, George M. Alexander, and Charles Powell, of Fairmont."

****

So many names of good friends from the past, names, we in Fairmont should remember, except one who later betrayed this giant of industry and his beloved family.

"Angels are bright still, though the brightest has fallen."

~ "Macbeth" Act IV, sc. 3

A RARE INSIGHT

On January 19, 1957, a few years before his death, C.E. "Ned" Smith wrote an interesting observation behind the coal demise in this area that had taken place thirty-seven years earlier. Many wondered why he took so long to divulge the truth.

"The weakening of the strong position of Consol Coal under Senator Clarence Watson probably can be traced to his purchase of a vast and expensive acreage of smokeless coal in southern West Virginia. The Watsons knew everything about the low sulphur coal here in Fairmont, except; it could not be successfully mixed with smokeless Pocahontas (county) coal. This hastened the day when Consol passed into the hands of Mr. Rockefeller, and ultimately to Pittsburgh Coal and the Hannah interests. In these deals Fairmont lost her identity as one of the principal coal capitals of the country, and her reputation for gracious living and hospitality, along with the ability to mine and market good coal.

"Personally we cannot speak as one of the sufferers of the collapse of the great coal boom. We had left town on the day after Harding was elected President (Nov.9, 1920). We were a partner in a very promising coal mine that was just getting in production and, while standing in the National Bank watching some of the Republicans cavorting around in celebration of the Harding victory, Sam Brady put his arm around our shoulder and told us not to give a thought to the coal business hereabouts while on our trip. 'This market is here to stay,' he said, 'and you will never see the end of it.'

"That evening we caught the train for New York and a day or so later boarded the Olympic with Senator Watson and a few others for Europe.

A week later when we walked into our quarters at the Ritz Hotel in London, Watson showed us a cablegram he had just received. It related that the coal boom, which was supposed to last forever, had busted higher than a kite. Watson had nothing more to say except to call a waiter and order up some rum and hot water. 'Good drink,' he commented when he smacked his lips over the brew. 'You can't beat it in cold weather.' It wasn't cold at all. A warm, drippy evening was what London had to offer. The cold he was thinking of was back in the coal fields here at home!"

****

In 1933, when the Democrats returned to power, "Ned" Smith was one of the leading figures in the party and was rewarded with a position as Secretary of the American Section, International Joint Commission, a quasi-judicial body which dealt with American- Canadian affairs, and frequently traveled to Ottawa where the Canadian section had its headquarters. Smith died on June 19, 1959 at the age of 73.

IN RETROSPECT

J.O.Watson, II, a son and grandson of coal barons, wrote in 1950:

> "I spent three winters in the late 1890's in Colorado. After 50 years in mining I returned to Cripple Creek and what a ghost town I beheld! I saw a ghost town, broken windows, vacant storefronts, and old residents deserting their hometown. A place where a few became enormously rich was now a ghost town."

****

As a granddaughter, and daughter of coal kings, I have seen the decline of Fairmont in the last 30 years. I pray that Fairmont has not become that ghost town of Cripple Creek. We have lost many businesses and factories, many connected to the WWII war effort. I went to the opening of Westinghouse Electric Company in 1942. We took Mammam who was amazed at such a huge plant. The main building was built for round the clock production in air-raid conditions. Westinghouse became Phillips and has been outsourced to Mexico.

We have also lost Domestic Coke Corporation (1918), which was sold to Sharon Steel in 1948 and now closed, Owens-Illinois Glass Plant (1929), and most of the Fairmont Aluminum Plant who bought the WV Metal Products, a brass foundry owned by the Hutchinsons, Watsons, and Camdens in 1919. Today, Novelis owns what is left of the aluminum plant.

Many local companies, Kettering Baking Co. (1921), Henry Oil Co. (1925), Fairmont Wall Plaster (1900), Jones Fur Service (1929), Fairmont Mattress Co. (1880), Monongah Glass (1903), and the Fairmont Box Factory (1929), have closed. I understand that the box factory was built to make and store ammunitions for WWI, but the war was over before it was needed and Monongah Glass moved into it, and in its final years, used it as a melt shop. Ralph Dollison bought the warehouse type building with all reinforced concrete slab floors, supported by cast concrete mushroom type columns- a big square, powerful, structure and unusual for Fairmont for it architectural style with its vestiges of ornamentation. Dollison developed Beechnut Packing Company in mid 1920. His sons, Charles ("Chud") and Richard kept it going until 1978. Today it is known as the Old Box Factory. Though empty and forgotten, it is still powerful enough to store ammunitions and too expensive to destroy.

The CEOs and leaders of these industries often transferred into Fairmont from larger cities, with new innovative ideas and interest in the development of their new communities just as David Morgan did in 1777; and Boaz Fleming, when he established his new County of Marion in 1842. These new trailblazers created the pathways in this northern section of West Virginia. They were a group of generous, selfless individuals who grew to love and help their community grow, often staying or returning here through their retirement and now buried at historic Woodlawn Cemetery.

Our Senior Senator, Robert Carlyle Byrd, erected the beautiful NASA building here in the 1990s with the support and vision of Fairmont's native son, Congressman Alan Bowlby Mollohan; the two also developed the High Technology Consortium. They did their best to diversify our businesses in the city, but many of the High Tech executives live in surrounding towns, choosing not to fuse with the townspeople of Fairmont.

The Consortium was a godsend to the city, as the area was annexed shortly before the first building, Huntington Bank, was built; and now the area provides a great tax benefit to Fairmont.

Our schools are exemplary. Historic Fairmont Senior High School (1929) has been classified for the past four years as one of the few Exemplary schools in the state. It's latest Principal, Chad Norman, was chosen as the 2010 State Principal of the year. In 2011 all new windows were installed, conducive to its historic lineage, and allowing central air conditioning. We also have a brand new Fairmont Middle School and two relatively new East High and North Marion High Schools in the county, after consolidating eight high schools into three.

The East-West Stadium and Municipal Pool, the first large pool in the state, built during the depression in 1937 by the Works Progress Administration (WPA), is large and modern enough for all sports' state tournaments. The Marion County Commissioners restored the pool where I grew up, but which has been closed for years, because of a leak.

But, we cannot buy a pair of shoes or many other necessities without traveling several miles on a dangerously busy Interstate 79 to the cities of Morgantown or Clarksburg. Retailers have deserted us, choosing to build two stores, one in Bridgeport, and another in Morgantown while closing their Fairmont business. A practice I have never understood.

In the five decades of the booming years, we had the best retail stores in the state. The large, five story Hartley's and the smaller Jones' department stores brought people from all areas. There were beautiful little dress and hat stores and several jewelry stores. A gemologist, Harry Dodge, whose reputation was impeccable and well known, owned one of the favorite stores. Harry, Junior, a good friend, had grown up in his parent's store, became a certified gemologist, and was the owner after his parents died. Dodge's had more than just exquisite jewelry, they also offered the top names of sterling silver, china and crystal - our town's little Tiffany's.

In the days before super markets with buggies, there were several family owned markets in the downtown area: Hermosilla's, Shumaker's, Pitrolo's, and Reitman's Markets, and Tino Potesta's Community Market on Merchant Street. Mother ordered from Shumaker's every morning and the groceries were delivered, before noon, by the back entrance at 741 and carefully unloaded onto the long white enameled table in the kitchen.

Hugh Fox founded Adams's Office Supply, two doors down from Hartley's, featuring office furniture and equipment. When Hugh died, Jack Wade, an old friend, bought and enlarged the store moving on down into the former Reitman's corner grocery store; and several years later moved into the old City National Bank. When Jack died, his long time clerk, and partner, Harvey Havlicheck, became the owner and this wonderful office supply business is still in downtown Fairmont. This unique store featured everything a business needed including candy bars, peanuts, and chewing gum under the counters, right at my eye level. Daddy and I spent hours at Adam's: me, eating and Daddy talking to all his old friends. Hugh Fox knew everyone in the state and the store resembled the old general stores of the past, without a pot-bellied stove.

Today, Fairmont's infrastructure is old and crumbling and the Water Department has had misfortunes, mainly over a new filtering system. We have always had the best water department in the state with the best tasting water. In the late thirties the City Water Director, Albert Robinson, wisely had fluoride added to the water, long before most cities had heard of it. My teeth are perfect. When the Junior League assisted the dentists who examined Head Start children at the Public Health Department, I was helping Dr. Sturm who declared he could tell exactly from which part of the county each child came because of his teeth. Those that had City water had perfect baby teeth; those who drank from well water from the outlying communities, had decayed or missing teeth.

Always interested in historic preservation, Congressman Alan Mollohan's efforts have designated an Historic Downtown District through the Vandalia Heritage Foundation. This is one of three historic districts in Fairmont; the other two are the Fleming Watson District and the Woodlawn Cemetery District. Through the Community Partnership Development Association, many of the beautiful old buildings in the city have been restored.

As Sonnencroft was completely destroyed in 1961, Vandalia Heritage Foundation restored Papa's first home at 700 Benoni Avenue in an attempt to keep historic homes alive and viable. It has been beautifully renovated and has accommodated the Vandalia Heritage Foundation offices for ten years. Currently the building is called the Hutchinson House.

Congressman Mollohan helped a neighborhood group save the garages of Highgate, J.E. Watson's Tudor style home, from being sold to Hardees's fast food restaurant several years ago. The group restored and equipped the rooms with kitchens and all amenities for special functions. Highgate has been the scene of several weddings, receptions, programs and parties, keeping solvent with rental charges for the various functions.

Our "Ink Stained Wretch", Oce Smith, wrote in his column:

The Times West Virginian
August 8, 1996

"It is still pretty difficult to accept for us Old Timers who grew up here, when Our Towne was one of the greatest industrial leaders in the tri state region; and when all highways paved with coal led to and from our Fairmont. But nothing lasts forever.

Consequently, it is our responsibility to retain what we can of our coal related employment and to recall with affection and respect the sunny days from our past...but not to relive them. We must concentrate our collective efforts now on another, less colorful, less dramatic and highly skilled era for our economic survival."

****

Jim Bissett of the Morgantown Dominion Post writes on Sunday July 25, 2010:

"All roads lead to Fairmont? City officials and other community boosters are hoping one road in particular, the $155 million Gateway Connector, can help put some progress in the passing lane for this Marion County city that has seen its economic fortunes stall over the past several decades."

****

City Director, Jay Rogers, in speaking of the new gateway entrance to the city, expressed hopes that, "The asphalt artery just might infuse new commercial life for the city, which has watched its neighbors to the north and south prosper as (Fairmont) has declined."

****

The 1.6-mile connector today called the Alan Mollohan Connector, opened right before Christmas 2010. What a gift to Fairmont! The entrance to downtown Fairmont is breathtaking, particularly after dark when our striking courthouse dome is illuminated. We have become a lovely bedroom community instead of the thriving, bustling city we once were; not yet a ghost town like Cripple Creek, but let us beware!

****

"The elk's call and the panther's scream

Once here so often heard,

Are now but shadow sounds behind the mind.

When, in imagination,

One remembers the long and long ago..."

~ Glenn D. Lough
"Now and Long Ago"

[AFTERWORD]

Alan Mollohan ran for Congress the first time in 1983 establishing his campaign from my husband, Paul's, law offices in the First National Bank building in Fairmont and successfully embarked on a long career. On May 4, 2010, Congressman Mollohan was defeated in the primaries by a Democratic challenger from Monongalia County who, in turn, lost to a Republican from Wheeling, West Virginia in that general election. Hence, Marion County and the entire First District of West Virginia lost 30 years of Mollohan's seniority on the Appropriations Committee.

Our beloved Senior Senator, Robert Carlyle Byrd, 92, died on June 28, 2010. Bob Byrd, the longest serving senator in American history served for 51 years and cast a record number of over 18,500 votes. Paul and I campaigned with him in every election since 1956 when he was a Congressman. In 1958, he won the Senator's seat by challenging Republican Chapman Revercomb. Byrd's mentors in the first year were Senate Majority Leader Lyndon B. Johnson and Carl Hayden, chairman of the powerful Appropriations Committee.

As a freshman Senator, Robert Byrd received the unique honor of being appointed to the Appropriations Committee, where he remained, often as chairman, for over 50 years bringing billions of dollars to his West Virginia. Our state was one of five states in the U.S. that was never assigned a major military base during the Second World War, while all our neighbors became wealthy, some with more than three installations.

As the senator often said, "When I am dead and they cut me open, they will find West Virginia written across my heart."

At the end of his services on the steps of the West Virginia State capitol building, J. Miles Layton eloquently reported in The Times-West Virginian:

"A twenty-one gun salute that thundered across the Capitol Square in Charleston was capped off with the immortal somber notes of "Taps". Thousands of people sang "Country Roads", an ending to a memorial service that must have made Senator Byrd smile as he watched from above."

****

In two short months, we lost our often criticized, but much envied position, having two senior congressional representatives who controlled spending decisions in both Houses of Congress. Hundreds of millions of federal dollars have been directed to West Virginia's First District during the 24 years that Representative Alan B. Mollohan has been on the House Appropriations Committee - all dried up with his loss in the Democratic primary in May. It will take a new congressional representative 25 to 30 years to gain the seniority held by Mollohan's defeat and he or she may never be appointed to the Appropriations Committee.

And the death in June of our senior senator, who served for over half a century, brought to the end a career that sent home several billions of dollars. Our Marion County son, Governor Joseph Manchin III, proposed a special election held in August 2010 and was nominated as the Democratic nominee against a Republican from Morgantown.

Governor Manchin was voted to fulfill the late Senator's unexpired two-year term as the Junior Senator of West Virginia on November 3, 2010. We wish him well.

"God alone beholds the end of what is sown;

Beyond our vision, weak and dim,

The harvest-time is hid with him."

~ Anonymous

CHAPTER FIVE

MOTHER'S DIARY
1914 - 1916

Graduation from Boise High School 1914
Ray Pefley at the age of 17

MOTHER'S DIARY

The following is a diary written by my mother, Ray Gumbert Pefley (Hutchinson), about her life at Mount Vernon Seminary in Washington, D.C. where she was sent by her godfather and uncle, Madison Smith, to study in the east, on the advice of close family friends, U.S. Senator and Mrs. William Borah of Idaho. At that time, Borah was "The Lion of the US Senate".

When Ray's father died of the measles, five weeks after she was born in 1897, Uncle Smith became her guardian. I was impressed that he had given her an electric car as a twelfth birthday present, and made sure she was educated and traveled with her mother, as a child. As he never married, he adored his ward as his only child, helping Lucinda and Mom to raise her to the best of his ability.

Excerpts of A Boarding School Diary 1914-1916 were published in the Mount Vernon Bulletin in February of 1975, eight years after Mother's death. I always loved to read it because she tells of the famous performers and Washington dignitaries that she knew, met or enjoyed. She tells of the animosity between her German teacher and her French teacher before the United States entered World War I; not until the Lusitania was sunk, did she worry about war.

Mount Vernon was one of the few finishing schools in the United States, although in Europe they were quite popular. Young men from affluent families attended prep schools followed by college; young women attended a finishing school, often a boarding school. Mount Vernon, founded in 1875, was a high school, which extended to a two- year course of training in cultural values and norms, which was very limited on the western frontier where Mother lived.

Most finishing schools were designed for women only, and as the name implies, girls that attended these boarding schools after their basic education was over, "finished" their education with instruction in how to live in the smart society of the east. Much of the schooling focused on refinement of existing skills, such as etiquette, sports, the arts, painting, dancing, and languages, ensuring that their graduates would be able to enjoy themselves and be accepted any place in the world.

The high school of Mount Vernon was closed in the mid-seventies and the college extended to a baccalaureate institution. The college was acquired by

George Washington University in 1999 and the 26-acre campus became the George Washington University at Mt. Vernon College.

Mother became friends with Fran and Kay Courtney, students from Morgantown WV, and would come to visit them over short holidays from the seminary, as it was such a long, tiring five-day trip by train back to her home in Idaho.

On her first visit Grace Courtney, another sister, set up a meeting - a blind date - for Mother with Daddy. Grace was dating his brother, Frank Hutchinson. Brooks Hutchinson, who was 10 years older than Ray, had graduated from Yale Law School in 1912 and was practicing law as the Hutchinson Coal Company corporate attorney. Brooks was seriously thinking of marrying Louise Breck, a girl he had known all of his life. Those plans disappeared when he met the beautiful little girl from the west.

A BOARDING SCHOOL DIARY

1914 - 1916

By Ray Pefley Hutchinson

October 6, 1914

It is such a long trip across the continent, from my dear loved ones and the sagebrush plains to the wooded hills of the East, to my goal -- Washington, D.C. and Mount Vernon Seminary where I am to attend school. This special train is made up in Chicago to accommodate the girls in that section of the country and from other points. I was first on board waiting quietly for my Pullman when I heard a bevy, a flock, a deluge of girls laughing and hugging one another. I felt very much alone. But not for long, as Miss Ashley herded them in and brought calmness out of the confusion. She lost no time introducing me to everyone and making me feel perfectly at ease. Soon it was time to go to the diner for dinner and every "old" girl asked a "new" one to join her. Mary Prince of Minneapolis invited me.

October 7, 1914

Next morning most of us had breakfast served in our berths. Later we went out to the Observation car and found several girls from Pittsburgh. Sarah Davidson, Florence Meyers were two I remember.

When we arrived in Washington we were taken to 1100 M. Street, most of the teachers greeted us and made us feel at home. Miss Harbaugh, who pairs us off with our roommates before we ever get to school, Miss Katherine Hill, Mrs. A.K. Payne our music teacher, Miss Cole, and Mrs. Hennsley, who is Mrs. Somers assistant. I was taken to my room and met my roommate. Much to our mutual surprise it was Florence Meyers of Pittsburgh. Our room is on the second floor, right in front of the elevator which is run by John, a Negro boy, who will always be remembered for his courtesy and good manners.

October 8, 1914

School really started to-day. There were classes in the morning, then a walk with an "old" girl in the afternoon. My companion and I strolled along M. Street to Massachusetts Avenue. There she pointed out some interesting places. The McAdoo home - Mrs. McAdoo was Eleanor Wilson, the president's daughter, and he is Secretary of the Treasury. Another place of interest is the house where the scene of action of the novel "The Man on the Box" took place. Then we saw the ugly red brick German Embassy, doubly interesting now because of the European War, which is raging abroad. I am told the Russian Embassy is really the most beautiful.

Washington is so lovely with its tree lined streets and Southern atmosphere. Even the traffic is different as they still use the old Victorias drawn by horses, as well as automobiles. The Victoria from the French Embassy just passed. The horses' harnesses were decorated with cockades of French tri-colors. All traffic gives an Embassy carriage right of way. We walked on to Dupont Circle, which is like Rome, they say, for all roads lead to there.

We have the best things to eat at school. Mrs. Dill the housekeeper prepares us wonderful meals, Zimmer - the baker, is unsurpassed! Nevertheless, every Saturday morning when we go to town, the thing to do is to go to Reeves and have something to eat. It was right after breakfast, but I had a Swiss cheese sandwich and chocolate pie with whipped cream. Then after shopping, we always go to Huyler's for a milk chocolate sundae and the half-pound of candy, we are allowed each week. Or, we might go to Brownley's for their famous "Trinities". Then to the California Fruit Store for the fruit we want to keep in our rooms.

This afternoon all the new girls went to Mount Vernon by boat. It was a wonderful trip up the Potomac, with the banks of Maryland on one side and Virginia on the other.

We went first to the tomb of George and Martha Washington. The old tomb was once broken into so this new one was built, the door locked, and the key thrown into the Potomac.

Next we went to the stables and saw Washington's old coach. Then, off to the kitchen. The copper and pewter cooking utensils and the table where all the meals were prepared are still there.

Then we went to the garden and saw the boxwood hedge that Washington planted. It is called a maze because of its labyrinth of twists and turns. There is also the Wishing Bush, so called because Nellie Custis stood by it when she became engaged. Whoever makes a wish and touches a leaf of it, the wish will come true. I took a tiny twig of it for my Memory Book, after making a wish.

Then we went all through the house, in every room. The room where Nellie Custis scratched her name on the windowpane with her diamond engagement ring is interesting as is the room where George Washington died. In one room there is a beautiful Aubusson rug presented to Washington by Louis XIV of France.

As we came out the front door and onto the huge veranda the sun was slowly sinking. It touched the soft grass, the stately oak trees, and the flagpole with gold and made the Potomac gleam as it glided silently onward. It was all so sacred and beautiful.

We went slowly down the path to the pier and got on the boat, rather quietly. Soon dusk descended and Mount Vernon faded from our sight but not from our memories. The lights of Washington soon came into view; the Monument, towering above all in gleaming whiteness.

October 31, 1914

Our Halloween party was held at the shelter of the new school to be. Hobgoblins, ghosts and witches danced around a huge bonfire, but soon vanished and became normal healthy girls when refreshments were served.

November 3, 1914

Instructions before the concert to-day were that under no circumstances must we remove our hats. It seems it simply is not done. People go to concerts to hear, not to see. I certainly hope I get behind a short person with a small hat. We must not turn around and gaze over the audience either, just as in church. I wore my black velvet suit trimmed in summer ermine and my small tricorn hat.

Finally! My first Boston Symphony Concert at the National Theatre. It was too beautiful! Pasquale Amato was the soloist, an Italian opera baritone.

Some women who sat near me knitted long gray woolen scarves or sweaters for the Belgians. How could they knit while that divine music was being sung! The war seems very remote.

November 17, 1914

Today we heard the famed operatic contralto, Schuman Heink. She is wonderful. Most of her songs were in German, but she gave "The Rosary" for an encore.

Walking back the chaperone pointed out the house where Lincoln visited and one day worked out one of the important battles of the Civil War with the tin soldiers belonging to the little boy who lived there.

November 23, 1914

Anna Pavlova to-day - I never even imagined anyone could dance as she does. She is like a disembodied spirit, floating on air. I liked the "Dying Swan" the best of all, perhaps because I had heard so much about it.

November 28, 1914

Mail Call is one of the thrills of the day. Letters from home produce either homesickness or contentment that everything is all right. No use for me to get homesick - twenty-five hundred miles to Boise is a long walk. Any way I am satisfied as I am getting just what I wanted. Everything is just as I imagined it would be, only better. The atmosphere of the school is peace and tranquility.

Saturday morning and sightseeing for the new girls. Many groans but we enjoy it just the same. It was the Printing and Engraving Building to-day, where we saw them making the new War-Tax Stamps. Surely this European War will be over soon. In another department we each had a dollar bill washed and ironed. It's difficult for me to get accustomed to paper money we have mostly silver out West.

December 4, 1914

We went to hear the Metropolitan Opera's mezzo-soprano, Louise Homer to-day. Flo, my roommate from Pittsburgh, whispered that Miss Homer was born in Pittsburgh too. Her first five songs were in German, then some in English, then one in French. As the United States is neutral, all were received with great applause.

The only war we notice at all is the growing coolness between the French teacher and the German teacher at school. They used to be such good friends both having lived abroad so long. But now all is changed and poor Fraulein has to go talk to Zimmer, our German baker. Madame hardly speaks to her.

War is difficult to realize. I always thought the Germans to be happy, jovial people. I can't believe they are doing the terrible things they are doing now. We are all beginning to hate the word "Hun" which is what the German soldiers are called.

December 9, 1914

To-day several of us attended a Red Cross meeting at the Shoreham Hotel in order to see President Wilson. He is not as tall as I thought he would be, but is quite nice looking, and has a good voice too. I have seen him in his large blue touring car several times. It has the seal of the United States on the door. It impressed me very much at first, but one becomes accustomed to seeing famous people in Washington. Congressmen and even Senators are hardly looked at twice.

December 12, 1914

Before we leave for Christmas vacation, we have Christmas for the servants and their families. We have a huge Christmas tree with Santa Clause to deliver the gifts; and then the families present us with a program of beautiful Negro spirituals.

January 16, 1915

Christmas vacation - just a dream and then back to the routine of school. My roommate and I, with a chaperone, attended a Peace Meeting to-night. I got tired of it and left. No use being so concerned about war. The Atlantic is wide and Wilson will keep us out of war.

January 22, 1915

My first trip to New York! Miss Ashley chaperoned ten of us up here for a tour of the Metropolitan Museum of Art. We tramped miles looking at gorgeous masterpieces all day. Saw the Rembrandts, the Fra Angelico's, the Sergeants, the wonderful Salt cup made by Benevento Cellini. This evening we managed to see Montgomery and Stowe in "Chin-Chin". Those two are so funny and the costumes were beautiful.

Also saw the Castles in "Watch-Your Step". Their dancing is wonderful. Mrs. Castle has bobbed hair, quite daring. I bought a new hat named for her. A flat little sailor of black silk with a pale pink rose in the front and two streamers of black ribbon in back. It looks nice with my black velvet suit.

We stayed at the Waldorf Astoria, another place of my dreams. It's just as I imagined. It is all red plush and gold. Peacock Alley is thrilling, where all the glamorous people of the world pass by. We had tea in the Palm Room just off Peacock Ally and had dinner in the famous Red Dining Room.

January 30, 1915

Two of my family's very best friends live in Washington, Senator and Mrs. William Edgar Borah. Mrs. Borah (Mary McConnell) was the daughter of Boise's Governor, William J. McConnell, in 1895. I have known them all my life. Today I had luncheon with Mrs. Borah at the Willard Hotel. She introduced me to Governor Cox of Ohio, and the Minister from the Philippines. I asked her if all the distinguished looking men she spoke to on the street were attaches of the foreign legations. She laughed and replied that most of them were waiters from the Willard, where she and the Senator had lived for seven years.

After luncheon we went to the theatre and saw Maude Adams in "Quality Street". It was a sweet play and I liked it immensely.

February 2, 1915

Miss Goodwin chaperoned eight of us to Congress this afternoon. She knows Vice-President Marshall very well and was going to introduce us to him, but just as we reached the Capitol, Senate adjourned. We heard some of the Congressmen speak on whether "Tipperary" is neutral or not. We had a suspicion they were doing it for our benefit, as they kept smiling at us up in the gallery. "Champ" Clark, Speaker of the House, was there.

February 12, 1915

Frances Courtney (from Morgantown, WV) and I went to a concert this afternoon, where we heard Frieda Hempel (German-Metropolitan Opera star) sing. She is supposed to have the best soprano voice since Adelina Patti (1843-1919). Sasseli played the harp beautifully.

February 14, 1915

Heavens - I am at French table for a month. We have to speak entirely in French. I will starve - even the servants, who have served here so long, understand it. Madame is so darling, but I am a little afraid of her. The "old" girls say she used to wear the most beautiful clothes and jewels, but now since her beloved France is at war, she wears only black. One touch of brightness today-- received a gorgeous corsage of orchids and violets for a valentine. Yale men are grand!

Le 24 Fevrier, 1915

La fete de Charlotte Wilson au table Francais. Nous avions un temps bonne mais le conversation ce n'est pas tres anime.

February 25, 1915

We are having a vacation this weekend, some of us thought we might celebrate the occasion and have dinner at the Willard. So, Fran and Kay Courtney and Flo Myers and I with Miss Kurtz (Aunt Annie) as chaperone went there tonight. We had <u>some</u> dinner! Didn't miss a course. I started all the giggling by asking for the "cute little puffed potatoes". I was informed by the high and mighty waiter that I meant "Potatoes soufflés". I agreed in a dazed fashion. So on through to dessert when Flo set us off again by ordering "Chocolate Cake parfait". We were all happy until the bill was presented! Eleven fifteen! Cash on hand, eleven five, but Miss Kurtz came to our rescue and we finally reached home, only to sink weakly on a davenport and laugh until we cried. We didn't have a penny left, so had to walk home.

February 26, 1915

Several of us attended Christ Church in Alexandria, Virginia where Washington used to go, and later General Robert E. Lee. The little old church is so impressive and fascinating. The same communion table, the seven-branched candlesticks and almost everything is the same as in Washington's time. The old-fashioned pews have doors to them, and a ridge across the back which is most uncomfortable, meant to be that way so no one can take a nap.. The pulpit is high above the congregation. Everything is painted white with mahogany trim, with brass plates on the entrance to the pews marking the ones belonging to famous people. The churchyard is filled with ancient headstones which are interesting.

February 27, 1915

This morning we visited the Navy Yards. We went to the Gun Shop first and saw them manufacturing the big cannons, 14-inch guns. Then we went to another shop where they were making the shells. We also saw one of the hydro-aero planes like the ones they are using in the present war. I am glad we are neutral.

The Mayflower, the President's yacht, where, we have heard rumored, President Wilson has been courting Edith Galt, is most interesting. The yacht was expropriated from the Navy in 1905 by President Teddy Roosevelt for his own personal use.

The President's suite is all rose and white. There are seven other guest rooms, all of them equally as beautiful. We saw the bathtub President Taft had made of a solid piece of marble. It is about life-size, as large as President Taft is. The floors of the yacht are all hardwood and good for dancing. On a cruise a marine band is employed.

I'd like to marry a President.

March 5, 1915

Today we saw Bernard Shaw's original production of "Pygmalion" with Mrs. Patrick Campbell, the great London stage star as Eliza Doolittle. It was very good and very unusual. It was snowing out so we had a special car. When we arrived home, we all rushed in and had some "Abend Brot" (bread or crackers with milk). Madame won't call it that any more, and very seldom joins us a ten in the evening when we have it because Fraulein comes often. I wish the war would end.

April 9, 1915

Went to a concert today to hear Alma Gluck (American Soprano) and Zimbalist (Violinist). She is the prettiest thing ever and I love her voice. She and Zimbalist are married and ideally happy.

In the evening Margaret Wilson, the President's daughter, came to school to sing for us. She has a very sweet voice. She was dressed in pure white satin and wore absolutely no jewelry whatever. We gave her a huge bouquet of American Beauty roses. We were told not to applaud excessively, but appreciatively.

April 17, 1915

Today we went to Baltimore on a special streetcar. Miss A. took us to the Walter's Art Gallery. We saw some Della Robbias and Raphael's Madonna. Flo Meyers made the prize faux pas about Donatello's statue of "David". Flo asked why "she" had a hat on!

About two o'clock we went to the Hotel Belvedere and had luncheon. "K" insisted on having plank steak and we had enough for a family of ten. Afterwards, we went for an automobile ride around Baltimore. It is beautiful.

April 21, 1915

We went to Arlington, Virginia, today in automobiles. We went by way of Fort Myer and the road was lovely. We saw the old mansion that Robert E. Lee lived in, an old southern place facing the Potomac with beautiful gardens surrounding it. One place was particularly beautiful- like and old Greek temple covered with wisteria.

Then we drove out the Speedway along the beautiful Potomac. The sun was just setting and made a broad path of molten gold over the water. The road was lined with flowering cherry trees in bloom, on both sides, a gift from Japan. The riverbanks were lined with beautiful green willows. It was all so lovely. I shall never forget it.

April 23, 1915

The seniors read their essays this morning. They were about the European War and very well done.

April 24, 1915

Sightseeing again - this time it was the Monument, the Pan-American building and the D.A.R. building, where their congress was in session.

In the afternoon we saw "Diplomacy" with William Gillette, Blanche Bates and Marie Dors.

May 7, 1915

Today we went to Kolb's on Connecticut Avenue for ice cream. We are not supposed to go that far, but their ice cream is so good. They are Germans and some of the girls won't go there. But I am neutral. Neutrality is best for the United States; at least everyone has thought so. As we were walking back to school this afternoon the newsboys were yelling, "Extra! Extra!" at Thomas Circle. The Lusitania was sunk today by a German submarine at two p.m. off the coast of Ireland, "One hundred and twenty four Americans on board." This may mean War! How can we let the Germans continue this way?

May 8, 1915

My roommate's mother, Mrs. Meyers, is here, so she took us to luncheon at the Willard, then to see Nazimova in "War Brides". The play only lasted twenty minutes but in that short time it brought us closer to the war than anything has so far. Nazimova, with her gorgeous, thrilling voice had the whole audience in tears, men not excepted. How terrible war must be to have your loved ones march off and leave you, perhaps never to see them again. Surely the war will soon be over. Everyone thinks it will last only another month or two at the most.

May 15, 1915

All the hurry, bustle and excitement of commencement will soon be over. Mothers, fathers, sisters, and - most exciting - brothers, have been arriving all week. All too soon this glorious year will be finished.

May 25, 1915

Class Day - and we almost wept our eyes out. The seniors sang all their old songs to us for the last time. Then came the Class Prophesy, then "K" gave the Class Statistics. Pat read the Class Will and said "Ruth Robinson wills to Ray Pefley the parlor for the reception of her numerous visitors and hopes she will make as good use of it as she has this year". They also willed us their "Butterfly Song" and Senior House. Then the Senior President handed her cap and gown to the Junior President and the seniors passed on, really away forever. All the girls were crying. Then we took the senior's' seats and sang our farewell to them.

May 26, 1915

Commencement is over - I am on my way to visit in West Virginia, Pittsburgh, Niles, Ohio, Indianapolis and Chicago. I may get home for the Fourth of July.

Mount Vernon students touring Washington in 1915

MY SENIOR YEAR AT MOUNT VERNON SEMINARY

October 1915

Back again, and this time- a dignified Senior - and the fun of Flag Week, making the poor juniors miserable. Having them stand when we enter a room. They jump up at table, too, and seat us as carefully as they do the teachers. They call us "Miss".

October 16, 1915

Flag Week ended with Senior House warming tonight. The juniors were very humble but they will soon become normal again.

November 9, 1915

I heard Geraldine Farrar today in concert. She is simply gorgeous, so beautiful and vivacious. Spanish type with blue-black hair. She sang wonderfully. I enjoyed especially the selection from "Carmen". She was gracious with encores. She sang "Mighty Lak' a Rose" and played her own accompaniment.

Mrs. Galt, Mrs. McAdoo and Margaret Wilson were there in the President's box. Mrs. Galt is always in "his" box. Usually his daughters sit across the theatre in another box. Mrs. Galt is quite beautiful with her marvelous clothes and orchids, her gorgeous diamond pin that President Wilson gave her for an engagement present. Everyone is naughty enough to wonder if he bought it at Galt's Jewelry store.

November 30, 1915

This evening we went to a French entertainment given by the French Ambassador at the Maison Rauscher for the wounded of France and Belgium. There were two plays of which all I could understand was "Quel est le prix?" which was asked over and over in one of the plays. Madame walked home with me and insisted on talking French all the way.

December 3, 1915

Heard Emmy Destin in concert today - "hear" is all one would want to do because she is most unattractive to look at.

December 9, 1915

Today we heard the Austrian born violinist, Fritz Kreisler in a concert. He is marvelous! He gave many encores as the audience stood and cheered him time after time. Madame wouldn't go but Fraulein did.

December 10, 1915

Saw David Warfield in "Vander Decken" tonight. The play has the same theme as the Flying Dutchman. It deals with reincarnation and is simply beautiful.

December 11, 1915

We had a lecture today about the Passion Play by Marie Mayer, who once took the part of Mary Magdalene.

December 16, 1915

Lucy and I went to see the stage actress Maude Adams who once played Peter Pan, in her new show tonight, "What Every Woman Knows". It was splendid.

[Author's NOTE: During the Christmas break, Ray's mother, Lucinda, became extremely ill, probably with pneumonia. She died in late January 1916; a terrible shock to Mother, Mom and Daddy Gumbert. Mother had to leave right after the funeral for her last semester, but she was convinced it was what her mother would have insisted she do.]

February 14, 1916

I received violets, a silver heart and American Beauty roses for a Valentine from Brooks today. He told me that Frank, his brother, had suddenly fallen for a girl he had met in Logan, Bonsall Wood, and said that his father had reported, upon his return from Logan, that she was pleasing, but a little timid.

Heard soprano Johanna Gadski and baritone Whitehill in concert today- liked both of them.

March 18, 1916

Saw Ethel Barrymore in "Our Mrs. Chesney" this afternoon. She was excellent, maybe the best actress the theatre has ever seen.

I made Star honor roll this month.

Brooks wrote that he saw Birth of a Nation at the movies in Fairmont and that a large symphony orchestra traveled with the film. He was very impressed.

March 23, 1916

The wonderful Russian Ballet Russe was given tonight. The President and his new bride were there and as they entered, the orchestra played "The Star-Spangled Banner" and everyone stood up, of course. It was perfectly thrilling! The boxes were filled with beautiful women in evening clothes and gorgeous Russian headdresses, jeweled crowns with long veils. There is to be a wonderful Russian ball to-night with everyone wearing the Russian headdresses.

Among the other famous people there was Alice Roosevelt Longworth, President Theodore Roosevelt's daughter, with her husband Congressman Nicholas Longworth. I could hardly watch the swaying colorful figures on the stage for watching the boxes.

When I wrote Brooks that the Ballet tickets were $49.78, he was absolutely shocked!

March 31, 1916

Heard the opera stars Pasquale Amato and Florence Macbeth in Carmen today. Amato was splendid when he sang the Toreador's Song.

April 1, 1916

Saw "Pollyanna" today, but it is too saccharine for words, I hated it!

April 4, 1916

I got back my Senior Essay today. It was one of the best on the Monroe Doctrine.

April15, 1916

Spent the day in Baltimore at the Walter's Art Gallery. This evening saw Ruth Chatterton and Henry Miller in "Daddy-Long-Legs". Loved it!

April 21, 1916

Went on a Senior Hike today, way out past Cabin John's bridge. Walked miles along the Canal, then boarded a canal boat pulled by mules and rode back to the city. It was such fun. We were caught in a thunderstorm and got soaked.

Received orchids and violets for Easter - thrills!!!! This evening we went to Keith's for dinner. The President and Mrs. Wilson were there in their box. He goes every week.

April 29, 1916

Spent the weekend at Annapolis. Stayed at Carvel Hall and had a wonderful time. Dances, with the pool plebes looking on wishfully, baseball games, lacrosse (the first I've ever seen). Rowing, I must say men in uniforms are most attractive. At the dance to-night I had bids for June Week.

Sunday morning, we saw the formation for chapel. Miles of men in black uniforms with brass buttons, white caps, and white gloves marching to stirring music and bugle calls. Afterwards we met them at Bancroft Hall and strolled out on the Promenade which commands a wonderful view of Chesapeake Bay, and this morning the bay was covered with sailboats.

May 4, 1916

All the seniors were invited to the White House to the tea this afternoon. We went first into the great East Room with its gold piano and crystal chandeliers, then to the Blue Room, where we were presented to the new Mrs. Wilson. She wore an orchid dress and was most charming. The President's aide presented each of us, and Mrs. Wilson distinctly repeated each name. The President was not in the receiving line because he had just received another of the numerous notes from Germany. We wondered if it meant War.

The President appeared later in the State Dining room where we had wonderful refreshments. We strolled out on the veranda overlooking the grounds. The gardens were filled with pink tulips and white pansies. Mrs. S. the head of our school, told us that she once walked out there with President Harrison, whom, she said, was most difficult to talk with.

Then just as we were leaving, Mrs. Wilson came out and got in the President's car. She smiled and waved her hand at us. Of course we were thrilled to death.

May 13, 1916

Tonight a gorgeous dinner and dance at Senator Borah's marvelous home. It was wonderful! I shall never forget the terrace in the moonlight. Far below were the lights of Washington and the Monument gleaming through the trees.

And so on to Graduation. School is over forever! No matter how often I return to Washington it will never be quite the same again.

This evening was the Junior-Senior Banquet. It was wonderful to be toasted and sung to as a senior. The decorations were American Beauties, the junior flower; and cornflowers, our class flowers. The whole program was carried out in war terms; the favors were silver vases with "1916-1917" engraved on them. The huge silver loving cup was filled and passed to each one while the others sang, "Here's to Ray Pefley, etc. Drink her down, drink her down - ".

[Author's Note: Alice Roosevelt Longworth (1884-1980)

Alice's marriage to Congressman Nicholas Longworth was a shaky one. Congressman Longworth was 14 years older than she was; and had a reputation as the playboy of D.C. carrying on numerous affairs with beautiful women. As reported in Betty Boyd Caroli's, "The Roosevelt Women", as well as in TIME by journalist Rebecca Winters Keegan, it was generally accepted knowledge in Washington that Alice also had a long, ongoing affair with Senator William Borah. The opening of Alice's diaries to modern historical researches indicates that Borah was, by Alice's own admission the father of her daughter, Paulina Longworth (1925-1957). Ray was unaware of this liaison until 1927, while visiting Washington and shopping with Mrs. Borah. There was a portrait of Alice Longworth and her two-year-old daughter, Paulina, in a store window. Mrs. Borah paused to look at it, and poignantly asked, "Ray... do you think she looks like Bill?"]

Ray at Mount Vernon in 1916

"White Roses"

"Reception at Sonnencroft"
The Fairmont Times
October 26, 1917

"Sonnencroft, the home of Mr. and Mrs. Clyde E. Hutchinson, was the scene of an afternoon reception at which Mrs. Brooks Swearingen Hutchinson; formerly Ray Pefley of Boise, Idaho, was introduced to her new friends here. Two daughters-in-law of the Hutchinson's, Mrs. Bernard Lee Hutchinson of Cincinnati and Mrs. Frank E. Hutchinson of Logan, W.Va., were in the receiving line."

****

Mother kept Daddy waiting for a year after graduation before a wedding date was set. She traveled to her friends' homes all over the country and would rave about their homes and the parties held in her honor. He would receive the copies of the hosts' hometown papers relating her visits, which I think, really worried him, as Mother was so much younger. Typical male! Mother always told us to, "keep them waiting. It works every time!" Daddy always countered this expression with, "He chased her until she caught him."

The article from the Los Angeles Graphic, March 3, 1917 stated:

"One of the most charming visitors in Los Angeles at present is Miss Ray Pefley of Boise, Idaho who is being entertained by Miss Grace Lobingier of 511 Westmoreland Avenue. Miss Pefley and Miss Lobingier were classmates at Mount Vernon College, Washington D.C. being graduated last June. In honor of this attractive young visitor, who is being accompanied during her stay here by her grandmother, a number of delightful social affairs are being given."

****

Mother finally set the wedding date for September 12, 1917. (This turned out to be the date of the Russian Revolution.)

The entire Hutchinson family followed Daddy, who preceded them by train, to Boise, Idaho for the wedding. They stopped at the Great Salt Lake and enjoyed the sightseeing along the trek west; so much easier in their new automobiles, than when Mom crossed those plains sixty years before.

According to The Idaho Statesman:

"An evening wedding was held in the Saint Michael's Cathedral with the Bishop of Idaho presiding. The decorations were unusually effective and beautiful and evoked the admiration of the guests before the bridal party appeared. They were executed and designed by the bridegroom's mother, Mrs. Clyde E. Hutchinson of Fairmont, West Virginia. Saint Michael's never looked lovelier than on this occasion."

Mammam had used quantities of the feathery Michaelmass daisies combined with small palms and pink asters used along the chancel rails and massed in Watteau baskets. "Tall sprays of pink gladiola arose from the altar, and the bridal pair spoke their vows beneath wedding bells of white roses suspended from an arch of roses and asparagus plumose. The white linen carpeted aisle, through which the bridal party passed, was bordered with daisies; and the white ribbons which garlanded the pews were fastened with a bunch of pink asters at each pew."

The Idaho Statesmen goes on with an elaborate description of the gowns, as you seldom read today. There was no Dior or Chanel yet, but there was Georgette de la Plante, a wonderful Parisian dressmaker who created a thin silk or crepe material, and named it Georgette for herself. Georgette was used extensively in the most elegant society gowns of the early part of the century.

"The winsome bridesmaids followed the ushers down the aisle one by one. They were gowned alike in short frocks of pale pink Georgette crepe over pink pussy willow taffeta, the bodices were made of taffeta with crepe sleeves, the full skirts trimmed with bands of taffeta. They wore large rose picture hats with brims of pink chiffon and black velvet crowns. They carried huge bouquets of pink Killarney roses tied with pink sash ribbons.

"Next were the two charming honored maids, Miss Vivian Slick of Boise and Miss Florence Myers of Pittsburgh, in pink Georgette evening gowns with silver hats ornamented with pink ostrich tips. They also wore silver slippers and carried big bouquets of pink roses and lavender orchids tied with pink satin ribbon; and lastly, the fair bride on the arm of her Godfather, Madison Smith, who gave her away.

"Attired simply in a Francaise, Empire gown of ivory white satin with a cathedral train and full-length veil, she was most beautiful. The upper part of the bodice was of tulle trimmed with seed pearls. Her veil was held in place with a circlet of pearls. She carried a large round bouquet of bride roses and white orchids with a shower of Swainsonia. Her only ornament was a diamond wristwatch a gift of the bridegroom.

"Eugene Farner at the organ played a processional from Lohengrin as the bridal party entered continuing the selection softly during the impressive Episcopal service which was pronounced by the Right Reverend Bishop Funsten, assisted by Dean Alward Chamberlaine. The organists played the Mendelssohn march as the party left the church."

The article describes the elaborate buffet served throughout the evening at the Owyhee Hotel ballroom and says that dancing to Tompkins' orchestra followed the reception.

"The bride is a native daughter and recognized as one of the most beautiful girls of the younger set. She met her future husband while in the east attending Mount Vernon Seminary in Washington, D.C., from which she graduated a year ago. The bridegroom is a graduate of West Virginia University and Yale Law School. They will make their home in Fairmont."

Ray and Brooks left on the night train for a tour of the northwest, including Portland, Seattle, Vancouver, and then off to Banf and Lake Louise. The close family followed the honeymooners on to Portland and Seattle and Mother always said she was afraid they would never be left alone as a couple!

"BEHOLD MY DAUGHTERS, MY DEAR"

Daughters-in-law playing golf at Deer Park; left to right: Katharine; Ray; Mammam; Bonnie and Margaret

CHAPTER SIX

THE MYSTERIOUS UNCLE CLAUDE

The Eight Hutchinson Sons

Left to Right
Front row: Jimmy and Robert
Back row: Brooks, Claude, Lee, Paul, Frank and Harold

"Claude Hutchinson Shot and Seriously Wounded Tues. Morning"
"Well Known Local Young Man is at Cook Hospital in Serious Condition"
"Bullet entered side, broke a rib and fractured intestines"
The Fairmont Times
May 13, 1919

"Lying at Cook Hospital in a serious condition Claude Hutchinson of this city, is suffering from the effects of a gunshot wound received early Tuesday morning, it is claimed at the hands of Mrs. Lester S. at her home on Center Street. At a late hour last night information received from the hospital was to the effect that his condition was considered favorable, but he was very seriously wounded. The bullet from Mrs. S's revolver entered his side it was reported, broke a rib, and then took a downward course, penetrating the intestines. An X-Ray picture disclosed the location of the ball, which was not removed last night. It was feared that the presence of the lead in the intestines might cause peritonitis to develop and the wound is being very carefully watched.

"According to the little information available regarding the affair, the shooting occurred about 12:30 Tuesday morning. It is said that Mrs. S, who is the wife of a fireman attached to the Central Station, and who was on night duty was awakened at that hour by a noise at her bedroom window. She saw a man with his knee in the opened window. She called out to the intruder who gave his name. She then ordered him away but when he failed to go, opened fire with her revolver.

"Three shots were fired one of which took effect. The police were then called and upon their arrival Mrs. S. told them practically the above story. Hutchinson had in the meantime been removed to the hospital.

"The police made an examination and say they saw marks where someone had climbed up on a coalhouse in the yard and from the top of this building had opened the window. They say the marks on the windowsill showed where someone had entered or attempted to enter the room.

"Claude Hutchinson is a well known young man about town. He is well known in social circles and has an unusually wide circle of acquaintances from all walks of life."

****

Daddy writes to Mother who, with Mom, is visiting her guardian and Uncle, Madison Smith, who had been ill in Boise. This was her first visit home to see him since her marriage.

June 2, 1919

"We brought Claude home from the hospital today. He seems to be doing pretty well, but they have not removed the bullet. Hope it won't be a problem in the future. We have hired a nurse to be with him at all times."

The following Saturday Daddy writes:

June 7, 1919

"Claude's condition became very alarming this morning. The nurse called me here at the office to say he needed to be taken back to the hospital. We took him back by ambulance this afternoon, for yet another operation."

June 8, 1919

"Claude's operation was very successful, and, by the greatest good luck, they found the bullet according to Dr. Howard. The bullet was shattered on the end leaving it ragged and would have caused him trouble. Talked to Father twice yesterday in Culver (where Lyda and Clyde were picking up their son Paul to bring him home for the summer vacation) and gave him the doctor's report. They had trouble with the Packard and had just arrived in Indiana that day."

"Claude Hutchinson Dies Suddenly at Cook Hospital"
"Young man was shot one month previous to his death."
"Warrant issued for Mrs. Anna S. charging her with murder."
The West Virginian
Friday June 13, 1919

"When physicians in charge thought he was recuperating from the effects of a revolver wound recently received, just one month ago today, Claude Hutchinson died suddenly at Cook Hospital where he was a patient. Following the death the body was removed to the Jones undertaking establishment to be prepared for burial while county authorities at once began their official investigation into the death.

120

"Prosecuting Attorney Walter Haggerty caused a warrant to be issued by Justice W.W. Conaway charging Mrs. Anna S., wife of Lester S., a fireman at Central Station, with the murder of Hutchinson. Mrs. S. was out of the city but made arrangements to appear at the office of the justice today to answer the charge.

"County Coroner Frank A. Lloyd empanelled a coroner's jury which viewed the body and then adjourned to meet Monday morning at 10 o'clock in the county court room to hold an inquest. The jury is composed of Fred Crislipp, Edward Franklin, Frank Murphy, June Clark, R.A. Cole and Floyd Hawkins.

"The shooting occurred early on the morning of May 13, last. Mrs. S. is said to have made the statement that she was awakened by noise at her bedroom window and she found someone trying to enter the room. She ordered the intruder away and when he failed to go, opened fire with the revolver. The person disappeared and a few hours later, young Hutchinson was admitted to Cook hospital suffering from a bullet wound in the stomach. He was apparently improving and was dismissed from the hospital. Later he became worse and the hospital performed an operation removing the bullet and he seemed to again be improving.

"This morning he was seized with a sinking spell and became unconscious. Dr. L.D. Howard was called and succeeded in reviving him. "I thought I was going to die," Hutchinson remarked. Then he suddenly exclaimed, "I am going to die." and sank back dead. A blood clot in the lungs is said to have been the immediate cause of death.

"His death occurred about 9 o'clock this morning and he was just preparing to eat his breakfast when the end came.

"Mr. and Mrs. Hutchinson, the parents of the young man together with their son Paul and a school friend of his were en route here from Culver, Indiana, where Paul had been graduated from Culver Military Academy. A message received here early yesterday morning said they were in Wheeling and would arrive here sometime tomorrow.

"Claude Ernest Hutchinson, 33 years of age, was the eldest son of eight sons born to Mr. and Mrs. Hutchison and his is the first death to occur in the family. The surviving sons are Attorney Brooks Hutchinson of this city; Bernard Lee, of Cincinnati, Ohio; Frank, of Logan, WV; Harold, Paul, Robert and James all of this city.

"The body was prepared for burial at the Jones Undertaking Parlor and later removed to Sonnencroft, the home of his parents. No funeral arrangements have as yet been made."

****

Daddy continued to keep Mother informed with the following sad letters,

June 14, 1919

My dearest Ray,

"No one can ever imagine what we had to go through yesterday and today. Briefly, I was in my office at 9 o'clock yesterday-Friday the thirteenth- the hospital called and said to hurry. I rushed over there to find Claude breathing his last. He was unconscious and did not speak. It was a total collapse.

"Fifteen minutes before, he was fine, asked for another piece of toast and was eating his breakfast with a relish. He called the nurse over to the bed and whispered, "I certainly feel sick", and slumped down. Only with the lung motor did they revive him. He awoke with the statement, ' I certainly thought I was gone that time!' He asked the doctor what time it was, and how glad he had been there to save him and sank back down again at ten minutes after nine when all efforts failed to revive him.

"I had talked to Mother earlier about how he was improving and was never better. They left the hotel in Wheeling to start on their last trek homeward. Can you imagine just what it was like to contemplate the family arriving at two-thirty and finding Claude dead in his room?

"Frank and Bonnie arrived last night and Lee and Katherine today. We are having the funeral tomorrow-Sunday the fifteenth- at 3 o'clock. We went to Woodlawn today and purchased thirty-three lots for the whole family on a lovely site. All of the brothers will be pallbearers.

"Today the house was filling rapidly with dear friends and it was one thing after another to make all the arrangements. I wanted everything to appear normal at home and asked everyone to go into the other rooms. Had Mr. Jones prepare the body and get it into Claude's bedroom by one o'clock. Then had the nurse and both the doctors- father and son- on hand to look after Mother.

122

"The family arrived and I guided Mother to her room without her suspicioning a thing, but just as she started to go into her room she sensed the general strain, or simply her mother's intuition and said, "What is the matter, Brooks?" Then she said, "Claude's dead" and collapsed to the floor.

"This evening she is calmer and I believe she will be able to attend the funeral tomorrow. When she went in to see him this morning, it was the most heart-rending scene I have ever experienced!

"It has been so terrible, my sweet, I am really glad you have not had to suffer through all this. Everyone has been so thoughtful and, of course, has such lightened the undertaking.

"Mother has asked for her dear Ray, but it is just as well, my love, that you are not here.

Poor Mother, she did take it so very hard. I have heard her say-so often, "a mother is only as happy as her saddest child." I am sure she will be a long time recovering her happy ways."

With all my heart, my love,
Yours devotedly,

~ Brooks

Claude had admitted all to Daddy and confessed he had been having an affair with Mrs. S.

In those days, as it still may be, firemen who were on duty for 2 weeks at a time were forbidden to leave their post for any reason. On Fireman S's post days, Claude and Mrs. S. were seeing each other at her home. It was thought the other firemen had taken an oath swearing never to tell that Fireman S had left his post on that fateful morning of May 13 and allowed him to sneak home, climb through the window and surprise the two lovers. Uncle Claude had jumped from the bed and was shot in the stomach. The gun was thrown to the floor and Mr. S., thinking Claude was dead, warned his wife to blame the break-in on Claude and threw the gun on the floor. Mrs. S. had followed her husband's dictates and waited to call the police until the fireman had time to return to his station.

Daddy told the prosecutor the whole story, who in turn told the coroner's jury and all murder charges were dropped.

123

When Mammam recovered from the shock of losing her first-born son she answered Mother's many letters.

July 14, 1919

" My precious girl,

"It is needless to say your dear letters have been appreciated. I have put off writing as I know Brooks writes to you daily. He has been so noble and wonderful, managing all the details; he is such a comfort to us all.

"I am so glad you and Mom did not have to suffer the loss of her son reliving it with me. You will never know how much I have suffered. The awful shock of giving up my first-born! He is never out of my mind I miss him so much - o'so much. When I go to call the boys his bed is empty. I hear his voice so often. Every time I speak to Paul I call him Claude - whenever I hear a car come up the driveway my heart throbs, thinking it is Claude. Only with time and God's help can we bear our sorrow.

"God spared his life for such a short time to let him think about what he had done. He did pray and asked God to forgive him. He says, 'Him that cometh unto me I will in no wise cast out." I am sure he will not cast my boy out-for he and he alone knows all of the poor boy's weaknesses. He tried so hard to do the right thing, but - oh well, God knows, I am trying to take His words for comfort.

"We are so eager for your homecoming and will kill the fatted calf! Brooks misses you terribly, but we know that your dear Uncle Smith needs you and Mom right now. Clyde joins me in sending you our love."

~ Mother

[AUTHOR'S NOTE: As a little girl we had such fun going to Woodlawn cemetery on Memorial Day. All the siblings and their wives would gather at Sonnencroft and take an assembled lunch along with peonies from Mammam's garden to our lots at the cemetery. We used a glass jar to bury at Papa's grave and my job would be to fill the jar with water from a spigot on the lot and put in the peonies. There were only two gravesites - Papa's and Uncle Claude's, which was ignored. We planted rose bushes and iris along the wall and shrubs of spirea behind the two granite benches and I got to water them in. I would be the only one to take a peony over and lay it on Uncle Claude's grave.

124

He had been buried in 1919 way over at the far edge of the lot, as if he was not one of ours. He was never mentioned and I never knew why the others - even his mother - ignored his grave, nor did I question the reason until I was a grown woman. Then I realized he was tallest of the group, handsome-with long dark eyelashes, an impeccable dresser, debonair, rich, and single; a true Don Juan. He was not interested in college or sports - just girls, perhaps resembling his grandfather, Jerry Hutchison. Claude was the mysterious Gatsby character - always in the shadows of life, and an enigma to his family. I still decorate his lonely grave.]

Claude Hutchinson

OTHER SCANDALS

Uncle Claude's death was one of several intriguing scandals of Fairmont during the roaring twenties and the dirty thirties - the Lost Generation.

Prohibition (1919-1933) - the eighteenth amendment of the U.S. Constitution forbade the manufacture, sale and transportation of alcoholic beverages. The amendment was a result of the Protestant churches led by the Women's Christian Temperance Union. The Anti-Saloon League of America reform movements convinced the government that it was their duty to protect free citizens from the temptations of drink by barring its sale.

The Fairmont WCTU group met in a building built for them in the early 1900's at the west corner of Fairmont Avenue and First Street. Mammam's church - The First Baptist Church was right across the street on Walnut Avenue. I told you that she had marched in a parade before she was married. And had little time after that to protest too much, but with so many sons at home she continued to preach against the evils of alcohol. Evidently, she and Clyde did not drink any alcohol nor serve it at their banquets or parties.

The only liquor in our home at 741 was apricot brandy that Mom made every few years. It was kept in a lovely decanter in the china cupboard and served only when there was company. Of course there were boxes in the basement I did not know about until they moved to Hawaii in the 50s.

Daddy leased a suite at the Waldorf Hotel in New York City on a yearly basis. During Prohibition the bellhops would buy French wines and liquors from the ship stewards and sneak their cache in to the Waldorf to those permanent tenants at a good price.   Daddy would tip the bellhops and carefully bring it to 741 and store it in the basement. When my parents left for Hawaii I inherited the boxes, but they sat in my basement on Coleman Avenue for 9 years, when we moved them to West End Drive. When I finally opened them after 70 years, the corks had rotted and crumbled and the liquor had evaporated, but I loved the beautiful empty bottles, remnants of an era we would never forget.

Congress finally passed the Volstead Act, which provided for the enforcement of the amendment in late 1919. Speakeasies, bootlegging and rum running all flourished under gangster elements. The "Wets" mounted a campaign to annul the law and were successful in 1933 when the 21st amendment was ratified, annulling the 18th and negating the Volstead Act.

My sisters and I would linger at the dining room table in the evening. Mother always said it ruined the conversation to move to another room and that is where we all learned about the other scandals from the past. Mother would warn us about drinking or running around with a "fast" crowd. She would exclaim how terrible it was to lose one's precious reputation - once lost –never to be regained, and then show us examples. I do not remember drugs being mentioned, probably because she mentioned "Coke" and we presumed it was Coca Cola.

During the Fitzgeraldesque era, a few of the cliques in different age brackets went wild on cocaine and alcohol and had adulterous trysts, enjoying the money boom, or so they thought.

The town was forever intrigued with the murder at a prominent household that involved six young couples, a few just out of college and well known in Fairmont.

A few were playing bridge; some were kibitzing, singing or dancing - all drinking, when a shot shattered the gaiety downstairs. The gunfire came from above and they rushed up the staircase. A man laid fatally shot on the bed and another man's wife was kneeling on the floor sobbing. They realized her husband was the guilty party.

The guests made a pact among themselves vowing never to reveal the truth. One guest was a close relative of the prosecuting attorney, who was called first; then police were told it was accidental.

As far as I know, that pact was never broken. There was no newspaper coverage, at least not in Daddy's Ledger - just an obituary.

All of the participants have been dead for many years. Two of them burned together in a nighttime house fire on Seventh Street, caused by what the firefighters called, cigarettes and alcohol.

Another murder I remember hearing about, as a child, was a married couple that, due to excess alcohol, never made it upstairs to bed.

When he awoke the next morning he found his wife, still in her blue velvet gown with her lapis lazuli beads wound tightly around her beautiful white throat, strangled to death on the living room settee. The murderer was never found and only her obituary was printed.

The next story was a mystery only a short time but it caused quite an uproar in the town.

"Blackhander Caught While Seeking Cash"
"Barbour County Lad Found Plenty of Folks at Home"
"Hutchinson Estate Gate"
The Fairmont Times
No date – Early 1920s

"After writing a Black Hand letter demanding $1,500 of C. E. Hutchison of Morgantown Avenue, Dorsey G. aged 19, Montrose, West Virginia was arrested and taken to the county jail near midnight last night when he called the Hutchinsons for money.

"The letter, mailed in Fairmont, directed that the money be placed at the entrance to the estate and threatened death to Mr. and Mrs. Hutchinson in the event of their refusal to comply with the demands. The letter was received yesterday afternoon. Mr. Hutchinson was out of the city but Mrs. Hutchinson communicated with her sons and the prosecuting attorney, Frank R. Amos, was notified. The money was to be at the gate at 11:30 last night.

"County and city officers were hidden about the estate and in nearby vantage points. It was a little later than 11:30 when Dorsey appeared. He walked slowly by the gate three times and was placed under arrest.

"Sheriff Charleton said he wrote from dictation the same letter, and all the same words were misspelled as in the original letter signed from The Black Hand. When confronted with this evidence the young boy admitted he had written the letter in the post office, but that he was drinking when he wrote the missive."

****

There were no follow-ups in my daddy's ledger; therefore it seemed a onetime occurrence in the city.

CHAPTER SEVEN

THE FAMILY

Clyde & Mary Lyda Hutchinson

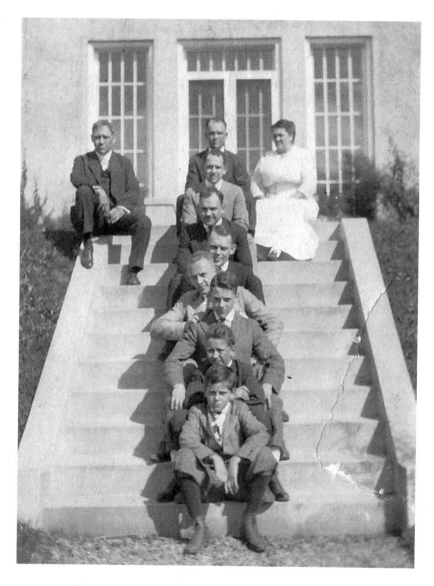

Claude & Mary Lyda pictured with their eight sons.

Top to bottom: Claude Ernest, Brooks Swearingen, Bernard Lee, Frank Ehlen, Harold Herbert, Paul Mason, Robert Jay and James Jeremiah

THE FAMILY

By Ray Pefley Hutchinson -1923

[AUTHOR'S NOTE: This chapter of vignettes relates Mother's intimate view of her large acquired family.

So many of the family had moved away or died before I was born, but through her perspective, I grew to know and love the characters, as intimately as Mother had.]

****

I was an only child, but when I married Brooks I acquired a family consisting of a Mother and Father, seven brothers, three sisters-in-law, and numerous nieces and nephews. I literally became a member of the family, for not a secret was kept from me. There were no conferences in corners, everything was discussed openly, and my opinion asked and listened to. I really could not believe it at first, and then, as I gradually realized and appreciated the joy of it, the story of Ruth and Naomi took on new meaning for me. Mother rejoiced at each son's marriage and took us to her heart, for she had always wanted a daughter.

The home of all these boys was an immense house which looked like a medieval castle— grey stucco, turreted, and draped with ivy. Terraced gardens, rose arbors, quiet pools filled with goldfish surrounded it (a gorgeous place in summer.) Inside all was cheer and comfort—not merely a house, but a home—dominated by a Mother who was the spirit of Ceres.

A large family is most delightful at all times, but at Christmas it is the most thrilling. The excitement began with decorating the whole house with holly, mistletoe and red candles. A great wreath was hung in the huge hall to welcome everyone. Logs of gigantic proportions were blazing in the living room fireplace. Everything in readiness for the welcome of those who were living out of town.

The first arrival was the quietest, for as more and more of the clan gathered, the more hilarious were the greetings. First Frank and Bonnie with their two little boys arrived from their home in the southern part of the state.

132

Next morning, Paul, a student at Yale, came dashing into the breakfast room-kissing everyone-glad to get home. Then Bob and Jimmy, the youngest, just home from military school and quite dashing in their uniforms. Many bear hugs and kisses again. Harold and Margaret drove up about dinnertime; the whole family trooping out to meet and help them unload their luggage, with much affectionate badinage.

The next day brought Katherine and Lee with their two children. Much laughter and many hugs and kisses for the babies. Many admiring comments on how tall Helen, the oldest grandchild, had grown; and how fat the baby was. Such a joy to be together again!.

In the dining room, with its tapestried walls and ivory woodwork, its clusters of long windows, looking over the terraced Italian garden, hours were spent at the long dining table. Sipping coffee, cracking nuts-anything to delay the departure of an impatient one. The most closely knitted family. Loyal to the last degree to each other, each secretly admiring all the rest. Everyone, more or less clever in the art of conversation. A word would start the ball rolling around the table, each adding a pun or a joke; everyone laughing as though it was the funniest in the world- so happy to be re-united again.

Mother, at the foot of the table, always calm, always pleasant, never impatient. Lyda was a large, handsome woman with soft brown eyes and beautiful black hair; and, that best of all gifts, a sense of humor. Tolerance is a word I always associate with her and kindliness.

Father, at the head of the table. A sturdy man, with ruddy complexion, grey eyes, and iron grey hair. Clyde was a perfect model for Rembrandt, a man, keen, clever, vital, and impetuous. Not talking much, but listening to everything. When he did have something to say, everyone else was all attention. A man who has cut and hewn the granite of life, from the farm boy to a well-known, respected financier throughout the East and a veritable Viking in business.

Henry Gray, the colored butler, in his spotless white coat, passing the plates quietly, answering a dozen demands at once, coming in for his share of jokes and questions, especially from the younger boys.

Much reminiscing of happy times from the oldest to the youngest. Times when Brooks and Lee roomed together at the University and were right and left ends on the 1906 -08 WVU football team. Then with much laughter, "Do you remember the time Jimmy slept in the newest automobile all night so Bob wouldn't get it first?" More teasing of Jimmy, "Why do you always sign your letters home to Mother and Father, 'Yours truly, James Hutchinson'?" "Remember when he wrote to Father and said, 'Ah. the trees are all abloom and here and there a dog would'". Jimmy blushes and there is more laughter.

Then finally when the three youngest have rushed away to keep engagements, and we simply can't linger at the dining table any longer, some drift into the conservatory, where soft lights are reflected in the fountain pool. The goldfish seem like tiny lights themselves as they dart through the water. Some of us wander to the music room and sounds of harmony, in spirit at least, are heard through the halls. Some go to the library, some to the billiard room for a game. But not for long do they separate. Soon the large armchairs on either side of the huge fireplace in the living room are filled. The davenport in front of the fire is easily accommodating six people.

Mother is sitting by the table so that the light from the lamp there falls on the sweater she is knitting for one of the grandchildren. She knits slowly and methodically. The sweater will probably be outgrown by the child it is intended for, and fit a much younger one when it is finally finished! Mother is always busy. This great room seems to reflect her personality with its warmth and cheer of mulberry velour draperies, gay, harmonizing chintzes on the furniture, and lampshades of golden silk. The great fireplace of bronzed tile topped by a mantle six feet above the floor, over which hangs a beautiful picture of the Canterbury Pilgrims. Great bronze lights flank either side, casting a soft glow over all. A copper kettle hangs on a crane and slowly steams from the heat of the fire.

Father sits at one side under a standing lamp, The New York Times strewn all around him on the floor. He is so impatient to find just the part he wants to read or having finished a section, to the floor it goes, to be picked up by someone else later. He reads and listens at the same time; sometimes breaking into the conversation to read us some article which especially interests him. Then- again he puts down the paper, holds his glasses in his hand, listens to us, makes some comment to the point or asks that some remark be repeated. Sometimes he gives his short, hearty laugh- then back to his paper.

Katherine and Lee are occupying one chair, as usual, much to the pretended disgust of everyone else. They were boy and girl sweethearts long before they were married, and have never gotten over their honeymoon days. Katherine is tall and slender, with sparkling brown eyes and bronze-gold hair. Vivacious, friendly, interesting personality. Lee is one of the two blondes of the family: one of the most happy-go-lucky persons in the world. "Hail-fellow-well-met," popular with everyone; simply radiating good-humor. Katherine says no one ever knows he has a surname.

Bonnie, blue-eyed, with beautiful blonde, wavy hair, in a big armchair, sits looking dreamily into the fire. She is a quiet, slow, lazy Southern type. She reads everything in sight; taking life as it comes, without struggling or striving for more than it has to give her, adoring Frank, who is her exact opposite. He is tall, dark, domineering; most certainly the undisputed head of his small family. He never allowed Bonnie to pack a trunk or even a suitcase, or choose a curtain for their home. But she likes that, so they get along perfectly together.

I am sitting next to Frank on the davenport, so suffice it to say, I am also blonde, and let it go at that. All these boys, so far, have preferred blondes. Brooks sits next to me. He is dark, too, and of course, most handsome in my eyes. He is not so tall but just the right height for me. He is broad-shouldered, powerful looking. When I say he has a disposition just like Mother's I can say nothing better. He is never impatient, never intolerant, and never loses his temper. He is the personification of thoughtfulness, kindness, and loyalty. That old adage about a good son making a good husband is true in this case. He is the eldest of the boys and the younger ones look up to him as a model, and really confide their troubles to him more often than to Father. I, who am so prejudiced, should not be writing this.

Margaret sits on a stool, toasting her back to the fire. She looks almost as small as one of the children. She has chestnut hair and blue-grey eyes. She is always well groomed, immaculate; an excitable, energetic, nervous type, with a keen sense of humor. Always ready to get down on the floor and play dolls or spin tops with the children, who adore her. She was from a small family like me, and at first it had been a trifle difficult for her to realize that she had married this whole family, and not just Harold. This is exactly what we all did, much to our surprise. But not one of these boys could be separated from the rest.

Harold sits in a chair near her; calm, quiet, brown eyes gazing at the fire, while he smokes a cigarette. We often laugh and remark that it is a good thing Margaret and Frank did not marry, for their wills are eternally clashing, while Bonnie and Harold would simply have drifted lazily with the tide. As it is, each has someone to spur him on.

It all comes back to me how much fun we had at Margaret's and Harold's wedding. Her home was in the small town of Montgomery in the southern part of the state. Harold, at that time, was superintendent at one of Father's mines in Logan. He and Harold Jenkins- another boy from Fairmont had a rambling old house at their disposal, so we all landed en masse for a house party the day before the wedding. The family had not been together for quite some time so everyone was hilarious. Everything seemed extremely humorous. We laughed and giggled until it was disgraceful. We danced until we were worn out and then played Bridge. At dinner, the dining table wasn't large enough to accommodate all of us, so Bob and Jimmy had to sit at a small table at one side. They pretended to be infants and such antics as they performed!

When Brooks and I were married, a good part of the family came out to my home in Idaho for the wedding. They almost went with us on our honeymoon, as we all took the same route through the Canadian Rockies. They followed us to Portland, Oregon, and spent a few hours with us, then preceded us to Seattle. When we arrived at the hotel there, we found the bridal suite of rooms engaged for us, and filled with roses! And we had hoped to fool everyone as to our being bride and groom! We were well advertised in Lake Louise and Banff, too, but from there on, they left us while we lingered in that Paradise.

Lee was the first son to marry, then Frank, both weddings before I joined the family. Now we always urge the younger boys to marry a girl who lives far away, so we will have a long journey to the wedding!

Paul, Robert and Jimmy are unmarried, as yet. Mother always spoke of them as her second generation. There are five years between Harold and Paul; the latter is the other blonde besides Lee. Paul had a very fiery temper, impetuous, flinging a golf club for yards after a bad shot; then very sorry for such a display. Loveable and charming, nevertheless rather a devil-may-care spirit. Yet he would leave a golf game early to rush home and hold the tiniest baby in the family for a while before it was put to bed! Quite a Don Juan with the girls. His very indifference seems to attract them all the more.

Robert, but how could anyone describe him? Driving the whole family to distraction with scrapes he seems unable to avoid; everyone worrying because of their very fondness for him. Family conclaves on what we would say to him after some affair, and then when the time came not being able to say it because he was so sorry, we didn't have the heart to. Or, at other times, turning away our wrath with some extremely funny joke or clownish act. Endearing himself to the children until it was understood by all, that Uncle Bobby was their favorite. The most witty, good-natured, clever person; he would don a white cap and apron and immediately become an excited French chef, demanding our wishes as to Sunday night supper, and he could cook it, too, if necessary. Or he would rough up his hair and talk exactly like the Russian artist who had just painted my portrait, "Ah, ze great art! Ze broad curve of ze brush," and so on, endlessly, much to the delight of everyone. Katherine said he was only amusing when in the midst of the family. That he never performed when he visited her, but was a total loss! I cannot say, for he was always interesting to me.

Jimmy was the baby; tall, dark, handsome, a perfect understudy for Richard Barthelmess of movie fame. Very quiet and retiring. He looked after Robert like a hen with one chicken. Jimmy was Robert's best audience, adoring him always. When Robert wasn't around Jimmy could be extremely witty himself, but with Robert present, he was only a foil for Robert's jokes.

Mother's father, Jacob Watkins, lives here, too. He sits in an armchair by the fireplace, opposite Bonnie. A patriarch of ninety winters; a giant man with sparkling sea-blue eyes, ruddy cheeks, and hair of heavy silver. He is very deaf and sits for hours just watching the rest of us. We thought to interest him in jigsaw puzzles, but after trying to fit several pieces together he would laugh, shake his head, and declare that it simply could not be done. Even after the puzzle was completed before his very eyes, he still seemed to doubt that such a feat had been accomplished.

As a stonemason, he had worked very hard all his life and the cost of things interested him greatly. The present-day expenses were simply beyond his reckoning. Just before Mother and Father left for a tour of the world he wanted to know how much it would cost. When told, he was sure they were going to buy the ship!

Repeatedly, he would ask Brooks how he ever met me, for my home was in Idaho. It was always a wonder to him why Brooks had to go so far from home to get a wife!

He lived in such deep silence that he was unnecessarily noisy himself. In church he would tap his cane on the floor at the most inopportune and embarrassing moments. Poor Grandfather, so old and yet so pathetically like a little child before he died. The house seemed strangely quiet and lonesome for months afterwards, without the tapping of his cane, as he slowly wandered through the halls.

But it's Christmas Eve, so around nine o'clock, after the children are asleep, "all snug in their beds," the Christmas tree is brought in, filling the room with the pungent, teasing odor of pine. It is a regal tree, towering to the ceiling. Mother brings down the ornaments and tells just how long each has been in the family. "This angel has been on the top of every tree since Brooks was a baby." "These we had in Chicago when Harold was a baby," and so on. We decorate all evening and about eleven o'clock discover the lights won't work, as usual. But after many suggestions to Frank, who always perched himself on the top of the ladder, presumably to decorate the difficult top branches, but really to hold forth in sidesplitting soliloquies, the tree is arrayed in all its glory. The mantle is hung with a row of red cotton stockings, trimmed around the top with cotton; a whole row in graduated sizes from the largest to a tiny one for the baby. The younger boys drift in from their various engagements. All the toys for the children have to be experimented with and inspected. Frank has brought himself a toy, and duly labels it as such, two little acrobat clowns who perform wondrous feats. He says it is too good for the children to break up, so he will enjoy it himself. All the packages are pinched and shaken and labels examined. Many wild guesses made as to just what each present might be.

Finally, we all repair to the kitchen to raid the icebox. Coffee is made by someone, sandwiches appear as if by magic, and some even find mince pie. Mother appears to guard the Christmas dinner. We all realize that it is after midnight, and everyone shouts, "Merry Christmas" and "Christmas Gift".

Great excitement next morning! Always the first to greet us as we rushed down-stairs was Father, who slipped a gold piece to each one. We girls always gave him a hearty kiss, which seemingly embarrassed, but really delighted him.

Then on to the loaded, glittering tree. The children, who had risen with the dawn, had the toys scattered all over the floor and are busily playing. Soon red and green tissue paper, ribbons of silver and gold, littered the room. Excited exclamations! Much rushing to each other with, "Oh, boys, you were dears to give me this lamp", "This cigarette lighter is just what I wanted", "Oh, this gorgeous luncheon set, Mother!" or "Gosh, these handkerchiefs with the monograms. Did you make them, Ray?"

Later the servants are brought in to receive their gifts and express their joy.

Ben, the gardener, pays his Christmas morning call. He is so dressed up we hardly know him. His eyes are twinkling with good will above his bright red necktie. His present is a new lunch bucket, and he is so impressed with it he insists in asking, "How much-a cost?" to the amusement of everyone.

The morning soon passes and dinner is announced. The table is a wonder for the children with its centerpiece of mirrors, representing a lake. It is surrounded by snow dotted with tiny pine trees. A miniature Santa Claus in his sleigh, drawn by little reindeer, is crossing it. Mother always had time to add a touch of beauty. The dinner was a culinary perfection, with everyone in high spirits, from the bouillon to the flaming plum pudding, borne in proudly on a large silver tray by Henry, the butler. Robert fusses him by casually remarking, "That pudding isn't burning very brightly, Henry. Are you sure you put all the brandy on it?"

By that time visitors are arriving to view the huge glistening tree and the gifts. The living room is aglow with soft lights and the roaring fire. Boxes of candy are opened; bowls of nuts, figs, and dates are passed to everyone. Much laughter, chatter, and music fills the whole house.

Evening comes and the children are dragged reluctantly to bed. The last one remarks, as he yawns and rubs his eyes, "I wish Christmas would come every day." So thought we all, as tired but deliciously comfortable, we gather around the fire Christmas night.

The words "East or West, Home is Best" in the leaded glass window on the stair landing, as we trail up-stairs to bed, seem perfect.

January1924 comes with Harold and Margaret, Brooks and me in New York with Mother and Father, all of us rushing around doing last minute shopping before they sail on their voyage around the world. Then, one midnight, standing on a pier, weeping and waving as the great new Liner- Laconia II -slowly glides out to sea. We watch her lights grow dim and then fade in the darkness. "How far is around the World?" My own little girl's question echoes in my heart, and I tremble to answer it.

Then, letters, first from Panama, next Los Angeles. We all longed to charter a plane and fly out there and stop them before they started on the Pacific, but sail they did. Stormy nights at home, and everyone's heart echoing the prayers lisped by the grandchildren to "Please, dear God, keep Mammam and Papa safe and bring them home soon."

Letters from Japan about the awful earthquake just before they reached there from Hong Kong, Shanghai, Singapore, Rangoon. How wonderful to even glimpse so many fairy-tale places. There is such a funny picture of Father and an Indian fakir. Father, with a sickly grin on his face, his hair standing upright; with a great python around his neck! When we teased him about it afterwards he always declared he was not the least bit afraid, that the wind made his hair look that way, but we always had our doubts!

Then we received pictures of them on camels in Egypt at the pyramids. Next Greece, then Rome, then Paris, and again we found ourselves in New York. This time it is June, and the ship sails in with bands playing and flags flying. Eagerly we scan the decks and locate Mother and Father. The gangplank is lowered, tears and kisses, and again the family is complete.

A gay week in New York, seeing all the theatres, shopping, and then finally home again. Mother and Father left with two trunks, they return with eight. We give them just the first evening to rest, and then the next day, we open the baggage.

Such excitement, wonder, and joy! Gifts from every country for everybody. Mother's bedroom turned into an Oriental bazaar. Four of everything for the girls. Gorgeous ceremonial bridal robes from Japan, shading from hyacinth blue to softest gray, heavily embroidered in gold. Mother's is black, lined in red with a red obi. Houri coats of heavenly blue from Kobe. "Ray, this one with the cherry blossoms and the doves on it is yours." "Bonnie, take this one with the lotus flowers," and so on.

From Japan, strings of pearls and square-cut crystals, and tiny bright-flowered kimonos for the children, and Chinese and Japanese dolls. Strings of turquoise-matrix and antique amber from Shanghai. Gorgeous Mandarin coats from Hong-Kong, and carved ivory combs. Strings of pink carnelians from Bombay. Lace from the Philippines, and a native costume. Velvet bags embroidered with gold peacocks from Agra. Batiks from Java. Silver toe-rings, silver anklets, huge earrings and a native robe from India. Interesting embroidered bags and donkey beads from Greece. From Egypt, tent work, silver scarves, scarabs and a Sheik's robe of pale blue silk shot with silver. Silk scarves from Florence, and marvelous beaded bags from Paris. For the boys carved ivory cigarette holders from China, amber cigarettes from Egypt, heavy silk robes from Japan, bill-folders of carved leather from India.

Such excitement and thrills at each new gift. Such tales of far-off lands and peoples! A picture of Father, sedately walking down the steps of a temple in India with a cow, not daring to drive it away because they are considered sacred there. He said he heard so much of reincarnation there, this must have been the reincarnation of old "Beauty", our old cow who died, from the way she followed him!

Then Mother told of the poor woman who died on the ship and had to be left in India, while her husband had to complete the trip alone. Of the time Mother almost missed the train in Agra for lingering at the Taj Mahal too long. Of the awful heat and how they hung wet sheets at the windows of the compartment to cool off the air; and about the burying towers in India, where the vultures sit. How cold it was in China, especially in the temples where they had to remove their shoes. We listen, but we cannot settle down for long, but must stroll around the room and gloat over our possessions.

Then during the remainder of that most gorgeous month, June, we simply revel in all being together again and bask in the sunshine of the garden. The children romp and race all day over the whole estate, resembling young Indians. We never knew where to look for them, in the fishponds or stables. At the latter place, Polly, the Irish setter, is a great attraction as she has again presented us with a large litter of adorable but worthless coal-black puppies.

Incessant splashing continues from the swimming pool as some of the boys decide it is just the right hour for a dip. Loud yells are heard frequently from some of the girls who have joined them.

The terraces are beautifully ablaze with color as seen from the dining-room windows. The heavenly blues of delphinium, mingling with the gorgeous shade of pink of the oriental poppies. Everywhere is beauty. We gather by the weeping-willow tree which hangs over the water-lily pond on the lowest terrace. The air is heavy with the perfume of roses. The golden day is slowly melting into the silver evening.

Jimmy, flat on his back by the rim of the pool, gazes dreamily at the clouds. Paul holds one of the children on his knee. Robert smokes and hums a tune. Everyone contented, restful, happy.

Henry appears with trays for each one of cold chicken, raspberry ice, delicious rolls, and tall glasses of iced tea.

"Oh, Mother, how did you know we all wanted to stay right here this marvelous evening and enjoy the sun-set?" Katherine exclaims.

Mother smiles and we all enjoy watching the clouds draw their gray chiffon over the crimson sun as it sinks behind the hills. The fireflies dart everywhere and the children begin chasing them. The dark descends slowly, almost lovingly, over this beautiful garden where we are all so contented. Someone hums "Carry Me Back to Old Virginia" and we all join in.

Father becomes restless and walks around the pool where the stars are now reflected. He is never still very long at a time. Finally he remarks that he thinks we should all prepare to go to the mountains of Maryland before the weather becomes too hot. We have spent several summers there in the cottage Father purchased for his grandchildren. The mountain air is most beneficial for them. His own sons spent every summer in that vicinity when they were small.

So without much discussion, we find ourselves in a few days on our way to the cottage. Cottage it was called, but it was really a rambling house of about thirty rooms. It had to be large to accommodate the family, which grew apace every year.

The men would drive us to Deer Park high up in the Maryland mountains in the suburbs of Oakland, then take the B&O back to Fairmont for the work week, leaving the younger boys with us, and return once again on the weekend.

Our summer neighbors always wanted to know who had the latest baby. My little Elaine (Sylvia and Diane had not been born yet) had been added to the list, and two more to Katherine's. Such happy hours they had together. So many happy ones, the childish quarrels and fusses didn't count.

We sisters played golf each morning, so rainy days were difficult. Shut in, seven or eight children can certainly create more noise than all the animals in a zoo. We were almost wild with the confusion until Mother suggested in her mild way that we girls go up to her bedroom and let the children have the down-stairs. This we always did after that, to the happy solution of the problem.

A woman once said to me, "It surely is not true that you four daughters-in-law can live for months in the same house together, with your mother-in-law, and never quarrel?" But that is exactly what we did. No one ever seemed to want to quarrel around Mother. There might be arguments or discussions, but never hard words nor hurt feelings. Her influence permeated the atmosphere of the whole house. Some one of the girls might get tired of the others, but she had her own room in which to retreat and enjoy her solitude. But by time for the next meal everyone would be present!

And such meals as there were! Made for men. Gigantic roasts surrounded by squadrons of potatoes, great bowls of gravy, and several species of vegetables, salads, hot bread and coffee three times a day. The luncheons were dinners and the dinners, banquets. Mother had raised her family before calories and vitamins and cod liver oil were heard of, and never thought of a balanced meal.

The dining table was always set for fourteen or sixteen at least. Usually there were several guests, as the boys felt perfectly free to ask anyone who happened to be with them. There was always room for more.

The children had their own dining room where their nurses looked after them. We saw little of the boys except as they passed and re-passed the house on the golf links that completely surrounded it. But in they would troop at luncheon and all conversation would stop. , "Did you see that drive I made on number nine?" or "I made a three on the fourteenth hole." We girls had a standing joke about them having the hoof and mouth disease. In fact, there were many family jokes, the mere mention of which would send everyone into gales of laughter. One joke we had about Bonnie was that all the things passed at the table finally surrounded her plate, for she never bothered to pass anything on, unless requested. We teased her about her Southern accent, too, which everyone copied at times, but she always remained calm as the summer sea.

After a leisurely luncheon, some of us would play a rubber or two of bridge or Mahjong on the side porch. The green velvet golf course brocaded with beautiful trees, spreading in all directions, the blue haze hanging over the mountains all around us. Gorgeous, languorous, carefree days! Nothing to worry about except, perhaps, the mail or the latest magazine or novel not arriving on time.

In the evenings we always had a log fire, for the mountain air was chilly. Sometimes the children popped corn or toasted marshmallows. Another time we all played their games with them or worked puzzles or had charades. Some evenings, after the children were in bed, we told ghost stories. My room was supposed to be haunted and many a time I have shivered as I turned out the light! One night after several particularly gruesome tales, I was slowly making my way up stairs, wishing the others would hurry and come, too, when something white fluttered in front of me, while someone grabbed me and groaned, "I want my golden arm!" Everyone was horrified at the scream I gave which even wakened the servants on the third floor. Harold had thrown a white Spanish shawl over the stair rail and Robert had grabbed me! They collapsed on the stairs and laughed until they were weak!

The golfers, even after their strenuous day, were always ready for bridge, so we usually had two tables. Mother was the most enthusiastic and tireless player of all. Once she and three of the boys played all night. She never lost the spirit of youth.

Breakfast time was always funny. We had the first and last bell, and Mother held us to the rule. The night before we always declared with much emphasis that we would not get up for breakfast but would diet. In that climate, though, ravenous appetites are chronic, so that the last bell always brought a great rush of the queerest assortment of dressing gowns. The girls usually arose early enough to insure their vanity by appearing in golf costumes, but the boys would rush in attired in pajamas and robes, demanding "Just a cup of coffee", but managing to eat everything in sight. Robert, always the comedian, would sometimes appear as a Chinaman, with Mother's mandarin coat and her sewing basket for a hat, jabbering in singsong Chinese, much to the delight of the children. Once he appeared all bent over, attired in a raccoon coat with a pillow stuffed under it on his back and announced in snarling accents that he was the Hunchback of Notre Dame!

Katherine kept the house decorated with flowers and sometimes I went with her. We would stroll through the woods and gather huge purple thistles, and Queen Anne's lace. She could find more ferns, ground pine, and prettier flowers than anyone else could. A drive with her was a constant stopping to gather golden rod or wild asters. She knew everyone in the village, too, the grocer, the postmaster, and the neighbors, and loved each and every one of them.

Meanwhile, the children, the sons and daughters, are growing up. They seem to have this same love of family. Though only cousins, they are as close to each other as most brothers and sisters. In retrospect, I can only hope that my own three little girls, when they marry, will acquire just such a family. I could wish for them nothing better.

Those were wonderful days never to be quite the same again, as the family circle is broken now. I wonder if we appreciated them as much as we should have. At least, we are rich in memories.

Last Picture Taken at Sonnencroft

Left to right: Ray, Diane, Mamman, Sylvia, Brooks, Elaine and Polly the Dog, 1936

SYNOPSIS of THE FAMILY

THE SONS

Here is a brief synopsis of the brother's lives. I have listed them in order of their deaths.

Claude Ernest

Claude Ernest, (April 4, 1887- 1919) Lyda's and Clyde's first-born son, preceded his parents in death at the age of 32. Claude never married and left no children. Claude's grave was the first in our plot at Woodlawn Cemetery.

Frank Ehlen, (October 10, 1892-1946) VMI, WVU, an engineer, was the next to die suddenly at 54, on July 4, 1946, a terrific shock to his family and many friends. Uncle Frank was playing golf at the Fox Hills Golf Club with office attaches of Inter-State Engineering & Constructors, Inc. where he was general manager. Attorney Jackson V. Blair, a good friend, brought him home and physicians were called, but another sudden attack took his life. He left his widow, Aunt Bonnie, my godmother, Bonsall (Wood) (November 7, 1894- 1982), and two sons who were still in the US Army, John Wood- with the U.S. Army Air Corps, and Frank Ehlen, Jr. with the U.S. Infantry-overseas. Uncle Frank is buried in Woodlawn Cemetery in Fairmont with Aunt Bonnie and youngest son, Jack.

Robert Jay

Robert Jay, (January 25, 1903-1969) He attended Peddie Institute, Hightstown, NJ, and Mrs. Kavanaugh's Prep School, Lawrenceburg KY, University of Kentucky and WVU where he was very badly injured in football. The dashing, darling, "favorite uncle" of all the nieces and nephews, was the next to succumb, after years of carousing and drinking, at the age of 66 on September 10, 1969. One morning in the thirties, Uncle Robert awoke in New York City with a strange blonde woman in his bed. There was a marriage license on the hotel dresser. He brought Aunt Maize home to Mammam and it was described in the Fairmont Times as, "a sudden and unexpected surprise for the Hutchinsons". Daddy had it annulled. I only remember seeing her once at Mammam's. During WWII, Bob joined the U.S. Merchant Marines. Uncle Robert is buried next to his mother at Woodlawn Cemetery, Fairmont.

Brooks Swearingen

My father, Brooks Swearingen, (July 10, 1888-1971) Staunton Military Academy, Staunton VA, WVU and Yale Law School. The next to the oldest, the attorney, the savior to the family, died in his daughter, Elaine's, arms in Pearl Harbor, Hawaii on February 11, 1971 at the age of 82. He was returned to Fairmont and buried in Woodlawn Cemetery with his wife, Ray. Mother had died in my arms at Fairmont General after suffering a heart attack at our home on August 18, 1967 while visiting my family in Fairmont. Daddy was coming to join her for their 50th wedding anniversary that would have been on September12. They left three daughters, Elaine, Sylvia and Diane.

Harold Herbert

Harold Herbert (April 1895-1973), Fairmont Senior High School, United State Navy, World War I, VMI and WVU where he played football for three years. Another engineer, the shyer, quiet, brother, died on February 15, 1973 at the age of 77 in Fairmont, leaving his widow, Margaret (Owens). Aunt Margaret was so much fun and, with no children, loved each niece and nephew.

Margaret was Sylvia's godmother and gave her a beautiful sheared beaver coat when she graduated from FSHS in 1945. Both Harold and Margaret are buried side by side at Woodlawn Cemetery in Fairmont.

Paul Mason

Paul Mason (July 7, 1901-1974) Culver Military Institute, Sheffield School of Yale, and postgraduate work at Columbia University and Colorado School of Mines in Chemistry and Mining Engineering. Uncle Paul signed up at the age of 43 in the US Army in WWII as a First Lieutenant with the US Army Signal Corp. He was stationed in London until 1946, retiring as a Major and receiving the Bronze Star and the Army Commendation Medal. Upon return to West Virginia, he worked for Monongahela Power Company (Allegheny Energy) for 30 years and served as State President of the West Virginia Professional Engineers in 1955. He died at the age of 73 on April 4, 1974, at the Clarksburg Veterans Hospital, leaving a widow, Pauline (Findley) and no children. He and Aunt Pauline, (1907-1984) who to me, looked like the movie star Gene Tierney, are buried together at Woodlawn Cemetery, Fairmont.

Bernard Lee

Bernard Lee (January 12, 1890-1974) always together, Uncle Lee died at 84 on December 15, 1974, just five days after his beloved Katherine (Race), (May 20, 1891). Aunt Katherine died on December 10, 1974. Uncle Lee was graduated from Staunton Military Academy and West Virginia University where he was an outstanding football player for four years and elected captain of the team in 1909. He was an avid golfer, and a competitor and champion of both contract and auction bridge. He was in charge of the Hutchinson coal interests in Cincinnati, Ohio. They left four children, Helen H. Light Drope, Bernard Lee, Jr., Ann H. Pechstein, and Mary Lyda H. Howe.

James Jeremiah

James Jeremiah (February 10, 1904-1980) Peddie Institute, NJ, University of Kentucky and associated with the U.S. Corps of Engineers until his retirement. The baby, sweet and shy, after a life of following Bobby and taking care of him, first married a beautiful red head and was hounded by her alcoholism for years; finally meeting and marrying his dear Lillian Bea (Gannaway) of Louisville, Kentucky in 1952 at the age of 48. He was the youngest and the last surviving son of Sonnencroft. Uncle Jimmy died May 14, 1980 at 76 and is buried with Bea who outlived him by 25 years. They left two daughters, Kathy (Mrs. Charles D. Boyer) and Pamela (Mrs. Ben Swift Wimsatt), who are approximately my children's ages being born in 1953 and 1954.

1925 Photo of the Hutchinson Sons

148

Although not a son, our dear friend, Henry Gray, the butler at Sonnencroft, was a part of the family and we were all so sad to read the following article in the Fairmont Times:

"Bullion Street Man A Suicide"
The Fairmont Times
Circa 1956

"Henry Gray, 56, of 107 Bullion Street was found dead in his home this morning by city police who said he was the victim of a self-inflicted bullet wound.

According to police, Mrs. Gray found her husband about 1:10 a.m. in the bathroom cutting his throat with a straight razor. She managed to take the razor from Gray and went to the neighbors for assistance.

A shot was heard as Mrs. Gray was returning to her home and Gray was found on the floor of the bedroom. The bullet had entered his head at the back of the right ear.

Patrolmen Richard Nigh and Jack Cox answered the call to the Gray residence. Coroner O. H. Koon also was called and said no further investigation will be made. Death was attributed to a self-inflicted wound from a 38-calibre pistol.

The deceased, who was said to have been in ill health for some time, had been a resident of Fairmont for more than 30 years. He formerly was employed by the C. E. Hutchinson family and was custodian of the headquarters of District 31, United Mine Workers of America, at the time of his recent retirement.

Mr. Gray was born in Piedmont, a son of Simon and Mary Ann Gray. In addition to his widow, he is survived by a sister, Mrs. Mary A. Perry of St. Paul, Minn., and a brother, Robert Gray of Summit, Calif. A nephew, Ronald Perry of Tuskegee, Ala., also survives."

****

Mrs. (Nannie) Gray called Mother and asked that she and Daddy greet and receive Henry's friends with her at the J. Lampkin Funeral Home, which they were honored to do.

Henry was loved by all the Hutchinsons and helped to raise "the boys" as much as any of the family.

Henry Gray, 1917

CHAPTER EIGHT

"LIFE IS OLD THERE"

Woodburn Circle, West Virginia University

WEST VIRGINIA UNIVERSITY: 1867

The Hutchinson and Parker families have been close to Morgantown and West Virginia University from the beginning. My father and mother met in Morgantown while Mother was visiting the Courtney family and my grandparents were friends of Elizabeth Moore (Principal of Woodburn Female Academy) and her family.

Paul and I loved WVU, attending many ball games over a period of several decades and as a family, are proud to claim twelve degrees and eight relatives or in-laws participating in varsity sports.

Our son, Eddie, was for many years ranked in the top four players of his age groups in the Mid-Atlantic Lawn Tennis Association, winning both singles and doubles throughout Maryland, Virginia, Delaware, Washington, D.C. and parts of West Virginia. In 1973 Eddie was appointed to the Junior Davis Cup Team by the Directors of MALTA and received a tennis scholarship to WVU playing under Coach Stanley Farr for four years. In his senior year Eddie was given the Outstanding Athletes award for tennis. He was presented with a gold watch that he still wears and cherishes today. He and his fiancée, Jan Carpenter, competing in mixed doubles, won the WVU Open Tournament in Morgantown. To this day they and their two sons, Brett and Brooks, still play the game on their backyard court.

Sylvia, our daughter, asked to start the first girls' tennis team in 1975 when she was not allowed to play on the boy's team that Eddie had started at Fairmont Senior High School in 1969. She had played in MALTA girls' tournaments since she was eight years old on the same tours as Eddie and was well experienced. She, in turn, received a scholarship to WVU and played under the excellent coaching of Martha Thorn. Paul was so proud when Sylvia was accepted into the Kappa Kappa Gamma sorority at WVU as it was his Phi Psi fraternity's sister organization. Sylvia was also a member of the Fellowship of Christian Athletes at the same time with Jeff Hostetler, former stand-out WVU quarterback and later NFL quarterback of the two-time Super Bowl Champions New York Giants.

Paul's family - all Methodists - lived in Buckhannon, Upshur County, WV, and most of them attended West Virginia Wesleyan University in Buckhannon. Paul's father, Paul Edward Parker, attended WVU, and played Varsity Basketball, 1918-1921, while getting his degree in Mining Engineering. Two of his teammates were Fairmonters, George Hill and Paul

"Biz" Dawson, who later became the coach at Fairmont Senior High School, taking over Frank Ice's Polar Bears.

Others on that WVU team as listed by Mr. Parker were: Braden Alleman (Charleston, WV); Ted Lewis (Charleston, WV); "Harnus" P. Mullenex (Morton, WV) who both played and coached in 1919; Earl Fisher (Canton, OH); Homer Martin, captain 1921 (Charleston, WV); Clem Kiger, (New Martinsville, WV); Columbus C. Pittsford (Charleston, WV) and John H. Behan captain 1920 (Cambridge, OH). The manager of the team was Thomas Nail and the Athletic Director was Harry A. Stansberry both of Morgantown, WV.

We love our State of "West-by-God-Virginia". We have the most beautiful mountains on this continent. The Appalachian Mountains extend from New York to Georgia, but in no state are they more majestic than in West Virginia. Our highest point is Spruce Mountain, in Pendleton County; 12 miles in length, the pinnacle, called Spruce Knob is 4,861 ft. and the view is breathtaking. With all these mountains we have many rivers. One the oldest river in the Western Hemisphere is appropriately called the New River that ends in West Virginia. Each year we have a Bridge Day on the New River Gorge Bridge over 800 feet above the river, the only standing structure in the US to allow parachuting and bungee jumping one day each year. And yes, we have West Virginia University.

"Montani Semper Liberi" – "Mountaineers are Always Free"

OLDER THAN THE TREES

In 1862, President Abraham Lincoln signed the Morrill Act offering grants of federal land to every state that agreed to establish a college for agriculture and engineering.

In 1864 Congress specifically extended the Morrill Act to include the new state of West Virginia (1863) born out of the Civil War. The state had less than six months in which to take definite action to establish a state institution of higher learning or fail to avail itself of the

Congressional Land Grant. This Act of 1862 provided government land script as an incentive to the creation of land-grant colleges.

Few ever knew that West Virginia University was offered to Fairmont and the offer was refused. Allison Sweeny Fleming, a direct descendant of Nathan Fleming, tells us they wanted to buy the old Nathan Fleming Farm, the long stretch of land now known as Edgemont and ending at the Locust Avenue junction. This entire area was inherited by Joab and Harrison (Harry) Fleming, and other surrounding farms could have been bought for expansion. This was one of Fairmont's most unfortunate decisions ever made. We declined the offer because: "we did not have faith in the new university". Today, of course WVU has exceeded all expectations, regardless of its location in very congested areas. Fairmont made a better decision later, in declining the state penitentiary, which was given to Moundsville, WV and is now closed.

The State Senate voted to have the new school in Morgantown, but the House of Delegates chose Charleston, the new Capitol. The Conference Committee could not agree so both bills failed. After much more bickering and Morgantown's offer of its two preparatory schools, the House vote was watched with great interest. The final tally showed Morgantown with 32 votes, Harrisville - 7, Frankfort - 7, Bethany - 4, and Greenwood - 3. The legislature wasted little time in passing an act dated February 7, 1867, accepting the Monongalia County offer and the first President, Alexander Martin, was inaugurated on June 27, six days before the deadline.

In a Times West Virginian article by Gail Marsh December 7, 1992, Dean Joseph Gluck, a special counselor to students at WVU and an authority on the school, said,

"The history of the University predates the Civil War by many years. Morgantown had something no one else had – two Preparatory Schools, the old Monongalia Academy was chartered in 1814 and drew students from seven states as far west as Indiana. The Woodburn Female Seminary was established in 1833 when Morgantown's population was about 700. The state had no money and Morgantown offered these two schools in exchange for starting the university there; the state took them up on their offer. The first building constructed on the new campus was called University Hall. The name was changed in 1899 to honor the first president Alexander Martin, a Methodist minister from Scotland who served from 1867-1875. His salary was $1600 a year. Woodburn Female Academy burned to the ground in 1873. The new Woodburn Hall was constructed in stages, the main part being completed in 1876. Chitwood Hall, named for a longtime history professor, Oliver P. Chitwood, was the last building constructed in Woodburn Circle, completed in 1893."

Professor Gluck continues, "A pamphlet from the National Register of Historic Places notes that Elizabeth Moore Hall, the women's Physical Education building was dedicated on November 28, 1928. It was a culmination of efforts by the WV chapter of the American Association of University Women to provide a building on campus especially for women. The building was named for Principal Elizabeth Moore, of Woodburn Female Academy. "

[AUTHOR'S NOTE: When confederate troops occupied Morgantown in 1863, Mrs. Moore invited the soldiers for bread and coffee and her hospitality is credited with preventing the soldiers from burning the Seminary. The Moore's daughter Susan Maxwell Moore, (my grandmother Lyda's good friend, who named Sonnencroft) served as Dean of Women at WVU from 1903 to 1923.]

IN THE BEGINNING: A TIMELINE OF WEST VIRGINIA UNIVERSITY

Land Grant schools were created in 1862. Congress provided tracts of land to states to support colleges whose mission was to educate the populace in agriculture, business and the trades.

In 1865, after the war ends, West Virginians embarked on building their new state, including institutions of higher learning. The State Legislature voted to put the college in Morgantown and move the state capitol to Charleston two years later as part of the deal.

In 1878 the College of Law was established as WVU's first professional school. A building to house this school was not built until 1923 and was later named "Colson Hall"

At this time the Law School was fully accredited by the American Bar Association.

[Author's Note: In 1951 my husband, Paul E. Parker, Jr., graduated from this law school. The new law school on the Evansdale Campus was completed in 1974; our son, Paul E. Parker, III (Eddie) graduated from the new facility in 1980.]

In 1884 the Board of Regents met with Elizabeth I. Moore, to, "ascertain the terms and conditions upon which the University might secure the use of the Morgantown Female Seminary building as a dormitory for female students and for other purposes in connection with the proposed plan for co-education". Five years later in 1889, after many disputes and much opposition, the Board of Regents voted to admit women to all departments except the Preparatory Department; and the first ten women came to study with 198 men.

The first woman graduate of the University was Harriet E. Lyon in 1891. She was first in the class, which included future WVU Law Professor James Russell Trotter, who maintained that WVU had lowered its standards by admitting women.

In 1891, students, Melville Davisson Post, who later became the first serial mystery storywriter, and Billie Meyer organized the first football team called the 'Snakes"; they lost their first game 72-0 against Washington and Jefferson College with Professor F.L. Emory as coach.

[AUTHOR'S NOTE: Melville Davisson Post was the brother of Aunt Maude (Post) Hutchinson, Uncle Mel Hutchinson's wife.]

My father, Brooks and Uncle Lee Hutchinson lettered in football 1906-07-08. In 1909 Uncle Lee was captain, but Daddy had to quit as he had been elected the University's Student Body President. Daddy was also chosen as the fourth Summit (president) of the Mountain, of which he was extremely proud and attended Mountain's 50th anniversary in 1954. The program listed John Guy Pritchard as the first Summit - '06, Paul H. Martin -'07, Ellis A. Yost - 08, Brooks S. Hutchinson -'09, and Roy O. Hall - '10. Any leader in Student activities could be selected to Mountain which was a social organization of students, "who had developed both strength and ability in college life and who gave promise of leadership when college days were ended." "Because Mountain acts but never speaks", many of its services to the University have remained anonymous and are never publicized.

In the Fairmont Times of September 1924, the donors for the current stadium drive were listed from Marion County. Writing about the interest shown by many of our family:

"One of West Virginia's best known families of athletes is the Hutchinson Clan of Fairmont. Until recently there had always been a Hutchinson on the Mountaineer eleven, and their unanimous response to the stadium drive has stamped them as builders of a modern plant destined to bring West Virginia out of disrepute. C.E. Hutchinson, prominent coal operator of Fairmont was the father of the mountaineer stars a few years earlier - Brooks, Lee, Harold, Frank and Robert. Another son, Paul attended Yale but he subscribed to the stadium feeling that, above everything else, he was a West Virginian."

The reporter notes, "Back in 1907, Brooks and Lee Hutchinson made a pair of famous ends. Older fans still compared varsity wingmen with the Hutchinson boys, and to be 'almost as good as Brooks and Lee' was quite an honor for future Mountaineer ends. Frank Hutchinson played on the 1914 team and Harold was on the 1914, 1915, 1916 teams."

****

Uncle Robert played as a freshman in 1918, but suffered a terrible football injury of a crushed nose, which gave him difficult breathing problems. Bobby had to be taken to the Mayo Clinic in the summer of 1919 to have a dangerous operation performed involving other crushed bones of the nasal cavity and never returned to football.

The old Mountaineer Field was completed in 1925 and recorded the first game as a win over West Virginia Wesleyan, 21 to 6.

In 1914 the Smith-Lever Act created Cooperative Extension; the primary organization for diffusing information from the colleges to the populace and to assist in the application of this knowledge. Today, West Virginia has Extension offices in all 55 counties of West Virginia.

On January 17, 2010, Ellen Hrabovsky, a member of the Dominion Post's Advisory Board writes, "The Master Gardeners Program was started in Seattle, Washington in 1972 to assist the county agents responding to the thousands of questions inundating their offices. They trained a core of knowledgeable volunteers to assist in meeting those demands. The WV Masters Gardener program began in 1993. Today there are 50, 000 volunteer Master Gardeners in 45 States, the District of Columbia and four Canadian provinces."

In 1928 a School of Physical Education was established and in 1936, a School of Pharmacy offered a four-year degree in Pharmacy.

In 1943 so many men were serving in WWII that women outnumbered the men - excluding soldier trainees by 809 women, compared to 592 men. Then in 1948, after the war, land for the Evansdale Campus was purchased and the Core Arboretum established; student population reached 8,069 as returning service men became students enrolled under the GI Bill.

Finally, in 1951 WVU was selected as the site of the state's new medical center. The university had a two-year medical school, but the students had to find medical schools in other States to finish their training. The beautiful new West Virginia University Hospital was built, from the taxing of the sale of soft drinks called the "pop tax". The building has since been renamed the Health Sciences Building, when Ruby Memorial Hospital was built in 1979.

[Author's Note: Bernie Sampson, an old friend, owned Nehi Bottling Company and swore that I paid for the school because all I drank was Royal

Crown Cola - one of his products. The glass and bottling plant owners throughout the state fought this tax yearly until the school was built.]

In 1960 the University Hospital opened and the School of Nursing and department of Pediatrics were established.

Both campuses were growing during this period; two more Towers of the Evansdale Residential Complex were completed; the Forestry building and The Creative Arts Center was constructed; while the new Mountainlair was built downtown.

It was disappointing to see that on a plaque in the new "Lair" listing the Student Body Presidents, the names went back only to 1925. How many other fathers' names were left out? Another faux pas occurred in the "new" Facilities building. The football pictures went back only to the mid-twenties.

It took the University ten years to complete the Personal Rapid Transit System (PRT), one of the first built in this country. Starting the process in 1970 the rails were completed between downtown and the Medical Center in 1979. Paul and I took his father, 82 years old, down to ride the PRT; but his mother refused, scared to death of it.

In 1980 the new Mountaineer Stadium was built. The beautiful new facility would hold 50,000 fans.

On September 6, 1980, Eddie, who had just graduated from Law School in the spring, Sylvia, who was beginning her senior year in Art Education, Paul and I were all in the stands. We were there to see our Governor John D. Rockefeller IV, accompanied by the University President Neil S. Bucklew and our guest, bespectacled, pageboy hair, John Denver, who wrote "Country Roads" in 1971, amble out to the center of the field to christen the magnificent new facility.

As the 325-member band, playing "Country Roads", formed an outline of the state of West Virginia around them, the President introduced the Governor, who was instrumental in getting the stadium built, and our adopted Mountaineer, John Denver.

As he sang the opening lyrics, "Almost Heaven, West Virginia ", Denver was joined by a sold out crowd of over 50,000 background singers - all loyal mountaineer fans; with the crowd's collective voices swelling to a climax at the conclusion. Denver looked around the stadium at the roaring crowd and realized this was no ordinary gig.

The crowd remained standing, cheering with appreciation as the threesome walked off the field. The West Virginia Mamas had tears in their eyes that day, including me.

The first football team (with an elliptical-shaped football) in 1891.

West Virginia University Magazine, Vol. 34, Number 1, 2011

I HEAR HER VOICE
Traditional State Songs

Just reading the words of each song depicts the love of native and adopted sons of our beautiful state of West Virginia. Each song brings back so many delightful, poignant, heart rendering memories.

Music strikes an emotional nerve every time I hear certain familiar tunes. No one can hold back the memories or tears when listening to the Star Spangled Banner or, if you are a West Virginian, "Almost Heaven – West Virginia" ("Country Roads"- c.1972).

Even though I followed my sister Elaine to Fairmont State College in 1950-54, graduating with an AB degree in Education, I married a graduate of WVU with two degrees - in Political Science and an LLD degree. Our children each received two degrees and with Daddy and four uncles plus a father-in-law, Paul E. Parker, who played varsity basketball for WVU and graduated in engineering; our family's degrees total twelve.

The songs I loved and learned as a child, Daddy and Mother taught us on our trips to Pittsburgh. They helped to pass the long hours in the back seat of a 1935 Chrysler, between two sisters, all cuddled under a grey, prickly wool car robe. I must start with the official State Song, which has two additional verses, which I have never heard, sung:

162

"THE WEST VIRGINIA HILLS "
Words by Ellen King, music by H.E. Engle- ©1896
Designated as the State Song in 1961

"Oh! The West Virginia Hills, how majestic and how grand,

With their summits bathed in glory, like our Prince Immanuel's land!

Is it any wonder then, that my heart with rapture thrills,

As I gaze once more with loved ones on those West Virginia Hills?

Oh, the hills, beautiful hills!

How I love those West Virginia Hills.

If o'er sea or land I roam, still I think of happy home,

And my friends among those West Virginia Hills"

"HAIL WEST VIRGINIA"
Words by Alumnus Fred B. Deem, Composition by
Alumni Earl Miller and Ed McWhorter- 1915-1916

"Let's give a rah for West Virginia,

And let us pledge to her anew.

Others may like black and crimson,

But for us it's Gold and Blue.

Let all our troubles be forgotten,

Let college spirit rule

We'll join and give our loyal efforts

For the good of our old school"

"It's West Virginia, Its West Virginia the pride of every Mountaineer.

Come on you old grads, come join us young lads,

It's West Virginia now we cheer!

Now is the time boys, to make a big noise

No matter what the people say,

For there is naught to fear; the gang's all here,

So hail to West Virginia, Hail!"

John Forrest "Fuzzy" Knight attended WVU in 1924 studying pre-law. He was a cheerleader and quite talented in music and theater and composed the fight song that is still sung today:

"FIGHT MOUNTAINEERS"

"Fight, fight, fight, fight Mountaineer

We're here to cheer for you.

Take that old ball down the field,

We're putting all our faith in you.

Play that team right off its feet,

You can't be beat, we know,

And when the game is through, we'll all cheer you.

West Virginia, West Virginia, rah! "

"Fuzzy" Knight was born May 9, 1901 in Fairmont, WV and after graduating from WVU left Fairmont and his wife, "Flo" who ran a hair salon in the Traction Office on First Street, and went to Hollywood. He appeared in over 200 western movies, usually as the successful comic "sidekick" to many top stars such as W.C. Fields, and Mae West ("My Little Chickadee") and Fred Mac Murray and Henry Fonda, ("Trail of the Lonesome Pine"). "Fuzzy" Knight died in 1976, at the age of 75.

WVU Music Professor, Frank Cuthbert, had suggested that someone write a song that could be used to open and close the Glee Club concerts. Louis Damarin Corson, then a junior at WVU, decided to try it.

During the 1936 Easter vacation, Lou sat down at the piano at his fraternity house (Phi Kappa Psi) and his fingers deftly picked out the slow somber chords and the single, stirring words found way under the notes.

In 1938, the students selected Corson's submission to be the official University's Alma Mater. The new Alma Mater was arranged by Lawrence Intravaia and was played for the first time on November 12, 1938 at the old Mountaineer Field." ("In The Bond, 100 Years Within West Virginia Alpha", written by David L. Woodrum- page 261)

"WVU ALMA MATER"

"Alma, our Alma Mater, the home of Mountaineers,

Sing we of thy honor, everlasting through the years;

Alma, our Alma Mater, we pledge in song to you,

Hail all Hail our Alma Mater, West Virginia U."

Both Lou 'Pop' Corson '36 (1915-1982) and Ed McWhorter, Jr.'11 (Hail West Virginia) were members of the Phi Kappa Psi fraternity and brothers of my husband Paul E Parker, '45.

Simple Gifts was written by Elder Joseph Brackett (born in Cumberland, Maine in 1797). Elder Brackett died in 1882, at the last remaining Shaker community in New Gloucester, Maine, now known as Sabbath Day Lake.

This is a beautiful, simple verse and tune that lingers with one, after every game.

I was always first in our seats, not to miss the magnificent West Virginia University Marching Band, "The Pride of West Virginia," perform the pre-game show.

"The Pride" began in 1901 with eight ROTC cadets. In 2001, celebrating their one hundredth anniversary at the Homecoming game, the 350-member corps was joined by 500 proud members of the Alumni Band for a rousing pre-game show with a tunnel entrance on to Mountaineer field. The 850 mass group covered the entire field and closed the special half time ceremonies with the most popular half-time selections in the WVU Band library, "Walk Him Up the Stairs/Old Man River".

The 350 strong in their new blue and gold capes performed their rendition of "Simple Gifts" as a climax of their pregame traditional show and do so to this day.

"SIMPLE GIFTS"

"'Tis the gift to be simple, 'tis the gift to be free.

'Tis the gift to come down where we ought to be,

And when we find ourselves in the place just right,

T'will be in the valley of love and delight.

When true simplicity is gain'd,

To bow and to bend we shan't be asham'd,

To turn, turn will be our delight,

'Till by turning, turning we come round right."

The Shakers are said to have danced to these instructions; but no one could have danced the way our band does to this moving melody. The entire WVU Band bursts forth from a huddle, holding their flags and instruments high in the air, much the same as the old Mountaineer football players did as they

166

entered the field from a long dark tunnel at the old stadium next to Woodburn Hall!

The song was largely unknown until it became famous throughout the world from Aaron Copeland's score for Martha Graham's ballet, "Appalachian Spring" which was first performed in 1944.

Our theme song or anthem, has become "COUNTRY ROADS"- ©1971. Words and music by John Denver, Bill Danoff, Taffy Niver; and initially released in 1972 by John Denver.

Denver first appeared before his adoring fans on September 6, 1980 at the dedication of the new Mountaineer Field. His performance also marked the first game for our new football coach, Don Nehlan

All these songs have played such a large part of Mountaineers lives. I could not help but think of all my beloved family members and how thrilled they would have been. The new stadium, the beautiful fall day, the flags flying, the youth, the exuberance, and the love of the fans for our West Virginia U! A scene never to be forgotten!

It was, "Almost Heaven".

[Afterword]

In early September 2001 WVU opened the football season with our new coach, Rich Rodriquez. Three days later, a Tuesday morning, 9-11-01, a little before 9 o'clock, while watching the TODAY Show with Katie Couric, we saw the terrorist planes hit the World Trade Center in New York City. Next we heard about the Pentagon and speculation about a third plane reported to be headed for the Capitol, but crashing in Pennsylvania. Our lives were changed forever and we realized that football was only a game. All games were cancelled for Saturday, September 8th.

Eddie invited Sylvia and me to the next game on September 22nd, against Kent State University. Taps was played before the game and at half time, thousands of fans stood and watched our West Virginia Pride surround an enormous 120-foot flag, unfurled and held by students, while we sang The Star Spangled Banner. The band played patriotic songs while forming an intertwined circle of love for our country. Once again we used music to interpret and ignite our memories, our love, our loyalty and allegiance, for our state, our country, and our fellow man.

CHAPTER NINE

"MAMMAM"
THE HEART OF THE FAMILY
1865 - 1943

Lyda Watkins Hutchinson
Given to Brooks S. Hutchinson by Madge Sample
"Mother in Winter, 1885"

"Reception at Sonnencroft "
The Fairmont Times

"Sonnencroft, the home of Mr. and Mrs. Clyde E. Hutchinson, was the scene of an afternoon reception at which Mrs. Harold H. Hutchinson; formerly of Montgomery, West Virginia was introduced to her new friends here. Three other daughters-in-law of the Hutchinson's, Mrs. Bernard Lee Hutchinson of Cincinnati and Mrs. Frank E. Hutchinson of Logan, W. VA., and Mrs. Brooks S. Hutchinson were in the receiving line."

****

Mammam was thrilled to have four daughters-in-law and had receptions to welcome them home after their honeymoons. Each year she held a grand ball during each Christmas season to celebrate them and her sons. Mammam entertained most of the brides in the area, either before or after their weddings. I remember hearing about Mary Hartley Greer who married a young engineer from Kentucky, Bernard Gilpin Sampson. The two had eloped and upon their return, Sonnencroft welcomed half of the town in an unforgettable reception.

In entertaining her civic organizations she would ask the young local talent to perform for groups in the huge conservatory where there was the Steinway grand piano. I have learned to play by ear on that same piano. My daughter Sylvia plays beautifully as she had piano every day at Miller Junior High School where they had electronic pianos. She studied under Mary Faith Conrad for two years.

Jean Billingsley Johnson (Mrs. Phillip) an old friend and neighbor of ours for 30 years on West End Drive played "Un Bel Die" (One Fine Day) from "Madam Butterfly" for us one Thanksgiving evening in the early 1980's. It was a poignant performance as she recalled playing and singing that same aria on this same piano as a guest of Mammam's at Sonnencroft. She had just returned to Fairmont after graduating from Julliard in voice and "Un Bel Die" had been sung for her final examination.

Mammam (Mary Lyda) was born to Jacob Martin and Ida Pauline (Swearingen) Watkins on March 26, 1865. Lyda was the only girl of five children that survived and helped her mother raise the four brothers - Charles and Augustus, who were older than she was, and the youngest were Bruce and Oaky.

170

Mary Lyda was a large framed woman, plump in her girlhood judging by photos. Her skin was olive and she had dark brown hair and soft brown eyes. She was always pleasant and never flustered or upset - a very tranquil disposition, always seeing the good - never the bad. Accepted everything as it was, and said she could do anything but have a daughter. Mammam was extremely capable, she could sew, needlepoint and embroider, paint china, cook, can, garden, all this while rearing eight active, handsome, charming sons.

Always quick to learn, she attended Fairmont State Normal School when it was on Quincy Street and graduated with a certificate in education. On a Wednesday evening, April 21, 1886, she married the only man she ever loved, Clyde Effington Hutchinson of Catawba, Monongalia County. The Fairmont paper reported, "The wedding was held in the bride's family home on Locust Avenue at eight o'clock before a large company of invited guests. The Reverend George McCollum presided at the ceremony and the words were soon spoken and the twain was made one."

Glen D. Lough, father of my close friend JoAnne Lough, gathering information for his renowned book, "Now And Long Ago", used to come to my Grandmother's on Gaston Ave each Saturday morning to deliver eggs. As he was gathering information for the book he was writing, he would question her about everything that she could tell him about the people and the town of Fairmont. That was the morning of the week when Mammam baked bread and I would often sit at the table with Mr. Lough and with him partake in a fresh slice of buttered salt rising with sugar sprinkled on top, listening to all the stories that she told.

When I was ten years old, I once again suffered another dear grandmother's death. I remember going with Daddy down to 107 Gaston Avenue, to the house, full of love and the smell of stale tobacco smoke still clinging to the walls. All the uncles and aunts smoked, but not Daddy or Mother. The smoky scent helped to remember the fun and games we all played; the uncles yelling and laughing over innumerable raucous games of Set Back - getting up and slamming their cards down shouting, "High-Low-Jack and the game!" I still love to smell any kind of tobacco - cigars, cigarettes, pipes, and I am reminded of those days we can easily recapture by scents.

She was lying in her huge sleigh bed from Sonnencroft. I knew this would be the last time I would see her. Daddy seemed so very sad. I wore my new red Chesterfield coat with a black velveteen collar and she smiled at me and waved her hand for me to turn around so she could see it from all angles.

Nodding her head in approval, she smiled, holding my one hand in hers. "Behold my daughter, my Dear!" She had had a stroke and was unable to speak. Daddy gave a resigned sigh and hurried me out to the car.

Mammam died on Wednesday, December 15, 1943 in the midst of WWII. She and her beautiful Sonnencroft seemed to deteriorate more rapidly after being parted. Mammam, the heart of the family, had been so strong through so much, but by the 40's, she had become melancholy, a weaker force in the family, victimized by her next-door neighbor - a jealous judge, and her only brother-in-law. A mother who remembered the First World War and had waited for sons to return and now had, not only two sons, but also three grandsons in the Second World War. Uncle Paul had enlisted as an engineer at the age of 42 and was a major serving in London and Uncle Robert had enlisted in the Merchant Marines. The three grandsons, Bernard Lee, Jack, and Frank, Jr. all enlisted in the Army. I remember how proud we were of Jack who had enlisted before Pearl Harbor, which entitled him to a special ribbon. He had a weak heart after suffering from rheumatic fever as a child and was afraid he would fail the physical.

Mammam often reminisced about the glorious days of Sonnencroft. The memories drifting out of the corners of her mind, she savored those moments, holding onto a life she loved and dared not forget. She spoke often of the receptions, the balls, the lovely gowns and the flirtations of all the beautiful young couples; assuring her listeners, that her daughters-in-law were the most beautiful of them all. "Scattered pictures of the smiles we left behind".

It was all so simple then.

Janet Chittum, remembers her mother, Gladys Halterman, who lived on Potomac Avenue –up the hill across from Sonnencroft, said her family would sit on their porch all evening and watch the ladies promenade over the grounds in their glamorous long gowns and enjoyed listening to the orchestra, their music wafting to every corner of Palatine well into the night.

In 1925, Mother and Eleanor Blackford Watson, tired of luncheons and bridge parties, had decided to do something worthwhile for the City of Fairmont and enlisted those playing bridge that day at the Country Club to join them in founding the Junior League of Fairmont. The charter members were Maxine Jenkins Brown, Mildred Robinson Carroll, Martha Dickerson, Mary Moulds Hurst Gates, Margaret Smith Guild, Ray Pefley Hutchinson,

Florence Hutchinson Ritchie, Mary Greer Sampson, Marjorie LeMasters Watkins, and Eleanor Blackford Watson. Together they started the Well Baby Clinic at the Miners' Hospital, which allowed all the miners, wives and any family who could not afford doctors to bring in their babies for checkups, formulas and free pediatric services. They donated to the Marion County Library after having their first fundraiser, a pancake supper. In 1926 they had their second ways and means project a "Dream Dinner". The women assisted, not only financially, but also with the organization and the production of the Times Christmas Fund for needy children.

In 1927, after two years of hard work, the group asked Mrs. Clyde E. Hutchinson, Mrs. Samuel D. Brady, Mrs. Charles Baird Mitchell, Mrs. Edwin Robinson, Mrs. John Gordon Smythe, and Mrs. J. E. Watson to become honorary members as the age for League membership had to be under thirty-five. The older women were delighted to accept and entertained the National Association officers who came to "inspect" the viability of Fairmont becoming a member of the National Junior League. After seeing the results of all of the needed projects and being entertained at Highgate, Sonnencroft, Pinelea and Homeacre, and the relatively new Fairmont Country Club (1912), Fairmont had little trouble being accepted as the 27th League in the Association of Junior Leagues, proposed by the Pittsburgh, Pennsylvania League and seconded by the Charleston, West Virginia League. The purpose of the Junior League has always been and remains today, "exclusively educational and charitable and is to promote voluntarism; to develop the potential of its members for voluntary participation in community affairs; and to demonstrate the effectiveness of trained volunteers".

I have been a member of the Fairmont League fifty-six years and I am still a volunteer in this community long after going sustaining in the League at the age of forty- exemplifying the quintessential volunteer. I learned very early how important it is to train good leaders for the community boards and to find a need in the community and fulfill it through active board participation. I have thoroughly enjoyed the challenges and basked in that feeling of accomplishment, attempting always to follow in Mammam's footsteps. In April of 2010, I was so honored by the Times-West Virginian who announced Diane Hutchinson Parker as Volunteer of the Year.

Mammam founded and was the first president of the Woman's Hospital Association of Cook Hospital. I was so proud to be elected as president of Fairmont General Volunteer Association in 1969, their 50th year and follow in her lead. She was the first president of the YWCA and Papa had provided the group's first home on Monroe Street. The big beautiful building on First Street, the YMCA-Young Men's Christian Association, still exists in Fairmont and today there is a big drive by the Community Partnership Association taking place to restore the beautiful building and its facilities-a swimming pool, bowling alley, work out rooms, a suspended ceiling for walking or running, for historic downtown Fairmont. The town has discovered that it once held dormitories on the top two floors for itinerant boys and young men who worked in town or were trying to find jobs, or to attend school and had no place to stay. When the dormitories were filled, Mammam had extended a standing invitation for those who were without a room to stay at Sonnencroft on her grown sons' sleeping porch and was delighted in having it and the pool occupied again. These boys stayed in touch with Mammam for many years after her generous gesture to them.

Mary Lyda epitomized the social activist of that period bringing to life the organizations of a community who, with great numbers, can, with time, effort, a heart and yes, large sums of money make things happen. There was no income tax then - no health insurance - she with Papa's help of course, gave back to their community and to those in need. The philanthropists of the past are too few today, but we have federal and state funds to help in some ways.

"Mrs. C.E. Hutchinson Dies Last Night in Home Here"
"Death Claimed One of Fairmont's Most Highly Honored and Beloved Residents"
The Fairmont Times
Thursday Morning, December 16, 1943

"Mrs. C.E. Hutchinson died last night at 11:10 o'clock in her home at 107 Gaston Avenue. At her bedside last night were three of her sons, Brooks, Frank and Harold.

"Mrs. Hutchinson's services throughout her long and useful life were not only to her family friends and church; they reached out to the community and elsewhere and influenced many lives. She was a pioneer in the Woman's Club of Fairmont. She helped to organize and served as the first President of the Young Woman's Christian Association, of this city. She was a pioneer leader in the Woman's Hospital Association; having organized the first old Cook Hospital Woman's Association in 1916, serving as their first President. She was an honorary member of The Junior League of Fairmont, Inc. and a charter member of Green Hills Garden Club and the Century Book Club.

"Mrs. Hutchinson was a woman of strong principles and fine Christian character. She had great charm and warm friendliness that endeared her to many. She stood for all things for the betterment of humanity and she gave her service and her talent and skills unsparingly throughout the years. Her home was ever the Mecca for young and old and she was delighted to entertain her friends, her church associates and her clubs. For her children and their children, to whom she was deeply attached, her home was a rendezvous at all time, and she had happy gatherings for many years, particularly at the holiday periods."

****

Mammam had been a strong, wise and discerning woman, quietly devout-devoted to the First Baptist Church, where her father, Jacob Watkins, had been one of the first trustees appointed in 1895. The congregation made sure Lyda was their first Mother of the Year, knowing of the many young people of the community she helped anonymously-beside her sons. She often acceded to Papa's wishes signifying he was the dominant figure in the home, but the sons and her close friends knew otherwise. She was unimpressed with her wealth, but thoroughly enjoyed the freedom to give to others.

"The West Virginia Baptist" issued each month by the State Convention and edited by Dr. Hugh D. Pickett, who had come back to Fairmont to conduct her final services, reported that,

"Mrs. Hutchinson had been chosen as the first Mother of the year by the State Convention. Her life had been devoted to her Christ, her Church, her home and her friends. In her death, the Fairmont Church and community and her host of friends everywhere, have undergone a severe loss."

****

In her handwritten will, scribbled in pencil, dated January, 1924, right before they left on their last trip around the world, she listed everything she owned. Every piece of her exquisite linen, handmade quilts signed and marked by her grandmothers, one dated back to the 1600s. One she specified had been made by her mother and given to Claude as a baby.

****

"My fine linens are to be equally divided among my seven children. Dear Clyde, I am sure all knew that my heart is full of love for you. That ever since our first-born son, I have worked so hard and prayed always to be a good mother and wife. I have prayed you will all live a right life so you can say He is your Savior too. I have lived and tried to appreciate everything I have had and I love. Our house has been my joy and my life. I know I am religious about things, but it is because I have appreciated and am thankful for it all. It has meant so much to me.

"Boys, your father has been most gracious, he never refused me money, clothes, or anything I would ask for. I tried to be to him a wife he could not find fault in and tried to grant him any favors, to do anything he would ask of me. How far short I came to all this, he and the Lord knows. I know I have my faults. I know I have not always done the right things, but it was an error of the head, not the heart; because of my deep love and gratitude I tried very hard to please. Now I trust if we are separated in this life, we may succeed in the Great Beyond where there is rest and peace. "

~ Lyda W. Hutchinson

A few days after her death on December 15, 1943, two long weary years of the roaring of cannons, the whining of bombs and reading of the men, women, and children suffering under smoke drenched stars abroad, Medora Mason writes again about a grandmother.

****

"Mary Chatter" column
The Times West Virginian
Sunday, December 18, 1943

"When looking back through the many columns I have written about Christmases we have known, it was with no joy in our heart that we looked forward to writing a column this week or to bringing our Christmas wish to you; but a number of things happened which changed the tenor of our mood. One of them was the receipt of a little V-Mail Christmas card from Italy, which scoffed at any reason for merriment in a muddy foxhole, even at Christmas time. Another was the death of a very grand woman to whom Christmas through the years was a wonderful celebration and our summing up of all the things she had meant in our life and the lives of her family, her community, and her state and country. And lastly, was an article we read in a magazine after coming from the home of this woman who loved Christmas and made them beautiful and sacred for her family and her friends.

"The article admonished that this year, more than ever, in all the bright valiant history of this great land of ours, Christmas should be celebrated with merriment and gaiety; that sad and unhappy things should be put aside and that we should carry out the old traditions and customs so dear to the hearts of everyone of us, and for which our boys are fighting and laying down their lives, or else- "what price glory?" Sitting there in the twilight, the gaudy magazine in its red dress, still opened before us, we took a little journey down the lane of memory and found a beautiful one, a way which should not be abandoned nor shall it be, no matter how muddy the foxholes in an alien land!

"And along the way, the friendship of Mrs. C.E. Hutchinson and the beauty of her life became a symbol of the true old fashioned American Christmas; a symbol of the loneliness and need in a mother's heart; the good things of this land of ours.... its standards and the hope and security for the future for which Christmas and the love and goodness embodied in mothers ever since that night, 1,943 years ago, on the Judean hillsides where American soldiers walk with reverence today, a young mother cradled a baby boy in her arms.

"And because her life was such as to symbolize all these things, there should be no unhappiness in the hearts of those she loved this Christmas time ... anymore than there was in those days soon after Thanksgiving when she started planning, plotting, and buying scads of presents boys would like; by making pounds and pounds of fruitcake, candy, cookies and popcorn balls and other good things; by having two large trees and never less than 2 huge turkeys; by having them come in later years from where ever they were with their families and making it a sacred trust that they be there, so that she could live it all over again with her grand children; and always- always being the mother with the rich and understanding heart ... the very core and strength and beauty and character of America and all America stands for! This year she will not be here in body, but her spirit will be here, and it will go on and on in all our memories- a shining, lovely thing just as the memory of Christmases of other days will go on and on and more and more will come, just as the spirit of America will go on and on until a great new glorious peace will come to all the world.

"Because of these things ... our memories and yours.... because America's mothers are all that Mrs. Hutchinson symbolized... because their sons, grandsons, and daughters too, are willing to fight for an old fashioned American Christmas and for a world made whole again, we wish you just that kind of Christmas! God bless our boys, every one, where ever they are, and make them know, somehow, that things are just the same at home this Christmas … lovely and bright and beautiful… as they would have them be."

****

"To live in hearts we leave behind is not to die"
~ Thomas Campbell
(Hallowed Ground)

THE OTHER MRS. HUTCHINSON

On the other side of Seventh Street and Fairmont Avenue, set up on a high walled bank with steep steps leading up to the front porch was an old weatherworn house that had not been painted in years with dirty windows, many broken and stuffed with brown paper bags. Some days when my sister Sylvia and I would walk home from Butcher School, an old woman in a long nightdress and a nightcap would come out on the porch and Sylvia would whisper, "There's Aunt Maud. She boils little girls and has them for dinner."

I never thought twice about this, taking off and dashing across busy Seventh Street, tearing for home and Mom's lap. That is why I would never go any farther than Mrs. Lively's on my tricycle.

Alice Maud Post Hutchinson was Uncle Melville Lee Hutchinson's wife, and was 10 years younger, born in 1867. She was a lovely and wealthy young lady. Her mother, Florence May Davisson was born and raised in Harrison County and married Ira Carpe Post, a cattle farmer and a native of Upshur County in 1866. The two had five children, Alice Maude, Melville Davisson (author), Sidney (doctor), Florence, and Emma, the second wife of Dr. William C. Ogden of Fairmont.

In 1878 the Post family moved into a large brick home, the neighbors called the "big home", but the Posts named "Templemoor", a name that it carries today over a century later. Ira Post maintained numerous herds of cattle and extensive pastureland on the old Clarksburg-Buckhannon Pike where cattle raising was a principal means of earning an income.

Charles Norton book, "Melville Davisson Post - Man of Many Mysteries" (1973) relates,

"A cattle raising project operated in this manner needed many extra helpers besides family. Among those with the Post family was an attractive Negress named Eliza Perkins who helped rear the Post children... she told them that, believable or not, that she could remember her grandmother in Africa "boiling a woman's head in a pot." [Author's Note: Perhaps that is what Sylvia remembered hearing and got Aunt Maude mixed up with Eliza.] "The Perkins family had belonged to the Post family since the years of legal slavery and had remained on in their service as an essential part of the cattle endeavor following the emancipation."

Aunt Maud's little brother, Melville Davisson Post (1869) was the first acknowledged mystery, crime-detective novelist and besides his many books, he wrote a series of detective stories for the Saturday Evening Post. He was known to have been very flamboyant and dramatic, but he graduated from WVU and became a lawyer. To help start the West Virginia University's first football team he called "The Skins", he directed and starred in the famous play, Shakespeare's "Richard the Third", and collected $160 to buy uniforms for his new team.

Melville and his wife, Bloom, had one child, a son, whom they lost at an early age, which had a dire effect on the two bereaved parents. Melville developed a deep depression and some degree of mental illness (paranoia) and he and Bloom spent months in the south of France trying to regain his health. Seeing himself as a man of mystery, Post revealed only a shadow of himself, seldom releasing any personal facts to the public. Some thought he used his "Black Dog", (as Winston Churchill called his depression) in his characters and plots and was often compared to the somber Edgar Allen Poe.

Aunt Maud and Uncle Mel Hutchinson had five daughters and two sons. Irene (Phillips), Martha (Colborn), Laura Lee (Carter), Dorothy - who died at birth, Clarence- who died at the age of five, Florence (Ritchie), and their last child, Melville Lee Jr. who was born in 1906, late in Maud's life at 40. The poor "change of life" child lived alone with his mother and father in the house on Seventh Street, as his sisters had either married or left for boarding schools.

Melville played with the little Faulkner girl who lived in a house a block away from his on Sixth Street and Fairmont Avenue. In 1912, at the age of six, he accidently shot his little friend while showing her a gun he had found in her house. Soon after the incident, young Mel was sent away to a relatively new school, opening in 1900, a preparatory school for affluent boys, the Jacob Tome Institute near Baltimore, in Cecil County, Maryland. The Carnegies and Melons had sent their sons there and Uncle Mel probably wanted him to stay there permanently. It took boys from kindergarten through high School and later - a college. Young Mel was there for many of his school years.

There was a mention of him attending his sister Martha's wedding in Fairmont when he was just 16 years old and attending Tome's Institute. Another mention of him was in his sister Florence's wedding description on November 7, 1923 and stated, at the age 17 he was visiting from St. Luke's College in Wayne, Pennsylvania. The wedding had been attended by only the immediate family and afterwards, forty guests were entertained at the Fairmont Country Club. His mother, Maud, was not mentioned.

Melville Lee Jr.'s obituary was so brief that all I learned was at the age of 22, in 1928, Melville Lee Jr. died in a Philadelphia hospital, which was close to St. Luke's school. There was nothing in Daddy's Ledger about how the young man had died; but one day I stood up after reading the Ledger and a little two-inch scrap of yellowed crackly newspaper fell to the floor - string too short to be saved? It had no date but read,

"Personal Estate Sold ----- More than $3,600 was realized at the Administratrix sale of the personal estate of Melville Hutchinson, Jr. in front of the courthouse this afternoon. A $1000 bond of the Hutchinson Coal Co. brought $850. A Packard Roadster was sold for $1950. One share of National Bank of Fairmont Stock brought $325, two shares of Peoples National Bank stock sold at $255 and two shares at $250. Two watches brought $85 and a silver tie tack sold for 50 cents."

It was well known there was a "strain" in the Post family. Poor Aunt Maud had lived alone, by choice, since her son had been sent away. Uncle Mel went out to live on his farm – where the old Fairmont Field Club was built in 1912. He sold some of his farmland to West End Development Company, who developed the clubhouse and golf course. In later years, he lived with his daughter, Florence, who had no children. Once Uncle Mel left, the house on Fairmont Avenue became more weathered, unloved and forgotten, as did its only occupant. The house had grown a grey tinge, casting an eerie milieu around the Seventh Street corner.

Mother always liked Aunt Maud who would call her now and then and relate the weird things she heard going on in the house, such as, "Men are on roof trying to come down the chimney." Mother would suggest she keep a fire going and that would prevent intruders from using that means of entry. One of Maud's grandsons told me that he and a friend would pick up all the sticks in her yard, ring the bell and sell them to her for kindling.

A total recluse, she never recognized any of her family and refused to have anything to do with them. Her daughters tried to take care of her but were spurned. She would speak only to her daughter Martha and her niece-in-law, my Mother. Packages of food and necessities were just left on her front porch. Today, sadly, she would have been institutionalized. However, she never did any harm and seemed satisfied in her own way. Mother was always empathetic with her and thought she was highly intelligent as was her little brother, Melville, and simply led the life she chose, withdrawn and isolated from a disagreeable, belligerent old man - an unforgiving hateful husband - who had sent her little boy away for life.

Aunt Maud died on August 1, 1942 in her home on Seventh Street. When the daughters found her there were U.S. postage stamps pasted on every wall of the downstairs rooms and, as she had died unattended by a doctor, the coroner was called. When her nightcap was removed, after so many years of neglect, her long, matted, moldered, grey hair clung to her head like wavy hands and could not be brushed. The daughters looked ruefully at the wasted body who had once been their mother.

So alone - so sad - so frightening ...

Aunt Maud's home on the corner of Seventh Street was torn down after her death in 1942. The land stood vacant for years and finally sold to Exxon where Harry Zimmerman built an Exxon service station. Today Rite Aid is on the site.

CHAPTER TEN

ROSES IN DECEMBER

741 FAIRMONT AVENUE

"God gave us memories that we might have roses in December."

~ J.M. Barrie

I was born at 741 Fairmont Avenue on the snowy night of Friday, December 30th, at 10:10 PM. Sylvia and Elaine had been taken to Mammam's - both praying hard for a little brother. Daddy called the Fairmont Hotel Ballroom and the glad news was announced at the Junior League of Fairmont's Charity Ball. The band leader was about to announce the Grand March, instead he announced that Brooks and Ray had another girl, and the crowd responded: "Oh, no! Not another girl!"

Mother – following her custom of a single name for a girl, named me Diane. Mrs. Joseph Hartley Greer came to call a few days later and when Mother told her my name, Aunt Ruth (McCue) said, "Oh Ray, pronounce it the way the French do- Dee –awn". Mother liked that, as Janet Gaynor, the star in the 1927 movie, giving one of the most famous screen performances of all time, was named "Diane". Gaynor won her first Academy Award as the mistreated Paris waif. The movie featured a beautiful love song, written by Erno Rapee and Lew Pollack: "I'm In Heaven When I see You Smile, My DIANE". I spent the early years having to correct teachers and new friends with the pronunciation. Today when someone calls and asks to speak with Di-anne, I know it is a solicitor and answer, "she isn't here" and hang up!

Elaine, Sylvia Jane and I were born at 741 and we were all three delivered by Dr. L.D. Howard. We all had Miss Ackerman as our nurse for the first six weeks. I was baptized on Easter Even, the 15th day of April in 1933 in the Parish House of Christ Episcopal Church by the Reverend Clarence W. Brickman. The Church at Ninth Street and Fairmont Avenue had not been built yet because of the "Crash of 1929" and would not be built until 1951. In fact the first wedding in the new Church, including the pews, was my sister Sylvia's on May 12, 1951, a year before I was married.

In reading through a very detailed pink moiré baby book that Mother faithfully kept, I was on stage at an early age. The Fairmont Women's Club arts department sponsored "Famous Madonnas in Tableaux" in the new, fireproof Fairmont Senior High School auditorium. The school had just been built in 1929 and was named Fairmont Senior High because the old Fairmont High School at Fifth Street became Fairmont Junior High School. East Fairmont High School was built in the early twenties behind the Shaw house. The school's Glee Club sang while the twelve portraits were depicted by live models. Mother and I were No. 9 - Madonna and Child. I do not remember the event, but I was told it was a beautiful production and I had performed admirably.

A "Mary Chatter" column by Medora Mason in The Sunday Times-West Virginian, Sunday Morning December 20, 1936 tells,

"The little story of a lovely curly haired Diane Hutchinson, who will be 4 years old the last day of this month, concerning Santa Claus. For several evenings she and her sister Sylvia have been listening to Santa Claus broadcast over the local radio. The other night Diane, peeved because Santa had failed to answer her letter, declared she was "mad at him", and when the time came for the evening broadcast she stuck a tiny finger in each ear and pretended she wasn't listening to him. Soon one of her parents said to her, "Diane you better not be mad at Santa Claus. He might not stop by here on Christmas Eve." Diane looked up whimsically, her fingers still in her ears, "She hear all right."

****

I did not talk until the age of three and then, they say, I never stopped. I talked in the third person, too fast and had trouble pronouncing words correctly. This baby talk often incited insensitive adults. A neighborhood friend's mother would teasingly say to me, "You talk Dutch!" and laugh at me. How embarrassing - for her! I would promptly head for home in tears, where Mother would sooth the hurt feelings while berating any adult who would treat a child so callously. This always made me feel relieved and exonerated. After all, even the telephone operators understood me. After dinner every night I was allowed to call Mammam to say goodnight. When the operator asked, "What number please?" I answered; "One tummy tick" (176) and Mammam would always answer.

When I wake up some mornings, the big red dial on my automatic time setting clock is at 7:41 and I know my mother is here with me. Mother loved our house on the corner of 741 Fairmont Avenue and Eighth Street, a huge 30-room house that was once owned by Dr. and Mrs. John R. Cook. I had heard the stories about Dr. Cook when there were no hospitals here yet. If a patient lived alone and was dying, Dr. John had brought them to his home – actually to die. The doctor, his wife, (Susan Olivia) and their daughter, Louise, had moved to this house from Rivesville where Dr. John had been the Montana Mines company doctor.

The house had a large garden, a carriage house, and a barn. Fairmont really needed a hospital and Dr. Cook and three other physicians purchased the land and house owned by J.W. Barnes on the corner of Gaston Avenue and Second Street where the hospital, now the Board of Education building, still stands. The Barnes' house was moved to the back of the property and later used as a nurses' home, where all nurses had to live and be on call 24-7. The nurses could not be married nor have children. Dr. Cook died of blood poisoning at the age of 45 in 1908, only five years after the new hospital opened.

When Daddy brought Mother home after their honeymoon in the fall of 1917, he took her to the Hillcrest section of Fairmont where he had purchased a huge portion of the undeveloped section of Fairmont. He wanted to build her another castle, but mother wanted a house on Fairmont or Locust Avenues, the hubs of the city. They started housekeeping renting the Carney Christie house. Carney, a friend of Daddy's, was a Broadway Shakespearean actor. The beautiful, stately, old stone house is still there today. Mrs. Christie, Carney's mother, tiring of the big city, wanted to come back to Fairmont to live, so Daddy rented 741, from Dr. Cook's estate.

Mother loved it! It was a bright happy house, with a large wrap-around porch where she could swing, read and gaze out over her beautiful gardens. She and Mammam would go to Grand Rapids, Michigan, then a manufacturing center that had been a trading post, settled by Dutch immigrants who excelled in furniture making. The two would buy large furniture suitable for Sonnencroft and 741 where all the ceilings were 12 feet high. We had wonderful Christmas trees, usually in the library. I thought Santa Claus brought the tree, because it was always a glorious surprise, beaming down on all the toys underneath when I came downstairs on that long awaited morning. I never knew that Daddy had to wait for the trees to go on sale Christmas Eve before he could afford to buy one. Our ceilings were so high the tree sellers would usually give him the tallest tree left on the lot, as they did not want to dispose of it.

One wonderful Christmas when I was four, and they thought I was suspicious about the "Jolly old man", Daddy dressed up in a Santa suit they had bought when Elaine was a little girl in the early 20s. The suit was made of red velvet with real white fur. Traditionally, we came down the stairs, the oldest first, the youngest last, but this year I was allowed to go down first. There he was! Sound asleep in the wicker telephone chair. I screamed for Daddy, whom I thought was upstairs shaving, and turned and ran back up, with Elaine and Sylvia trying to delay me. I ran into Daddy and insisted he come to see Santa; so "breathless Brooks" came dashing back down the back steps to the kitchen and ran outside looking for his counterpart. He showed me tracks in the snow from the eight reindeer, whose names I knew by heart.

I was totally convinced! Because of that little episode, I was the only child in all of Butcher Elementary School who believed in Mr. Claus until the fifth grade. I tried hard to believe in the man, not trusting my best friends who thought I was a little "slow", until Christmas Eve nearing my eighth birthday. It was always hard to fall asleep on this night of all nights, but I was almost there when I heard Mother ask Elaine, "Daddy has the tree up, aren't you coming down to help trim?" I did not even hear the answer. Santa Claus did NOT bring the tree, nor did he decorate it! I was relieved in a melancholy way, although it was hard to keep up the pretenses much longer. I simply was not sure I'd get everything I asked Santa for, if there was no Santa.

On the first floor of 741 there were four large rooms. Many old friends say they can remember every room of this house, having played with, danced with, or dated one of us. Jack Carpenter, my son's father-in-law, says during a pillow fight, he broke some of the crystal prisms on the elegant chandelier in the living room, the one to the left of the front door. This room is the one Jack Knowles describes in his book, "Vein of Riches", where Mother's seven-foot high portrait hung over a carved mahogany refectory table. Under the table was a wooden parquet inlaid bench where many friends would sit across from an enormous couch from Sonnencroft that was down filled and could seat eight small people, or sleep two adults. It was cobalt blue velvet and in the summer, Mother put cool white-on-white striped slipcovers over it and all other dark upholstered pieces each year. From this corner room you could see into the dining room and the hall, and from the windows to Fairmont Avenue and the side entrance to Highgate on Eighth Street.

Next to this room was a great hall or foyer where Mom sat and read and listened to Amos and Andy in a large brocaded wing back chair, the same chair I sit in today writing this book. In this hall was a fireplace, several arm chairs and a teakwood coramandel screen with panels of embroidered silk that Mammam had brought from the Orient. One Christmas morning this screen had hidden a console Stromberg Carlson phonograph player when I was in seventh grade. A wide staircase with two landings came down into the hall. The first landing was where we three brides threw our bouquets. This is the room where Mom could keep an eye on us and who might be coming to visit. This was where we sat on her lap and listened to all of the stories she would read or tell to us.

The third room was the library with leaded glass doors encasing hundreds of twice-read books. The Steinway parlor grand piano and a tall Victrola which you wound up to play the Red Seals records of Enrico Caruso and Alma Gluck, plus many other newer, popular 78 rpm records. This room was my favorite. This is where Santa Claus had fallen asleep and the Christmas tree stood each year. A large picture of Mother's godfather Uncle Madison Smith, hung above the mantle; a handsome man with white hair and a white goatee. He was Mother's paternal uncle who, after her father died when she was five weeks old, made Mother his ward. He was quite wealthy and had never married. I was so scared of that portrait because I thought it was "Doc Holly" (pediatrician Eugene Holland) of whom I was deathly afraid, as he gave me shots. I know I hurt Mother's feelings because she adored Uncle Smith as a father.

Although a baby doctor, I really do not think Dr. Holland liked children. He would not take you after the age of one or two when you were through with formulas. When we took rides around the Loop, Daddy and my sisters would tease me. When we got to Fourth Street and Locust Avenue, "Oh, Diane, here is Doc Holly's office." I would immediately get down on the floor of the car and hide between my sister's legs while Mother would admonish all three of them. As I look back on it, it was somewhat cruel. No wonder I was always scared of doctors.

I had two doctors right next door to me and I was scared to ride my little green tricycle past the long entrances to their front doors. Once I got past them I could safely go talk with my older friends who would not attack me. One day tall, handsome Dr. Amos Henry Stevens came out of what is now the only house still left on my old block. I panicked! With no turning radius I had to back up to get back on neutral ground which was rather difficult for a terrified three year old. He caught the handlebar and stooped down to speak to me - God forbid! I remember his very kind face with a dark, manicured mustache. He tried to help turn the trike around- my feet just flying, turning that front wheel as fast as I could. I never saw him again. He probably hid from me. I found a death notice in Daddy's Ledger that Dr. Stevens died in that house in 1939 at the age of 40. How tragic!

I once took my tricycle up a little hill on Seventh Street where the Go Mart is today and could not make it up to Lively's' driveway to turn. I went backwards right into Fairmont Avenue traffic. My neighbor and hero

George Peed, who married my sister Elaine 17 years later, picked me up and carried me all the way home. George was in uniform even then, as he attended Greenbrier Military Academy in Greenbrier County, WV, and then Annapolis Naval Academy. George reminded me of the incident often, telling Paul about it with much glee!

Two sets of French doors in the library led to the wraparound porch that held four large swings and several chairs and settees. A huge apple tree reaching up and over the porch railing shaded the west end. I remember an ice storm in April - the cruelest month - that encased each delicate pink and white blossom in a shield of ice. The west end of the porch was where our friends danced and sang and laughed through so many lovely summer evenings. All of us falling in and out of love and finally ending summer romances year after year.

There was a dining room that had a buzzer under mother's foot. It rang in the kitchen to a box that indicated from which room the call was coming, the dining room or perhaps from one of the bedrooms upstairs. There was a telephone room and cloakroom that incorporated a powder room off the kitchen area.

The kitchen and butler's pantry were unique. The kitchen became smaller when our first new Kelvinator refrigerator was placed in it in the late 30s, leaving the old icebox room a place to store jams and jellies and canned food. The butler's pantry had an oversized swinging door where the servants brought the food in to serve. After removing the dishes, they would be washed in a great copper sink. Long counters surrounded the pantry atop huge drawers for linens and utensils. Nannie McPherson, whom I adored, always kept a large red and gold fruitcake tin in the top, largest of the drawers, filled with a scrumptious cake or cinnamon rolls. I loved the tin; it had a royal pageboy dressed in a blue silk tunic with a gold tasseled rope surrounding his waist. He had blond hair in a pageboy cut and carried a large, festive and flaming plum pudding. Mother gave me that tin when Eddie was born. I bring it out every Christmas to store cookies and tell the following story,

One evening, Nanny brought into the dining room what looked like a chocolate cake, holding it high in the air with one big, strong, black arm and said, "I'm sorry Miz' Hutchinson", setting the cake down right in front of moi. It had funny marks, like little fingertips scraping off most of the icing. I could feel all those piercing eyes on me as I tried to scoot a little farther down in that tall youth chair. Mother said, rather sternly, "Diane, do you

190

know anything about this?" I braced myself, lifted my head off of my chest and, nodding, declared, "Me saw this little, teeny, tiny mouse run up and jump inside the cake drawer - Me think he ate that icing." For a three year old, I was rather proud of that seed of doubt I planted, as all of them were afraid to eat the rutted, pitted, delicious chocolate cake. Many years later Mother said I was so convincing that Nannie had to throw out the cake, as they simply were not sure to believe me or not. Mom and Daddy, taking no side in the inquisition, had enjoyed the whole incident.

Upstairs, there were five bedrooms. One was made into a sewing room and had huge linen drawers beneath a series of windows looking into the side gardens. Across the hall a large bathroom holding a sink big enough to bathe children until they were allowed in the biggest tub I have ever seen. Its controls were on the side with a 12" round showerhead coming down out of the ceiling with a large metal ring surrounding it, from which a heavy canvas curtain hung, enveloping one in a spa like room.

All these rooms had their own fireplaces which Daddy would light before he woke us for school. Then he would go down to the basement and stoke the huge coal furnace, hoping all the radiators would stay hot enough for the whole day. Elaine's room had a beautiful tall fireplace screen of asbestos that, when you lit it, the whole screen would flare into a beautiful red heat, until you would turn the key down to a soft warm blue, warming you immediately. My room had just a little gas stove, no asbestos, of which today I am most thankful.

The third floor was a fascinating attic filled with old toys, beautiful old broken dolls, rocking horses, piles of National Geographic, and old issues of Life and Time magazines from their first publications. There were books, hats of all eras and, of all things, a red velvet Santa Claus suit! There were beaded dresses and black velvet dancing shoes with rhinestone heels, the ostrich feather fan Mother had held on her lap in the large portrait - she certainly did not have feathers coming out of her hair as Jack Knowles had remembered, nor a jeweled "dog collar around her neck. There were old costumes hand sewn for Halloween, hand blown Christmas ornaments from Germany, and Easter baskets awaiting the Easter Bunny. Fans of all sizes joined the box of ostrich and peacock fans that were quite stylish to carry with beaded purses in the twenties. There were piles of handmade lace trimmed lingerie and soft little fur coats that I seemed to have outgrown each winter.

This wonderland attic was made into an apartment by Sylvia when she was in Junior High School. It had a small living room at the head of the steps, a study, a large bedroom with large twin beds, a full bath and a huge storage room, where Sylvia had thrown all of the toys and the things she did not want in her apartment. The bay window in Sylvia's bedroom held the 36-inch, square, three-story dollhouse that Daddy had won in a drawing sponsored by the Fairmont Times Christmas Fund show when Elaine was a little girl. What an awe-inspiring toy for any little girl. We three children, and our friends, thoroughly used and enjoyed it. The dollhouse was completely furnished and landscaped with trees, driveways, hedges and statuaries on a scale to compliment the house.

I would dress up in some of the dresses and high heels carry an old pocketbook, and put on Mother's old tri-corn hat and parade down Fairmont Avenue pushing my dolls in a beautiful, old wicker doll carriage, much to the neighbors' delight. The first house on my block at Seventh Street was Mrs. Henry Lively (Gladys) and that is as far as I was allowed to go. Attorney and Mrs. E. Forrest Hartley lived two houses from Seventh Street and would expect me to show them my latest outfits. Mr. Hartley seemed very old and ill but always smiled at me and, unable to speak as a result of a stroke, would smile and nod his head, approving my latest haute couture. Mrs. Hartley had been a Modderwell and was a sister of Louise DeBolt (the second Mrs. George DeBolt) and Mrs. J.E. Watson. She thoroughly enjoyed seeing what dolly I was mother to that day. I would wheel my dolls past George Peed's house and talk on the steps with his Aunt Mamie (May Fleming). She and George's mother (Roberta) were daughters of Robert Flavius Fleming, an attorney and brother of Governor Aretas Brooks Fleming. Mrs. Peed did not allow children up on her pristine front porch, so Mamie and I sat on the stone steps clear down at the sidewalk. Mamie had never married and had no children, and was not really too interested in doll play. But she was very sweet and always glad to have some company.

I seldom had anyone to play with, but I did not have imaginary friends as Elaine had until her little sister Sylvia was born. I had my dolls and Mom who read to me daily. Nannie was so good to me and let me help her bake and allowed me to eat raw ground beef until Mother found out. I loved sirloin steak bones and later dentists said that is why my teeth were so good. Nannie explained that she had scraped cooked steak for me as a baby; there was no baby food then. Mother insisted on high protein diets to nourish our skin and hair. It must have worked, because my skin and hair, for my age, are still pretty good.

The basement was rather scary when I was alone down there. There was an unfinished sub basement with shelves for canned goods, so deep and dark and cold even on a hot summer day, with clay floors that were never damp where Daddy stored lumber. The sub-basement had large doors that pulled up from the floors like cellar doors on the outside of a house. Mother said we were never to go down there unless there was a tornado.

Iona, the washwoman, would come twice a week, one day to wash and one day to iron. The washer was a large copper enclosed tub that rocked back and force by electricity. After the wash cycle, it then speeded up to shed most of the dirty water through a hose below into the laundry tubs. More clean water was added by a hose above and rocked again to rinse. The clothing was hung to dry outside or inside depending on the weather. The next day the dry muslin sheets would be fed through an enormous mangle which had been at Sonnencroft. I suppose the sheets were always softened by the extreme steam heat of the mangle ironing.

Nannie, who lived with us, had an apartment down stairs where she had a large sitting room and bedroom and a full bath at the foot of the basement steps. I would sit down there and play with her older children, Bayleise and Buddy, if they came to visit. They lived at Worthington with their grandmother. I often saw them after dinner when they would sit on the back porch steps and Mom and Nannie would make sure they had food to take home with them. Nannie's husband was serving time in the state penitentiary and Nannie always said it was the best thing that ever happened to their family.

I asked Sylvia to write me in her own words the story of the farm trip with Nannie and she wrote on Monday, August 15, 2011:

"I had been reading to myself since I was six years old...Diane had arrived and taken over Mom's lap. My favorite books were The Curly Tops, Honey Bunch and The Bobbsey Twins. They had all been to farms and Nannie had a farm. She had Thursday afternoons off and I begged and begged to go with her to the farm. Mother refused. Finally, when I was eight and Diane was three, Mother relented and said we could go. We boarded the big streetcar that went between Fairmont and Clarksburg and somewhere along that route, that only the conductor and Mom knew, he stopped and we got off. I remember climbing a huge hill and pulling myself up by the tall grass. I guess Nannie carried Diane because she was too little to make it on her own. When we got to the top of the hill there were several shacks, but I wanted to see the animals. There were no horses or cows, but there were several chickens and Nannie took us over to the pigsty to see the new baby pigs and Diane climbed in with them. I was so thrilled to be there I did not see where Nannie went so I went looking for her. I pushed opened the door of one of the shacks and there was a black man and a white naked woman sitting on the bed. I will never forget it! I was horrified - not at the mixed colors, but I had never seen a naked woman before. I backed out of the shack and, I guess Nannie found me. All I remember after that was the geese were chasing little muddy Diane, flapping their wings and honking. She was in tears running in circles as fast as she could. We never asked to go to the farm again. I still remember it like it was yesterday.

Love you... Sylvia"

Daddy sold 741 in 1953 and it was hard throwing away all the toys, magazines, clothes, many of mother's beautiful clothes were given to Mr. Lawrence Wallman and the Drama department at Fairmont State College as costumes for future plays. One dress we could not dispose of was Mother's bronze beaded ankle length gown. Mother had told us the story so often:

"We were in New York shopping for new winter wardrobes at Saks Fifth Avenue. I was trying on ensembles and your father was waiting for me on one of the silk couches. He was being entertained by several of the young, beautiful models parading before him in the gorgeous latest styles. I would come out of the dressing room attired in various pieces and your father would smile and nod his head at me approvingly, but seldom taking his eyes off those models. Finally I appeared in this spectacular, hand sewn, bronze beaded creation, and the clerk said," Mr. Hutchinson, this exquisite gown was just made for your beautiful wife." Brooks answered, "Yes, yes, that will be fine", smiling all the while at his models with just a quick glance at me. Later when the bills arrived from Saks, he was shocked to find a bronze beaded dress listed at $5000, and he knew very well why". Hell hath no fury!

Every old house has its own sounds as unique as its scent and its secrets. I remember coming home too late after a date and trying to miss the noisiest floorboards. Alone In bed at night was a time to wonder how many patients of Dr. Cook's had died in my room? I am sure, not many - there were no ghosts. It was such a safe beautiful room and, as I grew older, I had the entire wall over my bed filled with movie star pictures - Van Johnson, Tom Drake, Clark Gable, Robert Taylor, Cary Grant, Spencer Tracy and Katherine Hepburn, Susan Hayward, Bette Davis, Joan Crawford, June Allyson and Judy Garland. It was a large room and Daddy had a terrible time getting all those pictures down when they were readying the room for showing the wedding presents before my wedding, a popular custom done at that time. While Paul and I were on our honeymoon, Mother and Daddy had all my French provincial bedroom furniture, which had been in a guest room at Sonnencroft, moved to our new apartment we had rented at 827 Benoni Avenue - the old Hartman house. I would be leaving one castle for another, albeit, a temporary one.

Why do I remember the House on Eighth Street after all these years? What could be more important than the place you lived as a child, where you laughed more than you cried, where you were safe and loved? I still sleep in the bed I graduated to when I outgrew a youth bed. The one Sylvia had before me.

This is my December and I relish all the roses I have stored and enjoyed, reliving my youth at 741.

SYLVIA'S LETTER - 2000

When Paul died in 2000 my sister, Sylvia Jane Derby called from her home in Honolulu and asked me did I want her to fly in for his funeral and be with me then or would I prefer to have her come in October. I chose the latter. I had many dear friends to see me through this crisis, and wanted to be able to sit down and be with her, my only living sister who had not been to Fairmont since 1973. True to her word she visited us for several days late in October and then flew on to New York to be with her daughter Diana and her family for Thanksgiving. She learned where there is love, "you can go home again."

Nov. 15, 2000
"Dearest Diane,

Thank you, thank you, thank you, for a perfectly marvelous time and for letting me do exactly what I wanted to do. I saw dear Jack (Hutchinson) and Susan, I went to Woodlawn, I met Brooks and Brett, I heard Brooks play the piano, I saw Jean (Ireland) and I felt I honored Paul in a small way by going to the Air Force Association meeting which he had founded in Fairmont ... It was all just perfect!

I also felt so lucky to be able to "go back in time" to so many family "treasures". Each time I turned there was some touch of my childhood. I don't think any of my friends can do that. It's so wonderful that you've loved and cherished so many memories! I was surrounded by so many family pictures of happier times and each time I recognized a vase or a pillow, I pictured it at 741, and it gave me such a warm feeling. Even sleeping in my old bed was a treat.

I know we couldn't have done so much without our darling Sylvia. I will write her too and thank her for all her TLC. She is a marvelous person and I know she is happy. That is all we really want for our children - to be well and contented. It was so good to have so much of your time to just sit and talk and reminisce. I say I want to live to be a hundred, but I want someone left to remember with me!

Thank you again - dear one,
I love you,
~ Sylvia"

THE SHINNSTON TORNADO: 1944

I mentioned in the last chapter about the interesting sub-basement at 741, where Mother said we were to go in case of a tornado. Daddy would laugh, roll his eyes and, in general make fun of Mother's genuine fright of tornados which she had heard about from Mom, who talked freely about winds they had suffered crossing the prairies. "A tornado? In West Virginia? In these mountains? Mother would always call our mountains foothills, as compared to her "Rockies" which did not help the situation. She was right when you realize the highest point in West Virginia - Spruce Knob in Pendleton Co. is 4,861 ft, and Idaho's Borah Peak in Custer County is 12,662 ft.

There were doors in the floor that opened to steps leading down to a completely dry, clay dirt, floored sub-basement which held a lot of old lumber and half-filled paint cans, but where Mother always kept cans of food and a can opener. Daddy may have never known this, as he would have protested. That is until the night of the Shinnston Tornado, Friday, June 23, 1944.

Mother was sure a tornado was on its way because of the "eerie bright green light" in the hot evening sky. While she put her plants down off the porch tables onto the floor, Daddy was nonchalantly strolling around the yard. Sylvia was dressing for a date and I was helping Mother. Daddy was still laughing at Mother's "greenish light".

I had been called upstairs by Sylvia who was trying to curl her hair with a curling iron before her date arrived. She asked me to do the back of her hair which I proceeded to do and burned the inside of my left forearm. Not telling Mother about it, as she would scold Sylvia, I covered the raw burn with a bandage to hide it.

The telephone rang, the Red Cross calling for Daddy, the board president, to get to Joe Town outside of Shinnston. He left immediately and we did not see him for two days. Never again was the sub basement, nor the silly thoughts of tornados mentioned.

The loss of life and destruction was devastating to the entire area. The suburbs of Shinnston were the hardest hit. It took a week to finally read the news of the dead and injured and the terrible wrath and destruction on the small farming communities. It was if the Four Horsemen had created that wide swath down the mountainside, leaving nothing behind but famine, pestilence, destruction, and death.

"Shinnston Buries Her Beloved Dead"

"Tornado Reaps Heavy Toll of Death in Community"
"Fury of Storm Unequaled in History of West Virginia"
The Shinnston News
Thursday, June 29, 1944

"The tornado struck Shinnston about 8:30 Friday evening and while the people had brief seconds of warning in the unnatural noises immediately preceding the blow and in the appearance of a cone shaped cloud on the horizon, few of the victims had time to seek shelter, even in the basement of their homes. As panic seized everybody the crash of death was heard, the havoc was wrought and the devastating force moved on to spread its rage and destruction for many miles.

"Immediately after the tornado struck, calls were sent to Clarksburg and Fairmont for help. Amid the screams of ambulance sirens and general panic and confusion of the people, the rescue work quickly took form. The Coffindaffer Clinic, the only hospital here, was soon crowded with the wounded and stricken, while the Clarksburg and Fairmont Hospitals received the more critical cases.

"Many people report having seen the tornado approaching. Their descriptions are all about the same. It was the most terrifying sight of their lives, a monstrous mixture of fire and sulphur and blackness, forming its deadly funnel shape and carrying trees, lumber and debris. Results of its visitation are in many instances too horrible to describe. In its might, it performed such terrifying acts as sweeping the feathers clean off a chickens and leaving them standing stark dead, peeling the bark off of a tree and leaving them standing upright; carrying huge timbers which in some instances struck human beings to break their bones and disfigure them and all the while, in brief seconds, killing and leveling homes."

****

Time magazine, the July 3, 1944 issue reported,

"CATASTROPHE: They hoped for a storm"

"State trooper G.F. Randall, alone inside a concrete building beside the steel radio tower of the West Virginia State Police, got up to close a window against the wind and saw the spiral shaped cone sweeping over the hill toward him. "As it got closer I could see it was filled with wood, trees, and out houses. It seemed to be coming directly toward me. I was so damned interested I never moved. The tornado smashed in, the high steel pyramid doubled into an inverted-V". Randall straightened up, unhurt. Up Shinn's Run, the storm swirled across the countryside in a path 300 yards wide; leveling trees houses and fences as if an army of bulldozers had streaked through the valley. At Boothsville the tornado uprooted a new $250,000 pumping station and slammed it against a hillside. An 80- lb wrench lit in a field a half a mile away. Rescue workers counted 58 dead from the Shinnston tornado, "worst in West Virginia history. Every report lists a different figure for deaths from the worst natural disaster the state has ever seen."

****

Eyewitnesses swore that when the tornado crossed the West Fork River the water was drawn up and the bottom of the river was visible. The funnel continued for 40 miles, dissipating on Cheat Mountain. Many said hailstones were the size of baseballs.

The American Red Cross Chapters, in both Clarksburg and Fairmont, were busy for days trying to get families back together or at least located. Entire families, even entire neighborhoods were killed or blown away. Some bodies washed up later from the river, others were never found.

When Daddy returned to Fairmont, he slept for several hours and then drove us to Joe Town to see the ruins left by what the Almanacs report as the 14th worst storm ever to be recorded.

On our trip to see the devastation, I saw the cow that was split in half by a 2x4 beam - a scene I can never forget. The bloated carcass was lying in a filling station drive, next to the old fashioned pumps that were both standing upright where they were supposed to be, but upside down.

We saw rows of injured sitting in chairs and rockers being treated on front porches still left intact, the patient's faces heavy with death and disbelief.

Just a few days before on June 6th, the invasion of Normandy on the coast of France had taken place- the greatest invasion ever known. Thousands of our young men had died, many from Marion and Harrison Counties. The telegrams were starting to arrive. There seemed to be a milieu of death hanging over us all

The silly little burn, which I had covered with a bandage, became infected, teaching me never to cover a burn again. I had a bad scar on that arm for years, but every time I looked at it, I was reminded of the scars on the hills of Joe Town and Shinnston and what the dead and wounded had suffered on that hot and terrifying July night in 1944.

ILLNESSES: BLOOD POISONING & DRUGS

Some parents used to send children to the houses where there were childhood diseases so their child would be exposed and get it over with as children instead of often dying as adults. My maternal grandfather died of the measles 5 weeks after my mother was born.

Our son, Eddie, had the measles and developed post-infectious rubeola encephalitis. I remember Dr. Emery D. Wise coming to the house at 931 Coleman Avenue at one in the morning, sitting and staring at Eddie, who was in a near coma. He had no temperature and had been over the measles for a week. Dr. Wise called me the next morning and wanted us to take him straight to the hospital for Dr. O.L. Haynes, a pediatrician, to examine him.

Dr. Haynes admitted him to an isolated pediatric room immediately. No one was allowed in, not even me. I had to sit in the hallway and peek through a crack in the door. How frightening and sickening to see your 6 year old alone and unaware of the situation. He had not eaten for two days. I told O.L. how my children loved grape ice cubes and macaroni soup that I gave them when they were too ill to get liquids into them.

The next morning the nurse called and said that Dr. Haynes had brought Eddie a grape pop-sickle and wanted me to bring the macaroni soup immediately. The soup which Eddie and his family still enjoy every Sunday night in the winter is very simple:

Heat: 1 can of condensed tomato soup and 1 can of milk

Add: 1 cup cooked elbow macaroni to that liquid

Serve with salted soda crackers

Eddie began to eat as the special nurse, Mary Mangino, slowly fed him. Eddie progressed slowly in the next few days. Mary had been told to start reading nursery rhymes to him that might jump-start the brain to be more active and remind him of things he loved. Here was my brilliant Eddie, who could read before he went to kindergarten and, having been read the elemental rhymes as an infant, had memorized them before he was two.

Our Episcopal minister at the time was Tom Seitz. He would go up and see him at 7 am when no one else was allowed on the floor. Tom would then drop by our house to report and offer to run to the market for us. Tom proved his holiness, as he knew when a prayer was needed or when action spoke much louder than prayers.

Post-scare, we realized Eddie had not run a temperature, which would have burned out the virus attacking the base of the brain. Yet, if he had run too high a fever he would have gone home with lifelong residuals just as another patient did, who was packed in ice in another isolated room. His temperature had reached 107.

After ten days of special nursing care, we were finally allowed to bring him home.

He was still my beautiful, sweet, adorable and smart Eddie!

Dr. David Lindsay, an old friend, would check with me every morning about Eddie. His son Robbie was in Eddie's class and had suffered through mumps post-infectious meningitis.

I am so concerned about those who are fighting the newest vaccines to protect their children. I know the heartaches we suffered in 1962, when there were so few preventive vaccines.

In the early twenties, Elaine had Scarlet Fever, a streptococcal infection, an easily spread infectious disease of childhood causing a high fever and a wide spread bright red rash. The whole house was quarantined. Mother said a sign was put on the front door by the County Health Department to warn would be visitors, as doctors were required to report all incidences. Mother was told to burn all of Elaine's books that she had handled or touched and all toys that had been played with.

My sister Sylvia writes:

"I had whooping cough when I was three and gave it to Uncle Frank who never forgave me. I don't remember it much, but I do remember the earaches, and Daddy was always there.

I had German measles when I was 14 and broke out with a rash when I took a bath before going to a dance, so did not tell Mother, went to the dance and gave measles to every boy I danced with.

Elaine and I had chicken pox together. I was in second grade and I was allowed to sleep in her room - which I loved.

I also remember having my tonsils out when I was eight and I saw Mother crying as they wheeled me into the operating room, I was scared to death. I hemorrhaged a couple of weeks later and it was Mother's turn to be scared."

****

As a little girl I almost died of the whooping cough. It is an acute contagious disease of children, usually under the age of four, called Pertussis, the P in DPT shots today. I can recall the uncontrollable coughing in the middle of the night and fighting to catch my breath when I would hear that strange high-pitched whooping sound; hence, the title. Daddy right in the next room would come rushing in, and stand me up so I could hold on tightly to the bedpost with his big strong arms holding me, oh so gently. I would relax and feel so safe and, exhausted by the coughing spasms I would fall asleep in his arms in the old white wicker rocking chair. When we were ill as children, Daddy was always the patient night nurse.

Today we see a sudden return of whooping cough and they are once again advising young children and adults to be re-vaccinated. In September of 2010, the Fairmont Times reported that, "West Virginia health officials are investigating 60 reported case of whooping cough across the state. The Charleston Gazette has reported four new cases have been confirmed, three in Ohio County and one in Kanawha County. The office of Epidemiology and Prevention Services has said that only eleven cases were confirmed in 2009."

And it can be prevented!

The only other illness I remember, except for a light case of chicken pox caught from my sisters, was blood poisoning from my small pox shot when I was four.

The pediatrician of the day was a questionable stern doctor who had an office on Fairmont Avenue between Second and Third streets. His only child, Jimmy, was in Sylvia's class in school. I did not know him but he was very small for his age and extremely shy and withdrawn.

Sylvia remembers him well and wrote me, "He was in my grade at school and he weighed 30 pounds soaking wet...poor child. His father put me into the hospital for "observation" and diagnosed me with diabetes which was certainly not true."

My leg hurt and was terribly red, but I was scared to tell Mother, knowing she would take me back to the scary Dr. B.

I whispered to Sylvia, "My leg really hurts."

Looking at it, she immediately yelled, "MOTHER!"

So much for confidentiality!

Mother, of course looking shocked, composed herself and called Dr. John Paul Trach, the sweetest, kindest doctor in town, the only one I trusted. He was the father of three close friends, Jennianne, Julia, and John, Jr. This was long before Dr. John and his wife Opal had a second family: Mary Beth, Marty, and Mark. The latter three always reminded us of the first three children.

When Dr. John arrived, I remember how sober and worried he seemed. The good doctor injected me with another shot which I learned later was one of the first sulfa shots. It saved my life. Years later I learned that blood poisoning had started in the upper thigh where the small pox shot had been given. Girls often had shots on their legs so their pretty little arms were saved from disfiguring marks. Dr. John blamed the poisoning on a dirty needle.

Several years later I learned that sulfa preceded penicillin, the wonder drug, which came around 1940. Penicillin used by doctors for their patients before December 7, 1941 when WWII started, but was saved for the wounded during the war and not available to the public.

I also learned that Dr. B. and family had been literally asked to leave town when it was discovered the doctor and his wife had been drugging Jimmy most of his life to keep him quiet. In those days several doctors were addicted to the drugs of the day and it was not unusual, but to drug your children was unheard of.

Speaking of drugs, the torrid twenties produced many drug addicts, not just doctors of medicine. Many of the "flappers" were users of cocaine, the drug of the twenties.

The story goes that a John Smith Pemberton worked in a drug store in Columbus Georgia. Pemberton, a pharmacist and chemist, and a graduate of the Reform Medical College of Macon, Georgia, developed a coca wine in 1885 and called it Pemberton's Wine Coca. In 1886 when Atlanta and Fulton County passed prohibition legislation, Pemberton responded by developing Coca Cola, essentially a non-alcoholic version of French Wine Cola. The pharmacist told the Atlantic Journal, "It is composed of an extract from the leaf of Peruvian Coca, the purist wine, and the Kola nut. It is the most excellent of all tonics, assisting digestion, imparting energy to the organs of respiration, and strengthening the muscular and nervous system".

When the drink was originally launched the key ingredient was the coca leaf, chewed by the natives of Peru and Bolivia for 2000 years, the cola nut (caffeine) and some say damiana - a shrub native to South America considered to be an aphrodisiac- and was originally sold in drug stores as a patent medicine for five cents a glass. The cocaine was derived from the coca leaf and the caffeine from the kola nut leading to the name COCA COLA The k in kola was replaced with a C for marketing reasons.

Pemberton called for 5oz. of coca leaf per gallon of syrup. Indications that cocaine found in the kola leaf could prove addictive were generally ignored. Even Sigmund Freud enthused about the virtue of the leaf in his essay, "ber Coca - a song of praise to the magical substance". He claimed Coca Cola cured many diseases including morphine addiction, dyspepsia, neurasthenia, headache, and impotence, an array of ailments covering most people living in 1886.

In 1886 while still suffering from an on-going addiction to morphine, as did many other wounded Civil War veterans, Pemberton sold the rights to his beverage to Asa Griggs Candler who incorporated The Coca Cola Company in 1888.

The cola leaf was used in the formula for Coca Cola until 1929. By that time drugs and alcohol were rampant up and down the civilized society of the East Coast much as it is today. Many from Fairmont were addicted and one man, whom I remember well, always had a terrible red, runny nose, which Mother explained to us when asked why, "Bobby is a coke addict". This was long after the coca leaf had been removed from the drink but, sure enough, every time I saw him he was leaving the market with two cartons of Coca Cola!

Any one could get a prescription for cocaine, morphine etc. at a pharmacy where we called all pharmacists "doctors" and they gave you what they thought you needed. Daddy never had to pay a doctor for a prescription, he went in to Dr. Stotler at the H&H Drug store owned by Marshall and Glenn Hamilton, on the corner of Monroe and Adams Streets, and told the pharmacist what he needed. Voila!

DADDY AND DOORKNOBS

There is something frightening about doorknobs - of all things. I have seen them moving with no one knocking first, and I still have nightmares about it.

I was sitting in "Mom's" chair, waiting for Mother and Daddy to come home from the late movie. It was in the late 40's, no television yet, just reading and listening, unconsciously to the rattles and bumping of the huge house at 741, full of darkened rooms, supposedly unoccupied - just listening, yet trying to read. I had every light in the downstairs on until I thought it might draw too much attention and went around and turned them all off, except my reading lamp. Of course there were unexplained shadows everywhere.

The huge front door at 741 had a 4" round, heavily encrusted old brass knob. It was turning – ever so slowly, but the encrusted flower design on the knob was creeping slowly counter-clockwise. I could not move. I prayed the deadlock was in place, but was afraid to move because the intruder might see me through the old shaded yellow-orange panes.

I heard the garage door go up miles away at the back of the basement. Would Daddy make it up stairs in time to thrust his body against the door and save me? This is where I usually wake up but the night it really happened I ran through the library and the phone room to the top of the dark basement stairs and into Daddy's arms. I was safe! My father could answer any question with a short concise answer. For this incident he was positive I had drifted off to sleep and had a nightmare. He must have started the thought of a continuing nightmare. I have looked but no dream book ever lists doorknobs.

The death of his mother in 1943 really seemed to change Daddy. He would go to Woodlawn all most daily and often I would go with him. Mother did not like him going up there so much. She said it was just not healthy for him to brood. I often wonder if he did brood a lot. He had had so much responsibility since Papa died in 1926. I had never seen a picture of Papa smiling. I wonder if they both had a tendency to depression, a tendency that so many seem to have. He would just sit on one of the granite benches we brought from Sonnencroft's front porch and I would play or plant or read a book. I tried not to notice his tears or interrupt his memories. Daddy had been his mother's bulwark, her hope, her link with the past as she had been his. He was so despondent - I could see him age. It scared me. All my friends' parents were so much younger than mine. I always worried about him being around for the next Christmas.

Daddy survived Mother by four years; he died in Elaine's arms on Admiral's Row, Pearl Harbor, Hawaii on February 11, 1971.

"Do You Remember"
By E. E. Meredith
The Times West Virginia
July 10, 1956

"Brooks Hutchinson has heard a lot about the flood of July 10, 1888 for he was born on that day. His mother Mary Lyda, told him he had come down the river on a raft and she had plucked him out of that deluge saving his life, which he firmly believed for several years.

Meredith continues, "The great flood of the West Fork and the Tygart Valley Rivers came flooding into the Monongahela River (River of Falling Banks) and struck Fairmont. It was the greatest flood ever heard of in this area. It cut off all communication with the outside world for several days. The damage was considerable, amounting to $400,000. The Hunsaker covered bridge at Watson which, on its way downstream, knocked the railroad bridge off its piers; and several mills located on the West Fork and the Monongahela rivers went downstream. One of the mills was the Jackson's Mill and when it struck the F.M.&P., the railroad bridge a short distance down the stream, it is told that the "flour flew". Oliver Jackson is quoted as saying that a log went down the river with a coon on it and the animal was apparently enjoying the ride for it evidenced no anxiety. Another tale was of a haystack going downstream with a rooster on top of it."

****

Daddy was quite competitive and played championship contract bridge and usually won. He loved the game and recalled his experience at the Hotel Annapolis in Washington, D.C., which he owned. A group of men asked him to be fourth one evening and he obliged. When they were ready to retire Daddy was told they had been playing for ten cents a point! Daddy had won, but he never played bridge for money again.

Elaine, Sylvia and I were all taught Ely Culbertson bidding system before Charles H. Goren developed his point system in 1949. I was needed as a

208

fourth as the older girls were usually gone. We played three-handed bridge. What I really hated was the post-mortems, when we had to dissect every hand; what we had done wrong and what not to forget the next time. I did learn though and, once you have learned and played bridge, all other card games pale in comparison.

In 1942, Daddy was an air raid warden for several blocks of Fairmont Avenue. Each house had to have black draperies covering the windows in the house where a light might be used. Mother had made them for us and we used them ever night. When the sirens were tested from Palatine Knob every evening we would close the curtains and Daddy would put on his hard hat and check the block for any lights showing. He carried a small flashlight, as all the streetlights would turn off automatically. Our family was the youngest on the blocks so many of the others had retired for the night anyway. The sirens went off around ten p.m. announcing the curfew and I was usually in bed, lying there in the dark listening to the radio. Today I think how frightening that would have been for Daddy, all alone every night walking the dark sidewalks with no defense but a hard hat, but Daddy was not afraid of anything!

Today, it seems, so many hate lawyers...until they need one!

I have been the daughter of a lawyer, the wife of a lawyer, and the mother of a lawyer. Each one of these men - honest, good, kind, gentle, men; attorneys who loved the Rule of Law.

I am so grateful to have known and loved such men in my life.

"Brooks Swearingen Hutchinson"
Editorial
The Fairmont Times
February 15, 1971

"The death of Brooks Swearingen Hutchinson last week in Hawaii claimed the life of one of Marion County's foremost Senior citizens even though he had not resided here since 1958.

'It is always appropriate to reflect over the numerous activities of the deceased, and Mr. Hutchinson certainly carried a long list of important credits by his name. He was active in all phases of life in this County.

"His record at West Virginia University alone served as an indication of the high esteem in which Brooks Hutchinson was held. In addition to being a member of WVU's two ranking Honoraries- Sphinx and Mountain- he was the president of the student body in his senior year and also found time to letter in football.

"After graduation from Yale University College of Law, he returned to Fairmont to begin his law practice and was to be a member of the Marion County Bar Association for more than a half a century.

"Mr. Hutchinson was also active as a coal executive and served as president of numerous coal companies, but found time to serve as chairman of the local chapter of the American Red Cross for more than twenty years as well as being twice a president of the Fairmont Field Club.

"Because of his absence from Fairmont in recent years and his age, Brooks Hutchinson probably was not too well known among the younger generation of the community. But his death at the age of 82 was mourned by his many friends throughout the area who remember well his many accomplishments here."

My Mother & Daddy in Hawaii
September 1966

BRETT & ANOTHER BROOKS

Brooks Edward Parker

Paul and I were so thrilled with our first grandson. He was announced to us before going to a West Virginia football game in October of 1984. Eddie and Jan came in with a large beautifully wrapped box. I opened it and inside was a large red, yellow and blue soft furry ball with a card saying, "You will need this next June." Then Eddie proudly announced, "We're having a baby", and I burst into tears - completely delighted, but totally surprised. Eddie laughed and said that I got an A+ for the best reaction yet!

We welcomed Brooks Edward on June 9, 1985. He was named for his great grandfather (Brooks Hutchinson) and for his father and grandfather, Paul (Edward) Parker. Eddie had known and loved them all. I am sorry the grandfathers never knew Brooks or Brett Russell, born August 30, 1988. Brett was named for Jan's maternal grandfather, Russell Nichols. Russ Nichols was elected as Sheriff of Marion County and also as a Commissioner of the County Court. In 1940 he was appointed as the United States Marshal for the Northern District of West Virginia.

These two grandsons are now all grown up and as they have grown it has been fun to see the different personalities develop. Although Brooks was named for my father, Brett is the one who reminds me of him and of Eddie. Excelling in all sports, he quietly accepted many honors as a twelve-letter man, having played soccer, tennis and swim team, earning 3 letters each year for four years. Academically he excelled in math just as Daddy and Eddie had. Eddie took calculus in college as an elective to relax.

Brett majored in business at Belmont University in Nashville, Tennessee, where he received a soccer scholarship to play four years in the Division I, NCAA soccer program. After interning with the treasury department at Nissan at their national headquarters in Nashville TN, he was asked to join them after graduating, magna cum laude, from Belmont University in 2011.

Much like his granddaddy, Paul, Brooks is extremely extroverted, and, as Eddie says, knows everyone. When you pick him up at Pittsburgh International Airport, he has to greet many friends waiting to board the plane he just debarked. In Miller Junior High School he decided to participate in cross-country running - not because he enjoyed running - but because he enjoyed the spirited conversations with the team. Brooks treated all sports like this, just as fun. He and Brett played 4 years of tennis at Fairmont Senior High School and swam 4 years each on 8 years of state championship teams at FSHS. They both still play tennis and golf every chance they get. In his senior year of FSHS, Brooks was appointed on the Marion County United Way Executive Board as their first youth member.

He had composed their theme song when his father was chairman of the board when Brooks was five years old.

Brooks was a child prodigy. A virtuoso - playing the huge pipe organ at Saint Peter's Roman Catholic Church, where he took private lessons from Robert Ellis, an excellent teacher of piano and organ. Eddie built him a special bench that was low enough for him to reach the pedals, but still see the keyboard. His father stood beside him and learned when to pull the stops and turn the pages, as Brooks' little arms could not reach them. Brooks composed his first mass at the age of eight and played it at the 6 o'clock evening mass on New Year's Eve 1993. His Aunt Sylvia ("YaYa") had to rent a 4-wheel drive jeep to get Paul and me to the debut after a terrific snow and ice storm that day.

I had played by ear all my life. I can still play most any melody you hum to me, but I cannot read music. I would prop Brooks up on the seat next to me and play my grandmother's parlor grand and sing, "Can't help Lovin' that "Brooks" (Man) of Mine" from the Broadway musical "Showboat" by Jerome Kern and Oscar Hammerstein. Brooks would listen intently and watch the keyboard. When I finished, his little hand would take my hand and stroke it as if could feel the music emanating from my palm. When he was four he called me on the phone and asked how to play "His song". I gave him the letters, GGGC-CCGGG. The next time he came to visit he sat down and played the whole song with all the embellishment he loves to add. It is wonderful to watch and hear him play all the music I could never read. No one can play Beethoven's "Ode to Joy" or Bach's, "Jesu, Joy of Man's Desiring" like my Brooks. From his playpen he would say "Bach-Bach" I would play Bach's CD and he would conduct in perfect tempo.

When Sylvia and I came into his church here in Fairmont on Easter morning, I had not seen Brooks yet. When he saw us come in, he started to play "Jesus" and I knew he was greeting me with a hug, as only he can do!

Brooks Edward Parker

Eddie & Brett Parker

Brett Russell Parker

CHAPTER ELEVEN

SUMMERS IN FAIRMONT

Sylvia, Nannie, Diane

Sylvia and Diane

Diane in 1935

Sylvia and Diane, 1943

Diane in 1946

SUMMERS IN FAIRMONT

Summers at 741 were delightful. Fairmont Avenue has twelve blocks; each one is one-tenth of a mile, making it one mile from the South Side Bridge that runs from downtown Adams Street, over Coal Run Hollow where the General "Grumble " Jones' Civil War raid took place on April 29, 1863, to 12th street. The trees on Fairmont Avenue grew from both sides of the street, their crowns growing together to create a lush wonderland - a canopy of shade over the avenue, paved with the old yellow Hammond bricks made right here in Fairmont. The trees on one block would be maple; the next block might be poplar. The only ones still standing on one side of the avenue are in front of Highgate and they are the oaks between Eighth and Ninth streets. My block had poplar trees but the poplars are all gone. One block were sycamores, the only ones left standing today are at 12th street. These magnificent trees lined both sides of the broad avenue with the old city lines street cars going right down the middle.

In 2006, as a member of Green Hills Garden Club, I coerced Allegheny Power to replace some of the trees they had cut down for the placement of power poles all along Fairmont Avenue. I gave them the choice of putting all the power poles in the alleys where they belonged in the first place or planting trees. They chose the latter. There were only nine green areas left between the businesses that now line the grand old avenue, so I chose four species of 26 trees that were allowed to be planted on a state highway and most of them are thriving today, adding a little more ambiance to the town's major artery to the business area.

In the summers' scares of polio in the thirties and forties, they would close the movie theaters, the municipal pool, and the East West Stadium both built by the Works Progress Administration in 1937. The WPA brought all the cut stones by wheelbarrow from the George Ice's Quarry down on the (West Fork) River Road. Emily Ellen Ice Cather, his granddaughter, said he had two quarries, one on the river and the other at the top of View Avenue high above Locust Avenue. They have long ago been closed, but what splendid recreational facilities we have had for 75 years. Stonemasonry is quite a skill. The mason cuts, prepares and builds with stone, often in intricate, ornate designs, always leaving a "mason's mark" at the end of his structure. I know my maternal great grandfather, Jacob Watkins, built the wall still standing around the grounds of Sonnencroft, but I have never found his mark.

When we got too bored or tired of reading, Sylvia and I would hop on the streetcar since children rode free, to "go around the loop ". This route took us through town to Locust Avenue, which ran parallel to Fairmont Avenue and all the way out to Edgemont and back to Fairmont Avenue at Twelfth Street and finally back to Eighth and home. This trip took about an hour. Sylvia and I would pretend we were the little British Princesses. She had to be Elizabeth as they were about the same age; and I was Margaret Rose, the little sister. I always had to ride backwards and she would sit forward in front of me in our trolley-coach. We waved and nodded to our subjects all around the loop. Mr. Kraley, the car's conductor, would often stop over on Locust Avenue in front of a huge pond and let us go over to watch the fish for a few minutes.

Broad sidewalks ran in front of the houses, most set far back off the avenue. Our house had a huge six-foot high privet hedge all around it ending at the driveway entrance on Eighth Street. Daddy would have to trim that hedge about twice a summer dressed in old dress pants, a shirt and tie. He would not change for dinner, but would put on the old suit jacket that went with the pants. Mother would just shake her head. A gentleman of the old school, he felt a refined, courtly male did not sit down to eat with ladies, unless fully dressed! It took him a week to do all this trimming, as everyone who drove by had to stop at the curb and talk for a while. He put stakes in the ground with strings stretching between the posts to make sure the massive privet greenery was in an even line. He did this with the old long hand clippers; there were no gas-powered machines. No wonder his arms were so powerful.

In 1944, Sylvia was sixteen and allowed to get a job. She worked summers and Saturdays at Jones' Department Store for thirty cents an hour and was thrilled to get it. She got a percentage off the clothes she bought and seemed to enjoy Saturdays as she could work 12 hours. She still remembers that $3.60. I always thought her business acumen came from the old child's poem,

> *"Monday's child is fair of face*
> *Tuesday's child is full of grace,*
> *Wednesday's child is full of woe,*
> *Thursday's child has far to go,*
> *Friday's child is loving and giving,*
> *Saturday's child works hard for a living' (Sylvia Jane's day of birth)*
> *Sunday's child, the best day, is blithe and bonny and good and gay."*

Of course, I was born on a Friday.

Sylvia graduated from FSHS in 1945 and left to join Elaine in New York, leaving the "baby", the only child. I think Mother and Daddy were tired of parenting, as they were so much older than my friends' parents were. When I was attending Fairmont Junior High School in 1945, Mother had a frightening heart attack at the age of 48 and was not as active as she had been. Daddy worked in Clarksburg at the Federal Courthouse as W.V. Director of the Office of Price Administration. I had to walk a round trip - 12 blocks - home from school each day at noon to take Mother a lunch tray upstairs. Dr. Harold Jones said no steps and rest for at least 6 weeks. Each evening I would put dinner on at five and Daddy would get home around 5:15 and finish the preparations. I was scared to light the broiler unit of our old stove as it used to singe Sylvia's eyelashes when she lit it.

Worried to death, Elaine had come home for a few days after Mother's heart attack. She brought her a little yellow kitten on the B&O National Limited, all the way from New York City. Mother called her new companion, "Topaz" and she was our favorite for several years, presenting us with several litters of kittens, until "Addie", a neighbor who hated animals, killed her with some wicked poison. She poisoned all of our animals including a beagle, "GI Joe", who joined us for a short time until he was fed one of Addie's lethal doses and his back legs became paralyzed. Old Doctor Cramwell came to the house and put him to sleep.

Topaz just disappeared one day, and I searched everywhere for her. All the neighbors, except Addie, were on the lookout for her. Daddy would take a walk after dinner each night and the priest at St Joseph's Villa (Highgate), next door, stopped him one evening and said, "Brooks, I found Topaz inside the gates and I buried her under the Virgin Mary's statue near the fishpond." I still think of Topaz when I go past that pond on Ninth Street.

In the summer of 1945, Daddy and Mother were so glad that Uncle Frank Haymond, who married Susan Watson Arnette, (Daddy's first cousin-Aunt Lilly Jay's daughter) was appointed to the West Virginia Supreme Court. He replaced Chief Justice Herschel Hampton Rose who had died suddenly. Judge Rose had spoken to the American Legion Boys' State group the summer before in 1944, telling how good the practice of law had been to him and a great basis for any other profession. The Judge had encouraged my future husband, to run for the Supreme Court at Boys' State, which Paul had done and was elected as Chief Justice- the main reason Paul chose the law for his profession. Judge Rose was a well known and loved Fairmont son, and father of a highly respected attorney, Herschel Hampton Rose, Jr. who married C.E. and Elsie Smith's daughter, Elizabeth (Betty) His grandchildren are Ann, Attorneys Lisa Rose Lathrop and H.H. "Ned" Rose III. There is also a great grandson, H.H. Rose IV.

J. Harper Meredith was appointed as Circuit Court Judge to take Uncle Frank Haymond's place when he was elected to the WV Supreme Court of Appeals. Not until thirty-five years later, when he was 80 years old, was Meredith defeated by a newcomer in the primaries. The great judge died shortly after this defeat. I always felt his death was hastened by "good friends" who begged him to run one last time, and then caused his defeat.

The summer of 1946, during a polio scare, when we were more or less isolated from others, most of us stayed home and read. I kept track of the 35 books I read while sunning in a bathing suit trying to keep my tan. I would take an old quilt out and lie under the hawthorn tree in the side yard. I had required book reports for the entire school season. I would rummage through the attic shelves of old books and take them out to sunbathe. I loved "The Sheik", (E.M. Hull edition copyrighted in 1922) which had been a movie with Rudolph Valentino, James Fennimore Cooper's "The Last of the Mohicans", "The Feast" by Margaret Kennedy, and "The Touch of Nutmeg" by John Collier. I loved the Bronte's books and F. Scott Fitzgerald books. I remember Jack Knowles declaring that Fitzgerald's "The Great Gatsby" was the perfect short story, and how difficult short stories were to write.

My favorites were Margaret Mitchell's 1937 Pulitzer Prize winning, "Gone with the Wind" and Bram Stoker's gothic, "Dracula", the scariest book I have ever read. At night I would read in bed to fall asleep, but during "Dracula", I was afraid to turn off the bed lamp and finally fell asleep with the light shining in my face. I have read "Gone with the Wind" at least four times in my life and have had a different heroine each time. In high school it was Scarlett, when I was pregnant it was Melanie, when I was in my 30's it was back to Scarlett and recently it is back to Melanie again - an age telling sequence of choice.

The older I grew, the fewer novels I read. Self-help and medical books have finally won out as a matter of self-preservation for all the family.

Back to the spring of 1947 - I was asked to join the MYOBI Club.

MYOBI CAMP

Graduating from Fairmont Junior High and ninth grade began the summer of 1947. The disappointment of not being chosen Prom Queen of Fairmont Junior High School seems to pale by my invitation to join the MYOBI Club from the most beautiful, smart and exceptional group of Fairmont Senior High School girls. You had to be really popular to be invited to either the Skull Club or the Myobi Club and most of my friends chose Myobi if invited, as did I. MYOBI meant, "Make Your Owl Be Immortal ", signifying scholarship and wisdom.

Let me explain … The Skull Club and the Kibo Club for boys began in 1925. The Skull Club was a select group of 25, never any more, girls, chosen by their peers and their motto was, FHS meaning: Friendship, Health and Scholarship. Miss Ethel Hoult was the school advisor of the club and the first president was Mary Ellen Staggers.

The KIBO Club was founded in the same year of 1925 and was praised in the yearbook for, "bringing the school alive", by sponsoring a dance at the Fairmont Theatre Dance Hall. They held meetings every night and their purpose was to boost the school spirit at Fairmont High School by attending all the activities and cheering on the teams. Their logo was an Outhouse and their motto was "May the hinges of our friendship never rust". They became a non-sponsored social fraternity in the thirties, still sponsoring dances such as the "Bee-Bear Tear" each Armistice Day evening after the great rivalry of the East side Bees football matches against the West side Fairmont Senior Polar Bears.

The MYOBI Club was not founded until 1928 and was composed of a group of ten Junior and Senior girls who had made up the Campfire organization in the school, and their aim was to promote courtesy, good sportsmanship and friendliness in the community. Their advisor was Miss Carrie H. Boggs, the home economics teacher, and their first president was Marguerite Morris. Over the years, more girls were selected and it began to outshine the Skull Club that took in so few members. The Myobi Club finally became the outstanding group to join and became a non-school sponsored social sorority in the early forties, as did the Skull and Kibo clubs. The groups, by choice, became separate entities from the high school and had no sponsorship by the board of education or the school.

A group of boys started the Question Cl-?-ub in the late thirties competing with the Hi-Y Club established by the YMCA: Both of these groups had died out during WWII and when I went to FSHS in 1947 they no longer existed. I thank my good friend Warren Wysner, who had served as president of the popular group, for sending me pictures from his yearbook.

Each year the Myobi and Kibo Clubs rented homes at Benton's Ferry on the Tygart Valley River. My first year as a newly invited pledge was the most exciting. I was scared, but elated to be so accepted and wanted by this exceptional group of older girls. The graduated senior officers were our chaperones during the day, and Mrs. Gladwell, Anne's mother, came in the evening and spent the night.

The pledges had to cook, clean and fetch for the members while having fun ourselves. Friday night would be Hell Night, the final full day of camp. The pledges were to perform in a show for both the members and their guests, the Kibos, in my mind, the handsomest and most popular boys in the world!

I was to sing, "Put the Blame on Mame, Boys", which Rita Hayworth had made famous in the movie GILDA. I was scared to death, but had been in shows in the past so was fully prepared to be as enticing as a five foot, 15 year old could be.

On that hot Friday afternoon, a large group was sun bathing on the bank in the swimming area, but the sunrays were making it tempting to cool off in the shimmering, but dirty river and several of us were wading just knee deep. I had promised my mother I would not go near the water, as I had not had the necessary typhoid shot, but I had no intention of putting my head under water, getting my hair wet, or swallowing the dirty water. I stepped deeper into the coolness, "Oh how good the water felt!"

Before I knew it, I was too far from shore, getting the tips of my long hair wet, which would make it frizzy that night. Heading back, I looked up the high bank to the road and two uninvited boys from school -not Kibos- were throwing bottles from way up on the road into the river. I thought, "Are they throwing at me? Am I their target? No, they are friends, but what are they doing!" Right at that moment I saw a bottle wavering and hurtling down right above my face. I could see the HD stamp - for Home Dairy - on the bottom of the empty milk bottle. "What do I do now? I know, I will go under and pretend they hit me and stay under to scare them." I quickly turned, did a surface dive, feeling nothing but a hard tap on the back.

"There, that will scare them! How calm and serene it is down here, I don't even have to tread water." I could feel squishy mud, which felt like a little waterbed beneath my feet, and tall weeds quivering and tickling my calves, but I had no sense of gasping or struggling for breath, just profound silence and peace.

Suddenly a strong arm was around my waist drawing me up- up- upwards, and pulling me to shore. The strong arm belonged to Bob Cunningham, newly graduated football hero, and now, my lifesaver. Everyone was yelling, "Get this, get that", and a quilt was wrapped around me. No artificial respiration tactics… only a sense of compelling immediacy. I was carried to the car still wrapped, cocoon like, in the quilt, and placed carefully on the back seat and into Marva Jean Shaw's arms. I learned later the Kibos were yelling at the two boys to stop throwing the bottles and someone had asked, "Where is Diane?" Bob saw the blood floating on top of the water and dived in to rescue me.

My idol, Joan Spencer was driving and I felt safe, secure and warm. Marva Jean was in back holding my head. We were on the way to Mother's doctor, Harold Jones, in the heart of downtown Fairmont. His office was on the second floor of the Home Savings Bank Building. Joanie pulled half way in to a parking space and the two helped me out of the back seat in the dripping wet quilt, now soaked in blood, up to his office. I could hear drivers asking if we needed help, but the girls were on a quest.

A shocked Dr. Jones came running into the waiting room, exclaiming, "I am not a surgeon; get her to Bill Welton's office, now!" Off we go again in Friday's traffic, where police were holding forth directing the multitude of cars unable to get around our un-parked one. There were no rescue squads, ambulances or cell phones in 1947, just the fire department.

Dr. Welton spent two hours picking the shards of glass from the right side of my numbed back and shoulder where the bottle had exploded on impact. Joan and Marva Jean never left my side except when Marva Jean nearly passed out from watching. Joanie's father was a doctor and she seemed to be a little less sensitive.

All taped up and free of pain, I insisted on going back to the camp. I had plenty of time to tell Mother about the incident, and I had a performance that night. The show must go on!

In a new pair of corduroy shorts in a beautiful shade of coral and a new ruffled, off the shoulder, peasant blouse, I did a fair facsimile of Gilda and received lots of applause and bravos! My champion, Bob Cunningham, grabbed me down onto his lap, where I sat for the rest of the evening, absolutely thrilled with all the attention.

About 11 o'clock there was a commotion at the front door and in shot my sister Sylvia, crying, stamping her foot, and shouting, "WHERE IS MY SISTER?" How totally humiliating!

Mrs. Gladwell, Joanie and I took her into a bedroom and Mrs. Gladwell told her what had happened assuring her I was fine. Sylvia asked, "How many stitches did you have?" I calmly answered," Forty-five".

"FORTY-FIVE!"- More tears, more scolding. Evidently, Dr. Jones had called Mother about ten o'clock to inquire about me. He had told Mother about sending me to Welton's office –which, of course, was all news to the family.

Mortified, I was hurriedly putting my things in a bag to leave, as I was well aware that not only Sylvia was furious, but also that Daddy was outside, waiting to take me home, now!

When we left the camp, the party was over. All had dispersed.

What a night to remember! The drowning was so peaceful and I was having such a heavenly time on Hell Night!

BULLYING

"School was an unending spell of worries that did not seem petty and of toil uncheered by fruition; a time of discomfort, restriction and purposeless monotony." Winston Churchill

At the age of 15, these were my sentiments exactly.

My sophomore year, I met the best friend I had in high school, "Moe" (Richard). He was 19 years old, home on leave for his mother's funeral and was about to be shipped from Camp Pendleton to Japan with the U.S. Army Occupied Forces. He was in the eighth Cavalry and I fell head over heart for this blond, handsome young soldier. The war was just over and I was 15, an age when a young girl is always in love and between smiles and tears. As my friends were following me home from Sixth Street Pharmacy to the porch that late August evening, Moe came from behind, put his arm around me and started the march cadence "Hut-two-three-four-circle to the right with a slight hesitation-do it!" some silly march he had learned in basic training, but it impressed me. We only saw each other twice during this leave and off he went! He had asked his friends, "Jiggs", "Sax", "Buck", "Smitty", his class of 1946 Kibos to take care of me while he was abroad and they did just that. I never lacked for a date to a ball game, a movie, or a dance.

It was finally May and, having completed his stint in the US Army and over three hundred letters later, he was due home. He came straight to the high school and picked me up in the back drive in a beautiful brand new cream-colored Chevrolet. How thrilled I was to throw my arms around the returning hero once again. I did not know then how important it was to have an older benefactor who would defend me against the schoolyard bullies.

At the weekly Myobi meeting, jealousy prevailed; I was told I had to take Hell night over again this year, because Daddy had rescued me from the all-nighter in my pledge year. I was dumfounded, shocked, hurt, and embarrassed. Never would I go through that again, particularly, not as a junior with a freshman class of new recruits. Mother and Daddy had sworn, "No MYOBI Camp ever again!" I said, "Absolutely not!" A vote of the group was taken and I lost. I resigned.

High school life was miserable from then on. Several of those who were new seniors and juniors had voted for me in that vote, but not enough. The scary ones, the great big unattractive ones, mostly senior girls were really gang like in targeting me as easy prey. I was scared to walk to school; here again a Kibo from Chamberlain Avenue would pick me up on Eighth Street and another would join us on Benoni Avenue and Donnie and Ron would stay with me until I was safely inside the school. Teen-age girls are the worst. They are either your best friend or they hate you. The taunting and threats were whispered in passing throughout the hallways and I tried to ignore them all. One of the girls tried to trip me on the marble stairs. I never told Mother about this, as she would have tried to protect me by calling their mothers or worse yet, going to the school to see the principal, who would have done nothing, insisting it was just childish pranks.

Bullying has worsened in the schools today. Nothing has been able to stop it. The more the school or government tries to prevent it; teachers report more bullying after intervention than before. Assault and battery is a crime, civility must be restored, and communities must act. Because of the Myobi episode, I was fortunately sent to New York the next two summers; which I thoroughly enjoyed, creating vivid, happy, lifetime memories to this day.

HARASSMENT

As if bullying was not enough, students today, as yesterday, must, at times, undergo teacher harassment.

To enter college I had to have two years of physical education. I did not mind the exercises, the required cold showers, the bloomers we had to wear, the basketball games we had to play, but I was a single sport buff, and my sport was swimming. My sisters and I taught classes in swimming and diving each summer. I won all the girl's races at the Municipal Pool, even the 18's when I was 14; and performed synchronized swimming, which was totally new in the Fairmont area. I was an excellent diver, having been taught by Mrs. Ruth Leek, a championship diver. I excelled at back jack knifes off the ten-foot springboard. But- I hated the rings in gym class I had to fight each year.

Do you remember those horrible colored rings hanging far above our heads on ropes that we had to grasp and swing across the length of that hard floor like Tarzan and Jane? Ridiculous! Show me one reason that particular torture was necessary to matriculate into any college in the United States. My hands began sweating the minute I looked up and continued throughout the exercise, which I never completely finished, falling to the floor well before the assignment was completed. It never mattered much, Mrs. T., the stunning blond, tanned, statuesque, gym teacher was secluded behind her opaque glassed-in office, where you could often catch her shadow taking a swig from a bottle kept in her desk.

At the end of my junior year when grades came out I received a B-minus in Gym but only nine credits. At that time, ten credits were needed to apply for college entrance.

I was crestfallen; Mother was livid.

Daddy made the journey to Principal William E. Buckey's office, the principal who had opened the new Senior High School in 1929 and had been there when Elaine and Sylvia attended. That had been before his son was killed in World War II-enough to change any man. Mr. Buckey had lost much interest or pleasure in youth, or in life.

When Daddy related the complication he said, "Well, Brooks, we'll just ask Mrs. T. to explain herself". When arriving at the scene, she proceeded to explain how she felt the Hutchinson family had always gotten everything

231

they ever wanted and she was not going to renege on the little bit of power bestowed upon her to help them out in any way. Mr. Buckey said, "I am sorry Brooks, as she has tenure, I am powerless to change her mind."

Daddy went straight to the Marion County Board of Education and the Superintendent of Secondary Schools, Joe Straight, who assured Daddy I would have no trouble entering college.

I have no idea how much longer Mrs. T. lasted at FSHS, but I know when Eddie was a teen ager and interested in golf, Mrs. T. was one of the "mean, petty old women golfers" who would not let him play through their foursome.

I had no counselors at school, but today's children do. I am writing this to tell those young people, do not let the bullies win. Go to your counselors, go to your mother, go to your father, go to your siblings, go to your grandparents. Let the world know.

CHAPTER TWELVE

SUMMERS IN THE CITY
1948

Sylvia on right; head of the NBC Guidettes, 1948

Cadet Neil Kindig, West Point, 1949

Diane, 1949

"Moe" and Diane, May, 1950

Diane, 1946

Eleanor Labenthall and Sylvia were close friends and worked together as Guidettes at NBC at 30 Rockefeller Center where I spent most of my days when visiting my sisters in New York City. I would go to all the radio shows, free, of course. One day the three of us got off the elevator and saw Johnny Windsor and Danny Samples from Fairmont.

I said, "Hi, John." "Hi, Danny," and proceeded on with the girls.

Astonished, Sylvia asked, "Who were those boys? Did you know them?"

I explained that I went to school with them; then, quickly realizing how strange to see them in New York, we turned around and John and Danny were staring at us - mouths wide open. I went back and talked while the others waited.

Another time in the elevator a strange looking man got on with a Clark Bar. I said that it was one of my favorites. He asked, "Want a bite?" I replied, "Oh, no thank you, but it was nice of you to offer". He quickly broke off half and gave it to me and got off the elevator at the next floor. The other riders all said, "Do you know who that was?" It was Danny Kaye, the lovely comedian. I thought he looked nothing like Walter Mitty, but it was nice of him to share his candy bar.

I would watch the "Ole' Redhead Sports Interview" with "Red" Barber. One-day Red interviewed the movie "bad-man", George Raft, who had grown up on the streets of New York and who had a lifetime friendship with Owen "Owney" Madden, Benjamin "Bugsy" Siegel, and Siegel's old friend Meyer Lansky. Red, a famous baseball announcer who started out with the Cincinnati Reds, was interviewing Raft about the 1919 "Black Sox Scandal". Eight players from the Chicago White Sox (nicknamed the Black Sox) were accused of throwing the series that year to the Cincinnati Reds. All I could think about was how stunning George Raft was in person.

When I got bored, the guides would put me in Arturo Toscanini's Studio. "The great conductor was lured to NBC in 1937 by David Sarnoff, President of RCA, to lead the National Broadcasting Company's Orchestra. Toscanini had been such a draw that over thirty thousand people had requested tickets to his first broadcast." The studio was immense and on the large stage was a beautiful Steinway (eight foot) concert grand piano. I learned to play by ear on our own Steinway parlor grand (six foot) from Sonnencroft, so I would play my repertoire. My best one was my rendition of Tchaikovsky's Piano in B-Flat Minor that sounded like the popular "Tonight We Love". The Guidettes would bring the tours through and tell visitors that I was

Toscanini's granddaughter, which fascinated the visitors. I had a grand time impressing everyone, as long as it was just brief episodes.

All of the Guidettes were so much fun, and so beautiful; many of them were looking for Broadway auditions or just waiting to be discovered. One of Sylvia's first friends at NBC was Eva Marie Saint, an unheard of little junior student from Bowling Green University. She and Sylvia trained to be Guidettes together in the summer of 1945. Eva Marie returned to Bowling Green University in September and Sylvia entered New York University as a freshman.

Sylvia said, "After Eva Marie graduated she came back to New York and used the Guidettes locker room to come in and rest from her foot pounding day while trying to get a job on Broadway. She did get a part as understudy for the nurse in Leland Hayward's Broadway production of "Mr. Roberts", but the nurse always showed up. She would tell us about handsome Henry Fonda, whose wife attended every rehearsal and every performance."

"After one matinee performance, Millie and I went backstage to see her and it was the day she had heard she would play opposite Marlon Brando in 'On the Waterfront". Brando had sent her a huge bouquet of red roses. She was so thrilled. She was a darling girl and always herself. We lost touch after that, but know that she married before I did and had a boy and a girl."

[Note; "On the Waterfront" won eight Oscars in 1954, Brando won Best Actor and Saint won Best Supporting Actress. Today Sylvia and Eva Marie are both in their mid eighties and Eva Marie has been married for 60 years. She says in interviews, "Her most enduring co-stars have always been her family and her work."]

Some days, I would go to the Metropolitan Museum of Art where the great goldsmith Cellini's salt cup always greeted me. I loved to check out the great masters' art exhibits. A favorite was Sergeant's Madam X. I developed a love of El Greco, Goya, O'Keeffe and particularly Rembrandt. The light that emanates from his masterpieces has never been captured by any other artist. Upon leaving, I always checked the unwrapped mummy lying down in his crypt - never changing, but always fascinating to me.

I loved going up to the top of the Empire State Building, 1,472 feet tall according to my guidebook, and built in 1931, the year before I was born. From the observatory floor, I could see a distance of 80 miles. Today I love to watch the films, "An Affair to Remember" and "Sleepless in Seattle" – two of my favorite old movies, where the observatory roof is such an important feature. I would look over the other tall buildings and straight down, dizzy from the height and feeling my palms get clammy, as they do while I write this. I could see all the dots of people scurrying on the streets in dead silence, so high you are unable to hear a horn honk.

Often, going up or down 102 stories in the elevator, the visitors would complain of their ears hurting and I would calmly advise them to yawn as we did in the high elevations in West Virginia. The elevator operators loved that and started telling all their passengers my suggestion. The operators would tell us about one foggy morning in July of 1945, a U.S. Army Lt. Col. William Smith was trying to reach Newark airport to pick up his commanding officer, and because of the dense fog, lowered his B25 Bomber down a little finding he was in the middle of New York City skyscrapers. At 9:29 am he crashed the bomber into the 74th floor of the building killing eleven office workers, three crewmembers and injuring 26 others.

I would walk up one side of 5th Avenue to FAO Schwartz and cross over to the gorgeous century old, beaux arts Plaza Hotel, stopping to be entertained by the seals in Central Park and walk down the other side of 5th Avenue. Then meet Sylvia after work. One night, Ken Derby (her future husband) and Sylvia took me to Mama Leone's the famous Pizza Parlor, which claimed the first pizza in America. Mama Leone's opened in 1907 at 239 West 48th Street New York City. The un-pretentious pizzeria was only 20x40 feet and filled with stacks of pizza ovens, which they served as a free appetizer to all the customers. I usually filled up on the scrumptious pizza that could be ordered separately, but we usually got spaghetti as an entrée. The restaurant walls were filled with pictures of Broadway's greats – Lillian Russell, Ziegfeld, Anna Held, Billie Burke, Enrico Caruso, who had taken over the Metropolitan Opera House, and George M. Cohan of Yankee Doodle fame. Hundreds of stars who were constant après show diners.

Some evenings, Elaine, and I would go to see a Broadway show. My favorite was the revision of the first "musical", "Show Boat". We usually could afford only "peanut heaven" tickets, but Elaine, wanting me to see Helen Hayes "up close" in "Happy Birthday", spent a fortune for two seats on the aisle in the fourth or fifth row.

I was so disappointed, but I never told Elaine. The famous actress was too real and too old; I could see every wrinkle. There was no fantasy!

What a wonderful summer - I did not think about MYOBI once.

SECOND SUMMER IN THE CITY: 1949

I went to New York two years, 1948 and 1949. In 1949 Sylvia's friend, Eleanor Labenthall enticed her little brother Jimmy to show me his New York. Jimmy was maybe three years older than I was. He picked me up at Rockefeller Center in a black limousine, which was their family car. He drove all around his city including the clandestine Chinatown, one of the oldest ethnic Chinese enclaves outside of Asia. Jimmy pointed out the opium dens where long benches were used by the walk- in users to smoke and sleep. Next, to the Bowery, known for its flophouses, brothels, and clip joints. I had an excellent private tour and neither of us was apprehensive. Then we went on to a cocktail party at a friend's penthouse apartment. The guests were fascinated with a very young 16 year old from West Virginia and asked the usual questions,

"Have you ever been down in a coal mine?"

"No, no, bad luck to have women in a mine."

"I have a friend in Richmond". They had forgotten about West-by God-Virginia.

And they all loved my southern drawl, which seemed to get more pronounced as the event wore on. It was a wonderful evening, one I have always remembered.

I have seen James Labenthall on television financial shows. He is still a handsome man and, I know, still a gentleman. I am so glad I once knew him.

Sylvia's communication professor from New York University asked Sylvia to be a blind date for his nephew who was a Plebe (first year cadet) at West Point's Camp Buckner's summer camp on the Hudson River. Sylvia had a date in the city with Ken, so she had me take her place. Now, when I think about it, I was only 16 ½ years old going into my senior year in high school and my big sister sent me on a train to a freshman camp for soldiers! I was a little nervous, knowing very well that Mother and Daddy would have a fit.

I was met at the train by a camp bus along with several other girls who were beautifully dressed. We were driven to the campus and assigned dormitory rooms. I drew the top bunk in a room with two Smith College roommates. I introduced myself and they briefly looked at me, nodded, and then continued their unending chatter.

We were asked to change for dinner and a dance afterwards. I was going to wear a darling aqua summer dress with a yellow appliquéd trim around a boat neckline and puffy sleeves. The dress had a zipper all the way up the back which was impossible to zip. I hated to interrupt my chatty roommates, but finally got their attention and, without a break or a breath, one of them zipped me into the dress.

I slipped into my new Capezios, which Sylvia had bought me. The latest teen- age rage, handmade ballet slippers by Capezios - a company in N.Y. who made the first professional ballet shoes. I felt I had just left Bergdorf - Goodman!

Back to the bus and off to meet the boys. I was to meet a Neil Kindig who was waiting for his blind date since Sylvia was indisposed. He was a darling young man about 18 who was delighted to see a girl again!

We went through the receiving line made up of officers and their wives, then on to the dance floor. I had never seen a stag line as long as that one- before or since. Young men in dull grey uniforms, but brightened with vertical rows of shiny pewter buttons and black braid, white gloves and shiny black shoes; each one of them eager to hold a girl in their arms after being sequestered with plebes for several weeks.

I remember dancing, no longer than two minutes with each cadet, when it would be fair for another to cut in and ask the same questions, "How old are you?" I had been told by my sister to answer "17" as that was the desired age for the attending females and almost the truth. Guess they thought I was older.

"Where are you from?"

"West-by-God-Virginia."

"Ah, I should have known from the accent."

Another would say,

"I thought I saw some coal dust on 'that pretty face."

"Let's hear that southern drawl some more!"

I did not suggest to them, it was a "West Virginia twang".

What fun! What a dream of every 16 or 17 year-old girl! The boys took us back to the buses at midnight and I retired back to the "chat room" *"To sleep, perchance to dream."*

The next morning, breakfast with the boys before a row on the lake, pictures snapped, and time to go back to the train and the city. It was like a dream - too short - too quick to remember much - but oh, the glory of being a girl!

Sylvia reported years later, "You must have been a big hit!

I got an A+ in Communications!"

The three Hutchinson sisters; Elaine, 23; Sylvia, 18 and Diane, 13
Ray Stoker, photographer

IMAGES OF MY SISTERS

While writing this story, I realized my sisters and I spent very little time together as sisters. Elaine left home for New York in 1942, when I was just nine years old. Sylvia left right after her graduation from FSHS in 1945. I was in the sixth grade. They visited so seldom; I hardly knew them as a young teenager. I think Mother planned my trips to visit them so the three sisters might have a chance to bond as adults. I learned to worship Elaine all over again; Elaine, who had been gone the longest, had been my idol as a small child. After I returned home from that trip in 1949, we three never lived together again. Sylvia married in May of 1951 and Elaine came home to live; but I was in college at Fairmont State University and busy preparing for marriage, as was Elaine.

ELAINE

Elaine worked at Columbia Broadcasting System and then at United Air Lines as a reservationist and stayed in New York for ten years, always seeking that stardom that she had at FSC. She returned to Fairmont in the summer of 1951 and worked for J. Patrick Beacom as program director at "WVVW- 1490 on your radio dial". She joined the Junior League of Fairmont Incorporated and was a soloist as Eva Tanguay, in The Torrid Twenties Revue, produced by Cargill Productions for the League. She also starred in "The Night of January Sixteenth", produced by the Junior League - a murder trial which took place in the Marion County Court House, using townspeople in different legal roles, including a jury from the audience - a different one for each performance.

C.E. Ned Smith, the Editor of the Fairmont Times, who was cast as the judge, wrote the following review,

"Good Morning! May 15, 1951

"We are more than a silent admirer of Elaine Hutchinson, the charming daughter of Ray and Brooks Hutchinson because we think she has more talent than a whole bushel basketful of talented girls. Last January, when we played the part of the Judge in the Junior League production of 'The Night of January Sixteenth" at the Marion County Court House, Elaine was the villainous leading lady and we had the worst time in the world keeping our mind on our business while watching her portray her part. In brief Miss

Hutchinson was an artistic achievement in local theatricals and one of the most talented persons within the sound of my voice."

****

In 1952, while Paul and I were courting, Elaine reunited with an old child hood friend and close neighbor, Lt. JG George Pullen Peed. George was the son of Roberta Fleming Peed, (daughter of Judge Robert Flavius Fleming) and Col. George P. Peed, who had served as General John Pershing's physician during WW I. The Colonel earned many medals including the French Legion of Honor and the Croix de Guerre.

George was in New London, Connecticut at Submarine School when his Aunt Mamie Fleming died and he came home to Fairmont Avenue for her funeral where we all re-met. He and Elaine were the same age. He asked Elaine to go to dinner and Paul and I joined them. We drove to Mountain View in Taylor County- a bar and a jukebox. We let them dance the rest of the evening. Paul and I loved to dance, but George kept playing "Auf Weidersehen" over and over again so we just sat and talked, letting them dance alone. "My heart won't be the same, until we meet again Auf Weidersehen, my dear." It was another instance of love at second sight!

George had gone to Greenbrier Military Academy, then straight into the U.S. Naval Academy and from the Academy to the Battle of Leyte Gulf in 1944. The two of them were lucky to see each other again. Elaine had just returned from ten years in New York City and it seemed like another miraculous meeting. Or is this how love always happens?

Elaine and George were married on March 28, 1953 in Christ Episcopal Church in Fairmont. Elaine wore Mother's satin wedding dress with a cathedral train and carried an arm bouquet of white roses, just as Mother had. George was in full dress blues. As matron of honor, I wore a yellow lace gown and the bridesmaids Sylvia and Emily May - George's sister wore gowns of green lace. It was a formal evening wedding and Daddy was so thrilled he could still get into his white tie and tails. The best man was our cousin and old friend of George's, Melville Lee Colborn. The ushers, all stunning in white tie and tails, were brothers-in-law, Ken and Paul, Bob Tonry, Jr., William Wilson, Gordon Childs, all from Fairmont and Clark Doobie, Jr. and James M. (Brud) Knowles (Jack Knowles big brother) of Clarksburg.

The pair flew to California and luggage, car, and couple sailed to the groom's next assignment Pearl Harbor, Hawaii on the famous Matson ocean liner, Lurline, built in the year I was born for the Hawaiian –Australasia runs from the West Coast. We did not see them for four years when George's next assignment, shore duty as Assistant Officer in charge of Submarine Guided Missile Unit 51 at Yorktown, Virginia. They rented a beautiful home on the James River where Paul, little Eddie and I visited them to celebrate our first win for prosecutor after the General Election, in November of 1956.

Our brother-in law, George, was all Navy- an officer and a gentleman. He was born May 3, 1922 at Fort Monroe, Virginia. He graduated from Annapolis Naval Academy in 1944 and reported to the USS ALBERT W. GRANT (DD-649). On this tour he was in the battle of Leyte Gulf. The Commander was a student at the U.S. Naval Submarine School, New London, Connecticut, and. from 1947 to 1957 Commander Peed was a member of the Submarine Service, first qualifying in the USS CARBONERO (SS-337) and ending as Executive Officer in the USS SEA FOX (SS402). They went back to Hawaii and the Pacific fleet and he was commissioned as Captain. He served as Executive Officer in the USS FLETCHER (DDE-445), and Commanding Office of the USS BLAIR, (DER-147 and the USS RADFORD (DD-446), COMDESDIV-12 and was O-IN-C of submarine Guided Missile Unit Ten. His last assignment was as assistant chief of staff CINCPACFLT and retired June 30, 1974. We loved him, a true brother to us all.

Elaine and George had four tours of duty in Honolulu at Pearl Harbor. They insisted that Mother and Daddy move to be near them in the "Gem of the Pacific" and Ray and Brooks did just that after selling their home at 741 Fairmont Avenue and in October 1958. Paul and I drove them to the Pittsburgh International airport. It was hard to let them go. I knew they would be so much happier in the sunshine of Hawaii with Elaine, Sylvia and George, but would this be our last goodbye?

Elaine and George had three sons George III, (1954- 2003), Brooks Hutchinson (1956) and their special baby, Robert Fleming (1961). Brooks married Lori Dennison from Fort Pierce, Florida and they have three beautiful daughters: (Sarah, Allison and Hayley), Elaine often laughed as we thought of Mammam having eight sons-always trying for a daughter. Elaine thought she was just like her, but she preferred to stop with three sons.

Dear Elaine, whom I loved so much, died at the age of 67 on June 24, 1989 in Lawnwood Medical Center in Fort Pierce Florida. The family had retired to George's family winter home built in 1904, in Saint Lucie Village, Florida. She had been preparing to take a swim at her home, but when George arrived he found her on the floor. He carried her to the couch. The last words she uttered were, "I have the worst headache I have ever had in my life!" She suffered from an aneurism, a weak spot in the blood vessel of the brain, and had a subarachnoid hemorrhage.

Elaine was buried in Arlington National Cemetery on June 30, 1989 and we were all with her on that day. During the service, I held her first, 4-month-old grandbaby, the little girl she had wanted so much - Sarah Katherine, and the only one she had gotten to hold.

Captain George died May 5 of 2000, two days after his 78th birthday, and is buried at Arlington National Cemetery with Elaine and his parents.

Their first son, "Georgie", (March 15-1954) died suddenly on February 13, 2003 at the age of 48 of a heart attack. A master of trivia, of quotes and little known facts; we all encouraged him to go on Jeopardy. A loving son and nephew - it was too soon to lose him! His wife, Linda, scattered his ashes in his Indian River, just outside of his homestead's front door.

Elaine and Captain George
Georgie III, Robert Fleming, Brooks Hutchinson
1982

SYLVIA JANE

Sylvia Hutchinson Derby is one of the most remarkable women I have ever known. Sylvia married Kenneth Paul Derby who was a Guide at NBC. They married on May 12, 1951 at Christ Episcopal Church in Fairmont. As Ken was a Roman Catholic and his whole family was coming, Mother was worried about Sylvia being a protestant and his family's reaction to a non-catholic ceremony. After discussing this worry with the Reverend Graham Luckenbill, our rector at that time, the good reverend assured her, "I will take care of it!"

When the big day arrived, the Rev. Luckenbill stepped forward to conduct the services in his gorgeous gold embroidered scarf and vestments and a Bishop's miter on his head! The Derbys were impressed and our congregation still talks about it. Needless to say, Mother was relieved.

Sylvia and Ken had two children, Kenneth Paul, Jr. and Diana (Bell). Both children were born in New York City at Doctors Hospital.

Ken worked for BBD&O (Batten Barton Durstine and Osborne) a New York advertising firm, but soon moved his family to New Orleans.

After her husband, an alcoholic disappeared in 1957 leaving behind all his obligations to his family, abandoning Sylvia and their two adorable children in New Orleans with very little funds. Sylvia suffered her own "hard times"- so like Mom. She worked two jobs, daytime at BOAC, (British Overseas Airways Corporation), and at night in a hospital as a receptionist, taking the children to sleep on a couch near her desk. She told only Elaine about this. When Mother found out, she and Daddy headed straight to New Orleans to help with the children who were only five and two years old.

When Elaine heard about the separation, she and George sent for all of them to join their family in Hawaii. Mother and Daddy left in 1958, and Sylvia and her children followed in 1959. Elaine and George were living in Pearl Harbor at the time, but helped them find a small cottage right off of Waikiki Beach and life was good. The family was together again, all but Diane, but I was relieved and delighted for them all.

Sylvia, having worked for BOAC in Louisiana, applied at Qantas Airline, and they were thrilled to have her and her experience. Most of her closest friends today are Australians, who visit each other every year. She stayed with Qantas for over 30 years, retiring as manager of their Honolulu offices.

250

While in Hawaii, Sylvia entered both children in private schools, Kenneth at Iolani, a private Episcopal boys' school where both Brooks and George Peed attended. Iolani was established in 1863 by bishops and priests from the Anglican Church of England who were requested to come to Honolulu by King Kamehameha IV and his consort, Queen Emma. When our boys went to Iolani in the late 1960 and early seventies the school had moved to the present Ala Wai property. Today the school is co-educational and accepts children of all faiths from K-12th grade. Diana entered and graduated from Punahou, a private, coeducational, high school, the same school President Barrack Obama attended several years later. Punahou was established in 1841 and today, with an enrollment of 3,750, is the largest co-educational, independent school, on a single campus, in the United States. Kenneth received a scholarship to Yale University and Diana, to the University of Hartford in Connecticut.

Following graduation, Kenneth attended the Sorbonne University in Paris where he met his wife Milagros Manzano, from Madrid, Spain. Mila was born on November 27, 1950 and was only a little over a pound and a half at birth. Her mother, in order to save her life, kept her in swaddling clothes close to a warm oven. Therefore she was called Milagros, meaning "miracle" in Spanish.

Ken was asked to teach English for the ARAMCO, (an acronym for Arabian American Oil Company-- the largest oil corporation in the world). The ARAMCO compound with a population of 50,000 is in Dhahran, Saudi Arabia. Milagros graduated from the University of Madrid and today teaches Spanish for Adult Education classes in Dhahran. They have two beautiful daughters, Elena Christina and Ana Marie. The family has resided in Saudi for 30 years.

Diana lives in Seaford, New York with her daughter, Lisa Malia and her son, David Michael Bell. She received a BS degree in Education. Tiring of teaching and her children in college, Diana is an administrative assistant with the Nassau County Police Department (8th Precinct) on Long Island, New York.

Sylvia is in her early eighties and still goes around the world every year to visit her children, grandchildren and friends. She leaves Hawaii around the first of November and does not return for four months, taking five bags of luggage- one case filled with unwrapped Christmas presents so customs doesn't have to unwrap all the gifts for inspection.

When she visits my family in West Virginia, her namesake and I take her back to the Pittsburgh airport and we have to drop her off at the terminal. The air officer looks at her itinerary, which reads: Houston, Pittsburgh, New York, London, Bahrain- Saudi Arabia, Hong Kong, Bangkok, Australia and home to Honolulu; and immediately says "Please come with me", and wheels all of her five large bags inside for inspections; while Sylvia, in her little high heels, quickly follows him, smiling and waving frantically, "Aloha!"

August 1955
Front Row: Kenneth Derby Jr., Elaine and Georgie and George Peed
Middle Row: Sylvia and Diana, Diane and Eddie
Back Row: Ken Derby and Paul Parker

CHAPTER THIRTEEN

FAIRMONT STATE COLLEGE

First row, Left to right: Beverly Banko, Marie Murrin, Waneila Fisher, Eleanor Bennett, Nancy Lee Thompson. Second row: Joan Buchannon, Marilyn Krick, Mary Sue Sandy, Carolyn Crigler, Phoebe Schroeder, Mary E. Shroyer, Doris Lee Shaffer. Third row: Shirley Champ, Diane Parker, Elizabeth Dixon, Ann Forlines, Joan Hollen, Mary Ellen Heisey, Joyce Ann Flint, Dolores Haught.

GAMMA CHI CHI, founded in 1927, is the oldest sorority on the hill. Some of its annual activities include the Founder's Day banquet, Mother's Day banquet, the Tallow Tea honoring the faculty and staff, and the spring formal dinner-dance. The sorority maintains a trophy case in the main hall for the benefit of the student body.

Alpha Psi Omega

REPRESENTING one of the largest national honorary fraternities in the United States is the Alpha Psi Omega, honorary dramatic fraternity. It was founded at Fairmont State College in 1925 with Dr. Paul Opp as one of the original founders. As national business manager of the fraternity, Dr. Opp edits the *Playbill*, annual subscription of the honorary.

First row, Left to right: Diane Parker, Janie Sullivan. Second row: Dick Stewart, George Ann Bennett, Bill Andrick.

COLLEGE DAYS

Entering Fairmont State College in the summer school session June of 1950, I was elected President of the Freshman Class. I enjoyed the student government regimen and became knowledgeable of the college at the same time. FSC had been established in 1865 as a private Normal School for training teachers. Mammam graduated from there in 1885, my sister Elaine in 1942 and I, in 1954.

The Normal School was born out of the turbulence and strife of the Civil War and the formative years of the new state of West Virginia. Our public schools were sparse as there were not enough teachers to teach classes. The county superintendant of schools at the time was J.N. Boyd, who became the first principal of the new school, and ten-week sessions were held in the basement of the Methodist Protestant Church on Quincy Street.

In 1868 The West Virginia State Normal School at Fairmont opened under state auspices, with Dr. William Ryland White, a native Fairmonter and former State Superintendant of Schools, as principal.

A relative of friends, Jean (Blair) Ireland and Anne (Blair) Morgan, Dr. James G. Blair, a native of New York, a graduate of Wesleyan College of Connecticut in 1841, and a Methodist minister, was appointed principal in 1871. Under his able direction the academic program took a definite form. A normal course of two years of high school was offered to prospective teachers; and an academic department was offered to those wishing to go to college instead of teaching. Anne and Jean's grandfather, Jackson Van Buren Blair was sent to stay with the new president and take the two-year course for teachers, graduating in 1874. During James Blair's reign, opposition to the normal school arose and the legislature made no appropriations for salaries during the years 1873-1875. The school survived only because of the sacrifices of its teachers, the tuition of its students, and loyalty of the townspeople. Blair called the normal school, the "People's College". He died while serving as president in 1878.

Mary Rebecca Watson, J.O. and Matilda (Lamb) Watson's seventh child of ten, married the eighth principal of the Normal school, Conrad A. Sipe, a Pennsylvania native and a graduate of Adrian College in Michigan. Dr. Sipe, another Methodist minister, headed the school from 1883 to 1889. He enlarged the professional curriculum, secured larger appropriations, and saw a great influx of new students. Dr. Sipe retired in 1891 and became the head of the State Agency of National Life Insurance. Miss Lucy Lee (Sipe), their daughter, was born in 1882, never married and for one hundred and three years, lived her entire life on the grounds where she was born, outliving all the Watson's, except 2 grand nephews, Bart and J.O. II and a great grand nephew, J.E. Watson III.

Senator Joseph Rosier, the grandfather of a good friend, Patty Smith Huey, had been President of Fairmont State Normal School and Fairmont State Teacher's College from 1915 to 1945. No other chief administrator has matched his longevity in the office. He saw the Normal School move from Second Street and Fairmont Avenue, to the majestic building on Locust Avenue. He guided us through two world wars, helped us become more secure, offering a more varied curriculum, and after 1923 the college awarded the baccalaureate degree.

George W. Hand replaced the much beloved hometown son in 1945, with a mandate from the legislature to convert the teachers college to a comprehensive college. New buildings were built, the faculty and student body enlarged and the college earned accreditation from the North Central Associations of Colleges and Secondary Schools, all the necessary changes to keep up with the times. Dr. Hand was the president when I attended the "College on the Hill".

Daddy could not afford to send me away to college and I really did not want to go. Elaine had graduated from Fairmont State and had been a star for Lawrence Wallman- the best director in the state and head of the Speech and Drama Department. Elaine was voted as the first Junior Prom Queen and elected editor of the yearbook, "The Mound", in 1942. I loved trying to follow her example and was relieved not to have to compete with thousands at WVU. Also, dear Moe was here working for Interstate Engineers.

I pledged to the Gamma Chi Chi Sorority, the oldest local social sorority, established in 1927. There were three of these on campus, the Gammas, the Alpha Delta Chi, and the men's fraternity, Tau Beta Iota. These groups were formed during the depression, as most could not afford to go WVU. One could join a local sorority here yet still be eligible to join a national sorority, if times got better and you could attend a larger school. In 1950 six national groups had been added to the campus.

The three local groups would band together and produce the TAG (Tau Beta Iota, Alpha Delta, Gamma's) Show each year with Professor George Turley and "Pappy" Wallman as directors. The picture is of the United Nations year and I had a solo called - "I'm Sweet Marie from gay Paree', I love zee motor cars! It fills my heart with joy to see the Yankee boys." Mother took an old evening gown of Elaine's - a beautiful, one shouldered red faille ensemble, cut it off and added real handmade lace from the cedar chest to a crinoline petticoat I had worn in Jr. High School.

When I chose to join Elaine's old sorority, she sent me her cameo ring that had belonged to Mom. I loved the Gamma sisters and still do. I hope to attend their 87 Anniversary luncheon at the newly built Fairmont Field Club where we used to have our annual formals.

As a freshman, Mr. Wallman chose me to be his new "Claudia" and I was the lead in the three-act comedy drama "CLAUDIA", by Rose Franken, (1941). At the end of the first night's performance the Gammas presented their sister with an armful of red roses during the curtain call. A true night to remember!

At every rehearsal of "CLAUDIA", I fell a little more in love with my husband in the play. His real name was Rusty, a senior and a superb actor, having been directed for four years by Wallman. Rusty's stage name in "Claudia" [a very young lady and full of voltage] was David Naughton [A clean good-looking man about thirty] and at the end of the first act the lines were,

DAVID. [Knowing better.} You're a nice girl. I like you. [Catches her to him and cups her face in his hands.]

CLAUDIA. [A little tremulously.] That's not very exciting,--just to like me--?

DAVID. [{Huskily.] Don't you believe it, when you like the person you love, that's marriage, [Adds on a breath.] And it's exciting!

[Switches the room into darkness.] [Only the light from above stage shines down on them as they start up the stairs, her head on his shoulder.]

THE CURTAIN SLOWLY FALLS

Rusty sent me an armful of roses after the final performance. On the card was, "And it's exciting!"

I broke up with Moe and started dating Rusty.

On a double date after his fraternity formal Rusty whispered in my ear:

"I have a job in California starting next week and when I get settled I will send for you".

That shocked me into reality! I had no idea of marriage! I had just finished my first year in college and was just eighteen! As soon as Rusty left town, I went back to Moe.

"The Tag Show"
October, 1951

A NEST OF VIPERS

There have been books, plays and television series written about the Mundel-Loudin Case. I am no authority on the legal aspects or the reasons behind the $100,000 slander suit, but Charles Howard McCormick, a professor of history at Fairmont State College since 1970, wrote a riveting account of a local culture under stress, "This Nest of Vipers: McCarthyism and Higher Education in the Mundel Affair, 1951-1952 (1989).

I lived through this entire scandal, a political scandal of a college and a town. It drew unwanted national attention to both, because of anticommunism excess, and well before the Army- McCarthy hearings in 1954. I was affected in many ways, as both a student and a native of Fairmont. I knew all the people in this trial quite well, and was in church the morning our Rector, Graham Luckenbill, made the statement, which caused a mistrial.

Old friends were being maligned, hurt, and scandalized. The town was upset enough when the syndicated writer, William Manchester, came in to our, "grey and garish business district. Westward, past a mile of sore eyed frame houses pitched awkwardly on steep sloping hills, lies Fairmont State College, too remote to give the city a collegiate atmosphere, too close to be unobserved." It is true, Fairmont was not a college town, but Fairmont State was a town's college and still is.

Manchester had come to explore and describe an account of what he labeled a "second Scopes trial" for "Harpers Magazine" and the Baltimore Sun newspapers. Even the prominent Louisville Courier Journal made comparisons to Scopes trial and the Salem witchcraft furor.

In the summer of 1945 the State Board of Education was determined to rid the local college of deadwood. Thelma Brand Loudin, a native of Barrackville, a suburb of Fairmont, had been appointed by Governor M.M. Neely in 1941 to serve as Fairmont State's representative on the State Board of Education. In 1945, she sided with the board to enforce mandatory retirement at the age of 65, forcing President Rosier and six of his faculty members from their positions at the end of the school year. By September 1945, the Board had hired a new president, George Henry Hand.

The new president was inducted in 1946. Hand was a native of Wheeling, WV and a graduate of West Virginia University where he had starred in three varsity sports. After graduating in 1928, Hand moved to Ohio's

Denison University to be a professor of economics, next, to Ohio Wesleyan College and lastly, to the University of Vermont where he headed the Economics Department. From the very beginning his tenure at FSC was marked with controversy.

Joseph Rosier had been appointed by his good friend M.M. Neely to serve out his term as U. S. Senator; Neely exchanged his Senatorial seat for the Governor's seat. Under Rosier, the college was overly paternalistic. Old friends taught your children and treated them as their own. I thought I would enjoy the hometown atmosphere on "Rosier's Knob", but Dr. Hand had scoured the country, bringing in new blood. We knew too few to feel comfortable. To complicate the situation, the GI Bill brought in veterans and their families to swell the rosters and create more demands. These veterans were older, more practical and less tolerant toward the paternalistic authority and the more precious aspects of traditional campus life. Rows of barracks were built on the road below the College and rented to the vets and their small families.

Twenty-one of the older faculty members were lost during the year of 1947 by resignation, retirement or removal. Two of those removed were exceptionally controversial. The sharp tongued bursar, Miss Blanche Price, a fourteen year member of the business staff and well known throughout the town, and Medora Mason, the controlling public relations and journalism instructor who had constantly promoted the college in her charming and popular Fairmont Times daily column, "Mary Chatter " since 1929. Mason, a graduate of WVU, had been the fiancé of Uncle Gohen Arnold who was a State Senator from Buckhannon and well known as a business partner in the Hutchinson Coal Company. Uncle Gohen had died suddenly of a heart attack in the late thirties and Medora had never married, remaining at FSC until her removal.

"Much bitterness and acrimony was put forth by the townspeople, the faculty, and between Hand and Loudin. Although perhaps tactless, insensitive and too liberal for the local establishment mentality, Hand had shaken this sleepy college from its lethargy and provincialism."

It is generally thought that the accusation, President Hand had been employing communists and atheists, was thrust against Dr. Luella Raab Mundel. Manchester reported her as, "a frail, be-speckled, somewhat nervous Iowan in her late thirties who came to Fairmont in September of 1949 as Chairman of the Department of Art, bringing with her a Ph.D. from Iowa State University and a sheaf of teaching references from other

260

institutions. Her salary was $3,700 a year and she was on three-year probation, which she was never told. Her colleagues remember her as abrupt, independent and embittered over a three-year old divorce."

I remember Thelma Brand Loudin, a tall, stunning brunette, had raised certain questions concerning Mundel's religious beliefs, which clearly violated both academic freedom and her civil rights; but Mundel was denied any right to answer or respond. "The board had the legal right to refuse to re- employ Dr. Mundel and no remedy existed within normal grievance procedures." Therefore, on September27, 1951, Luella Mundel filed suit for $100,000 charging Thelma Loudin with slander.

Mundel received no help from American Association of University Professors (AAUP), or the American Civil Liberties Union (ACLU) who did put her in touch with a lawyer, Horace Spencer Meldahl, a Charleston attorney. The faculty at Fairmont State shied away from Mundel fearing for their own jobs and guilt by association. Meldahl insisted she hire a local attorney as co-counsel, which proved no easy task.

Eventually, the 78-year-old Tusca Morris, who had practiced law for over 40 years, accepted a retainer of $1000 to represent Miss Mundel. "As a young Prosecuting Attorney in town in 1909 he had won nineteen convictions against the members of the sinister Black Hand organization. From its hideout in the remote Killarm Hollow, this criminal conspiracy [allegedly] related to the Mafia, had been strong arming and extorting funds from Italian–Americans." Years later, Attorney Morris rose to be chief counsel for Consolidation Coal Company. Now in 1951, the late twilight of his career, after strong persuasion and a promise of 25 percent of damages, plus the retainer that cut sharply into Mundel's savings, he joined the litigation team.

The other major player was Fairmont's most famous citizen, the five terms U.S. Senator and one term Governor of West Virginia, Matthew Mansfield Neely and his son Alfred.

McCormick reports; "On a cold, blustery morning, December 17, 1951, began two weeks of humiliation and frustration for Luella Mundel". Mundel was being tried in front of a jury of all men, as women were not allowed to serve on juries in West Virginia until the fall of 1957.

In his opening statement, the graying Mendahl, from Charleston WV, quietly and logically laid out Mundel's case. He described the damage

Loudin had done to his client, leaving her in "poor health, nervous, sleepless, and with difficulty digesting her food". He promised to prove to this jury that Mundel had been, "properly qualified, properly hired and had performed well at the college".

Manchester describes the defense's opening statement,

"In a courtroom crammed with townspeople and students, Neely rose and stalked the all male jury- a chunky, jut-jawed figure in a double breasted suit and blue suede shoes, crouching over the jury box, delivering his open statement in phrases unmatched since the days of William Jennings Bryan.

" For over an hour he pranced before the awestruck twelve, delivering a thundering defense of the Board of Education's right 'to purge its school of teachers it believes incompetent, atheists, communists, horse thieves, murderers or just too ignorant to teach children'. Luella Mundel was a woman who would 'tear down the man from Galilee from the cross. A woman who boasted of painting pictures which arouse sexual desires in men...if that is reactionary,' he cried, 'make the most of it!'"

Dr. Paul Edwards, dean of community college at Fairmont State in 1990, wrote in a review of McCormack's book for the Times West Virginia February 11, 1990:

"The Jury trial was a travesty." Neely, the 70-year-old living legend became the dominant figure in the trial, defending his appointee, Loudin. "Neely's outrageous and bombastic buffoonery forced Mundel to defend her art, religious views and political implications." She vowed she was neither a communist nor an atheist. "Neely pressed on with histrionics, embracing the American flag, he railed, against any school that tolerated communism, atheism or any other godless philosophy in its halls." Mundel excused herself repeatedly to retire to the ladies' room where loud sobbing was heard; while Neely praised his client (Loudin) in liberating the college from; "agnostics, socialists, and screwballs, cleaning out this nest of vipers".

Dr. Edwards, speaking of William Manchester's view of Fairmont, referring to it as "Dog Patch," and describing "the outrageous trial as a heavy handed, melodramatic account of good guys" said, "Fairmonters were stung more by Manchester's harsh and unfair aesthetic criticism of the town than the substantive issues." I remember the scathing comments my parents made about Manchester, as did many other Fairmont citizens.

On Sunday morning, December 30, 1951, my nineteenth birthday, I was attending Christ Episcopal Church when our Rector, Graham Luckenbill, an outspoken clergyman known for his independence, paused in his announcements (at the Lectern, not in the pulpit) and denounced the Mundel trial as, "a farce which smacks loudly of all the bad traits of the Inquisition and the Crucifixion. State college teachers should not be chosen for their religious views", and asking us, his own parishioners, "To think and behave like true Christians". Up to that moment he had remained silent about the trial but he had recently offered the invocation at the college commencement so he was interested in the institution.

The Reverend Luckenbill opined, "Neither Neely or Mendahl understood the correct meaning of the words, 'truth', 'prove', and 'God'. Mundel made her point when she testified that she believes in truth, for truth was synonymous with God and righteousness."

"Days of Inquisition Not Over"
The Fairmont Times
Monday Morning, December 31, 1951

"After an hour and forty-five minute meeting with counsel in chambers, Judge Meredith declared a mistrial. He said that the priest's ill-advised remarks from the pulpit made it impossible for the jury to render a fair verdict.

"The obviously pained judge denied that the trial had become a farce. As the spectators left the courtroom, no one knew who had won or lost or what might happen next. He asked one of the Jurors, Walter Garrison, Sr. to step aside, explaining this is an 'old legal form we have to go through. It leaves only 11 men', he pointed out, 'which is not a jury'.

"No action was taken against the local minister at this court session. Judge Meredith had no comment."

****

"Mistrial Declared in Slander Action"
"Action Follows Sermon Given by Clergyman
By Logan Carroll- West Virginian Staff Writer
The Times West Virginian
Monday Evening, December 31, 1951

"Trial of the $100,000 slander action of Dr. Luella Rabb Mundel against Thelma Brand Loudin ended abruptly today when Judge J. Harper Meredith declared a mistrial.

Expanding on his remarks yesterday morning, Rev. Luckenbill said he also touched upon many infringements of personal liberties in this nation today.

'A teacher in a state supported institution should not be hired or fired because of religious or political beliefs,' he said, 'so long as she makes no attempt to teach those beliefs. Those beliefs are her own and should not be considered by her superiors. We must also fight for academic freedom in this nation', the Rector said, 'If we don't, we will turn out students with one track minds.' Citing a tenet of Catholic theology which holds, 'the Truth with a capital T is synonymous with God or righteousness and when Dr. Mundel said she worshiped truth she was considerably closer to God than Senator Neely, since God is Truth.' "

****

In what McCormack labeled a "sanctimonious pose of neutrality", twenty–four local clergymen of The Fairmont Ministerial Association censured Luckenbill and disassociated themselves from him, denouncing the trying of court cases from "the pulpit". The association president explained that Mr. Luckenbill did not belong to the organization and that membership is reserved to those clergymen who desire to co-operate.

Liberalist journalists rushed in where Fairmont clergy feared to tread. They charged that Mundel had not received a fair hearing, nor had been treated with common decency. A scathing editorial appeared in the Louisville Courier Journal, January 3, 1952, describing the trial as a scene of unreality echoing the Scopes trial and the Salem Witchcraft hysteria. The editorial pictured Mundel as a "nervous harassed young woman whom Neely had pilloried." The Courier Journal also blasted the Fairmont papers and the judge for timidity and inaction. (Grafton News, Jan.14, 1952; Charleston Daily News Jan.2-6, 1952)

Neither of our local newspapers responded to the out of town critics. C.E. Ned Smith believed that a newspaper certainly has no business trying the case in its editorial columns, nor should a minister try a case in his church. He did print The Charleston Gazette editorial on Jan 10, 1952, stating, "The reverend's remarks may have been a bit tactless in his denunciation of what he felt was persecution. Nevertheless, the remarks ...that resulted in a mistrial must be counted as particularly courageous, almost magnificent coming from the lips of a minister of the gospel."

The second trial opened with a new all male jury and the same cast of characters on July 7, 1952. The national press was absent, it was yesterday's news. The big story that week was the Republican National Convention and the newspapers were announcing General Dwight D. Eisenhower's nomination.

On July 16, the jury deliberated one hour and forty- three minutes and found for the defendant, Thelma Brand Loudin. "Overt slander was not established".

McCormack ends his chapter,

"Spewing bits of verse in all directions, Matt Neely held an impromptu news conference at the courthouse. He told the reporters that the verdict was one of the most important ever given in this state… it was a victory for those who wanted Christianity to play an active role in the schools. 'The verdict insured that we may sing in our colleges,

Long may our land be bright
With freedom's holy light,
Protect us by Thy might,
Great God our King!'

"'Now it would not become socially unacceptable for us to continue to return thanks

'To Him who stills the raven's clamorous nest,
And decks the lily fair in flow'ry pride.
Would the way His wisdom sees the best,
For all our wants provide'. "

****

The Charleston Gazette
July 17, 1952

"The ending was more than a courtroom triumph for Neely. It had serendipity, for in it he must have perceived a vindication of his Christian ideology, a legal precedent that would buttress the politicians' control of the board of education and the colleges and a resounding campaign statement that gave the lie to Republican claims that Democratic political leaders were not good Christian men."

****

In the next morning Fairmont Times, sharing the front page with Mundel's defeat and the grand opening of the Moose Club's new Antler Room (the décor was pastel greens, dark reds and flowed plastic wall drapes) was the announcement that Thelma Brand Loudin had been re-elected Vice President of the State Board of Education."

"Forgive but don't forget."

~ Elie Wiesel

CHAPTER FOURTEEN

ONE RED ROSE

The wedding of Diane Hutchinson and Paul Edward Parker
Christ Episcopal Church, Fairmont, West Virginia
November 22, 1952

PAUL

I worked at J. Patrick Beacom's radio station (1490 on your radio dial) through the summer of 1951 when Elaine came back to Fairmont to live. It was fun going up to Palatine Knob, the tallest spot in the area, needed to hold the tower signal and offices. All the broadcasts came from there. Elaine wrote copy for the announcers and I was program director. Sounds important, but my job was only to keep track of every record played during each 24-hour period and alphabetize the lists for the Federal Communications Commission.

I had a five-minute radio show for children every evening at five o'clock teaching walking and biking safety tips. As I was now majoring in elementary education at Fairmont State it seemed appropriate for me to be the teacher on the knob, as well as the student on the hill.

After shopping downtown one afternoon in January of 1952, I hopped on the bus at Adams and Monroe Streets and all the seats were taken. A young man in a grey trench coat and a stunning grey Homburg jumped up from the horizontal bench near the bus driver and offered his seat, which I accepted. He stood right in front of me holding onto the strap over my head while I sat in amazement, staring at his knotted belt, "Who was this gorgeous Adonis?" Suddenly he pulled the buzzer to get off and it was Seventh Street! He lived in the vicinity of 741? Where had he been? Who was he? What if I never saw him again? I felt my whole life was in jeopardy.

In March, Brooks Higginbotham called and asked me to read for "Harvey", the play that he was directing for the Marion County Little Theatre spring production. The tryouts were held at his home on Wednesday night at 7 o'clock. Daddy drove me to Brooks and Margaret's apartment house on Monroe Street, where I could hear music drifting from an upstairs window. I entered and recognized "Some Enchanted Evening", the Rogers and Hammerstein hit from South Pacific. Old friends Ray Stoker, the photographer, who had directed Elaine and me in "The Women" the past spring and his wife Gwen, were there, along with John Graham, who was to be the lead- Elwood P. Dowd - and Janet Wysner, an old friend from high school. I had no idea what part Mr. Higginbotham wanted me to read, but we got started and I was asked to read Nurse Ruth Kelly. Right at that moment, my January Adonis walked in from the kitchen with a drink in his hand and sat down in the only chair left, clear across the room. Brooks handed him a script to read Dr. Sanderson's part.

We were asked to introduce ourselves but most of us were old friends except Paul Edward Parker, Jr. who told us he had moved to Fairmont in the summer of 1951 and was an attorney with the Furbee and Hardesty law firm.

"You will meet a stranger across a crowded room."

The readings were fine and the cast chosen, rehearsals would begin on Friday evening at Christ Episcopal Church Parish House.

After the tryouts, Paul followed me down the stairs, offering to drive me home. Thanking him, I said my father would be waiting for me.

As I lay there trying to sleep that night-that glorious night - I could only wonder - had he heard the strains and the words of "Some Enchanted Evening". I wondered if he had heard the great advice, "Once you have found her, never let her go." Did he even really see that dark haired little girl with big brown eyes, or did he just see a sterile Nurse Kelly. He had no idea that his new friend had seen him several weeks ago on a city lines bus, and had been haunted by him for weeks, and here he was, sitting across a crowded room. This was truly destiny - God's will.

The rehearsals were fun and Paul and I enjoyed sitting and talking between our scenes. I learned he had graduated from WVU Law School on June 2, 1951. Two days later, he was admitted to the State Supreme Court and the State Bar Association in Charleston, and had moved to Fairmont immediately. He joined the firm of Furbee and Hardesty, but had recently rented a small office in the Home Savings Bank Building on Adams Street for private practice.

He had lived in two apartments since moving from Morgantown where his parents then resided. His first was in Fairmont Farms at "Ibby" Armstrong Meredith's stable apartments and another was in the Hite House on Fairmont Avenue, near Sixth Street. His parents, Betty and Paul Parker, had recently been transferred to the Fairmont Monongahela Power Company and were renting the Shinn house on the corner of Seventh and Benoni Avenue – diagonally across from Papa's first house and he was now living there with his parents.

We only rehearsed two or three times a week, learning lines, blocking the scenes; then I walked home leaving well before Paul, as I always had homework to finish. I was going to college in the morning and working at

WVVW in the afternoons. Daddy would pick me up at school and take me to Palatine Knob, always passing Paul's office on the second floor of the Home Savings Bank. I would ask Daddy to go very slowly so I could look back up at Paul's office and see if the lights were on, meaning he was there. Daddy would sigh and say, "Paul's in his office, all's right with the world".

One evening Moe and I were going to the movies and Daddy answered the door. Moe was standing there with a green tissue wrapped red rose from Hauge's Florists with no card. Moe just shrugged, shook his head and handed the rose to Daddy, who came back to the kitchen with the gift. I knew that one red rose meant passion and love, so presumed it must be Moe, but said nothing. The next night when Moe arrived, another red rose had been left at the door. Moe was upset. On our dates, the roses were never mentioned. Each evening a new rose appeared at the door. I had been dating Moe for years. He was a sweet, kind, gentle, man - more like a brother than a suitor. I was confused and worried. I did not want to hurt Moe again after Rusty - and yet…?

On the fifth night, a Friday, I had a rehearsal and confided to Mother,

"I really would love to go out with Paul, but he has never asked."

Wise woman-she, said, "Wear a rose in your hair tonight and see what happens."

Our scenes really jelled that evening and he was very attentive. After the rehearsal, as I was walking out the parish house door on Ninth Street, I felt an arm around my waist and he literally swept me off my feet, walked me home, holding hands, kissed me good night, and said, "You are beautiful", and left.

The next day, Easter Even, a tall, blue, soft, fuzzy, rabbit with not only long ears, but long arms and legs- somewhat like Harvey- was left on the porch table holding a bouquet of red roses. That did it! I was no longer confused.

The whole town had heard about the roses thanks to Mrs. Hauge, with whom Paul had made all the arrangements, and who had secretly been delivering the roses. Petty was such a darling person and loved being a part of a good romance. The cast knew about the exciting, charming courtship and left us alone at the Fairmont Senior High School rehearsals, when we would go sit in the back row of the auditorium and whisper together.

The performances were packed and it was a delight to hear a few applaud when our kissing scene arrived. We were certainly not the stars of the show- but it felt like it.

Fifty years later when the High School Foundation had all the old wooden splintered seats upholstered and were selling each seat with your name on the back, I bought those two courtship seats with Paul's name on one and my maiden name on the other.

"Who can explain it, who can tell you why..."

COURTSHIP

On June 4 of 1951, Paul had been admitted to the State Bar at the West Virginia Supreme Court. On June 4 of 1952 Paul called and asked if I would like a tour of his new offices in the Marion County Court House. He had been appointed as Assistant Prosecuting Attorney by Circuit Court Judge Harper Meredith on June 1, 1952. Mother was in New York with Sylvia, who was having her first baby, and Daddy and I were alone for a couple of weeks. I ironed a clean dress and caught a bus.

The Marion County Courthouse, a replica of the West Virginia State Capitol that resembles the National Capitol building, has been in continuous use since 1900. It is a magnificent structure with its Corinthian columns and gold dome with stained- glass windows and the blindfolded figure of Justice holding her sword and her scales atop a roman numerated clock that still chimes faithfully on the hour.

Arriving at the corner of Adams and Jefferson Streets about 1:30, I climbed the many steps up to the huge double oaken doors while remembering the four Hughes brothers. They were Alpheus, Zachary, Bert and Russ, who sat on those steps daily to receive their daily handouts and talk secretly to each other. Shabbily dressed, they were teased and tormented by the youths who lived along the familiar route they took each day from their shack on Washington Street extension, to their second home of many years, the courthouse steps. Too proud to accept anything but change they begged for each day, so when the odor of their clothes got too rancid, the sheriff would round them up and take them in to the jail for a wash down- clothes and all. Fairmont always took care of its eccentrics.

Then three more flights of worn marble steps to the third floor and the beautiful marble pillared rotunda, the circular waiting room looking down to the first floor, with the sun shining through the stained glass dome far above my head. The Prosecutor's offices were to the right of the staircase, connected to the Grand Jury room and on the left the Circuit Court room. I entered another heavy oak door to be greeted by Paul's secretary, "Sissy" Hopkins, Evan Hopkins' German war bride, both of whom attended my church. She said that Mr. Parker was expecting me and to go right in.

Paul had heard me and was holding the door, welcoming me into his new domain. I was so impressed by the spacious office with two arched windows overlooking Jefferson Street and the First National Bank. Several large dark red, leather, oak armchairs sat across from his desk and I sat in one, feeling like Alice in her smaller state. Tall, legal, glassed door bookcases, just like Daddy had, filled with rows of colorful matching spines of Michie's Jurisprudence and Southeastern Reporter flanked his executive desk. There was a handsome credenza and lamp behind his maroon leather executive chair. I was so impressed.

Without much small talk, he simply stated, "Diane, I would like very much for you to become my wife." With unhesitating surety, I answered, "I would love to be your wife, Paul." I now knew why it had never worked with anyone else.

He jumped up, led me over to the huge arched window, for all the world to see and we kissed, only to be interrupted by "Sissy" who stuck her head in the door and said,

"Mr. Parker, excuse me, but can you sell live frogs for bait?"

"Paul's in his heaven, all's right with the world"

MARRIAGE

What date for the wedding? I wanted to have it at Christmas holiday break, but Paul would have January term of court. We had heard that Dorothy Knowles, Jack's little sister and a friend of mine, was to be wed during the holidays and Mother did not want to compete with the Knowles, who would have a huge wedding and reception at the Field Club with practically the same friends. So Paul and Mother determined the date of November 22, Thanksgiving break- except we were going to Nassau on our honeymoon for three weeks which fit into Paul's schedule, but hardly a college student's. I had promised Daddy that I would finish my college studies, if he would just give me permission to marry at the age of nineteen.

Society News: *Diane Hutchinson - Paul E. Parker Jr.*

Betrothal Announced Here Today

Betty Sammons, Society Editor

The Times West Virginian

Sunday, July 20, 1952

"Mr. and Mrs. Brooks S. Hutchinson of 741 Fairmont Avenue announce the engagement of their daughter Diane to Paul Edward Parker, Jr. Miss Hutchinson graduated from Fairmont Senior High School and is now a junior student at Fairmont State College. She is a member of the Gamma Chi Chi Sorority and Alpha Psi Omega, national honor dramatic fraternity. She is the granddaughter of the late Clyde E. Hutchinson, pioneer coal operator in West Virginia and the late Mrs. Hutchinson. Her maternal grandparents were the late Mr. and Mrs. Ray Pefley of Boise, Idaho.

"Mr. Parker is the son of Mr. and Mrs. Paul E. Parker of 609 Benoni Avenue and grandson of the late Mr. and Mrs. John Edward Parker of Clarksburg and the late Mr. and Mrs. John Michael Shumaker of Buckhannon. Mr. Parker is a graduate of Morgantown High School and received his A.B. and L.L.B. degrees from West Virginia University. Mr. Parker is a member of the Phi Kappa Psi and Phi Delta Phi legal fraternity. During WWII he served in the U.S. Army and was discharged with the grade of Sergeant. He now holds a commission in the US Air Force Reserve. He is at present Assistant Prosecuting Attorney of Marion County.

The wedding will be an event of November."

****

I dropped to 98 pounds; Mother said I hardly ate anything between June and November. I was too excited- too in love to eat. Sylvia's wedding on May 12, 1951 was a dress rehearsal for Mother and all the arrangements flowed together flawlessly. Mother was always so gracious and unhurried, but when she was totally in charge, even General Patton would have complied with her directives.

The wedding was to be held at our Christ Episcopal Church at Ninth Street, just a block away from 741 where the reception would be held. The guests, who were parked on both sides of Fairmont Avenue, walked to the house for the reception. Daddy had the city police there to help with traffic, allowing the guests to cross to the Highgate side of the avenue and meander down to the reception. Mother had all the furniture moved out of two of the living

274

rooms where the receiving line was held so there was plenty of standing room for the 150 guests.

I knew so few of the Parker's guests as they came from all over the state, so the reception took a long time. Mr. Parker bought coal for Monongahela Power (Allegheny Energy Corp.) and they had been transferred often the past thirty years. Some of the sites were Parkersburg, Salem, Clarksburg, Morgantown, even Harlan, Kentucky, where Mrs. Parker said she had slept with a loaded gun under her pillow when Paul was a baby.

Mrs. Parker and my sisters, who were maids of honor, were to be in the receiving line and Mother coached them about who was who and whose spouse had died, and warned us all that, "If you meet with a "limp hand" it has to be a Watson." Sure enough, we recognized every Watson. Mrs. Parker had only been here a short time and Sylvia and Elaine had been in New York so long they were all grateful for the review of so many old friends.

"November two-two-fifty two", as Paul called it, was a crisp, sunny day, no snow, thank heavens. Daddy, Elaine, Sylvia, and I arrived at the church a few minutes before four and Petty Hague greeted us at the door, handing us our bouquets. Mine was of white orchids. Petty always recalled, I stood on my tiptoes to make sure Paul was waiting there for me. Miss Mary B. Price, chair of music at the college, was singing," I love thee, dear, for all eternity" and suddenly- the triumphal Lohengrin wedding march began. My sisters started down the aisle, Daddy offered me his arm. I said, "I think I have to throw up." I heard Daddy utter his strongest oath, "For the love of Mike!" And we started down the red-carpeted aisle to "Here Comes the Bride." All followed Mother's lead and were standing, all eyes on me! I was – once again - the star!

"Dearly beloved, we are gathered together here in the sight of God, and in the face of this company, to join together this man and this woman in holy matrimony…" Sylvia, my maid of honor, started crying. She cried through most of the service. Mr. Parker, Paul's father and best man, reached across Paul and me to hand her his handkerchief. I could faintly hear sniffling behind me, which was Uncle Robert, sitting on Mothers left, smelling of Bay Rum and liquor. Mother claimed afterwards, she was a wreck with both of them. Sylvia, whose only excuse was, "They are so young." To which Mother retorted, "Paul is older than you, Sylvia!"

I remember flowers were everywhere and Paul and I never sat down, much less ate. I ran upstairs after throwing my bouquet from the landing. I was not too happy about the result; I threw it to Elaine, and her future sister-in-law stepped in front of her and grabbed it. I changed into my three- piece going away suit of dark red wool tweed and a black velvet veiled hat. After kissing our parents good-bye, we ran out the front door, through a sea of rice to the Parkers' big new maroon Buick Roadmaster, which had been wildly decorated by the ushers. We drove it with the cans pip-popping behind off the brick road to Seventh Street and left it at the Parkers' house, picking up Paul's Nash which was hidden in their garage and left for Pittsburgh. Paul kept teasing me to stop at every motel, but I just giggled and said, "Onward to Pittsburgh".

Paul drove up a one-way street the wrong way to arrive at the William Penn Hotel, where the lobby was huge and opulent, and on the wall was the famous bronze plaque bearing the watermark of the damaging flood on March 19, 1936. The Monongahela River formed in Fairmont by the Tygart and West Fork Rivers and the larger Allegheny River flow together in Pittsburgh to form the Ohio River. The flood had paralyzed Pittsburgh creating $25,000,000 worth of damage. The floodwaters had peaked at 45.95 before beginning to recede. I remember the mark of the flood in the lobby was well above my head.

We checked in to our room with large windows overlooking the lighted city, and called down to make reservations for dinner. It was eight o'clock, but they assured us they would stay open for us. The dining room was beautiful, heavily draped in red velvet surrounding mirrors and stained glass. Very few people were still at dinner, but I felt they were all looking at us, realizing we were newlyweds. I had changed into a lovely iridescent blue taffeta dress and felt so grown up! I did not wear the white orchid corsage - a dead give-a-way of a newly wedded couple.

I have no idea what we ordered for dinner. I was still in a dream about the entire day. Looking back and reading about the experience, I realized that never again would I be the star From then on, I made Paul the leading light. I never tried out for another play again; I had fallen in love with my last leading man. We were beginning a life of forty-eight years together - so young, so in love, so confident, so comfortable with each other. This was surely a marriage made in heaven.

We went up to the room where I was surprised with a cold bottle of champagne waiting on ice, which had been delivered while at dinner. Paul knew how to open it and I saved the cork. I changed into my delicate, filmy, white nightgown and negligee – a gift from Aunt Susan and Uncle Frank Haymond. Paul toasted his new bride and I sipped my first taste of that delightful, heady nectar of the gods. Paul was writing something at the desk on William Penn stationery. Looking over his shoulder I read,

> *" Nay, but you who do not love her,*
>
> *Is she not pure gold, my mistress?"*

I sat down on his lap and answered, writing Elizabeth Browning's two most famous lines,

> *"How do I love thee, let me count the ways."*
>
> *"And If God choose, I shall but love thee better after death."*

On that enchanted evening Paul had "flown to my side and made me his own"-- never to let me go, until death us do part.

> *"What therefore God haith joined together, let no man put asunder."*

~ Mark X. 9

NASSAU

We had to get up early the next morning and board an Eastern Airlines new 88 passenger Super Constellation. Beautiful first air trip for me. Paul had flown and was so nonchalant about everything; I, in turn, was scared, but did not want him to know. He sensed it, holding my hand tightly at take off. Arriving at the Miami Airport, Paul thoughtfully suggested we send Western Union telegrams to our parents. I wrote,

"DARLINGS... LANDED MIAMI 9... FLIGHT EXCITING AND SAFE...NEVER BEEN HAPPIER... THANK YOU BOTH SO MUCH FOR EVERYTHING

LOVE FROM US BOTH... DIANE AND PAUL

Our second night as a couple we spent in the plush, luxurious Hotel Saxony on the white sanded Miami Beach. Returning to our room after dinner, we stepped out on our private balcony, high enough to almost touch the full moon. Paul pointed straight out over the horizon and said, "Straight ahead is Spain." It was my first glimpse of any ocean and to see the moon's silver rays glistening down on that sea of diamonds, disappearing with each huge wave tapering into the white sand, was mesmerizing to us both. A moment I still remember so many years later. I never was happier than on that balcony, high in the sky, in my beloved's arms on the night of November 23, 1952, with a warm southern breeze enveloping us both. Yet another enchanted evening! I softly hummed,

"Moon over Miami, shine on my love and me".

The next morning we left from the Miami Beach airport on a British Overseas Airways Corporation Stratocruiser, a much smaller plane for the 50-minute trip to the Bahamas. We were the lone passengers on board and the pilot invited us into the cockpit, which fascinated Paul. We could see those tiny islands, when suddenly we were getting ready to land on New Providence -one of those postage stamps below! I closed my eyes and prayed.

Calypso singers were there to greet us with Planters Punch served from a quaint white umbrella cart. The hotel had sent a limousine and when our bags were loaded, we were driven to the gorgeous, pink Fort Montagu Hotel, built in 1926 and located about a mile up the coast from the downtown capital of the islands, Nassau.

In 1952, Nassau had become the place for honeymoon escapes, as Bermuda had become so commercial. The native Bahamians were everywhere, still driving horse drawn carriages, for there were very few cars, just miles of beauty, white sand, and pastel colored Georgian buildings. The British Colonial Hotel was yellow and was the penthouse home of the once King Edward and his wife, Wallis Simpson, for whom he gave up the throne. Years later they moved to the penthouse suites at the Waldorf Astoria in New York City.

When we got to the desk to register there were two airmail letters to welcome us and addressed to Mr. and Mrs. Paul E. Parker Jr., an anomaly to us both. One was from Mother:

"Darlings,

So nice to have your wire from Miami. I am still marveling that you even thought to send it, as I know you are just living in paradise. There is no trip in a lifetime to equal the "honeymoon", so do enjoy it. Isn't it wonderful you could go to such a perfect spot.   Remember you are near the Equator and even the stars in the sky are different. Take a look at the Southern Cross for me. Happy Thanksgiving, my dears, and all our love.

~ Mother"

November 25, 1952

Elaine's letter,

"My dears,

One of the most glamorous and glittering weddings Fairmont has ever seen is over, and I hope this finds you both even more in love than ever and in perfect happiness.

Everyone is still raving about the beautiful bride, the handsome groom and the gorgeous wedding. In fact the telephone rings constantly with thoughtful souls wanting to know if we survived. Wedding presents continue to arrive daily. We have reached the 256 sticker which I will start with today. Mother is carefully placing each gift card in your scrapbook and adding to your list of thank you notes. People are delighted to receive those you mailed from Nassau.

Sylvia, (our crying sister, trying to steal the scene again), will be writing to you soon.

Don't be good but do be happy and have a simply marvelous, scrumptious honeymoon.

Best love to both our babies.

~ Elaine "

Every morning we rented bicycles from a vendor and rode down Bay Street, stopping to see all the natives' boutiques along the way, then headed to the beach each afternoon. I thought what fun it will be to go to "Doss" Knowles' wedding in December as the newest bride and the only one with a tan! A photographer from town came to the beach one afternoon and snapped several pictures of us that were later published in the Mid-Season, 1953 issue of NASSAU- Magazine of Life and Times in the Enchanting Bahamas, Page 25. The caption read,   "Mr. and Mrs. Paul E. Parker of Fairmont, West Virginia are shown on the beach of Nassau's Fort Montague Hotel during their recent honeymoon." (K.R. Ingraham) On page ten we found we had been sharing the beach with one of my favorite stars, Tyrone Power and his wife, Linda Christian and their young daughter.

Paul, a wonderful dancer, would lead me to the dance floor each night, dancing between every course, the band thoroughly enjoying our appreciation. One night as we entered, with many already seated and eating, the maitre d' led us to a newly assigned table, a prime spot right off the dance floor. Our band played the first few strains of "Here Comes the Bride", we both blushed, charming the group who had enjoyed watching us perform each evening. One night, the Calypso singers made up a story about, "Bahama Papa" and "Bahama Mama", which became our pet names for each other, the rest of our lives.

It was time to go home; the last morning in Nassau and we were nostalgic about leaving. Would it ever be the same? The manager came to see us off and orange blossoms were brought while waiting for the limousine. He toasted us and the Calypsos appeared to sing farewell to Bahama Mama and Papa, "wishing for you not only a good life, but also a happy, sweet one."

"God's in his heaven, all's right with the world."

~ Robert Browning

CHAPTER FIFTEEN

Hutchinson

IT'S CALLED MARRIAGE

Brooks and Ray Hutchinson, bride Diane Hutchinson, groom Paul Edward Parker, Betty and "Pep" Parker
1952

Paul gave me a little book by C.S. Lewis, "On LOVE", inscribed,

"To Dee Dee, My treasure, my gem of gems, my authority on love...

With love, Paul"

"What we call 'Being in love' is a glorious state and, in several ways, good for us. It helps to make us generous and courageous, it opens our eyes not only to the beauty of the beloved but to all beauty, and it subordinates (especially at first) our merely animal sexuality; in that sense, love is the great conqueror of lust."

I have heard and agree that in every marriage one loves more than the other, and one gives more than the other. Mother warned me to look pretty and well groomed even in a bathrobe getting breakfast. Her wise warning was, "Remember, he will get on the elevator and there will always be a couple of beautifully dressed young girls just waiting for him to wink!"

Today I realize a man usually loves more at first and continues, perhaps through boredom, for a few years while he climbs the professional ladder, waiting for the children to grow up, and finally getting his bride back.

That first Monday morning home from our honeymoon, Paul hopped out of bed, flung open the double windows and yelled "Good morning, world!" I hopped out of bed, put on my newest negligee and tried to cook Paul a fried egg over the candle of a carafe - a wedding present. I did not realize a 220 outlet was needed for the electric stove that was just sitting there, completely useless.

I sat and waited and waited. I could hear him brushing his teeth. He would soon be ready, but would the egg?

I sneaked down to the first floor apartment and asked my old friend Beverly Barrett Childs if she could finish cooking it, which she did while both she and Gordon laughingly admonished me for not realizing greater heat was needed to fry an egg. I ignored them and gratefully rushed "the first egg" - fully cooked - up to my new husband. Beverly took great delight in reporting this incident to everyone, at every gathering for the next 50 years.

Our kitchen was mainly a repository of repacked wedding presents. We had five toasters, so Paul chose which one to open and use first. We had milk and butter and a box of cereal ... but he ate the egg on a piece of Kettering's

283

salt-rising toast, and raved! This seemed unusual to me as most friends refuse to eat salt rising bread. Once the odor of the bread by heating is released, it resembles the very strong odor of Limburger cheese. I will not go into the many unsolicited, unpalatable descriptions we have heard in the past.

Paul had traded his Nash - 4 on-the-floor - in for a new green fluid drive DeSoto, which I could drive. He drove down to the courthouse jumped out of the car and left me alone to drive in early downtown traffic! I was scared to death but arrived at the college and found a parking place - finally. It was hard to come down to earth and get homework done again, but Paul could help with that, and did. Like Daddy, he could answer any question I would ask. That was part of his great attraction.

What wonderful neighbors we had during those first few impressionable years. Gordon and Beverly Childs, who had not been married too long either, lived on the first floor of 827 Benoni Avenue in the old Hartman house, a large imposing grey stone house that is still there. Mother, Daddy, Mom, Elaine and Sylvia lived there for a year, when Mrs. Cook would not sell 741 to Daddy after Dr. Cook died. Once the estate was settled we bought the Cook house and moved back.

Richard Dollison, son of Ralph Dollison, owner of the Fairmont Box Factory, bought the house and made it into apartments. His brother Charles (Chud) and his wife Dorothy (Dottie) Ashba Dollison lived on the beautiful second floor with three bedrooms; we lived up on the third floor which overlooked all the blocks to Fairmont Avenue. We had two bedrooms, a large kitchen and living room and a full bath. Mr. Parker (Pep) and I got four, 8ft boards and painted them white. I went to Altman's and ordered 48 bricks. The man looked at me as only a contractor could, and with exasperation hanging from every word said, "Lady, will you take 50?"

When the painting was done I had an 8 ft. bookcase with four shelves, held up by 48 red bricks. Beautiful! It did not take long to fill the bookcase and they are still holding many of the books I have referred to while writing this book… sixty years later.

Daddy and Mother had had all the furniture we needed moved into the apartment while we were gone, as Mrs. Parker (Betty) wanted us to come home to her third floor apartment. Mother did not think that was wise, and she and Daddy worked extremely hard to prevent that from happening.

284

Dottie and Chud would have little dinner parties for the "tenants" and we thoroughly enjoyed being with these ready-made friends. Dottie and Chud had two children "Pete", 10 years old, who developed a little crush on me; and the younger Nancy, who treated Paul as if he was Cary Grant and was enchanted with Paul's attention.

Gordon and Beverly had one little girl, Valerie, who was two years old. That first summer, I bought a plastic baby pool for her, and then would join her in the afternoons to get a tan. She never forgot that pool; it kept us both cool.

The third floor was stifling in the evening and Joe Currunchia, the Movie Man, gave Paul season tickets to his Starlite Drive-in, way out in Pleasant Valley. Gas then was only about 20 cents a gallon and Paul and I would go several times a week – get a hamburger or hot dog and eat in front of the movie. If we had all ready seen it, we would leave early when the apartment would be cooled.

Paul never did like the movies much. When "Ben Hur", with Charleton Heston, was first released in 1959, Joe Currunchia invited all the city and county officials for a private showing. Paul fidgeted all through the long film and on the way out, the local radio station shoved a mike in his face and said, "What did you think of the movie, Mr. Parker?" Paul answered a little curtly, "I enjoyed both of them."

"Of course feelings come and go; ceasing to 'be in love' need not mean ceasing to love. Love in this second sense- love as distinct from 'being in love' - is not merely a feeling. It is a deep unity, maintained by the will and deliberately strengthened by habit; reinforced by the grace both partners ask and receive from God. 'Being in love' first moved them to promise fidelity: this quieter love enables them to keep the promise. It is on this love that the engine of the marriage is run: being in love was the explosion that started it." (C.S. Lewis)

"When you like the person you love, it's called marriage, and it's exciting!"

~ David Norton ("Claudia")

GOOD MORNING, MISS DOVE

My student teaching was done in Jayenne School, classified as an urban school, with Geraldine Wildman as a critic teacher. She was a marvelous teacher and had been at Jayenne for several years. I would sit and observe from the back of the room and always noticed a darling little boy in the last row, who kept trying to hold hands with his neighbor, a little girl name Ginger Valentine, with the appropriate red curly hair. Changing at lunchtime, she wore two different dresses each day, both with beautiful big bows in back. The little boy, who loved to untie every bow, was Stanard Swihart, who grew up to be my doctor. He never forgot me, and as an adult, loved introducing me as his favorite first grade teacher.

My second stint of student teaching was a combined fifth and sixth grade at a rural school in White Hall with Principal Christine Palmer as the critic teacher. Here I learned how to treat a little girl who had an epileptic seizure. One of the children ran for Mrs. Palmer, who came back immediately, and the child was fine. All I remember doing was putting a wooden pencil between her teeth, but it worked! I got all "A" pluses from the two principals and the two critic teachers; but received a B from FSC supervisory teacher, Mrs. Margaret Willard. She was in charge of the student teaching and had been at the college for years. I had a private conference with her, questioning this grade. She peevishly informed me I had not joined her Future Teachers of America group, therefore she denied the "A's". When I protested, she said she would see to it that I would never get a job in Marion County.

When my grades arrived, I had all A's. Miss Wildman called to make sure and said that she and Mr. Floyd Prunty, principal of Jayenne School, had called the education department at the college and refused to accept any future student teachers if I did not receive the grades they had recorded and that I had earned. I thanked her so much and told her what Mrs. Willard had said about a job. Miss Wildman assured me that Mr. Prunty would call Mr. Glenn A. Keister, urban superintendent of the elementary schools at the Board of Education.

Because of a glitch in my advisor's office, I still needed Art 102, which was not available until the summer school second session; therefore, I received my diploma by mail in August of 1954. What a letdown! No "Pomp and Circumstance", no cap or gown, no proud parents crying in the stands.

The Marion County Board of Education called in August and hired me to teach one of the two first grades at White School on Locust Avenue. I was delighted, just what I asked for – either White, or my alma mater, Butcher. I am sure Mr. Prunty's call had something to do with it, but Sylvia and I had grown up with the Keister's daughters, Carol Jo, and Christine; and Paul, as assistant prosecutor, represented the Board of Education. Mr. Keister knew me better than Mrs. Willard did.

That same fall, Paul bought our first television set. Our old friend Bertram Cousins (Boots) had started a cable company, as in these West Virginia mountains; we could get only one channel. Paul brought the set home and we attached the four black wrought iron legs to it. The outside was a brown leather- look with a 19" screen, made by Raytheon. Mr. Parker gave us his Mon Power discount, to make it more affordable. Then we had to wait for the cable to be put in. It was installed just in time for the Army - McCarthy hearings. I would rush home from White School every day to listen and watch. What a wonderful, unbelievable invention.

I had seen my first set in 1948, six years before, at the RCA building in New York. The National Broadcasting Company had one on display promoting the future for the tours. It photographed the participants on the tour, but nothing else. Television still awed us after 45 years. During the Anita Hill and Clarence Thomas congressional hearings in 1991, Paul, who then was ill and just home from the hospital, said, "It is still a wonderment to me that we can be in a front row seat at these congressional hearings."

The 30 first graders were so young and many had never been to a private kindergarten. There was no pre-school in the early fifties and I had the first integrated class with two little black girls. No one noticed a difference. They fit right in. During the long Christmas holiday, when her out of town relatives had been visiting, one little girl whispered to me the first day back, "My uncle said I didn't have to go to school with 'chocolate drops.'" I had never heard that particular moniker, but I quickly responded, "Oh Betty, Missy and Annie are just two pretty little girls with long black hair just like yours." Betty took her thumb out of her mouth, looked me right in the eye and said, "Okay". End of problem.

Betty was one of the December babies whose birth date fell before January 1, when the cutoff date for five years olds to attend school ended. I was a December 30 baby and empathized with the children who seemed slower than their friends. I was the youngest in my class, a year younger than those born in January of 1932. When these December children returned after the holidays they began to catch up with the older students.

The students in 1954 were much more immature than today. They had grown to this age of five and six without pre-school, kindergarten or television. No Captain Kangaroo, Howdy Doody or Mr. Rogers. Several had never been read to, and were unfamiliar with children's books. When I asked them to get in line for the first recess they stood and looked bewildered. I had to place them in line placing their hand on the shoulder of the one in front. It was really a new experience. I had forgotten my student teaching of first grade was done in a spring session after they had been in school for six months.

With no pre-school or kindergarten, one little boy, Robin, started crying as soon as his mother left. He sat on my lap the first few days of school. Few knew how to put on their galoshes, so we had a class project of show and help. Only a few of them had known each other at the beginning of school and by November they were old friends. We had all bonded.

I thought it was just nerves, but in early October of 1954 I had a spell of stomach upsets, which Paul and I determined was nothing but anxiety over a new job. In late October, Dottie and Beverly suggested I see a doctor, as they were sure I was pregnant. Unbelievable!

Paul took me to see Dr. Emery D. Wise, a good friend of the Parkers and he pronounced it so. We drove directly to Mother's and Daddy's and made the announcement. We all cried for joy.

It was a little hard to listen to the "Bluebirds" try to read "Dick and Jane", as daily I had to run to the bathroom with morning sickness. I assigned one larger boy to be a monitor and answer the door. One day Paul came a little early to meet the children and take me to lunch. Dave Cannon went to the door and turned around and said, "Mrs. Parker, your daddy's here."

I told Mr. Byron Miller, the principal of White School about my pregnancy and, though sorry to lose me, he said he was glad I had told him as they were going to start painting the interior of the school and it might be wise if I quit at the end of the first semester- for the baby's sake. Mrs. Miller had lost a baby due to the strong chemicals in the commercial grade paint fumes. I asked the Board for a leave of absence so Mr. Miller could choose the substitute teacher. He suggested I not tell the children until after the Christmas holidays.

288

The first semester was ending and I had to tell them I was leaving. Each day it became harder for me. I loved each of those children and was vain enough to think they would miss me. Mr. Miller said that a Mrs. Haun would come on Wednesday, January 26, to meet her new students. My last day was Friday, the end of the first semester. I decided to tell them before Mrs. Haun's visit and get the shock over for all of us.

On Tuesday afternoon right after recess I told them we would have a visitor the next morning and nervously said, " Her name is Mrs. Haun and she is so excited to meet each of you as she will be your new teacher for the rest of the year. " Mouths fell open, the concern was visible. I continued, "Mr. Parker and I are going to have a baby and we have so many things to do to get ready to welcome a brand new little boy or girl into our home." Hands were waving high in the air. Many questions were asked and two adopted children told us stories about how their mothers and daddies had picked them out to keep from all the other babies because they were so special.

Many more questions ensued, "Are you going to pick out one of us?" Are you going to pick out only one?" One darling, bright little girl, Dianne, who thought we were related as we both had similar names, burst into tears. She put her head down on the desk and sobbed. All eyes were on her and it seemed a good time to end the subject. I asked everyone to draw a picture of what my new baby would look like; and took Dianne to the cloakroom and just held her. I assured her she would love her new teacher, but it would never be the same for Dianne.

Diane and her first grade class at the White School in 1955

MY FIRST GRADE TEACHER
By Dianne Richardson Oliva

[Author's Note: In the early seventies, Helen Richardson, Dianne's mother, brought me an essay Dianne had written for a WVU English class 14 years later that validated my hopes of being remembered.]

"She was the most wonderful woman in the world. Mrs. Parker was my first grade teacher. She taught me to count and I learned my letters from her. She was incredibly beautiful. Her hair was a luxurious brunette hue and her complexion was clear and rosy. I willingly left the safety of my mother's arms when I met this woman. When I looked into her kind eyes, I knew she thought I was special. She was the first person that I loved outside my family. She was my first mentor. I could not wait to go to school every morning. I dreaded the weekends without her, yet I had the satisfaction of spending a whole year in her classroom. When you are six years old a year is forever.

"In the middle of the school year, she told the class she had a special announcement to make. We were all very excited. I wondered what extraordinary treasure she would share with us. Could it be that she would tell the class how important I was to her? She made eye contact with me. This was a special look she saved for her favorites. "I have fantastic news for you. My husband and I are going to have a new baby in about five months. This will be our first child and we are so excited. I will not be able to teach after next week as we have so much to do to get ready for the new baby. You will be getting a new teacher and her name is Mrs. Haun. I know you will like her. She cannot wait to meet all of you. I have told her what extraordinary children you are..." She continued to tell us about our new teacher. It felt like she had thrown a knife into my chest. Why would she want a new baby when she had me? I looked at her, she was smiling at another student in the same way I thought she had reserved for me. How could I have been so blind? I felt wounded and betrayed. I looked down at my desk and tried not to cry I looked at the other students and I saw the sadness in their eyes. They couldn't possibly be as sad as I was. She meant everything to me. I started to sob quietly.

"She looked into my eyes and saw my intense pain and said, "Dianne, would you come to the cloak room with me?" I knew I had done nothing wrong, was I not allowed to love her? I asked if she was mad at me. She said "Dianne I am worried about you. Why are you crying?" I looked into her sweet face, and I knew that she loved me. "Mrs. Parker," I sobbed, "you cannot stop being my teacher. Surely it doesn't take five months to get ready for a baby. Just buy a few clothes and a bed and be done with it. I know I won't like the new teacher. She will be mean and couldn't be as beautiful as you. Please don't leave me."

"She tried to comfort and reassure me. Finally she said, "I have been saving a special gift to give you." She told me to wait until she got it for me. She returned with that entrancing smile, and handed me a wonderful treasure. I embraced that wonderful prize, and was able to smile weakly and ask," Is this just for me?" "Yes," she said, "You are a very special and sweet little girl and I will always remember that you cared enough about me to cry when I had to stop teaching." "Oh but I love you Mrs. Parker!" I confessed. "Yes I know you do, and I love you", she replied. My heart soared once again.

"I wish I could remember what token she gave me that day. It has been long forgotten and thrown away. Yet I will never forget my first love. As I grew older, I rode my bicycle by her house and remembered those remarkable days I spent in her glorious presence. The few times I ran into her she would look at me in her charming way and reminisce about the day I cried so passionately for her. I doubt if she still lives in that same house, but when I drive by I still look at it and smile. My beloved Mrs. Parker may be living there. If I went to her door she would remember how much I loved her as a little girl, and she would know that I still do."

"One hundred years from now, it will not matter what my bank account was, how big my house was, or what kind of car I drove. But the world might be a little better place because I was important in the life of a child."

~ Forrest Witcraft

CHAPTER SIXTEEN

A JEALOUS MISTRESS

Marion County Courthouse, built in 1900

"The Law is a jealous mistress and requires a long and constant courtship"

~ United States Supreme Court Justice Joseph Story -1829

Paul loved to practice law. His mother often said he had declared to her and his father that all he wanted to do was to practice law and love "Dee Dee".

Paul's uncle, Raymond Worth Shumaker, was an outstanding West Virginia athletic figure as player, coach and athletic director at Wesleyan College in Buckhannon. Uncle Worth was with the Americanism Committee of the American Legion at National Headquarters in Indianapolis, Indiana and was originator of Boys Nation and promoted Boys State at Jackson's Mills in West Virginia.

Paul had gone to the American Legion Boys State in 1944 as a junior from Morgantown High School and had run for the Supreme Court. Having won the seat, he was appointed as Chief Justice of the mock court. Judge Herschel Rose of Fairmont, Chief Justice of the West Virginia Supreme Court, had given the opening address to the boys, who were appointed from every high school and county in West Virginia. Paul, impressed with the stature and the words of Judge Rose, determined he would go to law school.

He majored in political science at WVU, but was drafted on December 12, 1945, his eighteenth birthday. He was sent to Fort Benning, Georgia for basic training and swore never to be in the U.S. Army Infantry again. He used to tell about night maneuvers, sleeping on that red clay of Georgia, and "in that deadly stillness you could hear two blades of grass rub against each other".

When he was discharged he returned to Morgantown and WVU - immediately joining the USAF- ROTC in 1947 - the year of its inception. Upon graduating, he was commissioned second lieutenant and proud to be an officer of the United States Air Force.

Paul graduated from WVU law school on June 2, 1951 and was admitted to the West Virginia Supreme Court two days later on June 4. At that time there was no LSAT (Law School Admission Test) and about 200 returning veterans, eager to get the excellent government education offered to those honorably discharged, were admitted to law school but after three years of rigorous training, only 50 graduated after taking the West Virginia bar examination as their final test. Paul used to say he was proud of being a C student as it was thought, "A students made law professors, B students made judges and C students made lawyers".

The day Paul proposed to me in his office was a very significant day for him. He had graduated from law school and been admitted to practice before the Supreme Court of Appeals a year before on this same date. I read the oath he took when he was sworn in as a new attorney.

"I do solemnly swear or affirm I will support the Constitution of the United States and the Constitution of this State, and I will faithfully perform the duties of attorney at law.

I will exhibit, and I will seek to maintain in others, the respect due to the courts and judges.

I will, to the best of my ability, abide by the Model Rules of Professional conduct and any other standards of ethics proclaimed by the courts, and in doubtful cases I will attempt to abide by the spirit of those ethical rules and precept of honor and fair play.

I will not reject, from any consideration personal to myself, the cause of the impoverished, the defenseless or the oppressed.

I will endeavor always to advance the cause of justice and to defend and to keep inviolate the rights of all persons whose trust is conferred upon me as an attorney at law."

Paul ascribed to this vow every day for the rest of his life.

In the spring of 1954 Paul joined the Air Force Reserve Unit whose forces in this area were represented by the 949 1st Air Reserve Squadron with flights in Fairmont, Morgantown and Clarksburg and headquarters at Fairmont State College. The squadron had been organized on a voluntary basis and had no training equipment, but it did have 17 officers and 6 enlisted men. Lt. Col. Andrew Hauge was the commanding officer in charge. Paul, a second lieutenant, really enjoyed the military significance and was appointed as the Marion County Civil Defense Director. Many today are not aware this agency ever existed in Fairmont.

The threat of the atomic bomb after those WWII years was greater than I ever realized. As we were only 93 miles from Pittsburgh, Pennsylvania, with great steel mills being a likely target for an enemy, Fairmont would be included in the "hot zone" for fallout.

On Monday, June 14, 1954, the Civil Defense Center, with Howard Stewart and William S. Schmidt in charge, was activated in the basement of the Federal Courthouse on Fairmont Avenue in connection with a simulated atomic bomb attack on the city of Wheeling, West Virginia - just outside of Pittsburgh, in our northern panhandle.

During the simulated attack, Radio Chief Thomas Haymond monitored all radio messages broadcasted in connection with the air radio defense test. Paul went to Wheeling to observe operations there.

As CD director, Paul organized the Marion County Auxiliary Police, which involved 600 men, into 12 field units in Fairmont, Mannington, Farmington, Barrackville, Millersville and Westchester, plus a communications division.

Two years later on April 13, 1956, a Fairmont Times front-page article announced Paul's resignation as CD director to run for prosecuting attorney of Marion County. He stated,

"I am particularly proud of my association with the Marion County Auxiliary Police and their Chief William Hamrick. Many of these men are specialists in power generation, radio transmission and equipment and each is uniformed and equipped, for the most part, at his own expense. The mobile communications truck is entirely a product of individual effort, the ingenuity and skills of these men in emergency situations has no counterpart in this state.

"Another group that has not received the recognition they deserve is our Ground Observer Corp. Some 300 men and women at 4 posts in the county formed a part of a nationwide spotting net of the United States Air Force. The Fairmont group is located on the roof of the First National Bank building and is connected with the Air Force Filter Center in Roanoke, Virginia by a direct phone line…all the volunteer spotters are to be congratulated for their indispensible service.

"A relatively new program underway is that of radiological defense under the direction of Dr. Rupert W. Powell. The American Legion, Post 17, is sponsoring a monitoring team for the detection and decontamination of areas subjected to radioactive fallout. Volunteer Legionnaires will be trained and the team will be equipped at the joint cost of Post 17 and the CD Council. This program has become essential in view of the threat of radioactive fallout in the area following a thermonuclear attack upon Wheeling or Pittsburgh and I deeply appreciate this fine contribution of funds and personnel to our defense."

"Parker said he 'resigned with great reluctance' and offered to work closely with the council in the future."

****

On June 7, 1955 our first child was born, Paul Edward Parker, III.

He was born two weeks late. The longest two weeks I ever remember. Paul was an absolute wreck after suffering along with me for twenty-four hours. After the birth and I was back in my room, the head nurse Albertha Rosier came in to see how I was. She held out her arms to Paul who literally fell in to them sobbing. No attention was paid to me or to my beautiful 9lb. 4oz. baby boy. She sent the new father home to get some sleep.

When Sylvia Elaine (8lb.14oz.) was born, 2 weeks early, on Sunday April 26, 1959, we arrived at Fairmont General Hospital around 6:00 a.m.; I sent Paul out for breakfast!

Sylvia arrived at 8:29 a.m.

When Paul got back from breakfast, he was delighted to hear of her birth and that I was fine.

"God's in his heaven, all's right with the world."

~ Robert Browning

Eddie and Sylvia, 1961

PASTA & POLITICS

Paul Edward Parker Jr.; campaign for prosecuting attorney for Marion County, 1956

Paul decided to run for Marion County Prosecuting Attorney against a 24-year incumbent-his old boss, Harrison Waitman Conaway, who had planned to run for judge of the criminal court. Paul resigned as assistant and filed in February 1956. Judge Miller did not retire and decided to serve another term. Conaway, therefore, filed against Paul to again run for his old office.

Paul ran as a crusader against the racketeers and promised to investigate the illegal sale of liquor and the flaunting of illegality in the heart of downtown Fairmont. Very few professional fees were coming in and several of the business people who really counted on Paul to win, carried us for months.

We lived on preparing others' income taxes until March 15, the due date in 1956; plus a few clients that followed him over to the Home Savings Bank building that had a rickety old elevator that scared Eddie and me. We could not afford a license for the Desoto and Paul walked to town every morning. On nice days I would wheel Eddie downtown in his stroller and meet Paul for lunch at Hagan's. It was fun to introduce Eddie to all the sales people and attorneys. Eddie, turning into a great politician, shook hands with everyone and particularly liked Rollo (Fritz) Conley, always offering him a bite of his saltine cracker. Fritz spoke several languages, including Japanese, and had served in the Diplomatic Corps during World War II. When he returned to Fairmont he attended Fairmont State College while I was there and then went on to WVU law school. He took great delight in telling everyone that he and I had graduated from college together in 1954, even though he was 30 years older than I.

Eddie was only ten months old and Mother and Daddy did a lot of babysitting. They would come to the house and Paul was relieved with free, "self propelled baby sitters". Eddie was thrilled with "Mony" and "Dah", his short cut from Grandmommy and Granddaddy.

Saturdays and Sundays were all pasta and politics. We attended two or three spaghetti dinners each evening, eating a few bites at each one to be polite. My favorite was the Immaculate Conception Church on East Side. Their sauce was scrumptious. Paul found out that Lena Fridley, the woman that used to clean his office at the courthouse, was one of the cooks who made that sauce. When he returned to the office as prosecutor, she would bring him sauce to take home about once a month.

We heard the owners of the illegal dives were fighting very hard against Paul, but we had been assured by the Democrats in Marion County, if we won the primary election against Conaway, we would be a "shoo in". Paul assumed nothing and fought as hard as he could, winning the democrat primary by only a few hundred votes.

Paul's platform announced under a large picture of him said,

DEMOCRATS   Nominate a man we can elect

PAUL E. PARKER Jr.
For
PROSECUTING ATTORNEY

EXPERIENCE:
Practiced law in Marion County for 5 years; served as Assistant Prosecuting Attorney for three and one half years resulting in a through working knowledge of every phase of criminal prosecution including investigation, preparation for trial and trial; acted as attorney for the Board of Education, State Road Commission (e.g. condemnation proceedings), the County Court, Department of Public Assistance and other governmental agencies.

SERVICE:
Veteran of World War II, United States Army; at present First Lieutenant United States Air Force Reserve.

PLATFORM:
I am firmly committed to the following:

1. Government by existing law as opposed to government by political and personal expediency.

2. Uncompromising prosecution of the professional gamblers, racketeers and bootleggers who now flourish defiantly in the heart of Fairmont.

3. Thorough investigation of all offenses.

4. Vigorous prosecution of persons charged with violation of the law.

5. Faithful protection of the rights, privileges and immunities of individuals.

"I rely solely upon the support of voters who favor impartial and proper law enforcement."

Sincerely, Paul E. Parker, Jr.

"This advertisement paid for by Democrats who believe Marion County is entitled to full value from tax money expended for legal services and law enforcement."

After a hard fought general election against his Phi Psi brother, Republican Harry Raymond Cronin, we were in!

"Marion County Officials Begin New Terms Today"
The Fairmont Times
Tuesday Morning, January 1, 1957

Pictures of the new officials were displayed on the front page that New Year morning in 1957. Criminal Judge Charles Miller, Sheriff, J. Max Gill, Prosecuting Attorney Paul E. Parker Jr., Circuit Clerk James C. Morgan, County Clerk Maria Haymond Clark, Assessor Alice Blanche Davis, and County Commissioners Harry D. Martin and Frank H. Conaway.

The afternoon paper read,

"New Prosecutor Taking Office in County Today"
The West Virginian
Wednesday Evening January 2, 1957

"Marion County has a new prosecuting attorney today for the first time in 24 years. Paul E. Parker, Jr. assumed his new duties this morning and immediately started preparations for the January term of court which opens next Tuesday. Parker was busy examining cases ready to be presented to the Grand Jury on opening day.

"Also assuming his duties today was H. Clare Hess, veteran Mannington attorney who will serve as Parker's assistant. Hess and city, county and federal officers were assisting Parker this morning in plans for the new court term.

"The youthful prosecutor succeeds Harrison Conaway who held the post longer than any other prosecuting attorney in the county's history. Hess replaces D.J. Romino, Fairmont attorney who was Conaway's assistant. Mrs. Yolanda Napple is serving temporarily as secretary to the new prosecutor."

302

Richard Parrish, Editor of The West Virginian, ran a series of articles soon after Paul was elected called "Marion County After Dark". The series featured the nightspots causing the most harm to businesses in the city and elaborating about the illegal gambling, sale of liquor, the numbers game, tip boards, and the lack of acknowledgement by either the city or county.

A year later on March 10, 1958, Richard Parrish's editorial in The West Virginian stated,

"The Mills of the Gods Grind Slowly, But..."

"It seems only yesterday that the racketeers were Kings in their own right in Fairmont and Marion County. They were rarely disturbed and then only by an occasional raid intended as a sop to eccentric citizens who had the notion that gambling, liquor and other rackets were supposed to be illegal and harmful.

"Here and there influential figures who had worked outside the law began to get their just desserts. A city board was elected on a reform ticket and a police chief resigned in a hurry. An attorney had the courage to run on a clean-up platform and he was elected prosecutor. A city curfew law was passed by the city board and upheld by the Criminal Court. Two civilian police chiefs took the handcuffs off the policemen and the rackets were hit harder than ever before. The city board passed an ordinance forbidding the playing of pinball machines by minors.

"Such steps represented solid gains toward the goal of a decent city and county, but they were, in their way, only temporary in nature."

****

"The rackets suffered their biggest blow here last year when temporary injunctions were issued by the Circuit Court and Kibbie's Place on Merchant Street and the Eldorado Club on Pleasant Valley Road were padlocked. Here was something really permanent, a thousand more times more effective than any number of "raids" on the illegal nightspots.

"It happened again last week when the Army Navy Garrison on Merchant Street and the Stardust room in Rivesville were padlocked.

Both of these places were notorious not only as lawbreakers but for their virtual defiance of city and county police. It has been charged that the Rivesville place was frequented by teen- agers."

****

"If these places are now out of existence for good then the whole community has made a gain. It will now be hoped that similar establishments will also be padlocked.

The many persons responsible for the padlocking are deserving of warm commendation. Clearly we have first-rate public officials among us. We believe they have the backing of the vast majority of our people."

****

And they were all padlocked for good. Soon after this editorial was published, the Ten High Club, that flourished a logo of a top hat and a glass of champagne, was padlocked- the last dive on Merchant Street. Mr. Constantine Potesta, owner of the Merchant Street Community Market, our first super market, would give Eddie, who rode up in the cart seat, a big bag of seedless green grapes to snack on while I shopped. "Tino" would introduce me to everyone as Prosecutor Parker's wife and exclaim that Mr. Parker had made it safe for women to walk on Merchant Street again.

Rider Pharmacy later bought that whole block and is still in that location.

After Paul retired as prosecutor he went into private practice and one of his principal clients was the Department of Highways. All the roads needed to be condemned that would lead into the new I-79 corridor. Paul became a master of Eminent Domain. Even judges would call him about the condemnation procedure. He wrote a textbook on Eminent Domain in later years.

He also handled personal injury cases. One of the most tragic cases was representing the husband of a woman killed in a furniture store fire.

In 1971- 1972, Paul came home one day and asked me to write down every single thing I did for each member of the family. This was rather fun and interesting and I proceeded with: the cooking, chauffeuring, nursing, teaching, mentoring, sewing and making of clothes and slipcovers, housekeeping, gardening etc-etc- He sent a typed list to Kent State University economist who put the going rate for everything on my list.

At the trial, the economist put a figure of money into the case, which proved the economic value of a wife and a mother to a husband, who, though self employed, would suffer from the loss of his deceased wife within West Virginia's Wrongful Death Act, and his pecuniary loss was compensable, where deceased performed all the duties as a housewife.

The Appellant appealed the case awarding damages for the death of the wife. His principle claim, that the husband was not her dependant distributee within the meaning of the Wrongful Death Act.

The United States District Court for the Northern District of West Virginia, Sidney L. Christie, Chief Judge ruled that he was and. Circuit Judges, Winter, Craven and Butzner affirmed and upheld the District Court's verdict. (Decided March 8, 1972)

Many years later, after Paul's stroke, he reminded me about the case in one of his love notes.

30 December 1994

Happy Birthday, Honey; being 62 is a great year and a great time- I know-I have done it before.

You've made me a millionaire in having such a gem as my love. Remember the furniture store fire case and the valuation of a wife we established and made law? Can you imagine an economist's analysis of your value? Makes Publishers Clearing House look like a piker!

As you mature you become even more valuable. As you once said, "Come along with me for the best is yet to be". You are right and I am trying- you certainly do mature well!

All my love, Paul

FINALLY!

On September 18, 1957, The West Virginian published a picture of a history making Grand Jury, the first Grand Jury in Marion County to include women members. They were welcomed to service yesterday by Judge Charles E. Miller. Pictured were Court Deputy Ralph C. Truman, Sheriff Max Gill, Prosecuting Attorney Paul E. Parker and jurors, Mrs. Patricia Maddox, Mrs. Lona Huey, Miss Mary Sturm, and Mrs. Ellen Horchler and matron, Frances Rowland. The male Jurors stood in the back of the group and one of them was our next-door neighbor, Anthony P. Cyran.

Before the vote "the little woman" was expected to raise the family, put food on the table and take good care of her husband. The more avant-garde pioneers formed the Women's Christian Temperance Union (WCTU) and fought for their platform from a little building they had built in 1897 at the end of the South Side Bridge on First Street and Fairmont Avenue.

These first feminists marched in the street and demanded the right to vote. They also demanded the "demon rum" be cast out of the home and peace would prevail. Mammam carried one side of a banner in a parade on Adams Street. The WCTU was incorporated in West Virginia on April 20, 1885; Mammam became 20 years old on April 21. She was married the next year in 1886, had Uncle Claude in 1887 and Daddy in 1888; she really did not have much time to march except that first year.

The West Virginia Encyclopedia, edited by Ken Sullivan (2006) states,

> *"Local suffrage clubs sprang up in the urban centers of West Virginia's northern counties, with the most active clubs in Wheeling and Fairmont. "*

A women's suffrage amendment failed to pass in 1913 because it called for a two-third majority needed in the Senate. Another attempt passed in 1915, leading to a statewide constitutional referendum in 1916. "The high hopes of the suffragists were shattered when the amendment failed by more than two to one. The women were not given the vote.

With a lot of in-fighting, the United States Congress passed the federal amendment in 1919, less than four years after the defeat of the referendum for state suffrage. It is thought that the, "West Virginia suffragists provided a crucial victory in the fight to win the 36 states needed to achieve women's suffrage nationally."

306

On March 10, 1920 the West Virginia State Senate guaranteed the right of women to vote by a close vote of 15-14. West Virginia was the 34th State to ratify the 19th amendment. But the right to serve on a jury still belonged to men only.

In 1954, the live TV production of "Twelve Angry Men" hit the boards and in 1957 the movie, directed by Sidney Lumet - his debut in filmmaking, was released. In the November 6 election of 1956, West Virginian voters finally approved jury service for women, the last state to do so; and Marion County elected Paul for his first term as prosecutor. It took 2 terms of court to collect all the data and the voter registration numbers of all the women in the county who were registered, and finally, Paul gladly welcomed the first four women jurors to the September term of the grand jury.

Paul's belief was that the women jurors were an essential component of a just and fair trial and he was adamant that our justice system may not always work the way we felt was right, but it was, by far, the best in the world.

While gathering data and information for this book I showed the children the newspaper clipping of the first women jurors. Jan, our daughter in law, exclaimed, "That was the year I was born!" It was hard for them to believe that women were not allowed to serve on juries until 1957, but our suffragists were no longer with us and "Twelve Angry Men" had brought the deliberate oversight to the feminist front.

HISTORY-MAKING GRAND JURY—Pictured above is first grand jury in Marion County Criminal Court to include women members. They were welcomed to service yesterday by Judge Charles E. Miller. Pictured above, left to right, front row, are Court Deputy Ralph C. Truman, Sheriff J. Max Gill, Prosecuting Attorney Paul E. Parker Jr., Jurors Mrs. Patricia Maddox, Mrs. Lona Huey, Miss Mary Sturm and Mrs. Ellen Horchler and Matron Frances Rowland; second row, Jurors James Clelland, Thomas Hamilton, Harry Thompson, Reese Mall, Vincent Vingle, Anthony P. Cyran, George S. Boehm and Assistant Prosecuting Attorney H. Clare Hess; back row, Howard Yoho, L. L. Eddy, Foreman William Thompson, Jess W. Jamison, James O. May and Circuit Clerk James C. Morgan.

History making Grand Jury; first jury with women, September 1957

JFK & THE 1960 PRIMARIES

Paul was prepared to run for one more term as prosecutor. He had made a real change in this town and his constituents were satisfied by the progress he had made. Due to his competency in his first term, he was considered a sure winner in the 1960 Primary election. Paul's' successful re-election was overshadowed by the exciting election of John F. Kennedy. The Kennedys bombarded West Virginia –a 95% Protestant State. Certain family members arrived several days before and helped the Democrat party set up dinners and functions, as we had done for Senator and Mrs. Hubert Humphrey, who had been here campaigning a week ago.

The Democrat women met with Teddy Kennedy in the Circuit Court room at the courthouse the night before his brother's appearance in Fairmont. Teddy came in to the middle of the beautiful stained glass windowed courtroom amidst hundreds of older women who thought him adorable and were eager to listen. He immediately took off his jacket and rolled up his dress shirtsleeves, to appear "just like home?" We all laughed with him and exclaimed how warm the weather was; he told us exactly the route of travel and the ETA, and to what we were to pay particular attention.

This group of women democrats had been doing this for the last 50 years or more and once Teddy was through with all his requirements and directions, he abruptly left with his coat slung over his shoulder. He was to meet with the Democrat Executive Committee for dinner at the Elk's Club. Aunt Fannie Haymond Arnette, president of the Democratic women, stood up and said, "O.K. gals, this is how we're going to proceed." Poor Teddy.

We all knew our jobs. Roberta Webb and I were in charge of decorating for luncheons and dinners during this election years and we had made plans for the Humphrey dinner at the Fairmont Hotel. Our committees used large silver candelabra and ivy on the speaker's table, interspersing the ivy around silver bowls holding masses of fresh flowers. However, Senator Kennedy would not be here for a dinner, only a rally at the Democrat Headquarters at the Virginia Theatre on Adams Street.

The motorcade, led by W.V. State police on motorcycles, took forever to come from Benedum Airport, as the streets were lined with Kennedy fans. After a quick luncheon at the sheriff's home next to the Marion County Courthouse, he took questions from all the national and local press. No observers were admitted, but Paul sneaked in through the back door leading to the jail and listened in quiet amazement, hearing him field every question with grace, dexterity and adroitness, just as a seasoned veteran of political wars. Paul met him afterwards and got his autograph on the back of his business card, which I had framed later.

Cynthia Woodward and I took Eddie and her daughter, Susan, both 4 years old at time, down to the theatre where he was to make his speech. When we arrived, there was no seating left inside and we were put in the line fronting his path into the double glass doors inside the lobby. It was a cold April day and Eddie was in his camel hair coat and leggings, looking very similar to Jack in his younger days. We had to lift the children up in our arms, as they were too little to fight the crowd building behind us. Susan had no gloves on and her hands were so cold. Cynthia remembers putting her gloves on Susan. The men guarding Kennedy and his staff came through first, pushing us all back to make room for the candidate. Kennedy came through, smiling broadly and stopped to speak to Eddie, patted him on the head and said, "Hello, young man", then tried to shake Susan's hand, laughing at the little hand in such big gloves. I was completely charmed! We did not go into the packed theatre; we forged our way out to Adams Street and took the children home for naps. From Fairmont, Jack and his entourage moved on to Morgantown, to meet Jackie for a large dinner at the Hotel Morgan.

The Kennedys invaded West Virginia en masse! All but Rose Kennedy, Jack's mother.

In her memoir "Times To Remember" (1974), she says that after Jack had won a surprising victory against Humphrey in Wisconsin, he sent Bobby, Larry O'Brien and Kenny O'Donnell to a West Virginia meeting of Democrat campaign workers in Charleston. Kenney O'Donnell described the welcome they received,

"Well", Bobby said to them pleasantly, *"what are our problems?"*

A man stood up and shouted,

"There's only one problem. He's a Catholic. That's our goddamned problem!"

Kenny continued,

"The room broke into an uproar with everyone yelling at us that no one would vote for a Catholic in a contested presidential primary... I looked at Bobby. He seemed to be in a state of shock. His face was as pale as ashes."

310

When they called Jack, he was taken aback by Bobby's discouragement and reminded him of the win in the pre-campaign poll. Bobby answered,

"The people who voted for you in that poll just found out that you're a Catholic." Overnight their whole situation in West Virginia had changed.

Poor Rose was all set to campaign with her family again, but in 1952 she had been made a papal countess by Pope Pius XII and in the terms of the scroll-delivered to her by Francis Cardinal Spellman - this was recognition of an exemplary life and considered a tremendous honor. But in West Virginia with "popery" suddenly the big issue, Rose Kennedy would have become counterproductive. Rose explains,

"So, I wasn't invited. I don't recall any discussion of the fact that I might be a problem. Bobby said I should go back to Palm Beach and rest for a week, we're booking you in Indiana, Nebraska and Maryland."

Franklin D. Roosevelt, Jr. was a valuable campaigner for Kennedy in West Virginia as Roosevelt's father (President Franklin Delano Roosevelt) had pushed through the National Recovery Act (NRA) legislation in 1933 giving the miners the rights to organize and get decent living wages. Jack decided to face the religious issue head on. He brought it up himself here in Fairmont while Humphrey was in southern West Virginia playing his campaign song, "Give Us That Old-time Religion", Jack was in Fairmont, contending with a smile,

"Nobody asked me if I was a Catholic when I joined the United States Navy."

We heard one old miner said he would love to meet Jackie, but could not leave his invalid wife. After Jackie left his home, he is quoted as saying,

"Now I believe in Santa Claus. She really looks like a queen."

Theodore H. White, a liberal journalist, described West Virginians, in his book, "The Making of a President, 1960 " as, "Handsome people... the best mannered and most courteous in the nation... these are the people who teach their children to say 'Sir' and 'Thank you' to their elders and speak in soft and gentle tones. Moreover, these are brave people - no state of the union contributed more heavily to the Armed Forces of the United States in proportion to population than did this state of mountain men; nor did any state suffer more casualties in proportion to its population. That they live as they do is a scar and shame on American life, an indictment of the national political system as well as of their own."

This was true. Remember - back in Afterword, Chapter 4 - West Virginia was one of five states never granted a major military base during WWII. Our neighbor, Ohio, had five installations. We hoped and prayed we could be responsible for Kennedy's election- believing him when he said he would never forget us if he won.

The national press had already conceded the election to Humphrey, but on Tuesday, May 10, 1960, West Virginia took great pride in playing a pivotal role in Kennedy's election. According to the West Virginia Bluebook of 1960, Kennedy received 236,510 votes to Hubert Humphrey's 152,510. Kennedy won 50 of the State's 55 counties.

We loved him. It was not a dislike of Humphrey, who was charming and delightful, but older-without the Kennedy élan.

It was a hard selection and a complete surprise to the country that a 95% protestant state would vote overwhelmingly for a Roman Catholic. Rumors were flying about the money spent, particularly in the southern coalfields, so unlike the northern counties.

Marion County, the home of longtime Senator the late Mathew M. Neely, and a strong Democrat county, finally had a winner after eight long years with a Republican in office. No votes needed to be bought here.

I think we were all in love with his youth, his glamour; he was bright, brave, funny and handsome. He looked like it was fun to be alive, to be a Kennedy, to be a politician and to be in West Virginia... for "one brief shining moment".

In the general election, with Frank Sinatra singing "High Hopes" in the background, Kennedy proclaimed, "I am not a Catholic candidate for President, I am the Democrat party's candidate for President, who happens to be a Catholic." It worked!

On a bitter cold day January 20, 1961, a young and vigorous new president stood before a shivering crowd and declaimed an unforgettable Inauguration speech.

"Mr. Chief Justice, President Eisenhower, Vice President Nixon, President Truman, Reverend Clergy, Fellow Citizens, we observe today not a victory of party, but a celebration of freedom --- symbolizing an end as well as a beginning --- signifying renewal, as well as change.

"Let the word go forth from this time and place, to friend and foe alike, that the torch has been passed to a new generation of Americans, born in this century, tempered by war, disciplined by a hard and bitter peace, proud of our ancient heritage, and unwilling to witness or permit the slow undoing of those human rights to which this nation has always been committed, and to which we are committed today, at home and around the world.

"Let every Nation know, whether it wishes us well or ill, that we shall pay any price, bear any burden, meet any hardship, support any friend, oppose any foe, in order to assure the survival and the success of liberty. This much we pledge and more.

"And so, my fellow Americans, ask not what your country can do for you, ask what you can do for your country. My fellow citizens of the world: ask not what America will do for you, but what together we can do for the freedom of man.

"With a good conscience our only sure reward, with history the final judge of our deeds, let us go forth to lead the land we love, asking His blessing and His help, but knowing that here on earth God's work must truly be our own."

~ President John F. Kennedy

[Author note]
A Topography of Faith Map 2012 from USA TODAY shows West Virginia:

Evangelistic Protestant	36%
Mainline protestant	22%
Roman Catholic	7%
Jewish	1%
Hindu	1%
All other religions	0.5%
Unaffiliated	19%

John F. Kennedy campaigning at a West Virginia coal mine, 1960

EXTRA! EXTRA!

A good conversation piece or icebreaker is the question, "Where Were You When?"

If we are old enough, we remember where we were on December 7, 1941. I was sitting in the Fairmont Theatre with my mother watching Bob Hope and Madeline Carroll, who played a spy in the just released, "My Favorite Blonde".

All of a sudden the movie went black, the overhead lights came on, the enormous red velvet curtain closed and a small, little man-extremely nervous- stepped out from the middle of the curtain and read from a shaking piece of paper, "The Japanese have just bombed Pearl Harbor." People were leaving the theatre. Mother started crying. I was eight years old.

When we came out of the theatre It was the first time I heard paperboys shouting, "EXTRA! EXTRA! Read all about it... Japs bomb Pearl Harbor!" The next time I heard "Extra Extra" was when President Roosevelt died on April 12, 1945. The little paperboys came out Fairmont Avenue to Twelfth Street shouting the news. The third time I heard it was November 22, 1963.

On November 22, 1963, our eleventh wedding anniversary, I had gone to Anne Morris Hupp's house across the street on Coleman Avenue. Sylvia was napping and Eddie was in Miss Edith Hall's third grade class at Butcher School. Anne had a radio on, but we were talking about a recipe. I thought I heard, "President Kennedy is dead." I ran back to the house and Paul was calling on the phone to tell me Kennedy had been shot. Paul was hanging out of his office window and heard the employees of the downtown stores who had rushed out yelling to the unaware what had happened "Kennedy Shot-Kennedy Shot!"

They did not have a radio in the prosecutor's office and I was the one to tell them Walter Cronkite's shocking announcement, Kennedy had died from a gunshot wound to the head.

I dressed Sylvia and we tore down to Butcher School. Eddie was one of the last to be picked up. Regina Cheney Cyran, our neighbor and his second grade teacher, was waiting there with him. Regina was eager to get home, as was I, but thought we should drive downtown to get a paper for ourselves. The town was deserted, stores were closed, but the horrible headlines were still being shouted. I stopped on Jackson Street and a boy ran over to give me an Extra edition.

Again, after almost 20 years , the frightening words: "EXTRA! EXTRA! JFK KILLED." The three-inch high, broad, black and bold banner headline proclaiming his death was placed above The West Virginian heading and date - November 22, 1963. We hurried back to our castle on Coleman Avenue. Paul was there - we felt safe.

Within minutes after the news, flags were at half-staff and employees of Jones Department store had removed everything from a display window on Adams Street and placed a picture of the late president on an easel, draped with black material. All activities were cancelled throughout the state, including a WVU Mountaineer game scheduled for Saturday afternoon, which was postponed until Thanksgiving night, November 28, the first game we had ever played on Thanksgiving Day.

We were in tears the rest of the day. No one left the house until the next morning, anniversary plans completely forgotten, just shock and sorrow enveloping the four of us. I do not recall what we ate for dinner, or if we ate. All I remember was the unsettling silence.

Paul called his parents to see if they were aware of the news and for two days we sat mesmerized by the gloom of television, as did the rest of the world.

On Sunday, the twenty-fourth, Paul was leaving to go back to his office to check and prepare the docket for the next morning. He was walking through the living room and we watched Lee Harvey Oswald being led through the basement of the Dallas Police Headquarters, being taken to the county jail. It was 11:21 AM; Jack Ruby stepped out from the crowd on the right, the sound of the bullets was heard by every American. Oswald was shot in the abdomen. A murder had been committed right before our eyes by Jack Ruby, a man no one knew. We had not even had time to hate the assassin yet.

No one seemed to care much about Oswald, who died soon after arriving at Parkland Memorial Hospital, the same hospital where Kennedy had died two days earlier. No one seemed to care about the police officer J.D.Tippit, who was slain by Oswald who had been hiding in a movie theatre and tried to leave when Tippet tried to arrest him. We were all hypnotized with the Kennedys' grief, which matched our own. The West Virginian, Monday

November 24, said on page 9, "Millions See JFK's Killer Murdered". "Police Close Books on Oswald". Only a short article followed.

On Monday the 25, all stores were closed, windows still draped in black. Two members from the Headquarters Battery of the 201 National Guard- the oldest guard unit in the country and still active in Fairmont, walked a guard of honor in front of the memorial wreath at the Marion County Court House, Warren Schrum reported Monday evening in the West Virginian,

"The few people on the streets of downtown Fairmont walked hurriedly on their way, none stopping to talk with a passing friend. Many stopped to look briefly at the memorial windows, but just for a second. Although the sun shone bright this morning, a blackness hung over the city."

That same funereal evening paper's editorial quoted Editor Richard Parish- while writing about Dallas,

"This is the Texas City in which the then Senator and Mrs. Johnson were nearly mobbed by radicals two or three years ago, where Ambassador (Adlai) Stevenson was spat upon and struck two or three weeks ago, where the president was assassinated and where the alleged assassin was fatally shot yesterday."

On Wednesday, November 27, 1963 - two days after the funeral, William Dent Evans, Editor of the Times-West Virginian repeated a syndicated column by Inez Robb,

"All America must share the responsibility for the President's death in a society, that scorning political assassination, still breeds it. There are factions that have not yet ceased to dance on the grave of Franklin Delano Roosevelt and there will be those, now mouthing pious platitudes, who will do the same on the grave of Mr. Kennedy. Television gave the nation a lesson in nauseating hypocrisy with a parade of the dead President's bittersweet enemies crowding the screen to protect their affection and respect. It was not their crocodile tears that linger in the memory but the bitter tears of an unknown Negro waiter caught by the camera as he cried into a napkin at the Dallas dining room where a shocked crowd first heard the news of the President's critical condition. For this terrible deed that has taken the life of a President, we should weep as much for ourselves as for him."

Evans ended the editorial elaborating on Parish's hatred of Dallas,

"Big D." as its citizens like to call Dallas, now has a new connotation, "Disgrace".

The town which egged and spat upon their fellow Texan, Lyndon B. Johnson when he was Vice-President of the United States; which heckled and hit with a protest sign, United Nation Ambassador, Adlai E. Stevenson; which was the scene of the assassination of our President, and which then permitted a gross miscarriage of justice in the Oswald case, has become an object of scorn. It might have happened somewhere else, as those who defend Dallas point out, but the fact remains that all these events occurred there and there alone."

I asked Eddie and Sylvia what they remembered of those four days in November, 49 years ago, when they were so very young. Eddie says he remembers me picking him up at Butcher School and hearing Regina Cyran asking me to fill her in on the tragedy; and he remembered Black Jack-the rider-less horse carrying empty boots, reversed in the stirrups in token that the warrior would not ride again.

Sylvia who was just four, remembers Black Jack, the boots in the stirrups backwards, and little two-year old John-John saluting, and of course, "Kenny in a box", which she had repeated each time the casket was shown.

Many years later in 2008, the country was proud once again. We elected another new charismatic president, another new president who revived our pride; who is respectful of intellect and the clear and subtle use of our language; who is respectful of our heritage and is now a part of it; who inherited a terrible legacy, but has tried to restore some hope, some pride for our future. His beautiful charming smile reminds us of our slain warrior so long ago.

"Don't let it be forgot,

That once there was a spot,

For one brief shining moment

That was known as Camelot."

~ Alan Jay Lerner (1918-1986)

318

CHAPTER SEVENTEEN

A PLEASURE TO RECALL

'FABULOUS FIFTIES' CHORINES'

The housing shortage—one problem of the decade—is solved by this group of chorines from "The Fabulous Fifties," who with their escorts build, landscape and decorate a dream house on stage. Left to right: Mrs. Kenneth S. Hobbs, Mrs. Paul E. Parker Jr., Mrs. M. E. McCarty Jr., Mrs. Bernard G. Sampson Jr., Mrs. Charles Hough, Bonnie Richards, Mrs. Walter Traugh and Mrs. Frank Clark.

"The Fabulous Fifties" will be presented Thursday, Friday and Saturday nights at 8:15 in West Fairmont High School auditorium by the Junior League of Fairmont, Inc. Reserved seats may be obtained by calling Mrs. James R. Kettering, 4518.

An all expense weekend for two in New York City will be awarded the holder of the lucky ticket. Three drawings will be made at each performance, with the drawing for the winner at the final performance.

The Junior League of Fairmont presented "The Fabulous Fifties" – a Jerome Cargill Production; 1955 (Photo credit: The Fairmont Times, October 26, 1955)

Inscribed over an old farmhouse in New Hampshire are the words from Virgil's "Aeneid",

"Forsan et haec olim meminisse iuvabit"
(Perhaps someday these things will be a pleasure to recall)

"Fairmont Fragments"

Junior League Newsletter, President's Message, November, 1970

While trying to cope with children, the cooking, the classroom, the pets and all the projects, a Junior League member invariably hears," I don't see how you do it!"

You do it because you want to do it. You think it is a good idea. You know that time can be made for any worthwhile effort. You also hear, "What does your husband think?" He does think and that is why I do these things. I want to keep up with his mind - with his viability.

League husbands are a special breed. They are men who actually feel that a woman makes a better wife and mother if she attempts to catch up and stay attached with the world around her home. Love and togetherness is not just sitting around gazing at each other, but looking outward together in the same direction.

If your family really does come first, do not neglect any of your duties as a mother. The work of today is beyond the back fence - keeping the environment clean; not just family relations, but race relations. Back in the Thirties it was "A chicken in every pot" to concern us, today-it is the "pot" tempting our children.

This is not the shrill cry of Woman's Liberation; it is simply the shouldering of woman's responsibilities. Explain to your family why you are a League member, why you attend meetings. Share your committee and placement experience with them. Each time I leave for a meeting, at least one member of the family says, "Have a good time at your party." I used to retort," It is a meeting not a party." I do not bother anymore, for they are more perspective than I; they know I enjoy it.

Be a wife, a mother and a volunteer in that order. Should any of you question your ability, or the time expended, remember," I am only one. I cannot do everything, but I can do something. What I can do, I ought to do. And what I ought to do, by God's grace, I will do."

Happy Thanksgiving,

~ Diane

I do recall with great pleasure all the involvement with the community the League offered me for 20 years. I became a member right out of college and had to go sustaining in the spring of 1973 at the age of 40. No one over the age of 35 was asked to join, as they would only be able to serve less than five years. You had to go sustaining at age 40 because you were supposed to be well trained to serve on community boards. Except, at the age of 40, we were ready for a rest after 15 to 20 years as league actives.

"The Purpose of the Junior League is exclusively educational and charitable and is to promote voluntarism; to develop the potential of its members for voluntary participation in community affairs; and to demonstrate the effectiveness of trained volunteers."

Once trained in parliamentary procedure and Robert's Rules of Order (Newly Revised), League graduates were chosen to serve on community boards and to become leaders in the community as trained volunteer board members.

After World War II, the girls came back to town, took off the white gloves and pearls and went back to work at making their community a better place. We were pleased to read an article in the "The Saturday Evening Post," February 1948 by Cleveland Amory who, after graduating from Harvard, became the Saturday Evening Post's youngest editor.

"The Junior League Gets Tough"
By Cleveland Amory (1917-1998)

"The current leader is Mrs. Ralph Jones (Margaret Linn Hamilton) of Charleston West Virginia and formerly from Fairmont, a 36 year old brunette, Smith College, Phi Beta Kappa, former teacher and wife of a doctor.

"Today the Junior League in action is seen, not in the large Leagues, but in the small ones. A model example is Fairmont W.Va. Fairmont is a mining town. Like other mining towns it is none too clean and there are cuspidors in every room of the best hotels. In a word it is not the kind of town in which you would expect to find a Junior League."

****

Yet Fairmont, which has a population of 25,000 and sneaked into the Association of Junior Leagues of America (AJLA) in 1927 just ahead of the 50,000 [population] rule, has not only a Junior League, but one of the country's outstanding ones. It is Mrs. Jones' hometown, and it has not only contributed Mrs. Jones, but also a Regional Director and a National Vice President. [Thelma Skaggs Shaw].

The majority of the townspeople have respect for this Junior League when it troupes its Children Theatre in station wagons. Fairmonters don't laugh because miner's children like the shows they put on.

The League thrift shop which is operated by Mrs. J .E. Watson, III - the original J.E. was one of Fairmont's biggest Coal Barons - has a sign that reads: VOLUNTEERS - DON'T FORGET THERE IS WORK TO BE DONE!

The only strictly social event the League has had in the last ten years was a dinner last January in honor of the new National President, Mrs. Jones. The dinner cost $100 for 175 people, and at the conclusion of the meal the Leaguers made their husbands buy the potted plants that had been used for table decorations.

C.E. Smith, editor of the Fairmont Times, feels that the town would not be where it is today without the Junior League. 'We have no 400 around here', he says. 'The League is the closest thing to it we've got, and it is an important influence. I suppose our girls join for the same reason most girls join the League anywhere else, because it is the thing to do, but when they get in - they work!'

The morale of Fairmont has not been lost on the current get-tough leaders. It was the Wilkes-Barre, Pennsylvania League which inaugurated the card system for liquidating non-workers and it may well be that the Fairmont League will be the one to revise social standards.

Of the 12 Provisional members taken in to the Fairmont League this year, only one went away to finishing school. No fewer than 10 of the 12 have regular jobs. Even the number of 12, considering the size of Fairmont, is indicative. If this proportion were applied to the New York City League, New York would take in approximately 3,600 members a year instead of 160 as it does today."

Mother, a founding member of the Fairmont Junior League in 1927, visited us in our new home at 5 West End Drive when she lived in Hawaii. Daddy would join her in September for their 50th anniversary celebration here in Fairmont. Our brother-in-law, George Peed, had driven her from Falls Church, Virginia where Elaine and he lived while on Pentagon duty. Mother had not felt well since her trip on old Route 50, a horrible, winding road with several horseshoe turns where you could see cars coming up from the same incline miles below you. We supposed it was the trip or jet lag.

On Tuesday morning, August 15, at 5:55 a.m. she had a heart attack.

I heard her pitiful little voice call me, "Diane, I can't breathe". I went tearing into her room and called Dr. Emery D. Wise, who said to call the fire department and he would meet us at the hospital. I was barely dressed when I heard the fire department emergency truck pull up my driveway. We have a staircase with a narrow landing so the firemen could not use a stretcher. I got Eddie's desk chair and they carried her down the steps and out to the makeshift ambulance. When I got to Fairmont General, a 212-bed hospital, they were just removing her from the fire truck and Dr. Wise arrived. There were no beds available. Therefore, she was placed in a bed with a screen around it on fifth floor hall. The firemen had administered oxygen, the only thing they could do while en route and she was transferred with it to the bed in the hallway.

On August 16, still no room. In the sixties the fifth floor was a private room floor, prior to the time of only three or four day stays before being released. A man with a broken ankle had a "good ole' friend," an orthopedic doctor who had allowed him to remain in the master suite for six weeks. His wife, a member of Green Hills Garden Club with Mother, kept peeking behind our privacy curtain while she visited her husband once a day. She would look at Mother then look at me and slowly shake her head. Aunt Pauline and Susan Hutchinson came up to check on us, but we had nowhere to sit but on the steps going up from behind her bed. They led up stairs to the doctor's lounge where her cardiologist, Jesse Jenkins, slept to be close by his patient.

Mesentery thrombosis developed on August 17. A thoracic surgeon was called, our trusted tennis friend Jack Kramer, who promised he would do everything possible to save her. Paul and I waited from 4 o'clock until after 8 p.m. when they wheeled her back up to fifth floor hall – again - no room in the recovery room! There was little hope.

Paul left to call Elaine in Falls Church and Sylvia and Daddy in Hawaii. I stayed until the end at 3:45 a.m.; it was Friday, August 18, 1967. She just slept away - holding my hand - in a bed in the fifth floor hallway - surrounded by monitors and other dying equipment. The man with the broken ankle in the master suite slept soundly.

Jesse Jenkins was so upset about this unconscionable situation; he demanded a two bed Intensive Care unit down on the third floor, which, after less than a year, extended to a four-bed unit. Jesse had found what he needed, but it took me four more years.

The Junior League had always searched the community for a need; started the project and turned it over to the community, after showing the evidence of how much it was needed. Our first project, in 1926, was the Well Baby Clinic at the Public Health Department where, during the depression, we hired the pediatrician and aided him with his examinations. This project helped prove our need and worth to the Association directors who visited us and asked us to join the National Association of Junior Leagues in 1927 - we really did not "sneak" in.

We started a Hearing Screening program, buying the audiometers for the BOE, and providing Dial A-hearing tests for all county residents. We assisted with Head Start dental examination with local dentists and we have read to blind students attending Fairmont State College, reading all their required textbooks onto tapes. We have purchased speech therapy equipment, tested for dyslexia and tutored children with learning disabilities.

We started a Children's Theatre Bureau and brought touring professionals such as Clare Tree Major productions for children, and produced several ourselves. The Masquers from Fairmont State College produced a few and I was in three or four of those when in junior high school. We also re-established the Community Concert Association and purchased hundreds of books for the Marion County Public Library while providing Story Hour for pre-schoolers. These are but a few of our projects which we have initiated and funded, showing the community the need and then turning them over and entrusting them to different agencies in Fairmont.

I was elected president of the Fairmont Junior League in April 1970 and on October 29, 1970, a supplement to the Times West Virginian showed pictures of some of the county leaders,

"1970 DAWN OF A NEW DECADE"

"THEY HOLD THE COUNTY SPOTLIGHT IN 1970 "

"PRESIDENT- MRS. PAUL E. PARKER, Jr. is serving as president of two women's organizations in Fairmont with a total membership of more than 500 women. Diane is president of the Junior League of Fairmont, Inc. and the Fairmont General Hospital Volunteer Association."

I was so proud to be following in the footsteps of Mammam and Mother - two of the strongest women I had ever known.

In the fall of 1971, Doug LaFauci, a professor at Fairmont State College from Connecticut who had been instrumental in starting a Rescue Squad program in his home state, called and asked if he could meet with me and a group of League members about Emergency Medical Service for Fairmont. We met at the college and he explained the need of community emergency medical care. How well I knew! Doug had spoken to every men's luncheon organization, Rotary, Lions, Elks, and Kiwanis, who all thought it was a great idea but had offered no ideas or assistance.

Mr. LaFauci admitted the League was his last hope. We were convinced and went to work. I knew well the need of Fairmont for emergency medical service after Mother's ride to Fairmont General in a fire truck with only very basic care by two firemen who did their best. Now I could do something personally to help, through the League and with their efforts. We could provide a sorely needed program to train Emergency Medical Technicians (EMTs) and provide a well-stocked emergency ambulance for our community.

On the floor of the U.S. Congress, West Virginia's First District Congressman Robert H. Mollohan, Alan's father, had presented a bill - H.R. 12787 - the Emergency Services Act on January 31, 1972 and sent me the Congressional Record for the "Proceedings and Debates of the 92d Congress, Second Session-Volume 118-Part 4, February 15-22 1972."

The Congressman had said that support for this bill had been growing, and so far he had twenty co-sponsors and the able assistance of Senator George McGovern who would be sponsoring the bill in the Senate. Congressman Mollohan told Congress he wished to present a newspaper article from his hometown of Fairmont West Virginia and how its Junior League has "rallied to the support of a volunteer rescue squad that I am confident will soon be filling the vacuum in emergency health care with quality service."

The article was from the Times West Virginian, February 13, 1972:

JUNIOR LEAGUE VOLUNTEERS AID RESCUE SQUAD

"Members of the Junior League of Fairmont Inc. have been assisting the Marion County Rescue Squad in numerous ways. Assistance has been provided in the areas of telephoning, film scheduling and distribution, typing and publicity. Future volunteer activities of the Junior League will be determined by the needs of the rescue squad. Members of the League's community research committee who initially researched this project in the fall of 1971 include Mrs. James Hales, chairman; Mrs. Peale Davidson, Mrs. Harry A. Dodge, Mrs. Gary Morgan, and Mrs. Charles Sinsel, with the assistance of Mrs. Paul E. Parker, Jr., President of the Junior League. Mrs. Emil Poshadel is the Junior League representative on the Marion County Rescue Squad Board and is also the Treasurer. The Junior League's contribution of $3000 to the Rescue Squad was made possible through the proceeds of the Bargain Counter on Washington Street and the annual Junior League Charity Ball. All money derived from these sources is put into the League's Community Trust Fund to be used for projects which benefit the community."

****

The Squad began with 100-trained volunteers, a rescue vehicle for which we raised $10,500 of the needed $12,000. The League contributed the $3000 putting them over the top. I was so proud of being a part of this sorely needed project and, today in 2012 the Rescue Squad is celebrating its 40th Anniversary.

The Junior League offered me involvement. How else could I, or the city, receive highly qualified emergency medical care that might have saved my mother's life; without fifty strong, determined, intelligent, trained volunteers behind me one hundred percent?

There is no such thing as separation of home and community, and at no time should one be torn between your responsibilities to either. Granted, the focus of our lives must remain in the home and we will rear our children to be sure, but so do the teacher, the preacher, the librarian, the doctor, the symphony conductor, the Children's Theatre producer, the grocer, the playground supervisor, the police and firemen, and the mayor. Yes. It does take a village to raise a child. Your home life will be as good as your community life, and I found we are all responsible for both. We buy the quality of life with the way we spend our energy.

The Valentine issue of the Fairmont Fragments the monthly newssheet was always dedicated to our husbands. The February issue of 1972 - Volume XXI, Issue VI- my last year as president, I asked Paul, my Valentine, to write my message to the members.

In lieu of the President's Message

PAUL'S EPISTLE

or Hear also what Paul saith:

Some of us most fortunate—whose matrimonial vows and affection run to wives bound by occasionally transcendent obligations to the Junior League— may liken our status to the hero of one of Lincoln's stories. Tarred, feathered, bouncing on a rail out of town, he was asked how he liked the ride. He replied that if it were not for the honor of the thing, he would rather walk.

Others among us are grateful that your boundless energies—and love of projects both small and large—are channelled away from our already happy homes and ever vulnerable checking accounts. If the League did not so efficiently gather these vital forces to attack and be absorbed in the changing problems of our town and people, the cumulative effect on the family might be frightening indeed.

Nevertheless, we are a toughly conditioned breed. Generations have taken and survived the walk, or the ride, and even the "sustaining" process with minimal distress and not inconsiderable pleasure.

Some of us find it remarkable that such lovely creatures, all Leaguers, with the inherent complexities of the feminine mind and personality, work so smoothly together, select current objectives and tasks so appropriately, and consistently achieve so much—even in areas where others fail.

All of us feel an enduring pride and admiration for your very real accomplishments and your knowledgeable competency. We cherish your grace, distinction, beauty, and charm, both individual and collective.

Persevere and continue ever so.

Paul Parker

GENERAL MEETING
MARCH 1, 1972
8:00 HEADQUARTERS
VOTING MEETING

BOARD MEETING—March 27
Jane Hales

329

[AFTERWORD]

The Junior League of Fairmont, Inc. holds a special place in my heart. In 1965, I was vice president and was elected to attend my first National Association of Junior Leagues of America Annual Conference in San Diego-Coronado, California. Edith Ann (McMillan) Wilson, the president and I had reservations at the Hotel Del Coronado. Edie Ann had a sister in Los Angeles and I had a whole family in Honolulu, Hawaii that I had not seen in eight years.

At that time plane fares were terribly expensive. The League paid airfare and our rooms to the west coast and Paul arranged the rest of the trip to Hawaii. Edie Ann flew to Los Angeles and visited with her sister.

When I landed on that tiny island of Oahu, Mother, Daddy, Sylvia, and her children, Kenneth and Diana were all there with hugs and kisses, placing beautiful leis around my neck. I spent three weeks with my dear ones, while Paul and his parents stayed with Sylvia, who was six and Eddie, ten.

The Junior League had given me the gift of three beautiful weeks, to be with my dear family after an absence of eight long years. This was a memory never to be repeated or forgotten. One I would never have had otherwise.

I will always be grateful. Those days are certainly a pleasure to recall.

From left to right: Diane, Barbara Cousins, Audrey Sidow, Helen Michele and Virginian Marvin

A Junior League Bargain Counter Bundle Tea at Field Club - to collect bundles of clothing to sell at our sustained Fund Raiser on Washington Street in down town Fairmont.

MOTHER: A WOMAN TO LOVE

A young Ray Pefley Hutchinson at Sonnencroft

Ray Pefley Hutchinson

Mother was not an ordinary Mother; in no way was she ever ordinary. Oh, she was impish and at times, jealous, but she admitted it. Her close friends were entertained by her frankness and enjoyed her candid, often shocking, but usually beneficent statements.

She had a beautiful face, surrounded by thick, naturally blond wavy hair. She told everyone that her mother put bleach on it as a child because she was afraid it would darken with age. It would have been a strawberry blond, but she went to Miss Starzman in the Masonic Temple and had it washed, with a little blond "Roux", a temporary tint, and set weekly. She usually wore it in three rolls, two around her face and one at the nape of her neck. Her eyes were always green. Some said hazel, but they were a beautiful golden green and her skin resembled fine china. There was no make-up foundation then, just a little Coty powder; the kind that you can buy in every drug store today and still comes in the same gold and brown print box it did in the thirties, and a little natural pink "Tangee" lipstick.

Men were always attracted to her, but she was in love only with her Yale man.

She was a great contract bridge player with a quick sharp mind; always bored with post mortems of a hand, or a rubber. When I came home from school she was dressed in a beautiful dress. Her adage was, "Never buy a "house dress" just wear your old, good ones." I was never allowed to wear blue jeans when I was I high school when they first became popular for city wear. Not that I ever wanted to; they were so unflattering, stiff and uncomfortable.

She wore stockings and high-heeled shoes every day - yes, old ones, even for gardening. If she were depressed, she would put on her pearls and go shopping. With her genuine pearls on, she would spend most of her time in the ten-cent stores looking at the costume jewelry, which she adored. Her diamonds were usually in the bank being used as collateral for loans, but rhinestones came out about then and she would buy many of this cheap great new artificial stone as brooches, necklaces, earrings, whatever she could afford. Today the vintage rhinestone jewelry is nearly as expensive as the real diamonds. She would ask, "Who can tell the difference? It depends entirely on who wears them."

I remember her silk stockings; they were a shiny copper on her legs. They had seams going up the back that had to be perfectly straight. The silk stockings would get runs in them and have to be thrown away, so she always

334

bought the same color and bought a box of three at a time. She had several pairs of nylon stockings she bought at Hartley's before WWII. The only pairs she could get until after the war. Nylon, the wonderful newly developed synthetic fiber, was created for parachutes. After the war, she swore they changed the process, as her first pairs never "ran" and the new nylons did. She was sure it was planned obsolescence.

An ardent reader, Mother devoured the latest books from the Marion County Library on the corner of First Street and Fairmont Avenue. Mrs. Waitman T. Conaway (Mary Willow) was the librarian and rented a room from Mammam in her house on Gaston Avenue. Miss Anna Briggs, the librarian at Fairmont State Teachers College also rented a room at my grandmother's. They kept Mother supplied with what they thought she would like.

A new book came out in 1944 called, "Forever Amber", by Kathleen Windsor. It was a lusty historical novel, but she could not afford to buy it. The book was banned in Boston and fourteen states banned it as pornography. Mother went down to the Marion County Library and asked if it was in yet. She was led to Mrs. Conaway's office, and the head librarian said, "Ray, you do not want to read that book." Mother was indignant and insisted she did.

Shaking her head, Mrs. Conaway opened a drawer of her desk and handed it to her with a look of disdain.

Mother thoroughly enjoyed the book, as did I, when I could sneak a glimpse of it while Mother was out. The same thing happened in 1948, when Mother asked for Norman Mailer's bestseller, "The Naked and the Dead"; she was sent back to Mrs. Conaway's office.

She hated sewing, but loved needlepoint and petit point, knitting, and crocheting. She made lovely placemats for her friends for Christmas. And she insisted we all learn to knit for the soldiers overseas. The Red Cross supplied the yarn and needles and we all knitted ugly Navy "submarine grey" or Army, "clay dirt orange" sweaters, but just the bodies, she did all the finishing touches, including the sleeves. I loved to do the ribbing –knit one-purl-two, and back, purl 2- knit 1, but the row upon row of the stocking stitch-knit a row -purl a row bored me to death! However, between the four of us, many boys were kept warm in the western theatre of war even with a few dropped stitches. Eventually Mother graduated to argyle socks, but Daddy would have nothing to do with them.

Mother was a good teacher, and taught us, as a good example, to be ladies; a title that even today needs to be earned. I am proud of her persistence in trying to perfect all three of us, not only culturally, but also in civility and graciousness. When, just to tease her, after dinner, we would answer, that we "were too full for another bite". She would sigh, roll her eyes and retort, "I have had a gentile sufficiency; more would be a superfluous redundancy." And we would all laugh. The writer, Gertrude Stein's mother, had made her say that, but all Mother really wanted us to say was, "No, thank you."

A cook, she was not! Mom, Mammam and Nannie had done all the cooking, and she neither asked nor wanted to learn. She would tell me, "Never learn to iron a man's shirt, you'll be stuck for life." After Mom was confined upstairs and we could not afford Nannie any longer, Mother gave up and tried to cook.

We had many sirloin steaks with the bone in. All she had to do was broil them a little. She loved the new oleomargarine, hoping it would reduce her weight, but she often did not bother to put the orange coloring in it to make it look like butter. I hated her spaghetti sauce that was mainly watered down ketchup with a little chili powder. Sylvia liked it though, which only encouraged her to make it more often. We had every kind of roast with potatoes and carrots roasted around it. During the war, Daddy would bring home what Mother referred to as sweetbreads, the expensive delicacies that were not sent to the soldiers, and sold to us cheaply. Mother must have finally read a recipe book for she made a fabulous kidney stew. I have no idea what was in it, but it was delicious. She would boil a beef tongue and served it like ham, which made scrumptious sandwiches.

Recently, while I was looking through her jottings, I found something I had never seen. It was in faded pencil, handwritten - never shown to Daddy to be typed. It reminded me of how much she loved and worried about us, but rarely displayed it, yet you knew you had no stronger ally. She was a woman to love and to miss.

"Oh, to be Queen"
by Ray Hutchinson
March 1950

"This modern waltz everyone is humming today has the quality of nostalgia about it. Just to close my eyes, I could be dancing to, "Meet Me Tonight in Dreamland" back in that western town I loved so. Wonderful days in high school - how happy I had been. I stood there with my hands resting in the warm soapy water full of dishes just remembering. Music is such a powerful medium to waft one back to high school days. Perfume could do the same thing. I wore White Rose or Lilac. We had little else to wear... none of these perfumes with names or numbers. Evening in Paris was one of the first new perfumes, but everyone smelled alike.

Just then a small whirlwind entered the house, our youngest daughter, Diane.

'Oh, Mother, I was nominated to be the Junior Prom queen at school today. Of course there are six or seven others and we will all be princesses in the Court of Beauty, but oh, if I could only be queen.'

Dark eyes glowing, pink cheeks, naturally curly soft brown hair- how could she help but win? But one never knows.

'Several of my friends say they will run my campaign, but I will have to have something new to wear. Oh, Mother, do you suppose I could have something new to wear the week before the vote?'

'My dear, you know how hard it is to buy anything right now.'

'But my friends who support me say I have to have something different to wear each day.'

'I know, darling, but you always look lovely, I'll try my best to see what we can do.'

Her high school days had been terrible! She was too short to be a majorette after practicing for hours all summer, throwing a baton high up in the air and catching it in a twirl every time. She had practiced and practiced to be a cheerleader, but only two had been chosen out of twenty-five want-to-be's. I haven't minded doing without things. As one grows older, the material things do not matter so much as the love of your husband and of your children and, as the minister says so often, 'the love of God'. The best I could do was two dollars.

'Why don't you go to town this afternoon and see what you can find?' I suggested.

After all, if they could just see your innocent, sweet, young beauty shining through, what difference would it make?

The cheap jersey blouse was bought. It had a pitiful little pink silk scarf; in some way that scarf did something to me. Every day it was arranged a different way, tied with care and flaunted valiantly. It became our symbol of battle, our flag to carry us on to victory.

But deep down in my heart, I knew it was not enough. I felt the prayers that were being prayed would be useless. That little blouse and scarf could never compete with the expensive outfits from the best stores. Children of that age are so impressed with the number of different dresses, the latest styles, and the small but expensive fads. I knew it was not to be.

Voting day arrived. Brooks and I were both nervous. Silly I guess, but when you love your children so much, you want them to have what they desire so much.

At noon she came home for lunch and the vote had been taken. She had lost by six votes. As the vote was so close, a recount had to be taken. There was still hope. She was so excited, pink cheeks and eyes sparkling.

'And Mother, even the other girls want me to win!'

'That, darling, shows your popularity, and your true friends. This will be something wonderful to remember even if you aren't elected queen. A real queen was a princess first.'

I prayed.

She gained two votes in the recount, but it was not to be and her faith was shaken - not in her friends - but in believing if you prayed hard enough, you would get what you prayed for.

She cried as soon as she got inside the door that afternoon and I cried with her, trying to explain it was for the best and that better days were ahead, but it just did not help. The jersey blouse and the little scarf were put away and never worn again. Something of her childhood- the firm belief you wanted most, must happen - were put away with them.

She was a dream princess in the Fairmont Senior High School Court of Beauty, in a beautiful layered blue lace gown from New York, lovingly sent by her sisters.

Many said she should have been the queen, even one of her favorite teachers, Miss Eva Mae Brown, whispered that sentiment to her as she came down the aisle, but it was not much comfort.

Perhaps this was to help her grow up. Ten years from now no one will remember who was Queen. In this checkerboard of nights and days, it was just not her turn to win."

[Author's Note] As my mother predicted three decades later, a girl I had gone to school with, now a grocery store clerk said,

"Diane, you were a beautiful prom queen in high school."

Flattered, I answered,

"Oh, thank you, Cathy, but I lost by four votes in a recount."

"That's funny, I always remember you as the queen!"

FSHS Junior Prom, May 1950
The second set of little Trach girls were flower girls-Marty and Merry Beth.
How beautiful we all were then.

LOVE, OCL

Mother and Daddy went to New Orleans in January of 1958 to help Sylvia with her little ones while she continued to work two jobs. We all missed them. Mother's friends would call to inquire how I was getting along without a mother and daddy, but we were doing fine. I missed them, of course, but was terribly busy with my family, the church and the Junior League. They left in October of 1958 for Hawaii, so the New Orleans trip was a dress rehearsal for me.

Mrs. Mathew Mansfield Neely, the Senator's wife, and close friend of Mother's, became a surrogate grandmother to Eddie and our new baby, Sylvia. Alberta Claire Ramage Neely was born on August 22, 1881 and was 16 years older than Mother, but she outlived Mother by ten years, dying on June 30, 1977.

She would call and say, "Put the water on." Ten minutes later she would fly in with a dozen ears of just picked corn from her back yard. She would never stay, just pat the children and tear off in a huge white Cadillac. She baked iced orange cookies for Eddie and Sylvia that were to die for! Neither she nor her daughter Corinne would ever give me the recipe. When she sent cards or flowers to us she always signed Love, OCL (Orange Cookie Lady).

Anne Blair Morgan, a cousin of "Bertie's", gave me the cookie recipe for Christmas, after Mrs. Neely died. I baked them, but I never found them as delicious as OCL's. All she asked for in return for her cookies were Mother's brownies that were so easy to make. The children and I would take them to 225 Watson Avenue and climb up those steep stone steps where she would be waiting for us on the front porch swing. She would tell Eddie and Sylvia how they should exercise every single day and proceed to show us how she could still, at 90, touch her toes without bending her knees- and that was in 2-inch heels!

In the winter months she would open a handsome camphor-wood chest, heavily hand carved from the Orient, with wonderful treasures inside. Donkey beads, Javanese toe rings, baby clothes from Belgium and small dolls from Germany- things that interested us all. I also recall the beautiful, unique cobalt blue glass table she used in the breakfast room.

Alberta Neely was a stunning woman. She had the bluest eyes I can remember, a periwinkle blue, and a porcelain complexion surrounded by an abundance of gorgeous white wavy hair. She would tell us about her Matt, our senior senator from West Virginia, who was born on a farm in Doddridge County in 1874. Alberta was seven years younger than Matt, as was I to Paul. She proclaimed a man should, "marry a woman half his age, plus seven", just as we had done... Paul was 25, half his age was 12, plus 7 made me 19, my age when we married.

She told us that every morning while shaving, Matt memorized verses of the Bible taped on the mirror and how, to the children's amazement, he always ate his dessert first, before his dinner. She would laugh and say, "He would stand here on the porch, which overlooks all of Fairmont and say, "Bert, someday I will be mayor of this fine city'." The state's champion vote getter of all time had not only been elected mayor, but also five times to the House of Representatives, five times to the United States Senate and once as the twenty-first Governor of his native state.

Leo Casey, who would often drive the senator back and forth to Washington, would call late at night and tell "Bert", "Set out the salt rising bread, we'll be there for breakfast." She would have the bread ready for their arrival early the next morning.

Mrs. Neely would speak about Washington society to Mother, and said she hated the pomp of Washington. She often had to go to lunches and dinners with the senator and would refer to the other wives and why she did or did not like them. She thought Vice President Alben Barkley's wife one of the most intelligent of the group and enjoyed sitting next to her at various functions. She seldom traveled to Washington when the Republicans were in power, but often when under FDR and Truman.

Her three children had been her life. Alfred Ramage Neely, the eldest, was an attorney like his father and in later years, circuit court judge- and one of our favorite attorneys in Fairmont. His wife Florence (Flo) and he had two beautiful little girls, Jill and Page. Alfred called his mother every morning to be helped in finishing the day's crossword puzzle and to keep her up on what the girls were doing. I doubt if he needed the help, but they were both very competitive and liked to gloat over knowing a difficult word.

Corinne was the second child and she was married to a radiologist, Harold Pettit and resided in South Carolina. Corinne wrote her mother a post card every single day and called often. The last child was John Champ Neely, the father of one of my closest friends, Matt Neely II., who lived with his grandparents and joined me in seventh grade at Fairmont Junior High

School when his grandparents returned to Fairmont from the governor's mansion in Charleston.

The senator died on January 18, 1958 and The Fairmont Times, on January 23, 1958, reporting on the senator's funeral, said,

> "Always a colorful figure and a master of political oratory the Senator drew in his lifetime the largest crowds that had ever attended campaign rallies in West Virginia. To his funeral he drew the most notable group of national figures to gather here at one time in the history of the city, and in the community where he began a 50 year career in public office as Mayor and lived to become its most distinguished citizen. Today Matthew Mansfield Neely was laid to eternal rest."

I went alone to his funeral at the First Presbyterian Church on Jackson Street. Mother and Daddy were in New Orleans, and Paul sat downstairs in reserved seats with the County Bar Association. A delegation of the senator's congressional colleagues sat in front of the closed casket, after hundreds had filed past it all morning. The streets were lined with mourners unable to get into the church. Mrs. Neely and the family sat in a private side room next to the sanctuary. The Reverend Frank Marvin conducted the services and read a eulogy from the senator's good friend, the Reverend Dr. Frederick Brown Harris, Chaplain of the US Senate who memorialized him as a "true friend of the laboring man." John L. Lewis, the international president of the United Mine Workers and good friend, sat in the row behind the congressional delegation.

The Fairmont Times had a squib about U.S. Senator Wayne Morse of Oregon, "who availed himself of the opportunity to go shopping after he arrived here yesterday to attend the funeral of his good friend, Senator Neely. The vitriolic-tongued westerner had come away from Washington in such a hurry that he did not pack a clean shirt. By the time he reached Fairmont he felt he should have a change and accomplished his mission in a downtown store immediately after arrival." (Maunz Men's Store right across from the courthouse).

After all her family had returned to their homes, Mrs. Neely wrote Mother in New Orleans on a beautiful thank you card engraved in Old English script,

Matthew M. Neely's family thanks you sincerely for your kindness and sympathy

She wrote,

"My Dear, We are sending hundreds of these cards, but other hundreds must have a personal note. I am very nervous and tense, but this work gives me something to do and keeps me from thinking of other things Rec'd your telegram and I thank you.

Was glad to get your letter yesterday. Green Hills (garden club) friends all there to help receive food at door and take the names of the donors. Elmira Jamison and Elizabeth Hardesty arranged flowers at the Church. I miss you and Brooks.

Pardon this kind of note but I'll write if I ever see the light before Easter - Nice long talk with Diane this morning - Eddie talked and said, "I miss you". D. had not told him to say it.

LOVE,

~ Bertie"

Mother and Daddy returned in the spring from New Orleans and prepared to go to Honolulu in October of 1958. Once again it was hard on us all. But our OCL continued to keep us close and taken care of with gifts of corn, zucchini and tomatoes from her garden and of course, orange cookies.

She never forgot our birthdays or holidays and all cards were signed, "Love, OCL".

Alberta Ramage Neely (November 22, 1952) pouring tea at the reception of Paul and Diane's wedding.

CHAPTER EIGHTEEN

TRADITIONS

Paul and Diane; Father and Mother of the groom, June 14th, 1980

When Mother and Daddy left in October 1958 to join Elaine and her family in Hawaii, I was pregnant with Sylvia, our second baby. My life was turned upside down. Christmas? What would we do for our very favorite day of the year? As it turned out the snow fell all of Christmas Eve and was so deep on Christmas day, that we were afraid to join Paul's parents in Buckhannon, where they spent every holiday. It was our first Christmas at 931 Coleman Avenue, our new castle.

Paul's parents had taught Eddie to call them Pep and Merr, and even though I had tried Grandmommy and Granddaddy for my parents, to Eddie they ended up as Mony and Dah. Pep and Merr had left on Christmas Eve, as was their custom, and were terribly disappointed that we were unable to be with all of Merr's family, the Shumakers of 15 College Avenue. John Michael Shumaker, Merr's father, had played the organ for many years in the Methodist church and his children had all been graduates of West Virginia Wesleyan University.

Christmas morning, Paul would go in to the living room and light the tree while Eddie and I waited to hear Paul say "Santa Claus did not arrive this year" and Eddie would run in and see if all his toys had been delivered. We had our presents to open and Eddie and Paul had a delightful time, both glad not to be whisked away from their new toys as in the past years.

Paul seemed to welcome the closeness and the warmth of his fireside without the presence of a large family. With two sets of grandparents to eat with in the past, but this year, we were orphans of a storm of snow. We braved the slippery streets to find a bite to eat, but not a store, market or restaurant was opened in the entire city. We had hot dogs and eggs and stale toast for our dinner and all of us cuddled together on the couch watching, "It's A Wonderful Life", I had seen it back in 1946 and had not thought much of the film at the time, but sitting there snuggled together on the couch it bought a new meaning to us all. Eddie fell in love with that story on his third Christmas. I don't think he ever missed the tinkle of that bell - Remember? "Every time you hear the tinkle of a bell it means another angel got his wings."

We were in dire need of new traditions and I tried to establish a new one with that movie.

The next night we celebrated down at Pep and Merr's as they had returned from her old homestead, but it really did not seem like Christmas. I had given Merr a white wax candle in the form of an angel and the candle had been placed on the edge of the mantle. Suddenly it fell off, breaking one of the angel's wings. Mrs. Parker hinted, that was a bad omen while patting my tummy. It really upset me. I got a match, heated the wing and stuck it back on the candle, while her innuendo stuck in my mind.

Paul's Christmases were never as happy as I tried to make them. Paul hated getting the tree and detested putting it up. We had to do it three times each year, for his mother, his aunts in Buckhannon and for us. The children and I loved to decorate the trees, but Paul resented his time away from his own home and the office. There are probably many other men who have suffered the same problem.

Mrs. Parker insisted we come to Buckhannon every Christmas morning and spend the night, but unless the weather was too bad, Paul insisted on driving home. I loved spending the night as Paul's two adorable aunts - Mrs. Parker's sisters - Nell Shumaker Post and Reta Pearle Shumaker - treated us as their own children. They always baked my favorite macaroni and cheese and yellow cup cakes with chocolate icing. It was great fun to be so pampered. Sylvia and Eddie adored Paul's little cousin Cyndy Post, Aunt Nell's grandchild, and she never tired of playing with these two little ones. Today Cyndy, and her husband John Guzzi, live in Clarksburg and have several adorable grandchildren. Cyndy is the only one of Paul's family left in the area.

If we drove home Eddie would always fall asleep, but not Sylvia, wanting to sing Christmas carols all the way home. We had no super highways then and it took an hour and a half to get to Fairmont on the best of nights. Funny, after the Shumakers were all gone, Paul was the one who, as attorney for the Division of Highways, condemned all the property for Interstate 79, which would have cut many minutes off our hundreds of trips to Buckhannon.

Many years later, in 1980 when Pep and Merr died within five weeks of each other, they left a houseful of furniture. I insisted on buying a condominium in Florida near where Elaine and George lived with their family. We went down and stayed with them in St. Lucie Village near Fort Pierce for three weeks while Paul recuperated from the shock and sadness of his parents' deaths. George and I looked at condominiums for sale and he would take us in his boat up and down the beautiful Indian River - a major east coast waterway linking to the Fort Pierce Inlet to the Atlantic Ocean. I found the place I loved on that inlet called La Entrada Del Mar (The Entrance to the Sea). Paul agreed. It had a dock and we could be in the ocean in two minutes. All the big freighters came into that inlet to bring produce from all over the world, and leave with huge cargos of Florida fruit. Paul kept an almanac by his chair to know what flag they were flying.

We packed everything at 818 Benoni Avenue to move. Only one item was left in the basement of the Parkers' house, a lovely mahogany sewing box.

"Oh, Paul, I thought I had packed that, we must take it with us."

He answered, "Leave it here; I never want to see it again."

He proceeded to tell me that when he was 15 years old he had asked for a Stromberg-Carlson phonograph player for Christmas. He had even bought a few 78-RPM records to play and hidden them so he wouldn't ruin his parent's surprise. A big box had arrived about two weeks before the big day. He was so sure that it was his new present and his mother hinted that it might be, giggling at his reaction. His father, if he knew, never took him aside to warn him.

Christmas morning arrived and they opened a few presents at their home in Salem and packed the car for Buckhannon, as was their tradition.

The whole Shumaker family was there. The turkey was about done and Paul played Santa Claus handing out all the marked presents, and there were several for him. The last present had a tag "From Santa" on it, so Paul opened it. The box was over 36' high and Paul removed all the packing carefully, and pulled out the contents. Mrs. Parker clapped her hands together and exclaimed,

"Oh, what I have always wanted, a beautiful mahogany sewing box! Thank you, Santa." Everyone laughed and applauded and went in to eat the turkey, except Paul.

"Lawyers, I suppose, were children once."

~ Charles Lamb

WHO IS SYLVIA?

Sylvia Elaine Parker was born the following April 26 with no wing missing, and was a perfect, beautiful, little angel who brought a totally new meaning to family – a daughter! Mother and Daddy had sent a gorgeous pink carnation lei from Hawaii which Paul hung over the mirror in my hospital room, next to his vase of red roses.

The garland of flowers was the hit of the maternity floor. No one had ever seen a real lei before and the nurses kept coming in to see and smell it; one even borrowed it to take on a tour of the hospital. We had made so many new friends and my room was filled with roses from Paul and other bouquets of fresh flowers, plus two of my favorite lemon pies that Betty Burger "Butch" Rymer had brought me. To make sure I got a bite, she baked one for the nurses and one for me. I took the lei home with me, but distributed the other flowers to several other new mothers. I was reminded of those many years later when Eddie's friend's mother told me those were the only flowers she had ever received.

When the nurse brought Sylvia in to me to dress to go home, I was afraid of her smallness, her delicacy. It had been four years since my big boy had arrived and he had been dressed and ready to go. I remember that morning how beautiful Coleman Avenue looked on our way home. I had been in the hospital a week and in that few days the maple trees had burst into leaves - that luscious, lettuce leaf green of spring. All I could think about that beautiful spring night in my own bed once again was how wonderful to have each room filled with someone to love.

Sylvia grew to be shy and sweet, speaking in monosyllables – "bow" for elbow. When a friend, trying to get her to speak, asked her what her name was she answered, to our surprise, "Tiltie", which we called her off and on for years.

She adored her big brother, who was always as ready to protect her, as she was to defend him. Eddie at 14 wrote a character sketch for an English class,

WHO IS SYLVIA?
English – Eddie Parker
December, 1969

"For Christmas she asked for a lipstick and a baby doll. She sets and styles her hair as well as a graduate beautician, but she can still be found in the topmost branches of the apple tree. In her pink ballet slippers she is a ten-year-old Pavlova, but takes just as much pride in out-shooting every boy in the neighborhood.

"She is a mischievous, eavesdropping, tattletale one minute and then defends you in the next breath. She will sneak into your room and mess up your record collection, but you are the one the bulk of her hard saved Christmas money is spent.

"You can be sitting engrossed in a television program and be hit in the head by her homemade paper airplane, but when you are sick, only a mother could be more sympathetic or nurse you any better.

"Part imp, part baby, part mother, part pest, part little girl, part woman and all sister - this is Sylvia."

****

When Sylvia entered Fairmont Senior High School she joined Robert Hawkins's Speech and Debate classes and with his National Forensics team, traveled to tournaments all over the state. As a sophomore she won her first West Virginia State award in Huntington at Marshall University for the "After Dinner Speaking" category, and went on the Nationals in Philadelphia, Pennsylvania with the junior and senior award-winning students.

She enjoyed Miss Joyce Flint's Choraliers and as senior, Sylvia's trio group sang in the first Madrigal production at an old English Fair held on the grounds at Loop Park. Sylvia played the guitar and the three girls sang while strolling the beautiful campus. Later the group became Doug Bunner's beautifully disciplined Madrigal singers. Our grandsons were in the Madrigals twenty years later. She was inducted into National Honor Society and won a coveted spot for the All State Chorus under Miss Flint's direction.

352

Sylvia started the first girls' tennis team as the administration would not allow her to play on the boy's team. The very team which her big brother, Eddie, had started. She was captain all three years, voted the Woman Athlete of the year and accepted two scholarships to West Virginia University for tennis and academics after graduating with high honors from high school. An English teacher sent the following essay she had written to the paper to be printed on Father's Day June 20, 1976 in the Times West Virginian:

A TRIBUTE TO DAD
by Sylvia E. Parker

"Who day and night scrambles for a living and feeds a wife and children and who had the right as master of the house, to have the final word at home? The poppa, the poppa-tradition!" Sheldon Harnick portrayed these thoughts of a father's role in the famous song "Tradition". Using the background of Jewish folklore and humor as a frame, Sholom Aleichem, author of "Fiddler on the Roof", attained his sights showing the general problems of a father and a husband. All the problems and experiences that are meaningful in this 1964 stage musical are universal ones.

"Who is up first in the morning letting the dog out and maybe mopping up little accidents before Mother comes down? Who sends auras of bacon floating skyward to sleeping rooms and who leaves for work before seen by his family to supply all the pennies for their needs? The poppa, the poppa - tradition.

"Who drives the longest on an eleven hour trip, and tolerates a blaring stereo for the greater portion of the time spent in the car? Who is the greatest and most willing tennis partner and who laughs triumphantly after stroking a solid backhand? "The poppa, the poppa - tradition".

"Who does the family Scotty fight over for attention, and who does she turn to for cookies and treats? Who has the strongest shoulder for comfort and crying and who do children dash to for a verdict of "yes" when Mother says "no"? "The poppa, the poppa - tradition".

"Who compliments Mother every night on an excellent dinner and comments, 'Why not?' if dinner is served at ten o'clock après tennis? Who hears all the little noises at night and gets out of a nice warm bed to investigate and who appears by your door at the first flash of lightening and before the first crack of thunder, which inevitably follows? "The poppa, the poppa - tradition".

"Who would do anything to make his family happy and who makes all of his little girl's wishes a reality? Who would even turn an All Star football game to the "Wizard of Oz"?

Who else - my poppa, my poppa - tradition!"

And this is Sylvia.

WHO IS EDDIE?

I thoroughly enjoyed the babyhood of my children, but I loved them more every year as they grew to become friends and comrades. They had great ideas and initiatives of their own and established many of our traditions.

I had read books to them nightly since their births, and taught Paul and them every song I had ever learned. Paul's family had evidently never sung in the car. I do not think today families do, with iPhones, iPods and iPads. A good friend took a granddaughter and her little friend shopping and there was no sound in the back seat. She turned to see why and they were twittering each other.

When Eddie was in second grade, on a trip to Buckhannon, we were all singing as usual and sang the first stanza of "America the Beautiful" by Katherine Lee Bates, but Eddie continued on with the other four verses. Paul and I had never heard the entire anthem ever sung before. Eddie had memorized it from Mother's copy of "A Treasury of the Familiar" edited by Ralph L. Woods, (1943) which I had inherited.

For Paul's 37th birthday - December 12, 1963 - after hearing it repeated during one of the Kennedy assassination programs and watching Paul tear up when it was read, Eddie, who was nine, memorized JFK's and Paul's favorite verse - a soliloquy from Shakespeare's King Richard II:

> *"This royal throne of Kings, this scepter'd isle.*
> *This earth of majesty, this seat of Mars,*
> *This other Eden, demi-paradise,*
> *This fortress-built by Nature for herself*
> *Against infection and the hand of war,*
> *This happy breed of men, this little world,*
> *This precious stone set in the silver sea,*
> *Which serves it in the office of a wall*
> *Or as a moat defensive of a house,*
> *Against the envy of less happier lands,*
> *This blessed plot, this earth, this realm, this England."*

All through their school life we did homework as a family. Paul was excellent in history and science and the law; I was good at English, drama and music but we were not too adept at math. Eddie, like my father, was the mathematician. In college he took calculus to relax.

The "new math" was introduced when Eddie was in fourth grade. Mrs. (Ruth) Fitch had urged me to teach the children the multiplication tables, which I did. The new math did not require it and the older teachers were disappointed with their results in the lower grades.

At Fairmont Senior High School, Miss Linda Huber, an excellent teacher of math, taught him so much and he referred back to her all through high school. Darlene Boyles, in his junior year, made math fun and interesting for him. It certainly did not come from home. I give all the credit to Eddie and those two teachers. One night Eddie was stumped on a geometry problem and asked Paul and his grandfather Parker, an engineer, to help him. The evening was ruined over their squabbling and inability to solve the problem.

Eddie was excelling in Fairmont Junior High as the captain of the basketball team under his favorite coach, Ron Everhart, who saw Eddie's potential and promoted it.

While in Mrs. Malcolm's seventh grade English class, her assignment was to memorize one or two verses of a favorite poem. Eddie, always exceeding our expectations, chose 15 verses of his favorite poem "The Highwayman" by Alfred Noyes.

For a month we had to listen to:

"The wind was a torrent of darkness among the gusty trees,
The moon was a ghostly galleon tossed upon cloudy seas,
The road was a ribbon of moonlight over the purple moor,
And the Highwayman came riding-riding –riding
The Highway man came riding, up to the old Inn door.

Every night Eddie would memorize a new verse and would repeat it at the dinner table. We had to hear the poem from the beginning each night and we would all join in as a chorus while Eddie said the new verse alone each time. Paul particularly liked the second verse and would overshadow us all even standing up to recite it,

"He'd a French cocked hat on his forehead, a bunch of lace at his chin,
A coat of the claret velvet and breeches of brown doeskin,
They fitted with never a wrinkle-his boots were up to his thigh!
And he rode with a jeweled twinkle, his pistol butts a-twinkle,
His rapier hilt a-twinkle, under the jeweled sky."

And finally the night before his school presentation we could all join in on the last verse,

> *"Back he rode like a madman, shrieking a curse to the sky,*
> *With the white road smoking behind him and his rapier brandished high!*
> *Blood red were his spurs in the golden noon, wine red was his velvet coat.*
> *When they shot him down on the highway, down like a dog on the highway,*
> *And he lay in his blood on the highway, with the bunch of lace at his throat."*

At this point, Sylvia and I were in tears. "Poor Bess, the landlord's daughter had watched for her love in the moonlight, and died in the darkness there."

Mrs. Malcolm was so impressed she wrote a little note,

"Eddie, I am so proud of you!" A +

After Paul had died, going through his wallet, I found this note all dog-eared and folded, and loved.

Allan (Fritz) Hauge, one of Andy and Petty Hauge's twin boys, told me at Eddie's wedding he remembered how Eddie always had to be the best. In eighth grade when Allan was picked to be Abraham Lincoln and Eddie was to be Stephen Douglas in the Lincoln – Douglas Debates of 1858, Eddie was very upset, as he wanted to be Lincoln, "Until I told him, Douglas won!"

In his senior year, at Fairmont Senior High School (1973), he was elected as president of the student body, president of National Honor Society, and was chosen the BPOE Elks Club, West Virginia Youth of the year. He was founder and captain of the tennis team and played varsity basketball at FSHS. He was offered the first scholar ship for tennis and an academic scholarship at WVU and graduated with highest honors from FSHS.

His first semester at West Virginia University, The Mid Atlantic Tennis Association (MALTA) of then the United States Lawn Tennis Association (USLTA) called and invited him to represent MALTA at the Junior Davis Cup in Poughkeepsie, New York. MALTA includes part of West Virginia, all of the District of Columbia, Maryland and Virginia. Eddie represented the State of West Virginia and another player he often played on the circuit, Roger Hamilton, represented Maryland. They were both finishing their 18-year-old season and would graduate to the men's category in USLTA, today called USTA. Eddie had been ranked in the top four players in his age group for the four years playing the circuit and he and Roger had won many sportsmanship trophies in the MALTA circuit. Bill Riordan, a director of MALTA knew these two would be great representatives. We drove Eddie to New York – a thrilling experience for us all. When Eddie was a six year old in first grade, he wrote a sign for his bedroom door announcing:

Office of Attorney Eddie Parker

I am a lawyer

I help people and I can help you too.

Office hours 7 to 8 am

In the beginning of his junior year at West Virginia University, in 1975, Eddie was chosen by his Political Science professors to attend London School of Economics in London, England, a prestigious opportunity for a pre-law student. We sent him to London three weeks early to find an apartment and to travel through Europe and to spend a few days with his first cousin, Ken Derby who was living in Madrid. He also toured the English coast and traveled through Scotland. We missed him terribly for it was a long separation. Eddie wrote us a beautiful letter from London,

Dear Mom and Dad,

"It's 2 am here and only around 8 in Fairmont, but I have a single purpose in writing this letter, to tell you that I miss and love you both very much.

My little adventure has made me realize what the family as a unit means. I have been blessed with the single most important factor in my life, parents that could be no better in any way. We all have our faults; but that is where the family comes in. We care- we understand- we accept what we are and work for each other.

All I am I owe to you. Yes, Mom, I have worked hard, but I am sure I would not be the person I am now or ever will be if it were not for you and Dad. You have given me everything, the intangible feeling of love, security and encouragement.

Please do not think I am just homesick, I am having a great time and enjoying the experience thoroughly! I only want you both to know, that even though I don't say it enough or show it enough, I love you both with all my heart."

Love,

~ Ed

And this is Eddie.

VACATIONS

The Fairmont Field Club was a second home to us and no one missed vacations. Paul spent two weeks on active reserve training at Lockbourne Air Force Base in Columbus, Ohio every summer as well as six days every three months. Lockbourne later became Rickenbacker Air base and today is closed. He had to learn to practice military law, which was different and interesting for him. Paul was always learning or teaching when on duty. He was always there to conduct courts-martial, which, as an old prosecutor, were easy for him. He was once sent to the southern part of West Virginia to depose witnesses in sonic boom complaints; several houses had lost all their windows. Often he was needed by the Judge Advocate for special hearings because of his experience such as divorce and spousal abuse cases.

This was in the late sixties. I remember the dates, as I only knew one couple that had been divorced before the Viet Nam War. One Saturday morning when our only judge, Harper Meredith, would hear only divorce cases, Paul apologized for bringing him nine new suits and Harper said, "Paul, I have all ready heard 34 complaints this morning; you will make it 43."

Paul often taught new air officers speech communication, particularly grammar and the use of power and flag words. When we lived at 931 Coleman and the children were still small, Paul had bought a new stereo and left for work leaving me to assemble the parts. I sat down and could not figure out the directions without pictures. I called Paul, who was with a client, and explained my dilemma. He abruptly suggested, "There has to be a schematic diagram, just follow it", and hung up the phone. After the client had left, he called me back and asked,

"Did you get it put together?"

I answered, "No, I did not, I couldn't find that schizophrenic diaphragm any where!"

Paul taught what he called, this "hilarious example" as a perfect malapropism and called me his "Mrs. Malaprop" (a comedy figure in the 1775 play, "The Rivals", by Richard B. Sheridan), on many occasions after that.

Each summer Paul spent two weeks at some base -where ever he was needed-on active reserve duty, and called it his summer vacation, while the children and I traveled all over Virginia and Maryland playing MALTA tennis tournaments. "Paul's farewell reminder was always, "Punch your volleys".

That first year Eddie was an unknown entity and was seeded in the top four but, after winning the top four tournaments that first year, the second year he was seeded #1 and often Sylvia was seeded #1 in the tens and under because of Eddie's status. She played one tournament with a little girl in Richmond our first year on the circuit. There was only a 10 game semi and a final for the little girls and she had made it to the finals. Paul flew down to watch her and Eddie, who was in the 14 and under final.

Sylvia, who was used to playing with her brother and daddy, would get bored with the typical baseline stance every little girl was taught to employ, and would rush the net and the opponent would just lob - never a volley retuned to punch. Sylvia would race back to get the lob, but seldom could make it. She was a real crowd pleaser and they clapped and whistled. The audience loved her and was on her side, but her poor little legs just wore out; however, she grew up to be a formidable woman player on the WVU women's team. She never won any of the MALTA tournaments, but she had a grand time helping the shaved ice machine vendors who adored her, particularly at the Home Beneficial tournament in Richmond at Byrd Park. This tourney was where we first met a lifelong friend, Betty Gustafson, whom we thought of as our "tennis angel".

Betty met us on our second year at this tournament and was impressed with Eddie's playing. Eddie had won many of the large MALTA tournaments the summer before and was seeded #1 at all of them the second year. Betty took Eddie, Sylvia and me under her wing.

When Eddie was asked by the other players "Who is your pro?" he simply said "My dad." Betty arranged lessons for Ed with the Country Club of Virginia tennis pro, where he learned a few more serves - ending up with a total of five that he never telegraphed. After the lesson, Betty would practice with him, making him repeat and repeat what he had just learned. She even played with Paul on one visit and could see why Eddie had learned so much from "his pro".

The other players would come on the courts with leather cases filled with several racquets intimidating their opponents and Ed had just two with him but the second year he had a black leather case with four racquets.

Betty taught gym at a high school in Richmond and was an excellent player herself and had played with Maureen "Little Mo" Connolly, the first and only woman to win all four of the grand slams in one year. We still keep in touch with Betty, whom the Parkers will never forget.

Paul stayed in the USAF Reserve for 25 years and was in the 302nd Tactical Air Lift Wing at Lockbourne and was honored to be nominated as the Strategic Air Command Officer of the year. It was announced the nominees had been narrowed to two, Paul and a surgeon general from another base. Lockbourne was so pleased their judge advocate nominee won.

Paul was flown to Offutt Air Force Base in Omaha, Nebraska, headquarters of SAC, to receive the award. He was thrilled to tour the major command post of which the newly formed United States Air force took command on November 9, 1948. Offutt gained international prominence when it became the host base for the Strategic Air Command, which was removed from Andrew Air Force Base in Maryland. Secretary of the Air Force Stuart Symington chose to locate the Air Force long range atomic strike force at Offutt because the base was more centrally located on the north American continent which was well beyond the existing range of long range nuclear armed bombers to (then) stay safely out of range of hostile missiles or bomber aircraft.

CITATION TO ACCOMPANY THE PRESENTATION

OF THE

SAC OUTSTANDING RESERVIST OF THE YEAR AWARD

TO

PAUL E. PARKER, JR.

THE SAC OUTSTANDING RESERVIST OF THE YEAR AWARD IS

PRESENTED TO PAUL E. PARKER, JR. FOR OUTSTANDING

ACHIEVEMENT IN BEHALF OF THE MOBILIZATION AUGMENTEE

PROGRAM DURING THE PERIOD 1 JANUARY 1971 TO 31

DECEMBER 1971. MAJOR PARKER'S INITIATIVE, SUPERB "CAN

DO" ATTITUDE, AND OUTSTANDING LEGAL KNOWLEDGE

CLEARLY DISTINGUISHED HIM AS THE OUTSTANDING

RESERVIST OF THE YEAR WITHIN THE STRAGEGIC AIR

COMMAND   DURING 1971. THE DISTINTIVE

ACCOMPLISHMENTS OF MAJOR PARKER REFLECT GREAT

CREDIT UPON HIMSELF AND THE UNITED STATES AIR FORCE.

In 1976, Paul had to retire from the Air Force as a Lieutenant Colonel after 25 years of active reserve service, but we finally had our first vacation as a family and went to Rehoboth Beach.

General J.E. Krysakowski and Major Paul E. Parker Jr., 1971

Omaha, Nebraska- July 21, 1971

Lockbourne's Major Paul E Parker of the 302nd Tactical Air Lift Wing, Air Force Reserve of Fairmont W.Va. receives plaque honoring him as Strategic Air Command's Outstanding Air Officer for 1971. The Major, a lawyer, works in Lockbourne's Judge Advocate office during his active duty-training period. General Joseph E. Krysakowski, SAC Staff Judge Advocate presented the award.

EARLY WARNING

When Paul went for his physical in 1976, he was told his test results showed that sometime in the past year he had had a massive, but silent, myocardial infarction. A massive heart attack? But when? We were both stunned!

Jesse Jenkins, MD had used Paul as a model under which to test pilots from Fairmont-Clarksburg Benedum airport and Hart Field in Morgantown. Paul was 50 years old and was the ultimate health guru to his friends. In good weather he played tennis every day. In the winter months he played with the Fairmont group in WVU tennis coach, Stanley Farr's, indoor courts. Paul jogged five miles every other day. He had not smoked in over 20 years. We were not 'partiers", and he seldom imbibed –I drank Diet Rite Cola and orange juice. He loved to practice law. He was a perfect example of a healthy, happy and contented 50-yearold male.

The only time in the past year that I could remember any complaint from Paul was a weekend in July of 1975. He called me in to the bedroom where he was sleeping; I was watching television in another room. He said he felt like someone was standing on his chest. I laid beside him and put my head on his chest, counting the heartbeats while taking his pulse. The beats were strong, steady and about 69 per minute. He said he was feeling better and I reported his heart sounded strong –no skipped beats. He immediately fell back to sleep. The next day, he played two sets of singles and two sets of doubles.

Dr. Jenkins sent Paul to the cardiac unit at West Virginia University Hospital and Medical Center, completed in 1960. This teaching hospital was replaced by Ruby Memorial in 1988. I drove Paul to Morgantown and waited for him three days in a row. I had located a little prayer book Mother had given me before she left for Hawaii. I carried that with me through those days of waiting in different lobbies all over the large hospital. I read each of those 365 prayers each day. I was scared.

On the third day the cardiologists invited me in to hear the final consultation and prognosis. They could offer no advice. They said he was in perfect health except for the EKG recorded heart attack and said he was doing everything he should and to keep it up. A reprieve!

On the way home, Paul strongly recommended we keep the whole week's happening to ourselves. He did not want to upset the children or his parents, nor did he want to play the victim on the tennis courts. He had no thoughts of becoming "the invalid". I agreed.

Paul was back in his heaven. Fourteen years later a doctor at Cleveland Clinic, being introduced to me, asked if I was the one who had talked her husband out of a heart attack.

In 1975 Eddie was in college majoring in political science and was sent to London School of Economics to study for a long semester. Paul and Eddie had gone to all the WVU games since Eddie was five and Sylvia and I would go shopping in Morgantown. The season of 1975 that Eddie was in London, I went with Paul to every game to keep him company, but I became an avid fan. I never missed a home game again for the next 15 years.

Sylvia's last year of high school, Paul suggested a family game, "Use a Word Three Times and It's Yours". On Sunday after church we exchanged words we had collected that week and asked each other the meaning by using in a sentence. Of course Paul often won. One of our favorites was schadenfreude. He pronounced it in German, "shah-had'-den-froy-duh", meaning "the malicious enjoyment of another's misfortunes", a word not even in the older dictionaries and used so often today. He would use some legal terms – caveat - a warning or proviso in the law - to suspend proceedings. Next would be - caveat emptor- the principle that the buyer alone is responsible, legally - "Let the buyer beware".

We all learned so much and in Sylvia's senior year in her last essay for Linda Morgan's English class, she used many of the words she had learned in an essay. Mrs. Morgan, an excellent English teacher, gave her an A and wrote – "Sylvia, don't do that to me again, I had to look up almost every word!"

I still have those words in an old yellowed file. Paul's handwriting was so bad I am glad we did not court by mail. But he did teach us to be aficionados of etymology.

Sylvia and Eddie were in college and we went back to Lockbourne, now called Rickenbacker Air Force Base, a few more times when they were in need of his services. In February 1979, we went to Florida to see Elaine and George and my sister Sylvia, who was visiting on her way back to Honolulu from her Christmas visit in Saudi with Ken and Mila. This was a first time reunion of the three sisters for several years.

366

Pep and Merr, Paul's parents, died in 1980 within five weeks of each other. Betty died of an aneurism on Friday, February 8, 1980. I had driven her to Morgantown on Thursday afternoon to see Pep, who was recovering from a minor operation at the WVU Hospital. We returned home about four. She said to me as we were driving down Jackson Street, "You have been a good wife to Paul, Diane." She had never said that to me before.

She called that night at eleven and said she could not breathe. I called the Rescue Squad and Paul rushed to her side. She was taken to Fairmont General Hospital emergency room where she waited for her doctor. Paul called me every hour. At around two a.m., her doctors had not arrived yet and Paul was on the phone with me. I heard a noise in the background - the blue Code and said, "Paul, go to your mother." Her heart had stopped beating and they had the crash cart bring her back. Her doctor arrived about fifteen minutes later and sent her by ambulance, with Paul following, to West Virginia University Hospital emergency room where she died that morning at five o'clock. Eddie was living at our duplex in Morgantown and Sylvia was living at the Kappa Kappa Gamma house. I woke them both and sent them to be with Paul.

Pep was upstairs in the same hospital sleeping peacefully. When told of Betty's death, he withdrew from us all. We arranged to have an ambulance bring him to the funeral service at Jones Chapel in Fairmont. He looked only at her with tears that were not even brushed away. He was oblivious of Paul, of family, or friends. He never spoke to any of us again. We got him back into ambulance and back to the Emergency Hospital on East side.

As an only child, Paul was naturally overwhelmed with losing his mother and now his father, both of whom were perfectly well in January. I went to the hospital daily and held Pep's cold lifeless hand and read articles from Time and Forbes, even the funny papers, that might create an interest, but no response, no squeeze of the hand, just his pacemaker beating in time with the bedside clock. Only once, while trying to feed him soup, did he open his eyes, look over at the empty chair and say, "Well, Betty, what are you doing just sitting there?" He died the next morning, a Saturday, March 15, 1980. I really believe Betty returned for him.

Back again to Heavener Cemetery in Buckhannon, West Virginia, where Paul and I had buried most of the Shumaker and Parker families, leaving Paul, devoid of close family, except my family of sisters, their families and, of course, Eddie, Sylvia and me.

So many life changes took place in 1980. Eddie graduated from Law School in June and was married to Jan Carpenter on June 14th. They left immediately for Pittsburgh to live as Eddie had accepted a position with a large law firm. Our little Sylvia was in her senior year at WVU.

We bought the condominium over the phone with our brother-in-law George's help in September. After attending the West Virginia Forest Festival in Elkins, West Virginia on October 3-4, where Sylvia served as a princess to Queen Silvia, we drove back to Fairmont and finished making arrangements to move to the condominium on the 11-12 of October.

Our Mayflower driver's name was Bill Farmer, an ex-lightweight professional boxer, and the strongest man I ever met! I wanted to see inside that huge moving van and could not reach the first step. Bill just picked me up and set me on the seat. It was just like a small apartment, with his bedroom and TV in back. Paul and I were both fascinated with the whole trip. Bill and his assistant met us at the beach a block from our new winter home and asked if we could wait until the next day to move in. He was staying at a hotel on Route A1A and it was then getting dusk. We went to Elaine's and met him at the townhouse at nine the next morning.

Bill knew just how to place things in every room so that I would have no trouble changing beds and he was an expert making room for all of Pep and Merr's furniture. We were so grateful for his expertise and will never forget our one big move to our new winter home in Florida.

We felt right at home, but only for a couple of days. We had to make the 16-hour trip back to Fairmont for a trial, but planned to return for Christmas when Sylvia's college break came in December.

Our traditions changed so drastically in 1980, our first Christmas without Eddie, who celebrated his first Christmas without us, but with his new wife and her family of twenty-one Carpenters in Fairmont.

It was the first Christmas I had spent with my sisters in 22 years.

It was our first Christmas without any of Paul's family, and at our age, the words "miss you" take on a different depth. It was a complete lifestyle change, distracting the old memories and creating new ones. My one goal in life at this point was keeping Paul healthy, happy, and alive.

The children were grown and Sylvia, after receiving her master's degree in 1982, in rehabilitation, moved to Towson, Maryland to work for a private case management group as a Supervisor. Eddie had moved back to Fairmont from Pittsburgh and was practicing with Paul. And we had ten more years of a wonderful life ahead.

Paul and Diane on their boat, "Tug Dad"; Fort Piece Inlet, Florida

CHAPTER NINETEEN

A TEN-YEAR JOURNEY

Paul and Diane, 1990

THE BEGINNING: 1990

The beginning was really the early warning - the silent MI in July of 1975 - 15 years before, at the age of 48. We had worked so hard to keep him alive and he was doing so well. Perhaps this is why we were so shocked on June 8, 1990, after a fun Florida winter of jogging and tennis. He had laughingly protested, there was not as much oxygen on the courts, and had played more doubles than singles, but I was proud of him for recognizing he was growing older.

I had been shopping in Bridgeport and Eddie was waiting for me in the driveway when I got home. Paul had had a massive heart attack and was at Ruby Memorial in Morgantown; Eddie had come to drive me to his side. I knew my life had been changed forever. I was a little girl again at 741. Alone, but this time - his life was in my hands. I would not let my Love die this early! I was not ready to say a final good bye.

Paul had not felt well when he went to work that morning, but Eddie had joined him for lunch in his office. About 2 o'clock, he drove himself to his doctor's office and had a massive heart attack. The Rescue Squad drove him directly to Ruby Memorial, the huge medical facility in Morgantown, where all his past records were. The doctor's office was unable to reach me and called Eddie who left immediately for Ruby, returning soon to pick me up. Eddie, as nervous as I was, drove me straight to him.

It was not good. He needed a triple bypass of the three major arteries which were 99% blocked. They could not operate for two weeks, as his blood coagulation time was 20 minutes.

We had to allow the beta-blocker and the aspirin he took daily to ward off blood clots, to dissipate in his system. I drove him home where he spent the next several days talking to friends and getting advice as to hospitals and cardiologists.

Many said Cleveland Clinic, which did not suit either of us. I had taken him there in 1988 and 1989. They said his arteries were 60-40 % blocked and did not see the need in 1989 to repeat with another catheterization. After talking to Dr. Bob Nugent, a neurologist and an old tennis friend, Paul was convinced Gordon Murray, a thoracic surgeon at Ruby, was the one.

We waited patiently for two weeks, neither of us realizing he was forming a stress ulcer while he watched me mowing the grass with his father's old

Lawn Boy mower, which only he could start, and doing all the chores he usually did. We were both apprehensive, but tried not to let the other notice.

On June 26, 1990, Paul underwent a triple by-pass. Coronary artery by-pass surgery, which began in the late 1960s, was one method used in 1990 for treating coronary artery disease. The procedure increases the nourishment and circulation to the heart muscle. The large vein, called the saphenous vein, is removed from one leg or both and attached to the aorta and the other end is connected to the coronary artery below the blockage by passing the obstructed area. This procedure eliminates chest pain by supplying blood to a deficient area of the heart. In Paul's case, three pieces of the saphenous vein were connected to the right coronary artery, the left anterior descending artery, and the circumflex artery - thus a "triple by-pass".

When he came out of the Cardiac Care Unit (CCU), he was in A-Fib. A tall, turbaned "fellow" from the cardiology department tried to convert him back to a sinus rhythm, but was unsuccessful and I took him home, reluctantly, with atrial fibrillation on July 6, ten days after surgery.

Atrial fibrillation (A-Fib) is a dysrhythmia- a rapid or irregular heartbeat due to chaotic electrical activity that can occur after surgery, and Paul had it. He had been on the telemetry floor (10 East) and one or two times nurses ran in, "Mr. Parker, are you all right?" and he would have flipped into Ventricular Fibrillation, scaring those monitoring his heart. He had to go home on Coumadin (Warfarin) and be monitored weekly for his A-Fib.

Paul was simply not well enough to be home. He was so pale, his skin the color of paste, paler than pale. He showed no signs of recuperating…no hunger… no "good morning world"… no interest in being alive. I made him go outside to walk around the yard in the sunshine. Dina came with food and Cynthia came with more. Dina said, "Diane! His coloring is terrible!"

On July 8, Tim Ireland came with Jean's homemade cinnamon rolls that we love. Joe Woodward came later with new jokes to cheer him…but not much laughter.

Monday, July 9, I called the Physicians Office Center (POC). I told them he was breathless and sweaty and he needed to be seen. I took him to POC at two o'clock. They took him off some meds and put him on others. I brought him home.

On the 12th, Paul stayed upstairs in bed all day. Kept his feet up and took all the new and some old meds. Cynthia came with more food, even buttermilk pie. He sat up to eat but very little, and then back to bed. At three o'clock in the morning I had to wake him to give him his Procanimide. At four, he went to bathroom, called, "Dee Dee", and passed out. I went tearing in and blood was everywhere. The Rescue Squad came once again; his blood pressure was 80/41. I called Eddie to meet me at FGH emergency room where they insisted on stabilizing him. FGH sent him on Ruby. Eddie followed the ambulance; I beat all of them there. It was the morning of Friday, the 13 of July.

Poor Sylvia was working in Charlotte, North Carolina. I had sent her back after his return home from the by-pass surgery; I did not want her to lose her job.

Dr. Timberlake was the chief of the trauma unit at Ruby. A navy doctor who had served on board an aircraft carrier in the Pacific. He took charge and called in the head cardiologist on duty in July. He arrived and introduced himself as Phil Maxwell. Paul lying there – bleeding to death - his hemoglobin was down to eight; opened one eye and said, "Phillip Leman Maxwell?" The doctor looked stunned. Paul said, "Your mother was my first date". That resulted in a very close bond between these two men.

Dr. Maxwell left the room to procure more units of blood. On his return he said he had also called his mother in Salem, West Virginia and she had verified Paul was her first date back in Salem Grade School. Paul's father had driven them to the movies and back to the drug store for sodas afterwards.

After receiving the blood transfusions they moved Paul to surgical intensive care unit (SICU). Eddie left for Fairmont; I stayed until 10:30pm and felt safe to leave him with Karen, the R.N. in SICU.

I stayed in Sylvia's empty apartment again on Elm Street in Morgantown and did not have far to go. I had just gotten ready for bed when Karen called to alert me. Paul was hemorrhaging again and doctors were discussing cauterizing an ulcer that had perforated the stomach. I dressed and raced back to hospital. I was sitting in a little cubical for SICU family and called Eddie at midnight; he arrived at 12:30. Timberlake came in to see us about 2:30 and said nothing could be done but surgery. The ulcer was so close to a large hematoma on his left side they were afraid to cauterize. Eddie - the attorney - asked how old was the hematoma and the physician answered,

374

"About a week." Evidently it had been done during the attempt to convert the heart out of atrial fibrillation.

If Paul remained stable during the "quickie" operation, they wanted to do a hemi-gastrectomy, a splenectomy and a vagus nerve resection, which meant they would cut the vagus nerve, remove his damaged spleen, and cut out the bottom of his stomach!

I was freezing to death while he explained all this to us - probably in shock. The O.R. nurse wrapped me in comforting hot towels. Of course we gave our permission to operate and then we waited. Eddie kept disappearing, coming back with candy bars. He did nothing but pace the floor and eat the candy. I did nothing but shiver and pray.

It was Saturday morning, July 14. At 8: 30, Dr Timberlake said that he had done all that could be done and to go home and get some sleep while he was in recovery. Eddie drove me to Fairmont to get clothes and sleep a little, assuring me he would take me back to Paul in a couple of hours.

I remember coming up stairs and lying on top of the bedspread in a fetal position. I was sobbing so hard I gasped for breath. I had to talk to Sylvia and called her in Charlotte. I remember saying, "Please come home, darling, or you may never see your daddy again."

I drove myself back and stayed with him in intensive care. There were no objections. The nurses said his "numbers went down when I was there". Sometime after midnight the nurse called a security guard to walk me to the car; I stopped at an all night diner and got a hamburger to take back to the apartment. I slept - Sylvia was on her way.

Sylvia arrived the next morning after driving through a terrible rainstorm and went in to see Paul and felt faint. I sent her to her apartment to get some sleep.

Fluid had built up around Paul's left lung, which caused atelectasis; a collapsed lung, and the fluid had to be drained in order for him to breathe without extreme pain. Dr. Schmidt explained the lung lining was like cotton candy and was stuck together preventing oxygen from entering, and a bronchoscopy would remove the fluid and allow the lung to expand. After the procedure, he was resting more comfortably, but they told me not to let him get up or do anything. I hummed softly to him until he went to sleep. I hoped Sylvia was sleeping too.

Around five o'clock a new nurse reported to SICU. She insisted I leave his side; she had to change his bed. I tried to explain, but she would not listen. Taking my arm she directed me out of the larger double doors and shut them tightly. I was scared to death. I was unable to see Paul, I could not even see in his room. An orderly finally came and opened both doors to wheel in dinner trays and left them open. I saw Paul slumped over in my straight back chair struggling to keep his balance, but leaning perilously to his left, in great pain. No one was with him!

I went tearing out to the receptionist station in the lobby but it was closed. I burst into tears and waited for the elevator to creep up to my floor. Dr. Maxwell stepped from the elevator and asked, "Mrs. Parker! What's wrong?" I explained through tears what had just happened, how the nursing staff at Ruby had been so exemplary, so efficient and so wonderful to us both, but Paul was all alone because an unknown nurse had escorted me out. He spun around saying, "It will be taken care of!"

I sat in the window-bench overlooking the vast parking lot far below; the magnificent stadium towering over it all. We had such fun at tailgate parties at the WVU football games in that parking lot - the blue lot. Would we ever be able to go again? I did not care as long as he lived!

Twenty minutes later Dr. Maxwell said, "Paul is back in bed and all is well. This will never happen again!" He explained that a contract nurse had been hired, as a regular nurse had become ill during her shift. The substitute had not taken the time to review her patient's history. That night at the apartment, the head nurse at SICU called and apologized, I remember her name was Diane with a long i- and was always kind and professional. What may have been a small gesture to others restored my faith and confidence in the nursing staff.

On Sunday July 15, Sylvia returned to Charlotte and on July 20, Eddie and his family left for ten days in Florida. Paul healed slowly and moved twice to step-down units on eight-west, the surgical floor.

On July 24, I brought Paul home again. It was a very emotional time for us both. Flowers, fruits, friends, and food started arriving. Our dear friends Cynthia and Joe, Dina, and Jean and Tim brought in food and great conversation every day. What would we have done without this support group? We were on our own once again but not alone.

This time we were free of Coumadin, but still in A-Fib. They did not want him to "bleed out" again. When looking back, this is a frightening thought.

The dog days of August arrived. He was still ill, not eating and patiently tolerating my nervous chatter. I would take him a tray every morning and read the Times-West Virginian to him. He then would go back to bed, always sleeping on his left side. At noon I would try to get him dressed-thank God it was summer and he just needed a tee shirt and shorts. I would help him down the steps and out to the porch where he would lie on the couch and sleep most of the day. In the last seven weeks, his weight had dropped from 183 to 135; the only thing he seemed able to tolerate was Ensure, which probably saved his life.

August was hot and humid and he chose to stay in the air-conditioned house getting very little exercise. Our friend Bernie Sampson was in the hospital again and Dina, afraid to stay alone, stayed with us at such times. It was August 24, a Friday. We had been home one month from the last operation. We had eaten and Dina was expected any time. I kept her dinner warm and she arrived about ten o'clock.

While we were in the breakfast room discussing Bernie's health there was a loud thump from above. We both went tearing upstairs and Paul was on the floor, having fallen from our high master bed. He had pulled the sheet and blanket off the bed with him. His mouth was drooping on the left and his speech was slurry, as he said, "I got caught up in the bedclothes."

I had never, in recent history, heard the term bedclothes used by him or anyone else. I left him with Dina and called the Rescue Squad again. I had to move the furniture off the landing to help the squad each time they were due.

They arrived and knew the way up stairs. George Yost, an old basketball friend, was the first in the room and said, "Well, Paul, what are you doing on the floor with a pretty woman?" Paul looked up and said, "Well, George, we don't need you, what are you doing here?" I called Eddie and we all arrived at Fairmont General Hospital together.

The doctors and staff just stood and watched him. I kept asking, "What are 'we' doing for him?" There was really nothing any one could do to stop a stroke in 1990. They admitted him to a room about 3 A.M. and Eddie, Dina and I went home.

The next morning, Saturday August 25, Dina had gone up to be with Bernie and I checked on Paul, who was about the same. A new neurologist introduced himself and said he had been in Fairmont only six weeks. He had done x-rays and said there was nothing he could do, after repeating he had been at FGH only six weeks. I asked to have Paul transferred to Ruby and took the X-Rays with me.

He was admitted for the fourth time, from the emergency room. Our old friend, Phil Maxwell, had him assigned to the telemetry floor10-East again. Phil had called in neurologists who diagnosed a massive bleed to the right frontal lobe with 30-35% brain damage. I finally told them all, "Please keep him this time until he is well enough to go home."

Ruby kept him from August 25 to October 1, when he was transferred to Greater Pittsburgh Rehab Hospital in Monroeville, Pennsylvania. There were no rehab hospitals in the northern part of West Virginia so we went 100 miles north to Pittsburgh. Dina and I took a trip up to inspect the place and see about my apartment and meet the staff. Bernie had been there for several weeks and Paul and I had visited him there.

On October 1, Eddie drove me to Monroeville with suitcases, cooking utensils and sheets and Harry, the cat. Eddie's father-in-law, Jack Carpenter, followed us. Jack and Eddie moved in all my belongings and went back to Fairmont. I stayed at the Ivanhoe Apartments very close to the hospital for the next three months, spending each day with Paul and making friends with all his new caregivers.

He was still on a feeding tube and unable to walk, hence, his rehab was all for the upper body. At 7 o'clock in the evening I would tuck him in, clean his feeding tube, and kiss him goodnight. On the way to the apartment, I would stop at the market and get something to eat. Arriving after dark, I would scurry in the back door and climb the poorly lit steps to the second floor's lonely hallways. Once inside and safe, I would eat dinner - usually Lean Cuisine, watch the news and call the children and either Jean or Cynthia or Dina.

Each night I would push the snooze button and go to sleep listening to WISH FM (WSHH-FM, 99.7 FM), a favorite old music station in Pittsburgh. I would listen to the old songs that were popular back in the eighties-"Mack the Knife"- which we loved to dance to, "What I Did for Love", which had new meaning for me at this point. I cried myself to sleep some nights, awakening to any strange sounds; I would push snooze again and the old love songs would drift me back to sleep.

[Author's Note: WSHH-pronounced Wish - had a contest going as Christmas neared, "Why do you like Pennsylvania". I posted an entry exclaiming how wonderful people had been to a rival West Virginian; all had been so kind, courteous and empathetic to my husband in Greater Pitt Rehab Hospital and to me. I ended the letter with reference to their new license plate logo - I knew I "would always have a friend in Pennsylvania". I did not win the contest but a few days before going home, a huge red poinsettia arrived with a card, "Good luck! Your friends from WISH".]

Paul became very depressed in the hospital. He still was not walking and refused to go to the dining room with the others. I would feed him his dinner in his room. I had read so much about strokes and knew the victims of heart attacks and brain attacks often became clinically depressed. I asked the doctors at Greater Pitt to administer an anti-depressant. "Oh! My! No way!" They would have to call in a psychiatrist! I suggested they do just that.

The next day a pompous little man introduced himself as a psychiatrist and I told him what Paul needed. He insisted on interviewing Paul alone and I said fine, but he will want me there. Again- "Indeed not!" I sat and waited for an hour and the little man came over to me and said, "That man is terribly depressed!" I was sure he had not heard the whole story, but he got the picture.

He prescribed 10 mg of a drug called Pamelor and the next day one of his favorite nurses met me, pointing down the hall behind me, she said, "You just missed him, he's gone for a walk." He was walking down the hall waving to patients stuck in their rooms.

From then on he went to the dining room and tried to make friends with all the patients, who then seemed more ill than he was. At Thanksgiving, which was also our 38th wedding anniversary, I arranged a table for those without families to sit with Paul and me and brought fresh flowers and place cards for them. Paul was the hit of the cafeteria!

It would soon be Christmas and I arranged to bring him home. On December 20, Jack drove Eddie back, and the two packed us both and home we flew, delighted to be free of the routine of a hospital and back to Sylvia, our dear friends and to our castle on West End Drive. It was Paul's first glimpse of his home since August 24.

379

Sylvia was there to meet us and had the house all warmed and Jan had brought our dinner. The little ones were sick and she was afraid to bring them, as Paul was so fragile.

Sylvia had arranged Eddie's old bed, a much lower one, for her daddy; he was no longer able to crawl in or out of the high master bed any more. Sylvia had rigged a device with a long strap with which he could pull himself up and out of bed.

"We give Thee most humble and hearty thanks."

The Book of Common Prayer (1928)

THE END OF THE BEGINNING

In January of 1991 Paul and I did not go to our Florida townhouse. We were both disappointed but he was too weak to make the trip. He was back on Coumadin and could hardly raise his left arm. Doctor Maxwell wanted to cardio convert him as soon as Paul was able. He wanted to do it himself this time.

Back in August, I had seen an ad in the Dominion Post asking for qualified rehabilitation administrators to apply for jobs at a new acute care hospital to be opened in Morgantown on Van Voorhis road in March. I sent this to Sylvia who, unbeknown to me, had already applied while we were in rehab in Monroeville rehab. February 1991, she came back to Morgantown to live and helped to open MountainView Rehabilitation Hospital, today owned by HealthSouth. Sylvia became its first Director of Admissions.

Paul's appointment to convert was arranged for March 4 and, once converted, he would be admitted to MountainView as its eleventh patient. I had to have him at Ruby Memorial at 6 AM - not an easy task! I had to get up at three, get him dressed and drive twenty-five miles to the hospital in Morgantown. We got there at six, and they put him in bed where he immediately fell back to sleep. The procedure would be done around 7:30. The nurse came in at 7 to take his blood pressure and temperature, and was shocked to find his temperature so low - 92.7. She flew around saying, "Oh! We can't have that. Dr. Maxwell will have to postpone this conversion for another day". Once she had left, I jumped on top of Paul and said, "Warm up Paul, I can't go through all this again!" Paul started crying (his stroke caused him to cry instead of laugh).

It worked. His temperature shot up to 98 degrees. Dr. Maxwell knew just what to do and Paul was out of A-Fib and off Coumadin for the next four years.

We went to MountainView and an old friend Richard Taylor, recovering from a terrible automobile accident in Ohio, was admitted at the end of the week. His wife, Jean, and I had been in the Junior League together for many years; she had preceded me as president. For a couple of months, we four ate dinner together in the cafeteria. Sylvia would bring us Eskimo Pies and join us. Jean and Richard taught us to play UNO, an old card game we had never learned. Jean would have to be back in Fairmont before dark, so we would get the boys both back to their rooms and in to bed. I would stay and watch TV with Paul until he fell asleep. We did this until April 25, the day before Sylvia's birthday, when they sent Paul home. He could now lift his left arm up to his shoulder and was able to do the little ordinary things that he had not been able to do.

The neurologist at Ruby told me Paul had lost what was called the executive function of the brain, another term for cognitive process, involving planning, attention, problem solving, memory or mental flexibility. He could not dial a telephone number, nor remember his clients' names or their cases. He had to give up his law practice and Eddie and I went to his offices, which he had in association with Pete and John Higginbotham, on the corner of Adams and Monroe Streets in downtown Fairmont. After 40 years of practice, it was a difficult task.

Paul thrived and gained a little weight. Tim Ireland would pick him up and take him to senior men's golf every Wednesday at one o'clock. This gave me a free afternoon to go shopping or do whatever I wanted to. An old friend, John Veasey, Editor of the Times West Virginian, would take him to his club to play golf. Eddie took his father to Continuing Legal Education (CLE) courses at the Law School on some Saturday mornings, which he thoroughly enjoyed. I felt it was imperative for him to be with his peers to keep him interested in life and the law.

Tim would call two or three times a week to play golf and Paul was always up for that.

He would be ready and waiting in the sunroom an hour before Tim was due. He would sit patiently and wait for him. Tim drove a Mercedes Benz. He would yell in to me and say, "He's coming!" He could hear the diesel motor turn off Country Club Road to West End Drive. I do not believe Tim ever played much more tennis after Paul could not play. These two tennis buffs always swore they were saving golf for their old age; neither tennis nor old age was ever mentioned. Today the Field Club tennis courts, where we all grew up and had such wonderful healthy fun, are no longer. The tennis courts were sold and demolished for a doctor's office. It pains us all to look from the club down to a black top parking lot.

Not remembering clients' names was a real concern to Paul; he loved people. When someone would come up to him at a mall and say, "Paul, "I bet you don't remember me." Paul would say, "No, I don't", and start to cry (laugh) which would upset whoever it was. I suggested he just say, "I'm sorry, I have had a stroke and you will have to tell me your name". Or, "Just stick your hand out and say I am Paul Parker, and they should say I

382

am so-and-so". This must have worked for him, as I heard no more complaints.

He complained his driver's license had expired and I told him he would have to take a State Police exam all over again to renew it, which would make him furious with me. He wanted to drive a motorized car at Sam's Club and got on it - against my advice - started it, and went down the aisles saying, "BEEP-BEEP", with people jumping out of his way. He claimed he did not know how the brake worked but thoroughly enjoyed the ride. The brake was on the left and he could not lift his left foot up high enough to reach it. Oh, well, we lived and learned.

He pleaded for a tricycle in Florida and we bought a terribly expensive one for adults. I thought if he could not use it, I would and did. George and I got him on it and he drove it right into the garage door! He could not steer left or peddle with his left foot.

He started to write a book - a legal textbook on Eminent Domain, a subject on which he had become an expert. Judges often called him to ascertain the law in condemnation cases currently before them. Paul had been on retainer from the WV Department of Highways since 1963 and had tried literally hundreds of condemnation cases to build the new Federal highway I-79 in the state. Thank God he had learned why he could not drive anything, any more. The only further comment he made about a driver's license was, "Well, if I thought I might endanger others, I don't want to drive."

I leaned over and kissed him.

That first Valentine's Day after his stroke he wrote me a dear note on his old Tandy computer…

> *"When to the sessions of sweet silent thought,*
> *I summon up the remembrance of things past,*
> *I sigh the lack of many a thing I sought,*
> *Then can I flood an eye, as yet unflowed,*
> *But if I think on thee dear friend*
> *All losses are restored and sorrows end.*

Love, Paul …and Wm. S.

Sonnet XXX"

383

SEA FEVER

While we were waiting to return to Florida I cross-stitched the first and last verse of a poem Paul loved,

SEA FEVER, by John Masefield,

"I must go down to the seas again, to the lonely sea and the sky,
And all I ask is a tall ship and a star to steer her by,
And the wheel's kick and the wind's song and the white sails shaking,
And a gray mist on the sea's face and a gray dawn breaking."
"I must go down to the seas again, to the vagrant gypsy life,
To the Gull's way and the whale's way, where the wind's like a whetted
knife;
And all I ask is a merry yarn from a laughing fellow rover,
And quiet sleep and sweet dreams, when the long trick's over."

We went to Florida in January of 1992 and it was so good to be back. I hung the poem in the kitchen and he would repeat it every day, perhaps trying to memorize it.

Things were once again difficult to accept. He had played tennis daily at the Pelican Yacht Club with a wonderful group of men he had met at the courts. Many of them were retired lawyers and doctors. Paul would jog to the courts every morning and they would play until noon and then Paul would lunch and take a nap and, after work, someone invariably called him for a fourth.

I took him down to see everyone that morning in '92 and it was really old home week. They hardly recognized him; he had lost many pounds - from 183 down to 134. The men insisted I leave him there and they would bring him home when they were through playing.

I had not been home an hour until I was called. He had passed out on the courts! I really thought they were all big boys and knew better than to let him try to play.

When I got to the courts he was wrapped up in jackets lying there in the hot sun. They thought he was in shock. I took the jackets off and said he might have had a heat stroke. The culprits were waiting for the Rescue Squad to get there, frantically running out on the highway to keep traffic moving. I gave him some orange juice and he was fine. We got him to the car while assuring the crowd he would be better. What a day!

We had to sell our bow-rider, Tug-Dad, but that was no trouble. Our old friend Bill Jatazak, owner of Modern Marine on U.S.I where we had bought the boat and stored it every year when we went north said he would take care of everything. We had such fun with Bill and his wife Jan, an operating room nurse at Lawnwood Medical Center, who always included us in their big Super Bowl parties and introduced us to some of Paul's tennis friends.

Too soon, it was May; time to go home. We went down to the beach to say goodbye to the Atlantic, and Paul said, "Why don't we move to Ocean Village", a gated community a couple of miles south on A1A. "We could get a condo in one of the three Seascapes and use the elevator. We could see the ocean every day." Which I knew meant the little town house I loved so had two sets of stairs that would be harder for him to climb next year.

We went straight to Hoyt Murphy Real Estate office on the beach and asked to see Doreen Cowles, a great realtor who lived in Seascape 41. She started looking that day. At the end of July she had three on the market, one in each of the three Seascapes. With faxed pictures of each apartment, we chose the third floor in the 4100 building. We called our brother, George, and Doreen took him to see it and he heartily approved. We drove down for the closing on August 3, 1993, and moved in after 2 weeks of packing. She had the new place painted and ready to move right in. The moving took about six hours although we moved only five miles away on A1A. We even had old Fairmont friends, June Haymond Fox Cheplick and her husband Joe and Willa Jenkins Shingleton and her son Bob, living there in the winter months. Young Bob was part of the security group at the Village community, which was comforting.

The fresh air and sunshine was wonderful for us both. By our 1994 visit Paul put on some weight and sat at the pool with me and sunned. He played golf about three times a week on a three-par course at Ocean Village. I would drive him to June and Joe's golf cottage and off the two boys would go...no golf carts, they walked the course with Joe carrying two golf bags, bless his heart!

June Cheplick and I were old friends and had gone to college together. June was a niece of Jack Hutchinson's wife Susan (Haymond). We would go shopping and were often joined by Willa Jenkins Shingleton, close friend and widow of WV State Senator William "Shang" Shingleton. What fun we had! Joe would take Paul back to his cottage where we three girls would join them for drinks on their porch overlooking a putting green, often staying for dinner. It really seemed as if we were almost back to normal but - it was too good to be true.

His anniversary note to me that year was,

Nov. two-two, 1994

To Dee Dee- My one and only love:

"On this 42nd anniversary when I called you Bahama Mama, or when we stopped in Gettysburg returning from our trip to Ken's and Sylvia's in New York, or even later flying home in your new mink coat, did you think that our joint efforts–synergistically- would produce 42 happy years, two beautiful, talented, successful children, and make you my own - one and only love? You make me rich in having this dear gem - as twenty oceans if all their sands were pearls, all their waters molten silver, and all their rocks solid gold.

Happy forty-second anniversary, I love you."

~ Paul and Wm. S"

THE NECKLACE

On our way home from Florida in May of 1989, before Paul's illness, we stopped and spent the night with Sylvia and her good friend Tina Proveaux who were working in Charlotte, North Carolina. Tina and her family had lived on Elm Street and Maple Avenue above Sylvia when she lived in our duplex on Elm Street in Morgantown. We bought the building for the children to stay in while at WVU. Sylvia and Tina both worked at Things Remembered at the Morgantown Mall. When they both graduated from graduate school they moved first to Towson, MD and then in a year moved to better jobs in Charlotte, NC.

We landed on Saturday evening and the girls had made homemade white pizza for us. It was the first we had ever had and we became devotees. On Sunday morning – Mother's Day, Sylvia presented me with an 18-carat gold necklace with my name - D I A N E - in Arabic attached to a thin gold chain. I was thrilled. She had asked Tina's parents, who then lived in Saudi Arabia, to have one made for me months before. From that day on, I never took it off. Often, a stranger would say, "Hello, Diane" using the French pronunciation and smile at me, which usually shocked me, until I remembered the necklace.

In 1995 we left for Florida January 8, a Sunday, stopping in Columbia, South Carolina for the night. Fred and Sharon Cyran would drive over from Augusta, Georgia, 60 miles from Columbia and take us to California Dreaming in the old Atlantic Coast Line Railroad Station, on the edge of the University of SC campus. It was always so good to see our old next-door neighbor from Fairmont. Fred was in Fairmont Senior High School at the time Eddie was born and our back yards joined. When Fred got home from school, Eddie and I would be out in our yard and Fred would join us. Eddie would grab his car keys like a rattle and cut his teeth on them. Poor Fred never seemed to mind. Regina Cheney Cyran, Fred's mother, was such a big help to have next door – a true mentor to me the rest of her life. She taught both Eddie and Sylvia in second grade of Butcher School.

It was good to see our ocean again. Paul loved the sea and to be able to hear the waves all night often putting him to sleep. Things were back to normal – Paul and George went to the driving range about every day, working slowly into their old forms. George was a beautiful golfer. He had learned from Sam Snead when he was a student at Greenbrier Military School and Snead was the Pro at the five-star Greenbrier Resort. George still carried his first club made from hickory for luck.

June and Joe had not arrived yet and it was fun just to relax and look at the ocean. I would go to the pool each morning and take my "Walkie Talkie" with me and leave Paul's set right by his bedside so he could call me if I was needed. Sylvia had given them to us before we left, hoping I would not worry about him as much. I sunned and read until 12, fixed lunch then we would go shopping or to the range and hit balls.

On Sunday morning, January 22, I heard the coffee pot turn on, it was only 7 o'clock and I tiptoed into the kitchen. I heard Paul say, "Dee Dee?" I went back into the bedroom and he could hardly breath - He said he had not wanted to wake me but he had trouble breathing all night. He had been unable to urinate and was in pain. I called the Rescue Squad and told them I would call the gate. I dressed and waited for what seemed like hours and the squad appeared. They got him to the ambulance and told me to meet them at Lawnwood Hospital out by the Orange Blossom Mall. I could not follow them because of all the stoplights on US1. I found Paul at the emergency room; the squad had left, and Paul was lying there with oxygen, which seemed to have relieved the pain somewhat.

The ER doctor on duty asked who our doctor was and I answered we did not have one in Florida. He said he was sorry but could not call for one unless I gave him a name. I asked if he could recommend a good cardiologist – "No indeed!" I would have to find one.

It is difficult for me to write this. I have never heard of this lack of care or compassion, before or since. The man knew we were what Floridians scornfully call, "Snowbirds". He seemed to be enjoying my dilemma. He did not even have a phone book!

I knew George's number and called him. He said he would call his daughter-in-law, Lori, who had been a nurse at Lawnwood before she married Brooks Peed. He called me right back and said, "Margie". I ran back to the emergency room and told the doctor, "Margie". By this time it was one or two o 'clock in the afternoon. The good doctor was unreachable as he - or she - was on the golf course. I did not want to scare Paul, but I was livid! We had been there for hours, it was a Sunday morning; I could not make any enemies, but I asked if they would let me clean him to make him more comfortable.

Around six o'clock, Dr. Ziad Marjieh took one look at us and said to the ER supervisor, "Get this man into an examining room!" I followed them and filled Dr, Marjieh in on his record of illnesses and what he had told me that morning. The handsome tanned, steel grey haired man looked up and said abruptly, "Where did you get that necklace?" I answered, "Can you read it?" He said, "Diane" –with the French pronunciation! "O young Lochinvar is come out of the West!" I was so relieved, as was Paul. They admitted him to the Telemetry floor and found from an EKG that there had been a heart attack and he was back in A-Fib. He was put on Heparin and Paul insisted I go home. About 8pm when they came to take him to X-Ray, I left. He was stable and I was exhausted. It was dark but very little traffic. I called George to thank him and went to bed. "Oh God, make clean my heart and take not thy holy spirit from us!"

Dr. Marjieh had called in a urologist, Dr. Bogdan Marcol, who informed me that this was "A worst case scenario", but he would try to save his life. He was a young man who, when the older men in the Urology Association were not interested in tackling this case, spoke up and said he would attempt the needed procedure, a transurethral resection of the prostate gland (TURP) which would require anesthetics, then determined it would be safer to use a saddle block because of Paul' stroke.

388

On Monday, February 6, Dr. Marjieh converted him back to a regular sinus rhythm and on Wednesday the 8, he flipped into Ventricular fibrillation (V-Tec) and back into A-Fib. He was on all kinds of drugs and one made his throat to become swollen. Paul had quit eating, becoming weaker and weaker.

On Friday, February 10, Dr Marjieh came in and spoke to him about going to a nursing home for a couple of weeks to heal more before the TURP was attempted. I had my arm on the rail of the bed, and Paul sat up on one arm, grabbed my arm and looking straight at Marjieh and said in a loud, strong voice, "If it were not for this little girl I'd just as soon be dead!", and fell back onto his pillow.

We were shocked - Paul's sweet, tireless patience had worn thin. Dr. Marjieh motioned me to follow him to the hall out of earshot, "He is in a deep depression!" Being fully aware and having heard this song before, I suggested Pamelor. The good doctor said, "Get me the strength and he'll have one for dinner." I called Sylvia and she checked his records and it was nortriptyline -10 milligrams. After dinner there it was in the little white cup with his evening meds.

February 20, he was stable enough to go to the Skilled Nursing Unit (SNU). We had delightful nurses who were told to feed him anything he wanted to get him strong enough to have his operation. When they asked him what he wanted for dinner he asked for a steak, a baked potato and a beer. He did not eat much, but it was a start.

Paul had lost ten pounds since entering Lawnwood five weeks before. He had been admitted at 142 lbs. and when admitted to SNU he had dropped to 132. Julie, the head nurse ordered him a filet and a baked potato several times while on her floor, but no more beer. Paul loved milk and seemed to be better every day. They even helped him shower, and made him walk back to bed that second week. What angels of mercy they were. I even wheeled him outside for some sun.

On Wednesday March 1, Dr. Marcol thought he was improved enough and planned the TURP for Friday, March 3. I arrived at the hospital at 7:15. They took him down to the operating room at 8:30. Our friend, Jan Jatazak, the operating room nurse and Dr. Marjieh were both waiting for us. I was relieved to see them. Dr. Marjieh said he wanted him back on his floor in a private room following the procedure.

Immediately after it was over Dr. Marcol came in and said he got along fine. He smiled and continued, "He and the anesthetist kept us all entertained discussing medieval history!"

We arrived home in a wheel chair after forty-five days on Tuesday, the 10th of March. A Home Health nurse visited us three times a week for blood tests. Evidently the first test for prostate cancer (PSA) showed Paul's number was 63. A healthy number would have been four or below.

In the follow up appointment with Marcol, he explained the Gleason Scale prostate cancer of 1 to 7, Paul was at 5 and he wanted to prescribe a CAT and bone scans. Except for the cancer – everything else was ok and we should now follow up with Dr. Marjieh.

After what we had been through, the rather frightening news did not seem to scare either of us; I was as optimistic as Paul. We followed through with Marjieh who had arranged for the scans and after receiving those, suggested radiation to prevent the cancer from spreading to the bone.

Monday April 3, we met with the doctors at the cancer center and Paul was tattooed for radiation treatments, which would begin on Wednesday, April 5. Another routine was adopted. I went to the pool in the morning while Paul slept and then to radiation at 3 o'clock, afterwards, to the driving range to hit balls. George would often join us. The radiation did not seem to tire Paul and the boys had fun. Sometimes George would go home and pick up Rob and join us at Norris's Ribs on U.S. 1 for the best ribs and onion loaves we had ever eaten.

In the past years, Jan, a teacher, and Bill Heckenhauer, a mechanical engineer from Bucyrus, Ohio, our good friends who lived in the penthouse of our building with a beautiful view of the coastline, which always thrilled us both, would have us up for dinner. They often included June, Joe, Willa and Gerry Smith, a retired Food Editor for the Pittsburgh Press who lived directly below us. Paul and I hosted Easter parties, birthday parties and receptions for our guests from Fairmont, with this group and my pool friends, Corrine and Jim Buchannan from Indiana, Jean and Ken Edson, an attorney from Brooklyn and Lois and John Pawley, a retired four-star general in the Air Force. We were a diverse and interesting group who kept our minds from dwelling on dire predictions. These dear people were our support group during this crucial year alone in Florida and those few years we had left for us. I shall never forget them. They had all gone home in April and early May but as we had to have 9 weeks of radiation (38 treatments) we did not leave for Fairmont until after the Memorial Day weekend, arriving home on June 4.

Sylvia saved us, once again. The necklace - her Mother's Day gift of love - created a bond between a total stranger and me. Together we saved Paul's life.

In 1995 my late Valentine read:

March 11, 1995

Dearest Dee Dee
When I am lonely, dear white heart,
Black is the night, wild is the sea,
By love's light my foot finds
The old pathway to Thee.
Thank you for everything, I love you, Paul

Christmas at the Fairmont Field Club, 1995

CHAPTER TWENTY

THE FINAL FLING

"There's a ship lies rigged and waiting in the harbor,
"Tomorrow for old England she sails"
and dear Dee Dee, we shall be aboard that ship tomorrow,
"For I have loved you deeply, more deeply than the spoken word can tell."

Paul's note was on my pillow the night before we sailed for Southampton.
He would sing Roger Whittaker's famous "Last Farewell" to me when he
was happy and exhilarated, defying the last few words of the song he sang in
earnest, "Though death and darkness gather all about me".

Dina and Warren Wysner had just married in Cancun, Mexico in July and
this trip was their honeymoon. It was our second honeymoon after 45 years.
What fun, just to be together. We spent the night near the Pittsburgh
International Airport and the next morning flew into Newark, New Jersey,
where a bus awaited to take us to Pier 90 in New York Harbor. We had to
wait to board the liner while they loaded the cargo. This was the 30th
anniversary trip of the Queen Elizabeth II, the only super liner in the world,
a ship that represented the all but vanished luxury travel at sea. We sat with
red, white and blue balloons everywhere and English tunes playing while we
observed all the boarding passengers. A lovely English couple with a baby
in a stroller were shipping all their furniture and two cars. They had been in
the United States for two years and were excited to return home to England.

I thought of Mammam and Papa who sailed out of the same harbor seventy
–three years ago in 1924 on the Laconia II.

We boarded and walked, surely miles, to our cabin 4021. Paul was starving
and we found the Lido that was serving tea, but Paul wanted a beer, which
shocked us all. It was teatime not beer time. We returned to the cabin where
a lovely bouquet of flowers had been delivered from Eddie, Jan, Brett,
Brooks, and Sylvia, wishing us "Bon Voyage and God-Speed!" The
Stargazer lilies perfumed the cabin and reminded us of home, and the
children. We cried.

Hardly had time to sit down before lifeboat drills - scenes of the Titanic
wavering though our thoughts. We struggled with the vests and found deck
chairs for sailing out of New York Harbor – The Statue of Liberty looked
majestic and we threw her a kiss. I thought of the huddled masses yearning
to breathe free; all the Italians and Irish we knew from home that came to
Ellis Island and kissed the ground. Paul and I had never left the United
States except for Nassau on our first honeymoon. We took many pictures,
including one in front of the twin towers, standing so majestic and so grand.

394

Many tears shed while saying goodbye to our country and our children. I, too, prayed for Godspeed and safe journey for us both.

I kept a log of the trip across the same path as the Titanic:

Wednesday, September 17 - Each morning we were reminded to set our watches up one hour. I dressed for a swim in the deck pool and asked the steward which elevator to take. He advised me to use the indoor pool as we were in the North Atlantic and it was only 40 degrees out on deck. Listed a lot today, large swells and much cooler. While Paul slept I toured Harrods on another deck and bought several little things with my Cunard credit card. Also went to the photography shop and bought pictures of all of us boarding. Will buy two sets and make albums for both couples; we could never have gotten this far without our dear friends. Our dining room was the Mauretania table 306. Met Dina and Warren and had "Carre D'agneau Boulangere", (roasted rack of lamb) and "Tarte De Pommes au Caramel" (crepes with caramelized apples). We went directly to cabin and to sleep.

Thursday, 18 - Went to immigration where they stamped and checked passports to facilitate debarkation in Southampton. On to the library where Michael Leyton, our tour director, gave us pounds for $13.50 ($26.00 in our currency) for tube and bus passes. Met Dina and Warren in Lido for lunch and to a Revue in Grand Theatre. Paul had to excuse himself, lost his way and sat clear across the huge auditorium. He sat there and waited for me and quipped, "I knew you'd find me." I had been worried to death about him. It was formal dress for dinner the second night. We had Chateaubriand Béarnaise and on to Barnaby's Magical Show. Later, we danced in the Queen's ballroom. Sea was quieter tonight.

Friday, 19 - We are 1049 nautical miles from New York. We just passed the coast of Newfoundland and were steering toward Bishop's Rock of Cornwall. I wrote too many postcards to mail aboard ship and the swells got to me. The steward brought a little pill and Paul and I slept for several hours. The Wysners came by bearing seasick wristbands - somewhat like shutting the barn door.

We could not miss the Captain's Ball that night. I wore a copper sequined gown and probably resembled the color of my frock, but what fun it was! Had picture taken being greeted by the ship's Captain. Dina had to retreat to the smoking area and met a new friend. She brought Henrich Schultze from Hamburg, Germany over for a drink. He told us there were about 280 Germans on board this trip, plus the international USA Ryder Cup Team of pro-golfers headed for Madrid. Paul was not impressed with Dina's new smoking companion and later said, "Interesting fellow but not as anti-Nazi as he would have us believe." We had slept most of the day so danced and listened to Wayne Fontana and the Mindbenders – a Top 60's British band, until one in the morning.

The next day, September 20, is the Thirtieth Anniversary of the QE2 and we are 1854 nautical miles from New York, longitude 78 degrees. In the afternoon we attended the lecture in the Grand Lounge by the senior officer of the Cunard Liner, Commodore John Burton Hall who told interesting tales of building the magnificent ship. Then, to the theatre to hear George Parker, who was in charge of the 1967 launching. He and the others pronounced Cunard, "Que'-nard" unlike us. He said the name of the new ship was a mystery until Queen Elizabeth II announced, "I christen thee " Queen Elizabeth the second". He showed the films of the launching and it was fascinating. Last night to dress for dinner, I wore my silver and gold striped jacket and black crepe slacks. We met Dina and Warren for dinner amid festive balloons. The surprise dessert- all the stewards entered the great dining hall holding aloft flaming baked Alaska. Danced in the festive Queen's ballroom where celebratory champagne was flowing until midnight.

On Sunday 21, of September, it was announced at the church service those wishing to renew their wedding vows were invited to the Grand Lounge stage at two o'clock. Paul proposed we do just that and asked if I would. I answered yes; I would love to, just as I had so many years before. We stood with several other couples about our age and the Anglican vicar repeated the same words from the 1928 Episcopal prayer book that Graham Luckenbill had used 45 years ago. A beautiful gold scrolled certificate of marriage was blessed and presented to all the participants. A beautiful, sacred, unforgettable ending to a trip of a lifetime. That evening on my pillow Paul's note read;

"When we first were in love, it was a most happy thing. If you had said no, we would not have known what was to be and is - the happy beauty of our lengthy Christian marriage. It has been a remarkable journey. As a sick old man, I feared your refusal this second time, but you signed on for another 45! As you always say -'The best is yet to be'

Love, Paul."

Warren Wysner, Dina Shoal Sampson Wysner and Paul Parker, Jr.
I, Diane, took this treasured photo on our way out of the New York Harbor.

LONDON CALLING

Each day Paul kept his own diary, not of the ship, but of London. He saw a few things we did not notice:

"Sept. 22

The countryside of Surry - bus coming from Southampton to London pretty with sheep and horses. One herd of sheep was put to pasture in the right of way of the Mainway (four-lane interstate). 'Chatty Cathy' (Guide) described countryside for two hours.

Driving to the Grosvenor Thistle Hotel on Buckingham Palace Road in London was rather like driving in downtown Pittsburgh; exciting to see the opposing traffic coming head on!

Bus Tour upon arrival London town - Black taxis recommended for all travel. Taxi took us through Belgravia…rows of white columned townhouses, very nice. Occupied by ambassadors and such. Solid rows of red brick townhouses facing the British Museum very nice. Going past Buck House, driver told of Prime Minister, Benjamin Disraeli, when terminally ill, was asked if his beloved Queen Victoria be told of his near death, he answered, 'No, she would just give me a message for Albert'.

"What did we see? Thames River scenes - 2 times. Cold! First time entered the Tower. Not sure why the second trip, but saw Parliament from the river. Still cold. Buckingham Palace interior and changing of the Guard. British Museum and Madame Tussaud's Wax Museum - stopped at Victoria Pub, near our hotel. Not good - out of bread you know. Albert's pub - very good and had bread. I liked Clarence Room at our hotel – The Grosvenor. At breakfast when Linda welcomed me, ordered two poached eggs without asking…she remembered I did not approve of their coddled eggs. At dinner, Italian waiter, Ivan, and waitress, Manuela, did fine job. The Harvard Bar at hotel has lounge and tables, serves Beck's inter alia in walnut paneled room with plaques and oars, etc. of Harvard Crew on walls. View from Grosvenor of Buck House Road. Reminds me of the old William Penn Lobby in Pittsburgh. I will miss that milieu.

"Sept. 23

At the Tower, I particularly enjoyed the Royal Regiment of Fusiliers Museum, (British Infantry Regiment). Their original duty assigned by King James II in 1685, was to protect the Royal guns kept within the tower. The museum displayed the uniforms, weapons, and battlefield displays, including Sudan. The regiment mounts the guards at the Tower wearing short red tunics, black pants and high boots and full dress sentry wearing hats of bear fur, pacing a prescribed route. Reminded me of walking post for demerits at Fort Benning for not making bed tight enough or rifle dirty. The beefeaters, soldiers or yeoman at the Tower dress like ads for the Beefeaters gin and conduct tours. The BE we drew was a husky six-footer who explained the execution process at the Tower. The prisoner was hanged by neck, but was cut down when blue - before dead and hanged again. He said the English were very good at this. The body was stretched and quartered, and the quarters were hung in different locations of London as a warning to other culprits."

[NOTE: Paul and our beefeater carried on a long gruesome conversation about Guy Fawkes being quartered, which the rest of the group thought extremely funny. Dina and I left them and strolled over the Tower Green to the Bloody Tower. Saw the Queen's Jewels and shopped for replicas in the gift shop.]

"Sept. 24

Madam Tussaud's Wax Museum has great exhibits, but the last section of horrors, dungeon atmosphere, and guillotines is a bit much for me. I would not take Brett or Brooks there. The basement atmosphere of Westminster Abbey with cobblestone floors, stone walls and cemetery feel should be seen but then pass on to sunshine or pub, no loo at Abby, so did both.

Left D and W doing brass rubbings at Abbey and on to Victoria and Albert Museum, Italian - Greek sculptures including Michelangelo's David in plaster...very impressive. One day to British Museum wanted to see Great Round Reading Room, we weren't allowed to go in without prior ID... Dee Dee took little girl aside and she led us in to have IDs made and took us into the Great Reading Room (1857) where Marx, Tom Hardy, Kipling, Gandhi, Lenin and G.B Shaw read and wrote. Green reading lamps at each individual desk, and books surrounding the entire walls up to top floor where dome begins. Dee Dee can do anything.

"Sept 26

Shopped Harrods, Diana and Dodi's portraits on easel draped in black beside a grand piano with a vase of white roses - Dodi's father - Al Fayed owns Harrods...They died on Aug. 31 and hear they will take up an entire department store window for a year. Tonight, "Phantom of the Opera" at Her Majesty's Theatre-spectacular. Searched for black cab - it was midnight and they all shut their vacancy lights off and would not stop - sailed by, eyes straight ahead. Dina and Warren looked for bus stops - back hurt, Dee Dee said, sit down on curb... she flagged a handsome Mercedes - Asian driver, polite, stopped – asked if we could afford ten pounds Dee said yes – Dee in front 3 of us in back. Takes us home and worth it.

[NOTE: This was the first complaint I heard of Paul's back hurting.]

"Sept. 28

Felt queasy in Buckingham Palace, i.e. Buck house, and sat down on gold silk settee. "Pep" tired - back hurt. To Buck House emergency room in wheel chair, soft drink and soft chair. Nice people - exchanged jokes. Dee found me again. Off to change of Guard. Next on to Hyde Park and Park Lane Hotel antique sale, Diane found a Gucci buckle bracelet for $50.

"Sept.29

Up early, Bus arrives, loads baggage and off to Gatwick The countryside of Surry green and lovely. Passed through Battersea on way. Virgin Atlantic flight 17 took us to Newark, 33,000 ft. 450 mph - service splendid on Boeing 747 - Warren said, 'Bigger, faster, and better service than Boeing B17.' (Warren- waist gunner on Boeing – B17 during WWII - US Army Eighth Air Force Base - station 128 at Deenethorpe, near Corby, England - there to bomb Berlin 1944-1945)

"Sept. 30

Warren drives all to Fairmont, first and only rain on trip. Dreams are now memories. I couldn't have gone without Warren and Dina; of course, I wouldn't be at all, without Dee Dee. My prayers at Westminster and Warren, got us home safely. How nice to hear at Customs, 'Welcome to your home country'. Good to be back"

The Captain's Ball on the QE II
Paul, Diane, Dina and Warren

MEMENTO-MORI

Upon our return, I warned Paul's internist, Christine Kincaid, at Ruby Memorial about his back complaints in London. She scheduled a bone scan immediately and we went down for a checkup. He had not had a scan for bone since November 1996 when Dr. Kandzari had done a vaporization of the prostate gland. That bone scan was clear.

I dreaded to hear the results, which she telephoned the next morning. The cancer had spread from the prostate. There were ten "hot" spots on the spinal column, the base of neck and on the right thorax.

Dr. Kandzari prescribed a three-month Lupron Depot shot, which he administered at Ruby Memorial. Eventually, in 1999, Lupron Depot became too expensive for the hospital to absorb and I had to order it from Rider's Pharmacy in Fairmont, and hand carry it Ruby. The precious medicine was in a hypodermic needle and inserted into Paul's arm by a doctor. This shot kept him alive for two years with the PSA falling back to normal for a month or two and the hot spots calming down - with no new additional ones. We continued to go to Florida in 1998 and 1999, with all doctors taking wonderful care of him.

In 2000, against my best judgment, we returned to the Sunshine State. Our brother-in-law, Captain George, had a triple by-pass, just as Paul had ten years before. Neither of the boys was able to play golf or fish or do the many things they loved to do together these many years. Joe and Cynthia Woodward had returned for their last trip to Titusville just a couple of hours north of us. None of us visited with each other that year. Paul's back was too bad, George was recuperating and Joe was on dialysis. This was our 20th year in Fort Pierce and it was good for Paul, both physically and spiritually, to be there - at least a little closer to his brothers. He so enjoyed the ocean - even hearing the waves lapping up on shore at night. The Masefield poem I cross-stitched was still on the wall. I heard Paul whisper, "And all I ask is a merry yarn from a laughing fellow rover". This year there were no fellow rovers.

Joe Woodward died on April 10, and we were not able to help Cynthia, but her children flew down. She had formed many friendships in Titusville as I had in Fort Pierce. Our nephews, having discovered George had developed a brain tumor, were, of course, too busy with their father, families and jobs. Sylvia, always on call, would return to bring us home anytime. But, we still lingered.

June and Joe Cheplick had returned to Bath, New York and Jan and Bill Heckenhauer and their dear little dog, Buddy, had gone home to Bucyrus, Ohio. Cynthia had returned to Fairmont to have a memorial service for her Joe, and George was dying from a brain tumor. Paul thought it was now time to say goodbye to the south. He said, "I want to see the mountains and a real tree again."

With Sylvia's help, we arrived home on May 1. We sent George flowers and love on his birthday, May 3, and he died on May 5. "Georgie" called us and said he was at peace. Sylvia attended the funeral at Arlington National Cemetery and filmed the proceedings, complete with military honors, a horse drawn caisson, a gun salute, Taps and a military wrapped flag, given to Rob. Through the tears, all I could see was my hero, George at 14, in his Greenbrier Military uniform, rescuing me and my little green tricycle off the streetcar tracks on Fairmont Avenue and carrying me home to 741.

Between Paul's stroke, his cardiac condition, and the spread of the prostate cancer, his daily functioning continued to be compromised. He started sliding his left foot; the stroke affected side, and would stumble over it. He slept more and more each day. He never complained, but I could tell his back pain was increasing in frequency and amount. Sylvia, writing to an old friend of hers in the medical field asked, "We were just hoping there was something else that could be done to make him more comfortable and/or functional at home. My mother has performed miracles with him, but even she admits that he is getting worse each day." There was little response - No new suggestions or ideas. I think we knew that, but it was worth a try.

Two "fellow rovers "called him after we arrived home. On June 23, Tim called to see if he felt like playing golf and he answered, "Why not?" He could only play two holes, his back hurt so. Tim brought him home and I gave him a Darvocet and put him to bed. A couple of days later John Veasey called to play and he said yes again. I was not going to interfere; I knew John would take care of him just as Tim had. I really think he needed to say farewell to these two, faithful, old friends.

The many doctors and specialists had done all they could for ten years, but Dr. Christine suggested seeing an oncologist to leave nothing unturned. She sent us to a Dr. H. at Mary Babb Randolph Cancer Center, a part of Ruby Memorial.

On 30 of June we waited and waited to see the new doctor, two hours in a wheelchair in the hallway. We spoke very little. This was not the time for

402

inane chatter. Paul sat and looked at the floor while I got more upset every hour. They had called us out of the waiting room where – at least - there were windows. Once in a while a nursed stopped and shook her head and asked, "Still waiting?" I asked for a blanket for him. It is so cold in hospitals.

The futility of it all! I was angered at this last trip for what I knew would be bad news. I knew the doctors who had treated him for ten years had never given up and had cared for us both. Now, here we sit, cold, uncomfortable and scared for three long hours.

When the doctor was free we were ushered in and introduced to Dr. H., I never knew his first name. He was a large man, very apologetic about keeping us waiting and kindly reported he had looked over Paul's history, but there was very little left to do. I explained that Dr. Kincaid had thought chemotherapy might help with the pain and looking at Paul, he eagerly suggested it might give him a few more innings. Paul looked right at me. I said, "Paul, darling, this has to be your call. " Paul sat up straight in the wheelchair, raised his right arm into the air and said, "Let's go for it!"

Dr. H. administered a dose of chemo on July 7, at 12 Noon. We returned home at four. Sylvia had had a hospital bed put in for him. We helped him into the much higher bed and he slept soundly until morning. I gave him his pills regularly but he refused all food. On July 10, he was so weak I had trouble getting him in and out of bed. On Tuesday the 11th, Alan Mollohan called and asked to speak to him. I told Alan about the chemo and how weak he was, but Alan insisted. I handed the phone to Paul. Paul whispered to him – I could hear Alan talking and heard him say, "Let me talk to Diane". He was upset and told me to call the rescue squad. I called Sylvia, who was at Fairmont General Hospital – keeping close - and she called Eddie and the Jan Care Ambulance Service. All came to the house immediately. They rushed him to Ruby and I beat them there one last time.

Paul was in a room with a young man in terrible pain. A Dr. Auber from Oncology was on-call and had us moved to a private room.

After a modified barium swallow test, we found he could not swallow any more. Aspiration pneumonia! On Wednesday, they asked permission to put in a G tube, which I should never have done. He hated it and now, I think it was unnecessary. I was still fighting to keep him alive and he was trying to give up.

Our private room was lovely and flowers were everywhere. Jean and Tim came to see him. Eddie and Jan came by and stayed for lunch in the cafeteria. Sylvia came in the evening to stay the nights to relieve me so I could go back to the apartment to sleep. Then I would relieve her in the morning so she could go to work. Dr. Christine and her husband, Kenny Kincaid, Paul's fraternity brother and dear friend had come by. So good to see everyone; not much conversation, but their presence was felt and appreciated.

On Thursday July 27, Paul had a seizure - an episode. Sylvia had come to relieve me but as I was leaving, Paul pointed at the curtain that hid the door, looked terrified and kept pointing at the curtain and saying "ju-ju-ju-ju". Sylvia jumped in front of him and said, "It's ok, Dad. Nothing will get by me". Gasping for breath, he fell back in the bed and was calm. He had gone into ventricular tachycardia and never awoke from this comatose state.

From then on, he was seldom alone. Eddie came to relieve me at dinnertime, Sylvia arrived about 9 o'clock to spend the night and when our favorite nurse came in the 7 am shift, she or Eddie relieved Sylvia to go to work. Prudence was one of the many nurses who loved the story of our courtship and the "one red rose".

He was on a morphine drip which Sylvia and I monitored; if we felt he was in any pain we could raise the number of drips one degree at a time. There was nothing to be done but wait. Each day I sat listening to the piped in music on the TV set and held his hand. No feedings were needed, no nurses came in. I felt in limbo with him. I had been told to tell him it was all right to go and I had whispered this several times in his ear. I assured him that over the past ten years he had taught me how to get along without him. This was the most precious gift he could give me.

The death certificate said he died at 10:05 AM-08-02-00. They did not report that Prudence had gotten him ready for grand rounds and he had died in their presence. (I have a feeling he did it on purpose.) Or that the receptionist was holding me in the lobby until the doctors had escaped, or that Prudence had come down the hallway in tears - too much happening for her all at once. I held her and we cried together. I went in, put my head down on his chest, hugged him, gathered his things and said, "See you later darling", and left.   That night I slept with his last poem to me taped on the bed lamp,

"Dear Dee Dee, If fate should dictate that we part,
Then when rain rattles hard against your windows; know then
that is my soul searching for you, to hold your hand,
to dance with you, to comfort you.
Love, Paul "

The Marion County Bar Memorial Service was on the 4th day of August. The six of us attended and it was so enlightening and healing to hear his peers honor him.

The funeral was on Saturday morning the fifth at 11 o'clock. How cathartic to see so many old friends; every room of the R.C. Jones Chapel was filled. Clyde Judy had one room filled with AFA members. Paul was the founding president of the Air Force Association "General Pete Everest" Chapter here in 1998 and Clyde had followed him as president. Alan and Barbara had come from Washington. Alan came to the hospital the night before Paul died and sat with me for 2 hours. We reminisced and he was such a comfort.

Against the children's wishes, when I saw my beautiful Paul, I left the casket opened - he was at rest in his navy blue blazer and red tie. Unbeknownst to me, Sylvia had brought an appropriate "Miracle Flight" golf ball with "Love Tiltie" on it – Paul's nickname for how she first pronounced Sylvia when she was little. Brooks came in with another golf ball with "Brooks and Brett" on it. The three took them to show Eddie and he drew from his pocket a fluorescent green tennis ball, on it was, "Punch your volleys": Paul's favorite encouragement before each tennis match.

Before the service, the casket had to be closed. I bent to kiss him and, for the first time, saw the three balls tucked under his right elbow in the fold of the tufted white satin. To this precious cache of mementos, I added one red rose.

"Paul's in his heaven, all's right with the world."

CHAPTER TWENTY-ONE

THE FOURTH DAY OF AUGUST

The Marion County Bar Association, circa 1985
Photo credit: Buffington Studio

IN THE CIRCUIT COURT ROOM OF MARION COUNTY, WEST VIRGINIA

DIVISION I COURTROOM

IN RE: Memorial Service of PAUL E. PARKER, JR., ESQUIRE DECEASED

PROCEEDINGS HAD BEFORE THE MARION COUNTY BAR ASSOCIATION SPECIAL MEETING.

In regard to the Memorial Service of Paul E. Parker, Jr., Esquire, deceased, on the 4th day of August 2000 at 10:00 o'clock a.m.

TERRI R. CHESLOCK, C.C.R.

Official Court Reporter, Division I

Marion County Circuit Court

Fairmont West Virginia

P R O C E E D I N G S

BE IT REMEMBERED that heretofore, to-wit: on Friday, the 4th day of August, 2000, at 10:00 o'clock, a.m., In Regard to the Memorial Service of Paul E. Parker, Jr., Esquire, deceased, at the Special Meeting of the Marion County Bar Association held in the Division I Courtroom, Marion County, West Virginia; the following proceedings were had:

* * *

PRESIDENT JEFFREY D. TAYLOR: I'd like to call this Special Meeting of the Marion County Bar Association to order. On behalf of the Bar Association, I'd like to welcome each and everyone of you here this morning. We're here for a truly solemn purpose, and that purpose is to honor the memory of our fellow member, Paul Parker, Jr., who passed away on August 2, 2000.

Mr. Parker will truly be missed by his family, by his many friends, and by each and every member of this association.

As is the tradition of this Association, Mr. Scott Tharp will present a Resolution of Respect that has been drafted in honor of Paul Parker, Jr.. This Resolution of Respect was drafted by attorneys Scott Tharp, Kenny Miller, and Alfred Lemley.

Mr. Tharp.

MR. J. SCOTT THARP: Mr. President.

The Members of our Association are saddened once more by the death on August 2nd, 2000, of one (1) of our prominent and able

1   members, Paul E. Parker, Jr., who until his last illness was an
2   active practitioner of this Bar.

3   Paul E. Parker, Jr., was born December 12, 1926, in
4   Buckhannon, West Virginia, the son of Paul E. Parker, Sr., and
5   Betty Shumaker Parker. He graduated from Morgantown High School
6   and received his Bachelor of Science degree from West Virginia
7   University where he was a member of Phi Kappa Psi Fraternity. He
8   received his Bachelor of Laws Degree from West Virginia University
9   College of Law in 1951.

10   Upon graduation from law school, he was associated with the
11   firm of Furbee and Hardesty in Fairmont for a while and was later
12   appointed Assistant Prosecuting Attorney of Marion County in 1952,
13   serving under Harrison Conaway. He then succeeded Mr. Conaway as
14   Prosecuting Attorney by being elected in 1956 and reelected in
15   1960. After leaving the Prosecutor's Office, he opened his law
16   office as a sole practitioner and continued as an active
17   practitioner for many years until a debilitating illness caused him
18   to close his practice.

19   He was inducted into the U.S. Army in 1945 and participated in
20   the ROTC program at West Virginia University. He served in the
21   U.S. Air Force Active Reserve Judge Advocated General Corp for
22   twenty-two (22) years, retiring as Lieutenant Colonel. Recognizing
23   his dedicated and enthusiastic service, he was honored as a U.S.
24   Air Force Strategic Air Command Outstanding Reservist for the year

1 1971.

2 Several months ago he showed to his interest and devotion to

3 the U.S. Air Force, he spearheaded the local effort resulting in

4 the formation of the General "Pete" Everest Chapter of the Air

5 Force Association for the Northern District of West Virginia based

6 in Marion County. He was elected and served as the Chapter's

7 Founding President.

8 Mr. Parker served as a representative of the Fraternal Order

9 of Police Lodge on the City of Fairmont Police Civil Service

10 Commission, and served several years as its President. He also

11 served as Civil Defense Director for Marion County and was a member

12 of Family Service Board of Directors.

13 Mr. Parker was a member of the West Virginia State Bar, the

14 American Bar Association, and the Marion County Bar Association,

15 having served as its President.

16 He was a member of Christ Episcopal Church in Fairmont and

17 served as a member of the Vestry for several years.

18 He was a member of the Fairmont Field Club where he was an

19 avid, competitive, and accomplished tennis player.

20 Mr. Parker was devoted to his family, consisting of his wife,

21 Diane Hutchinson Parker, who survives; two (2) children, Paul E.

22 Parker, III, and Sylvia Elaine; and two (2) grandsons, Brooks

23 Edward Parker and Brent Russell Parker.

24 While engaged in the private practice of law, Paul Parker

1   represented a varied of clients and was an excellent litigator.

2   After spending several years in criminal litigation as Prosecutor,

3   he returned to private practice where he acquired an expertise in

4   condemnation law representing the West Virginia Department of

5   Highways in hundreds of cases in Marion County and surrounding

6   counties.

7   He displayed unflinching loyalty to his clients and was a

8   determined advocate, who never wavered in his zeal to see that his

9   clients' interests were served.

10 He enjoyed the practice of law until an unfortunate illness

11 struck him down. He had a zest for life, which enjoyed to the

12 fullest measure.

13 Unfortunately, because of his illness many of the younger

14 members of the Bar were denied the association of Mr. Parker, and

15 a chance to observe a competent and outstanding practitioner ply

16 his trade.

17 The Marion County Bar has lost a valued member, a wide circle

18 of others have lost a loyal friend, and the community has lost a

19 citizen whose memory deserves and will always have the highest

20 respect.

21 Now, therefore, be it resolved that these Resolutions of

22 Sorrow and Respect are hereby adopted by this Association as

23 testimonials of our affection and respect for Paul E. Parker, Jr.,

24 and further that these resolutions be entered in the records of the

1   Circuit Court of Marion County and that a copy thereof be furnished

2   to the family and the <u>Times-West Virginian</u> for publication.

3   Mr. President, I move the adoption of the Resolution.

4   **PRESIDENT JEFFREY D. TAYLOR:**   Thank you, Mr. Tharp.

5   At this time, I would open the floor for comments from anyone

6   who may wish to speak.

7   **MR. RODERICK DEVISON:**   Mr. Chairman, I must take

8   this opportunity to mention another one of Paul's accomplishments

9   that took about a year of his professional life at least part time.

10   In the 70's we got into a problem with being overextended and

11   Harper Meredith, in his wisdom, appointed Paul to be our Receiver.

12   I told Paul he was the best Receiver I ever had. I don't reckon

13   anyone can afford more than one (1) Receiver.

14   Clear up until the time he was still around and a little bit

15   active I mentioned things that happened during that approximate

16   year that he had operated as Receiver, and he remembered things and

17   -- and I had to compliment every time about the professional way

18   that he handled matters, and as it turned out, he was able to

19   convince the creditors to be patient, and as a result, he saved the

20   properties and had it all paid out and everybody got their money.

21   They didn't get all the interest owed them, but got their money,

22   and he handled it in a very nice manner.

23   I think that's a credit to him, possibly a little known

24   accomplishment of Paul. We liked him very much. He was a good

1   man, and we'll miss him.

2   **PRESIDENT JEFFREY D. TAYLOR**:   Thank you, Mr. Devison.

3   **MR. JAMES A. LIOTTA**:   Mr. President, members of

4   Paul's family.

5   Nearly twenty (20) years ago I had the fortune of trying a

6   civil case with Paul on the other side, and why I know it was

7   nearly twenty (20) years ago was Judge Meredith was still on the

8   bench at the time. And as he was likely to do during his final

9   years on the bench, Judge Meredith would doze from time to time

10   during the course of the trial.

11   And in this particular case, Judge Meredith dozed, and it

12   happened in either in my direct examination -- although I don't

13   think there's a correlation between his going to sleep and my

14   asking questions, but Paul objected to one (1) of the questions I

15   asked. I don't remember the detail. Of course, I stood silent,

16   Paul stood silent, and the Judge stood silent. So Paul objected a

17   second time a little louder, and about the third time the Judge

18   opened his eyes and looked up and heard Paul's objection and ruled

19   in Paul's favor. I never quite knew why or how, but he did and the

20   trial proceeded, and I had the good fortune, and of course at that

21   time, I was a young, relatively fresh lawyer, inexperienced but

22   lucky. Being in my favor, I had the good fortune of the jury

23   seeing things my way at the end of the case.

24   A day or two (2) later I got in the mail a letter, return

1 address said Paul E. Parker on it, and I thought it would be a

2 Motion for a New Trial or some such thing. Instead, there was a

3 very kind, very nice letter from Paul both congratulating me on the

4 outcome of the trial and also complimenting me on my handling of

5 the case. And as a young lawyer newly starting out, receiving that

6 from -- from Paul was very meaningful, and it just exemplifies the

7 kind of gentleman and kind of person he was to serve as a mentor

8 and to help and to be so kind.

9   That has always stuck with me over the years, although it was

10 nearly twenty (20) years ago, I think it pretty well exemplifies

11 the kind of person Paul was, and those who haven't had the

12 opportunity to practice with him and know him, you truly have

13 missed something.

14   Thank you.

15 **PRESIDENT JEFFREY D. TAYLOR:**   Thank you.

16 **HONORABLE FRED L. FOX, II:**   Mr. President. I came to

17 this Bar thirty-three (33) years ago this summer, and after meeting

18 other members of my firm, one (1) of the first lawyers I met was

19 Paul Parker. That was because we played basketball together every

20 Wednesday night at the episcopal church. We played tennis together

21 all the other nights.

22   Paul was a great competitor, and he had that unique ability,

23 which most of us don't have and I certainly don't have, to enjoy

24 athletics even when he was not doing well. Paul Parker never threw

1   a racket, and I'm not admitting that I never threw one.

2   We played -- we played basketball for years.   Chuck

3   Critchfield, Stormin Norman Kronjeager, and Paul started when Eddie

4   was probably ten (10), started bringing Eddie, and Eddie played

5   with us until he got to be fourteen (14) and then he was too good,

6   and wouldn't let him play anymore.

7   Those are some of the things I remember.   I can remember in

8   one (1) of the stories that Paul and I recounted many times.   I

9   remember presiding over one (1) of the first criminal cases I had

10   in which the Prosecuting Attorney was Frank C. Mascara, and the

11   defense attorney was Paul Parker, and everybody knew that Frank and

12   Paul clashed in the courtroom.

13   We were trying the case which took about three (3) days to

14   try, and it was a very acrimonious, to say the least, occasion, and

15   at one (1) point in the -- during the trial I did something which

16   you can't do any more, but you could do then because Judge Meredith

17   set the precedent.   Paul kept objecting to Frank's questions, which

18   I thought was proper, and I kept overruling it.   Finally, I said to

19   Paul, sit down, don't get back up, you've got an objection to every

20   question hereafter on the record.

21   The case lasted three (3) days, and the jury came in, and I

22   don't even remember what the verdict was.   I know, however, that

23   that evening about 6:30 we were playing tennis, Paul Parker and I

24   were partners against Chuck Critchfield and, I think, Mel Colburn,

1   and one (1) of the jurors who we all knew drove by. Nobody noticed

2   him, but he turned around and came back and parked. And we saw him

3   and went over and said something to him, and he said, "I can't

4   believe the way you guys behave towards each other all through the

5   last three (3) days in court and now you're out here playing tennis

6   together, and you're even partners."

7   That was sort of the -- that was sort of the relationship we

8   all had with Paul.

9   One (1) of the finest things that Paul Parker ever did was to

10 marry Diane Hutchinson. And I -- it cannot go without saying that

11 Diane, your support of Paul during the last ten (10) years has been

12 something which is amazing to me, and I respect you so much for

13 that.

14   To the very end -- I quit playing tennis twenty (20) years

15 ago, and Paul used to tease me about it. He quit ten (10) years

16 ago and took up golf, as did I. And we no longer then referred to

17 golf as an old man's sport, because we were both actively playing.

18   He was an upper. Paul Parker was -- always had a positive

19 frame of mind about everything and no matter how bad you felt, if

20 you sat down and talked to him for a while, you were over it. We

21 don't have very many people like that, and we're sure going to miss

22 him.

23 **MR. PHILIP C. PETTY:**   Mr. President.

24 **PRESIDENT JEFFREY D. TAYLOR:**   Mr. Petty.

1   **MR. PHILIP C. PETTY:**   After hearing of Paul's

2   death while I was out of town the other day, I had time to think

3   about what I wanted to say about him at this ceremony, and a couple

4   of stories come to mind that point out some of qualities that Judge

5   Fox mentioned, and that's that his competitive spirit not only on

6   the tennis court, but in this court.

7   And again back probably about the same time Jim was talking

8   about when I was a young lawyer, Paul and I had a divorce case that

9   was pretty hard fought, and is probably one (1) of the reasons I

10   don't do divorces anymore. I think it lasted ten (10) years or

11   more. Bur during the initial stages of that divorce proceeding, we

12   were trading motions back and forth and writing letters back and

13   forth, having hearings. And I'd just go home and complain or moan

14   about all these things this old -- this lawyer was doing to me. I

15   was just starting, you know, just terrible, and of course, I'm sure

16   you're saying the same thing.

17   Well, it was either a Bar social or a Bar picnic or something,

18   and my wife and I went, and we're young lawyers in the bar. And

19   while I was off talking to someone, Paul introduced himself to

20   Cathy and at the end of the evening she said, "That's Paul Parker?"

21   I said, "Yes." She said, "Well, he's a delightful man. He's a

22   gentleman." And that really kind of sums it up because he could

23   really be a tiger in the courtroom on behalf of his clients and

24   probably on the tennis court as well, but he was truly a gentleman.

He went out of his way to make us feel welcome as young people into the community, not only of Marion County, but also the Bar Association. And that competitive spirit is -- stayed on as he went through the last ten (10) years of illness. Things that would stop other people, he just made himself go through, and his spirit as a gentleman gave him the grace to accept that and not give up and continue to do what he liked to do, which was thinking the law and working the law.

I can remember a few years back running into him at the bank, and he had just had a bad spell, and you could barely hear him talk, but he brought me a folder or pamphlet that he had made up on the changes and the new Rules of Civil Procedure and the different amendments. He said, "Here's something I think you might want to use." And I used it for several years. He had given it a lot of thought, so you never -- he never quit. He never gave up. And I think that sums him up well.

MS. ELISABETH H. ROSE: Mr. President, I want to echo Mr. Liotta's comment and also Mr. Petty, approximately twenty (20) years ago as well, I tried my very first case against Mr. Parker, and that's what I called him for a long time. It was here in this courtroom in front of Judge Meredith, and I was terrified, but that could have been partly because, Alfred, you represented the co-defendant. But at any rate we all know, that was a very big event, and it was a very stressful thing for me. Unlike Mr.

1   Liotta, I did not come out victorious.

2   But the thing I remember about him, in addition to the

3   scariness of the whole thing, was the graciousness that was

4   displayed to me by Mr. Parker. As Mr. Liotta said and Mr. Petty,

5   that was sort of the signature part of his personality. I was new.

6   I was inexperienced, and no one would have known it more completely

7   than my opponent, but he treated me as an equal. He treated me as

8   a contemporary and it made the experience one that I remembered

9   positively, and I appreciated that so much. And that graciousness

10   was never absent from his demeanor, even after his health betrayed

11   him, he had such battles to fight.

12   I don't remember exactly when it was that I last saw him, but

13   I remember he was still a gracious, gracious gentleman, and that is

14   how I remember him.

15   **MR. PHILIP A. PRITCHARD:**   Mr. President.

16   **PRESIDENT JEFFREY D. TAYLOR:**   Yes.

17   **MR. PHILIP A. PRITCHARD:**   Yes, I'm sort of repeating

18   what a few others have said. I started a few years before Phil and

19   Lisa, but I didn't do many civil trials, but when I started out, I

20   met Paul, and I knew his reputation, and that he was a very

21   competitive lawyer, good lawyer, and a gentleman. My early

22   experience I remember the work on the flood control up in

23   Mannington, which we are sort of just finishing up now. And he --

24   you know, he did some of the project, and I would go to him for

1 advice and I was amazed at the things -- the real estate things

2 relating to that.

3   I tried to stay out of court as much as possible against Paul,

4 but one (1) time we did have a case, and it was not a real big

5 case, just a new car, and it worked out and our client returned it,

6 and he represented the auto dealer. I had -- at the time I met

7 Glenn Schumacher as a senior in law school, and he was legal clerk

8 for me, and he did a lot of research on it and go the things lined

9 up, even had a professor at the law school help out, and we thought

10 we had the law entirely on our side and the facts on our side, but

11 we still had to go against Paul Parker, so we were kind of nervous

12 so Glenn sat at counsel table and so forth, and we got through the

13 case and weren't sure how the jury was going to come out. They did

14 come out on our side. We didn't of course get all the extra things

15 we asked for, the basic coverage, and as has been said by others,

16 Paul was so gracious and kind, and he did file some motions and

17 ruled in our favor, but after that he was also very kind.

18   I remember one (1) time, I knew he did play tennis, and my

19 tennis game wasn't much better than my golf game, which isn't very

20 good, and George May once gave me a big lesson golf. But anyways

21 he had offered, and I said, "Well, I need to practice some more

22 before I go out with you," which looking back I'm sure I would have

23 enjoyed a lesson from him anyways.

24   We will sure miss him, and he's a true gentleman.

1   **MR. DAVID R. JANES:**   Mr. President. It was my

2 honor and privilege to know Paul Parker in many of his different

3 roles. First, as a friend of my parents; next, as a fraternity

4 brother, that's as a mentor and a role model.

5   In 1977, fresh out of law school, I came to Fairmont to

6 establish my practice, and it was my distinct honor to work in the

7 office with Paul Parker and George Amos. I worked with them for

8 several months, and that was my first direct look at the practice

9 of law as practiced by two (2) excellent practitioners, each in

10 their own right.

11   What I learned from Paul that I remember most, one (1) of

12 which has been said here today, that is that he was a zealous

13 advocate of his clients no matter what the outcome might be

14 expected to be.

15   The second thing that I learned from Paul I thought was very

16 important was to observe him in dealing with his clients, and he

17 had a remarkable way of dealing with clients when things were going

18 well and when things were not going well. The clients always

19 seemed to leave his office with a smile on their face and a hand

20 shake, and they was always very appreciative of him for the work

21 that he did on their behalf because they knew that he did

22 everything that he possibly could to present their case to advance

23 their cause. I think that's something that I have tried to keep

24 with me over my twenty-three (23) years since that time I spent

1 with Paul Parker. I much value and appreciate that time with him.

2   **MR. D. J. ROMINO, SR.:**   Mr. President. You have

3 heard a lot of these lawyers this afternoon, and I can't help but

4 sit here and listen to the beautiful remarks.

5   I do want to tell you that several years ago, it was several

6 years ago, he made me his Assistant Prosecuting Attorney, and it

7 was joy working for Paul. It really was. The only thing he said

8 in my presence, he said, "When a case comes to me, it's mine. When

9 a case is otherwise, it's yours." That's how it would be most of

10 the time until I got in trouble, and he would help me.

11   A tremendous man. His family well known to me, his wife, his

12 son, his grandson. He's got a hugely talented grandson who plays

13 in our church many days -- many times.

14   Paul's manners were just perfect. He never said anything that

15 was out of the ordinary. I tell you one (1) thing, when he said the

16 law was the law, it was the law. He was a tough competitor. He

17 knew what he was doing, and when he got up there and told the jury

18 something he was telling them the truth, and I respected him for

19 that. I respected him for his love of his family, his

20 grandchildren, his son, and his whole family. A beautiful family.

21 Thank you.

22   **PRESIDENT JEFFREY D. TAYLOR:**   Thank you.

23   **BRENT E. BEVERIDGE:**   Mr. President.

24   I'd like to relate two (2) aspects of Paul Parker's practice,

1 his life and so on. Many of you know or some of you older members

2 of the Bar recall that my wife Beverly worked for Mr. Parker for

3 fourteen (14) years, and I married her while she was in Mr.

4 Parker's employment, and she continued for a year and a half (1½)

5 or so until we had our first child back in 1982.

6   And you know, it's kind of unique, I came home the other night

7 and when I came into the house, I was passing through to do

8 whatever I was going to do, and Beverly said, "Mr. Parker died."

9 That's the first thing she said to me as I came through. And

10 somebody, I think -- somebody else mentioned here, I think Lisa

11 referred to him as "Mr. Parker," and she's always referred to him

12 in the past when she started working back in 1968 or so for him,

13 and during the past thirty-two (32) years, she's referred to him as

14 Mr. Parker out of respect. He generated that.

15   And I've heard through the years when she's mentioned him or

16 she said, "I saw him the other day," or she said she saw some of

17 his family members and maintained at least that contact. And I

18 think, you know, Mr. Parker, and I think several people here would

19 use that word and use it out of respect and deserve that type of

20 respect.

21   There's a couple other words and another aspect that I want to

22 address. Judge Fox used the word "acrimonious." Scott Tharp, in

23 his Resolution, used the word "unflinching." And when they use

24 those words, and my -- somebody would say, "What do you remember

1 Paul Parker for?" And it was kind of insignificant, but it

2 illustrates his unflinching positions that he took and the acrimony

3 is sometimes generated, and I recall a case in which I represented

4 a woman in a family dispute over either a right of way or a piece

5 of land or some -- some trash or something out in Fairview, and

6 Paul represented a scoundrel, and Ken Simons represented a

7 scoundrel. My woman was kind of in between, and she was standing

8 by watching all of us. So, I got to go to depositions and all the

9 hearings to see the acrimony and the unflinching positions taken by

10 Paul and Ken Simons. My client, one (1) time that I can remember

11 -- I can remember where everybody was sitting, and this was

12 probably in 1985, 1980, somewhere in the late 70's, early 80's I

13 can remember where everybody was sitting, and I can remember almost

14 what everybody was doing, where and the whole thing because here's

15 Ken, Paul, and two (2) scoundrels arguing, fighting, objecting in

16 the deposition, I believe, and my client's sitting there, and

17 finally she just reached the point that she had to cry. And I

18 don't know who caused it or what, but it was acrimony and the

19 unflinching position taken by all of these individuals.

20   And, you know, as what now becomes one (1) of the older

21 members of the Bar, you remember and appreciate some of these

22 things, and you can, as we sit right here and look around the room,

23 we talked about Frank and his classic battles with Paul, and Alfred

24 over there with Sax getting into, and Herschel and, you know, those

1   things that I think this an opportunity to remember some of those

2   things.   And particularly Paul brought about the unflinching

3   acrimony.

4   MR. KENNETH R. MILLER: Mr. President.

5   PRESIDENT JEFFREY D. TAYLOR: Yes, sir.

6   MR. KENNETH R. MILLER: When I came to this Bar in

7   1972, we tried lots of civil cases, we tried lots of cases of all

8   kinds, somewhat different today. We mediate more. We try fewer

9   cases. But I had the privilege of trying several cases against

10   Paul. And I also, at that time, delved a little bit into domestic

11   relations work. Most of us had a general practice. I always found

12   Paul, as I've already stated, to be a very formidable adversary

13   both in the courtroom and on the tennis court where I also had the

14   privilege of engaging in combat with Paul on numerous occasions as

15   Eddie and Diane and Jan and all the others know.

16   I guess the unfairness of life seems to be even more evident

17   in Paul's circumstances because he seemed to be the epitome of

18   physical conditioning. He was an excellent athlete. He played

19   tennis everyday. He jogged. Then suddenly when he was stricken, it

20   just didn't seem fair to the rest of us, and I'm sure to the family

21   as well, and yet that is a lesson for us all. Perhaps it was his

22   good health that allowed to remain with us for ten (10) years or so

23   since his stroke or early problems. But that's not really what I

24   remember most about Paul. What I remember most is his infectious

1   smile and his laugh on the tennis court or on the street.

2   As others have emphasized, he was always upbeat, optimistic,

3   a very enjoyable person to talk with. Not necessarily in the

4   courtroom did he have that demeanor, but outside and it was that

5   laugh that you could hear really a distance away even if you're up

6   at the swimming pool was Sylvia was probably swimming and her dad

7   was down at the tennis courts, you always knew what his frame of

8   mind was. His frame of mind was always -- it seemed at least to us

9   as outsiders, but he may have had a bad day, but he always seemed

10 to be happy and upbeat, and it was always a joy to talk to him.

11   And even after he was stricken and ill, I saw him in church on

12 several occasions, also at seminars, and he always had that same

13 smile and was always in good humor, and I think that that's what I

14 will remember most about your husband, your father, and

15 grandfather, and your father-in-law. He had a quality about him

16 that made you feel good just by being associated with him and just

17 hearing him laugh. I'll miss him.

18   **MR. ROBERT F. COHEN, JR.**:   I just want to very briefly

19 echo what Ken had to say. I last saw Paul at a continuing legal

20 education seminar just last fall, and he was obviously very sick,

21 and yet he was there, the education, going there, and being

22 connected was important to him, and it was his warmth, his

23 friendliness, and his desire to still remain part of the legal

24 community.

1   **PRESIDENT JEFFREY D. TAYLOR:**   Is there anyone else that

2   would like to comment this morning?

3   **MR. J. SCOTT THARP:**   Mr. President.

4   It is difficult to say anything without reiterating what has

5   already been said, but one (1) thing I would say, of course, I

6   practiced with Paul many, many years, but back in the old days when

7   we used to do most of the domestic relation work on Saturday

8   morning, Paul would always be seen coming to the courthouse, and

9   that's when you didn't have to have Family Law Masters back in

10   those days. Judge Meredith could resolve ten (10) or fifteen (15)

11   cases on a Saturday morning without worrying about that.

12   But the thing that I think exemplifies his personality in the

13   courtroom most was in condemnation cases. Paul probably tried more

14   condemnation cases than any lawyer here, and maybe any lawyer in

15   West Virginia, because when I-79 came through, that opened up lots

16   and lots of cases in court and lots and lots of land and it seemed

17   like there was always condemnation cases being tried. He would try

18   cases in Monongalia, Preston, Harrison, Doddridge, other counties

19   as well, but when you're a condemnation case and you're

20   representing the State, you're representing the bad guy really as

21   far as the jury's ordinarily concerned. But Paul had a personality

22   that he was able to make the jury feel like he was representing the

23   good guy, you know, and he tried enough cases and he always had the

24   disadvantage of having this appraiser come in from Wheeling or

1   somewhere that you're having to use, you know, and the other lawyer

2   railing about that sort of thing, but Paul was able to, and I think

3   that was shown in his personality, that in a condemnation case,

4   which he tried so many, he was able to make the State of West

5   Virginia Department of Highways look like they were the good guys

6   and your poor property was the bad guy, and that was typical of the

7   way he could litigate.

8   One (1) other thing I remember, he always had a pension for

9   getting everybody's full name. When I would see him, he wouldn't

10 just call me Scott, it was Joseph Scott. That was the way he would

11 always greet me. But we will miss him. He had a great -- in the

12 condemnation case, I think I will remember that more than anything

13 that you thought you had the advantage going in, but he always

14 seemed to take it away from you.

15   **PRESIDENT JEFFREY D. TAYLOR:**   I'd like to thank everyone

16 for coming here this morning and thank you for your kind comments

17 about Mr. Paul Parker, Jr.

18   To the family we say that we are truly sorry for your loss.

19 Please don't hesitate to let us know if there is anything we can do

20 for you.

21   Certified copies of the Resolution of Respect that was drafted

22 by Mr. Lemley, Mr. Miller, and Mr. Tharp will be provided to the

23 Parker family and also provided to the <u>Times-West Virginian</u>

24 newspaper for publishing.

1   Thank you all again for coming. This· meeting is now

2   adjourned.

3   **MR. PAUL E. "EDDIE" PARKER, III:** Mr. President, before we

4   adjourn, I would like to thank you for convening this Special

5   Session of the Marion County Bar Association. I'd like to

6   personally thank each of you for coming this morning.

7   Judge Fox, I think, with the possible exception of being home

8   with us and on the tennis court with Kenny and myself and others,

9   I think this is the one (1) place where Dad wanted to be in this

10   room, and I think it's entirely appropriate that we remember him

11   this morning.

12   I thank you all for your very kind comments and gracious

13   support of us at this time. Thank you again.

14   **PRESIDENT JEFFREY D. TAYLOR:** Thank you, Eddie.

15   * * *

16   (Whereupon, 10:36 o'clock a.m., the Special Meeting of the

17   Marion County Bar Association for the Memorial Service for Paul E.

18   Parker, Jr., deceased, was concluded.)

19   * * *

20

21

22

23

24

1 STATE OF WEST VIRGINIA,

2 COUNTY OF MARION, TO-WIT:

3   I, Terri R. Cheslock, Official Reporter of the Circuit Court

4 of Marion County, West Virginia, do hereby certify that the

5 foregoing is a true and correct transcript of the proceedings had

6 and testimony taken in the hearing in the Special Meeting of the

7 Marion County Bar Association for the Memorial Service for Paul E.

8 Parker, Jr., deceased, as reported by me in stenomask.

9   I hereby certify that the transcript within meets the

10 requirements of the Code of the State of West Virginia, 51-7-4, and

11 all rules pertaining thereto as promulgated by the Supreme Court of

12 Appeals.

13   Given under my hand this 29th day of September, 2000.

14

15   Terri R. Cheslock
16   Official Reporter, Circuit Court
17   Of Marion County, West Virginia

18   * * *

19

20

21

22

23

24

25

REFLECTIONS

Christmas, 2010
Brooks, Sylvia, Brett, Diane, Jan and Eddie Parker

"Nay, we are seven!"
~ William Wordsworth

While reading this morning my eyes darted to movement on the top of the clear glass coffee table where my book was laying. The movement was a reflection of our 500 plus-year-old sycamore tree's fluttering leaves reflected from the sky light above. It reminded me of a lifetime of memories and stories as reported through the press and the public's eye, and then followed by my etceteras, as in a prism when it refracts the colorful truths.

Looking back down at the reflection in the table, it has moved away from me, as escaping from my thoughts. I clutch them as I would a child trying to dash away from me.

I go upstairs and look in the mirror. I see an older person that has grown from the writing of these memoirs, one that I still like and even admire.

I have written and finished a book - not just talked about doing so. It has taken me four years, but I have finished it – 21 polished chapters. I am proud of what I have accomplished and enjoyed every hour - every year, I only regret I did not start writing ten years ago.

I have become my own strong being. I do not want to look as young as possible; I want to look as good as possible for my age. I have lost my beautiful dark brown, wavy hair; I have let it become a steel gray, but still thick and wavy - thank God! I wanted to see what I really looked like at my age today. I like it and pray the color depicts my strength and resilience.

I have loved each member of my immediate family, unconditionally. Paul and I literally spent our lives loving and making sure that Eddie and Sylvia would grow up prepared to take care of themselves and their families.

The greatest gift I can give them now - at my age and theirs - is my attitude toward life; to keep on being a role model, even if they have not been aware that my - or their father's - behavior had much impact on their lives.

I hope I will be remembered as a strong woman with a sense of humor, and a gift of words; after all, words are symbols and the significance of these symbols will vary with the knowledge and experience of the mind receiving them. How could one write a memoir at twenty-five? Only those entering their teens would be interested.

One must live awhile to remember a life of happiness and woes. I hope I have warned my readers of life's pitfalls and subtly advised them how to create happiness and beauty by never giving up hope, with the belief and trust that everything really does happen for the best.

As my daughter, Sylvia's, published story for my Mother's Day present so aptly stated:

"There is the strength of womankind in these memories. The strength of mothers and daughters. The strength of family. Perhaps the true essence and heart of these mountains is matriarchal.

The soft powerful feminine voices resonating through the hills, echoing through the generations. Leading and teaching each of us the way to lead our lives."

There will be no end to this saga, it will live on with my children and I hope, yours; perhaps reminding them of the elegance, graciousness and civility of not so long ago, when scandal would lose one's reputation never to be regained. A lesson hard to find in a few hundred words, but certainly worth remembering in this new world of scandal-less, boorish, crassness. I pray "This, too, shall pass away."

I will be grateful if I have passed the test that Mr. Caulfield suggested and you consider me "a great friend you could call up at home".

LOVE,

Diane

ACKNOWLEDGEMENTS

Founders of the Air Force Association "General Pete Everest" Chapter,
July, 1998

Clyde Judy, Andrew Hauge, Warren Wysner, Paul Parker, Don Robinson
(AFA), Gary Cox and David Nuzum

To the many people who have contributed and enhanced the lives of five generations of my family, "I give my most humble and hearty thanks for all thy goodness and loving kindness to us", most particularly to:

Sylvia Hutchinson Derby, my dear sister. She is the only one I have left of my 741 family. Thank you, darling for adding your memories to mine.

To my dear daughter, Sylvia Parker, who urged me to "write - write - write" and she would take care of the rest and my son, Eddie Parker, my legal consultant.

Kristen Heiser, friend and advisor, without whose technical and graphical expertise this tome would never have materialized and I am forever grateful.

Mrs. John Wood Hutchinson (Susan Haymond Hutchinson) my beautiful first cousin in-law, who, with my first cousin Jack, traced the Hutchinson family to the McDonald Clan of Scotland and provided many of the dates and interesting facts and stories over these many years about the family.

My two excellent editors and dear friends who were so patient:

Cynthia Taylor Woodward (Mrs. Joseph D.) Copy Editor

Jean Meredith Taylor (Mrs. Richard R.) Story Editor

My dear friends who became my sisters and brothers in adulthood,

Anne Blair Morgan (Mrs. William B.)

Jean Blair Ireland and Thomas DeWitt Ireland (Tim)

Diana Scholl Sampson Wysner - (Bernard G.) and Warren B. Wysner

Elaine Markowitz Pollock, among her many attributes, is a superlative knitter, who knitted me a swath of ribbing (Knit-one, Purl-Two and 6 inches of row one-Knit and row two-Purl) giving me a glimpse into my past and what I had knitted for those cold soldiers in WWII.

Carol Ballah Amos

J.C. Amos, Esq.

Eddie O. Barrett

Delegate Mike Caputo

Caroline Richards Carlot

Emily Ellen Ice Cather

Roger D. Curry, J.D

Carol Lee Bobet Gilmore

Donley C. Kennedy

Carol Sorenson LaFollette

Marion County Bar Association

Dianne Richardson Oliva

Robert H. Quenon

James C. and Mimi (Tucker) Tarleton

John R. "Jack" Carpenter

Rosemary Brunetti Tennant

Richard S. Wagner

Elaine Bennett Watson

Carole Jenkins Wilburn

The Times-West Virginian:

John C. Veasey, Editor

Misty Poe, Managing Editor

Writers:

Mary Wade Burnside

Oce Smith

Jonathon Williams

Photographers:

Tammy Shriver

Danny Snyder

Connie Price Talbott

A special acknowledgement to:

JoAnn Lough, a dear friend since our days at Butcher Elementary School, and the best history teacher I have ever had. We pursued the "bright lights" of the theatre throughout our schooldays not realizing our common and underlying interest in history. Back in 1947, taking Miss (Lucile) Jenkins' Public Speaking together, we knew it was connected with being on stage, but we did not understand how important the section on Parliamentary Procedure would be later. We will not forget our stint together in theatre at Fairmont State either. The play was "Claudia". I was delighted to be cast in the title role with JoAnn as my mother.

Following JoAnn's retirement in 1997 from the Fairmont State College Speech and Theatre faculty, she concentrated on the organization of the Masquers archives. Since 1923 the Masquers has been the Fairmont State University play production organization. This work led her to FSC history and, at the same time, she was managing a second publication of the popular *Now and Long Ago, a History of the Marion County Area*. Her father Glenn D. Lough, then deceased, was the author. She combined her theatre and speech background with that of her father's life-long research by writing articles, presenting one-woman shows, creating public celebrations, etc. in order to bring area history "alive".

In 2000, I founded the Woodlawn Cemetery Preservation Society. As a member, JoAnn and I researched and she wrote the application, which helped place the Cemetery and its Chapel on the National Register of Historic Places in 2004 as an Historic District for the City. Our investigation included such personages as Francis H. Pierpont, Governor of Restored Virginia (1861-68), and his wife Julia plus those of my family and other great leaders of the coal industry.

We also worked together to establish Julia Pierpont Day, which is now in its eighth consecutive year, and I was pleased to assist with the dedication of the six West Virginia Civil War Trails markers, which JoAnn was instrumental in securing for the City of Fairmont.

Our high school parliamentary procedure held us in good stead during our fight to save the historic Marion County Jail in 2004 from being torn down to provide five parking places for the Marion County commissioners. JoAnn led the fight to save this mighty fortress, which still stand and is being used for storage and a holding facility for those awaiting trial.

Many honors have been bestowed, including in 2006 a Doctorate of Fine Arts granted by Fairmont State University and a West Virginia History Hero Award by the West Virginia Division of Culture and History.

JoAnne and her father's book *Now and Long Ago* were indispensible to me in my writing. I always knew the dates were right and all the other facts factual. We thank her for being "our hero", teacher, director, and a person who remains committed and dedicated to sharing her knowledge with us all.

~ D.H.P.

BIBLIOGRAPHY

Bartlett, John, FAMILIAR QUOTATIONS, Tenth Edition Revised-Nathan Haskell Dole, Little, Brown and Company, 1920

Bartlett, John, FAMILIAR QUOTATIONS, Sixteenth Edition, Edited –Justin Kaplan, Little, Brown and Company, 1992

Birmingham, Stephen, THE GRAND DAMES, Simon and Shuster, New York, 1982

Birmingham, Stephen, THE RIGHT PEOPLE- A Portrait of the American Social Establishment, Little, Brown and Company, 1958

Byers, Robert J., Project Editor, PROFILES-West Virginians Who Made a Difference, "Clarence Watson", p.57, The Charleston Gazette, 1999

Carroll, Eleanor Watson, "FORTUNES MADE AND LOST by MARION COUNTY COAL BARONS", Column in The Fairmont Times, Monday, September 20, 1954

Comstock, Jim, Editor, The Comstock Load, "FROM SONNENCROFT TO HIGHGATE", The West Virginia Hillbilly, Sept. 22, 1988

Constantine, Tony, asst. by Dan Miller, MOUNTAINEER FOOTBALL, Athletic Publicity Office West Virginia University- 1891-1969, 1969

Cook, Tony, Editor, and Barbara J. Howe, West Virginia University Alumni Magazine, "YEAR BY   YEAR 1862-2000", Special issue, Winter, 2000

Dallek, Robert, AN UNFINISHED LIFE-JOHN F. KENNEDY-1917-1963, Little, Brown And Company, 2003

Davitz, Lois Leiderman, Ph.D. & Joel R. Davitz, Ph.D., GETTING ALONG – almost-WITH YOUR ADULT KIDS, Sorin Books, Notre Dame, ID, 2003

Dunnington, George A., Publisher, HISTORY OF MARION COUNTY -1880, Fairmont WV, 1880

Edwards, Paul, "Critique of McCormack's THIS NEST OF VIPERS", Times West Virginian, Feb.11, 1990

Ehrlich, Eugene, AMO, AMAS, AMAT and MORE, Harper and Row Publishers, New York, 1985

Ernst, Harry W., West Virginia UNIVERSITY-A Pictorial History, West Virginia University, 1980

Ewen, David, THE HOME BOOK OF MUSICAL KNOWLEDGE, Grolier Inc. New York, 1954

Fairmont High School Class of 1916, MARION COUNTY IN THE MAKING, 1917

Fenwick, Millicent, Vogue's Book of Etiquette, 1948

Fleming, Allison Sweeney, My Own Home Town, Feb. 28, 1950 Pub. Local Rotary Club

FORBES MAGAZINE, October 9, 2000, page 78.

Gale, William, and Christine Peyton Jones, Editors, INDUSTRIAL FAIRMONT, August 1993

Gibran, Kahlil, THE PROPHET, Alfred A. Knopf, 1923

Lewis, C.S., C.S. Lewis on LOVE, Compiled by Lesley Walmsley, Thomas Nelson Publishers, Nashville, 1998

Lough, Glenn D., NOW AND LONG AGO-A History of the Marion County Area, Morgantown Printing and Binding Company Co. 1969

Holdforth, Lucinda, WHY MANNERS MATTER - The Case of Civilized Behavior in a Civilized World, 2007

Kennedy, Rose Fitzgerald, TIMES TO REMEMBER, Doubleday & Company, Inc. Garden City New York, 1974

Knowles, John, A VEIN OF RICHES, Little, Brown and Co., 1978

Knowles, John, Taped Conversation with John Knowles-with permission, March 14, 1978

Kashner, Zoe, Editorial Editor, New York Times, the WORLD ALMANAC AND BOOK OF FACTS, 2007

Lough, Glenn D., Now and Long Ago-A History of Marion County, McClain Printing Co. Parsons, WV, 1969

Manchester, William, "THE CASE OF LUELLA MUNDELL", Harpers Magazine 1952

Marion County Historical Society, A HISTORY OF MARION COUNTY, Wadsworth Publishing Co. Inc., Marceline, Missouri, 1985

MARION COUNTY CENTENIAL YEARBOOK- 1863-1963, Fairmont Printing Co., 1963

MAROON and WHITE, FSU Alumni Magazine, "A Look Back at Fairmont State Presidents", Fall, Volume 27, 2010

Mason, Medora, "MARY CHATTER" Columns, The West Virginian. 1930 - 1950

McCormack, Charles S., THIS NEST OF VIPERS- McCarthyism and Higher Education in the Mundel Affair 1951-1952, Published by Board of Trustees of the University of Illinois, 1989

McMillan, Debra Ball, AN ORNAMENT TO THE CITY, Headline Books, Inc., Terra Alta, WV, 1996

Meredith, E.E., Editor, "DO YOU REMEMBER" Columns, The West Virginian.1920 -1945

Norton, Charles A., MEVILILLE DAVISSON POST: MAN OF MANY MYSTERIES, Bowling Green University Popular Press, Bowling Green, Ohio, 1973

Okrent, Daniel, GREAT FORTUNE-The Epic of Rockefeller, page 364, Viking Penguin, 2003

POCKET OXFORD AMERICAN THESAURUS, Second Edition, Oxford University Press, 2008

Reeves, Thomas C., A QUESTION OF CHARACTER- A Life of John F. Kennedy, The Free Press, A Division of Macmillan, Inc., New York, 1991

Rogers and Hammerstein, words and music, Broadway Musical "SOUTH PACIFIC", 1949

Roget, Peter Mark, M.D., THESAURUS OF ENGLISH WORDS AND PHRASES, 1911, Enlarged and   improved by John Lewis Roget- new edition revised by Samuel Romilly Roget, 1921

Salinger, J.D., the CATCHER IN THE RYE, Little, Brown and Company, p.25, 1945

Shrager, David, and Elizabeth Frost, THE QUOTABLE LAWYER, 1986

Smith, Clarence E., Editor, "GOOD MORNING COLUMNS", February 21, 1926 - 1959.

Smucker, Anna Egan, A HISTORY OF WEST VIRGINIA, 1997

Sommer, Robin Langley, NOTE BENE, Guide to Familiar Latin Quotations and Phrase, 1995

Sullivan, Ken, Editor, THE WEST VIRGINIA ENCYCLOPEDIA, The West Virginia Humanities Council, 2006

Toothman, Fred R., GREAT COAL LEADERS OF WEST VIRGINIA, Vandalia Book Co. Huntington,   WV, 1988

Watson, James Otis II, "THE VALLEY COAL STORY" The Monongahelan Magazine - Monongahela Power Co. supplement to the Times West Virginian, February 3,10,17,24, 1957

Williams, John A., WEST VIRGINIA- A HISTORY FOR BEGINNERS, 1997

Withers, Alexander Scott, CHRONICLES OF BORDER WARFARE, The Robert Clarke Company, 1895, reprinted, McClain Printing Company, Parsons W.Va., 1961

Woods, Ralph L., Editor, A TREASURY OF THE FAMILIAR, Macmillan Company, New York, 1942

APPENDIX

The only interior picture in Daddy's ledger of Sonnencroft

Sonnencroft on right; Morgantown Avenue on bottom of page; Shaw House on bottom far left

Architect's rendering of Sonnencroft

Architect's rendering of Sonnencroft

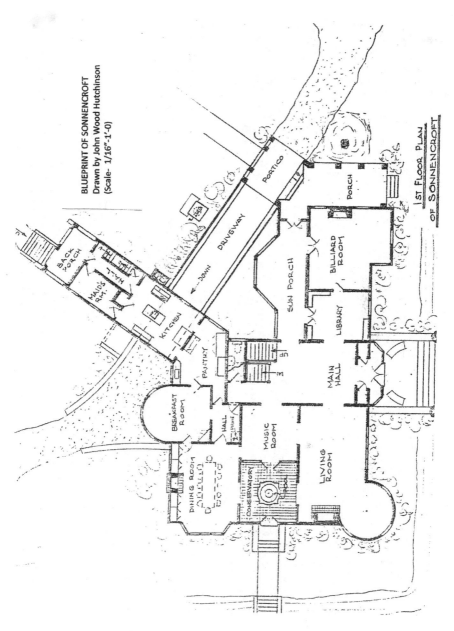

Blueprint of Sonnencroft's first floor
Scale = 1/16" = 1'0"

447

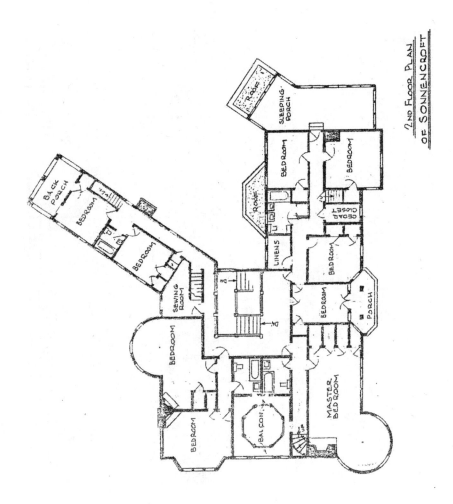

Blueprint of Sonnencroft's second floor
Scale = 1/16" = 1'0"

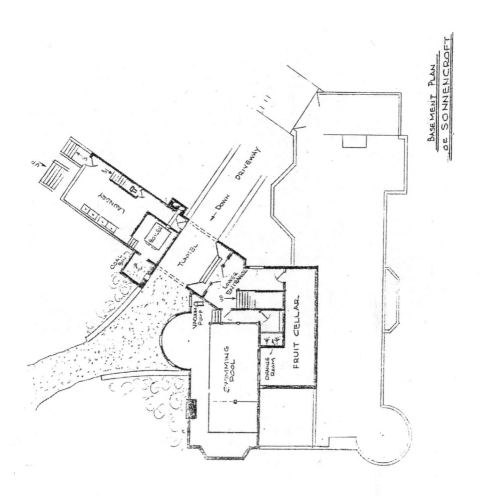

Blueprint of Sonnencroft's basement
Scale = 1/16" = 1'0"

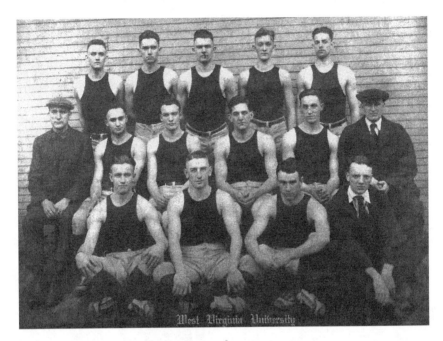

West Virginia University Varsity Basketball Team, 1919
Front row, left to right: Paul Edward Parker, Braden Alleman, Ted Lewis
and manager Thomas Nail
Middle row: Coach "Harness" Mullenex, Earl Fisher, George Hill, Homer
Martin, and Paul "Biz" Dawson, Athletic Director Harry D. Stansberry
Back row: Clem Kiger and others

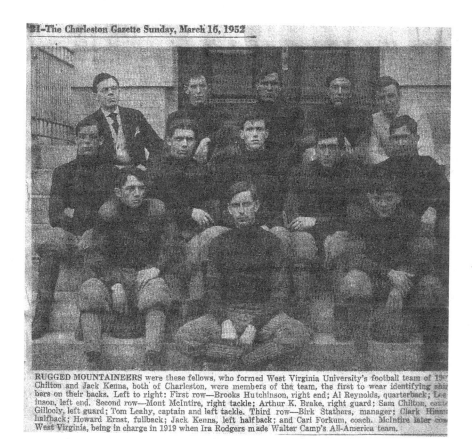

RUGGED MOUNTAINEERS were these fellows, who formed West Virginia University's football team of 19?? Chilton and Jack Kenna, both of Charleston, were members of the team, the first to wear identifying ??? bers on their backs. Left to right: First row—Brooks Hutchinson, right end; Al Reynolds, quarterback; Le? inson, left end. Second row—Mont McIntire, right tackle; Arthur K. Brake, right guard; Sam Chilton, cen?? Gillooly, left guard; Tom Leahy, captain and left tackle. Third row—Birk Stathers, manager; Clark Hin?? halfback; Howard Ernst, fullback; Jack Kenna, left halfback; and Carl Forkum, coach. McIntire later co?? West Virginia, being in charge in 1919 when Ira Rodgers made Walter Camp's All-America team.

West Virginia University Football Team, 1908
Brooks Hutchinson, pictured first row on far left, played right-end.
Lee Hutchinson on far right; played left-end.

ELWOOD DOWD AND FRIEND—Elwood P. Dowd sits for a portrait with his six-foot, four-legged, long eared friend, Harvey, a pooka. John Graham will be seen as Elwood and Harvey either will or will not be seen, depending upon the imagination of the playgoer, in the forthcoming production of "Harvey," the recent Broadway hit, to be presented Friday and Saturday, April 25 and 26, by the Marion County Little Theater.

452

Paul and Diane fell in love during this production of "Harvey"

Newspaper clippings promoting the play

Paul Parker Jr. and Congressman Alan B. Mollohan, 1996

Diane Parker, Senator Robert C. Byrd and Paul Parker, Jr., 1996

The Hutchinson Family Reunion in Fairmont, West Virginia, June, 2012
Former C.E. Hutchinson Residence on Benoni Avenue, where the family
lived while Sonnencroft was being built

About Diane Parker

I was born December 30, 1932 a 741 Fairmont Avenue. My parents were Brooks and Ray Hutchinson and Daddy was president of WV Cole and Coke. His father Clyde E. Hutchinson was founder and president of Hutchinson Coal Company, a nucleus of CONSOL.

I have been a lifelong resident of Fairmont, West Virginia and a "cradle" member of Christ Episcopal Church at Ninth Street and a sixty-year member of the Fairmont Field Club.

In 1952 I married Attorney Paul Edward Parker, Jr. and we had two children Paul E. Parker, III, born in 1955 (1980 - married Jan Carpenter). In 1959, a daughter, Sylvia Elaine Parker was born. I have two grandsons Brooks Edward and Brett Russell born to Eddie and Jan in 1985 and 1988.

Graduating from Fairmont Senior High School in 1950, I am a Lifetime member of the FSHS Foundation serving 6 years on the Foundation board of directors. As chairman of our 1950 Class Reunion, I organized our 60th on August 27, 2010.

I graduated from Fairmont State University in 1954 with an AB Degree in Elementary Education and taught first grade at White School on Locust Avenue in 1954-55. While at FSU I was elected president of my Freshman Class and was active in Professor L.A. Walman's Drama Department, performing in FSC Masquer's productions from second grade throughout my college career; because of this I was elected to the national honorary drama fraternity, Alpha Psi Omega at a very early age. I am still a member of the 85-year-old local Gamma Chi Chi social sorority.

An Active member of the Junior League of Fairmont, Inc for twenty- one years, I went sustaining at the age of forty, after serving as president in 1970-72. While president I was instrumental in getting the Marion County Rescue Squad started in our city of Fairmont. Doug La Fauci met with a committee and said the Jr. League was his last hope to start a squad in Fairmont as he had in Connecticut.

The late Congressman Robert H. Mollohan acclaimed in a February 16, 1972 issue of The Congressional Record of the 92nd Congress that, his home town of Fairmont, WV and its Junior League Community Research Committee, with the assistance of the President, Mrs. Paul E. Parker, Jr.,

"This group rallied to the support of a volunteer rescue squad by sending forth speakers in the community, film scheduling and distribution, phone calls, typing and newspaper publicity; and by adding a $3000 donation to the$10,500 collected, taking the needed $12,000 over the top for the first equipped ambulance of the "Save A Life project."

The Congressman had introduced H.R. 12787; the Emergency Medical Services Act, on January 31 of 1972 and support had been growing across the country for a federal effort to save the lives of thousands of highway and accident victims by upgrading the quality of ambulance and emergency room care.

I started the Flower Service of the Fairmont General Hospital Association; and in 1954 was appointed by the Women's Hospital Auxiliary, to attend the National Hospital Association's Convention in Chicago, IL, with Administrator and Mrs. Cheney Ellerby, the FGH CEO that preceded O.B. Ayers. My grandmother, Mrs. Clyde E. Hutchinson, had started the first Woman's Auxiliary at Cook Hospital in 1916 and served as its first president; and I was elected to serve two 2-year terms as president of the Fairmont General Hospital Volunteer Association 50 years later. The volunteers were then 500 strong and we contributed thousands of dollars to the new (1970) Fairmont General Hospital through our lunchroom and gift shop business that we had operated on the premises since 1939.

I have served three, two-year terms as president of the Green Hills Garden Club, founded in 1929, the oldest garden club in the state of West Virginia, succeeding my mother who was president in 1935. I have written a history of the organization that includes many names of old Fairmont and all the projects we have had in the past 83 years. In the thirties, we planted a mile of sycamore trees out Locust Avenue to beatify the newly paved road to the new Fairmont State Teachers College. Many years later in 2006, I persuaded Allegheny Power Company to plant $5000 worth of a variety of trees along Fairmont Avenue, where there were once canopied trees lining the Avenue. These trees had been struck down for huge poles and power lines that should have been put underground or in the alleyways as they do today and preserved the beautiful ambience of this major artery to the downtown of Fairmont.

After my husband's death, I realized the need for a restoration of the cemetery where five generations of my family are buried. I founded and served as chairman of the Woodlawn Cemetery Preservation Society in 2001. After three years, we were successful in placing the Cemetery and the old Chapel building on the State and National Historic Register that made it possible to receive State and Federal grants.

We worked hard to establish a legal board of trustees, appointed by the Judge of the Marion County Circuit Court and have since finished the newer building on the premises and completely cleaned up this historic district.

My husband and I established the General Frank K. (Pete) Everest Association of the American Air force Association (AAA) and this group of veterans have provided several $1000 scholarships to Junior ROTC Cadets and one to FSHS Frankie Baker who received an appointment to the Air Force Academy. After Paul's death in 2000, I stayed on as historian and treasurer for 11 years.

In March of 2010, I was elected as Volunteer of the Year by the editorial board of the local newspaper, the Fairmont Times West Virginian. In July, 2010, I was interviewed by the Times-West Virginian for a front page issue about the book "Daddy's Ledger" that I had started to write in February 2009 and have finished in June of 2012.

I have worked all these years for my beloved Fairmont and its people to make this a good, safe, and pleasant place to live and to raise our children; I have loved every minute of it.